Co. rus

You shall not dwell in tombs made by the dead for the living. And though of magnificence and splendour, your house shall not hold your secret nor shelter your longing. For that which is boundless in you abides in the mansion of the sky, whose door is the morning mist, and whose windows are the songs and the silences of night.

Kahlil Gibran, *The Prophet* (1923)

Daniele Nunziata

Colonial and Postcolonial Cyprus

Transportal Literatures of Empire, Nationalism, and Sectarianism

palgrave
macmillan

Daniele Nunziata
St Anne's College
University of Oxford
Oxford, UK

ISBN 978-3-030-58238-8 ISBN 978-3-030-58236-4 (eBook)
https://doi.org/10.1007/978-3-030-58236-4

Cover image: © Getty Images, Image ID: 488791109, Location: Nicosia, Cyprus.

This Palgrave Macmillan imprint is published by the registered company Springer Nature Switzerland AG
The registered company address is: Gewerbestrasse 11, 6330 Cham, Switzerland

For my parents,

My grandparents,

And my brothers.

Preface

Six decades ago this year, the eastern-most island of the Mediterranean gained its independence from the British Empire. Or rather, it *mostly* gained independence. For many people living beyond its shores, the colonial history of Cyprus is something of which they have little knowledge, as though this uncomfortable aspect of the island's past—and that of the UK—is a fact best forgotten. The bloody reality of its modern history is an uneasy truth not marketable for holiday brochures of golden beaches and turquoise seas. Nonetheless, every Cypriot today still reckons with a century's worth of violence and dispossession, much of which is rooted in the island's bitter colonial shackles and extends to the continuing legacies of it post-independence partition in 1974.

This is also a history which has seldom featured in global historiographies and the many unusual aspects of Cyprus' geographic, cultural, and political status have resulted in reservation when studying this location. Cyprus cannot be easily moored to pre-existing ideas of geography, culture, and politics—or, at least, not with the critical tools which currently exist. It was for this reason that the paradigm of *transportal literatures* was generated to understand culture from this island in ways which are highly indebted to the existing postcolonial discipline, but which also aim to expand the latter's theoretical parameters further. It also serves to pay due diligence to the often-forgotten colonialist structures which have informed the development of Cyprus and its modern culture as they exist today—torn, broken, sectarian—as a move towards some future resolution.

This book began life as my doctoral thesis at the University of Oxford. I was encouraged to commence this project by legal cases which were brought against the British government from 2012 onwards demanding justice for the atrocities committed by the empire in the 1950s through torture and internment camps. This was the 'Cyprus Emergency', so-called to echo similar events in Algeria, Kenya, and Malaya. This act of resistance resulted in a trickling open of archived documents relating to this suppressed era of British, Commonwealth, and Mediterranean histories, and monetary compensation began being provided for victims. In 2019, a mere one million pounds were split between 33 people who were, as they exposed in their court testimonies, tortured and, in some cases raped, by British officials. These cases offered to closest Cypriots have ever been granted in the way of recognition of the island's violent political past, from any of the countries complicit in its modern history of death and displacement. It was a modicum of the type of process facilitated in post-apartheid South Africa through the 1995 Truth and Reconciliation Commission. For Cypriots, truth and reconciliation have long been denied. The silences continue and the very limited publicity which these recent court cases generated signals further denial and cover-up.

As we move into a decade marked by renewed calls to decolonise academia, and to recognise and correct the colonial legacies of the world's major powers, there is need for comparable action in relation to Cyprus and Cypriots. This urgency informed my research which sought to apply the invaluable tools of postcolonialism to study the literature of, and about, Cyprus in order to investigate the colonial residues which remain interwoven into its cultural being. Politics and culture feed-off each other in ways which sustain, or repudiate, social conventions. Words are the units of both storytelling and government doctrines, and these two forms regularly blur into one another in a site as politically unstable and fragmented as Cyprus.

The island first came under British control in 1878, chosen to function as a stepping-stone in the midst of the Levant, allowing the empire further manoeuvrability between the three continents meeting on the shores of the Middle East. This political decision was followed by an outpouring of Anglophone travelogues about Cyprus and featuring accounts of British travellers arriving at the island to assess its usefulness for the empire. This began with Samuel White Baker and his *Cyprus, As I Saw It in 1879*, in which he surveyed the economic merits of controlling the island's resources while also passing judgement on the 'Oriental', 'savage', and 'primitive' nature of the 'native' islanders and their culture. This was supported by succeeding newspaper accounts, cartographic reports, and travellers' guides which veered from warnings of malarial and venereal infections to romantic accounts of an Eastern site of otherworldliness and exoticism.

Exactly one century later (and only several years after Cyprus had been nominally decolonised and then partitioned into incongruous segments), Edward Said published his famous scholarly resistance to colonialist literature: *Orientalism.* Like more than a quarter of Cypriots in the 1970s, Said was a refugee of the Eastern Mediterranean and his work focused an unprecedented lens on the ways in which literary depictions of this part of the world (the 'Orient') had been produced according to set motifs of powerlessness, moral decay, and exotic otherness to justify the need for paternalistic colonial protection by the imperial powers of Western Europe. His work forever changed the study of diverse fields—from literary criticism to anthropology—and gave life to the framework of postcolonial theory as it exists today. His notion of the *imaginative geography* of the colonial imagination influenced the concept of the *imagined communities* of nations (to quote Benedict Anderson) and of the ways in which these colonial and national spaces of domination create subject positions of *subalternity* for its marginalised inhabitants (to paraphrase Gayatri Spivak).

This field offers an important stepping-off point from which to begin to consider the situation of Cyprus. This island has been under the sway of various transcontinental empires since prehistory and has existed as a unified and independent island for *only fourteen years* (from 1960 to 1974). This is less than two decades of a lifespan of several millennia, dating back to the advent of agriculture when the first humans sailed across from the Levantine mainland approximately 12,000 years ago. Nonetheless, this claim of complete freedom for fourteen years is a generous suggestion. It is necessary, here, to return to the opening sentences of this preface: Cyprus *mostly* gained independence in 1960.

After formally decolonising the island, the UK retained two sizeable military bases on the island which remain to this day: the Sovereign Base Areas of Akrotiri and Dhekelia. As their very name suggests, the sovereignty of the newly 'independent' Republic of Cyprus was not complete. Some was retained by Britain. Despite the decision to include a copper-coloured map of the whole island on its national flag, the real political situation meant that internal borders cut the island into political territories of independent land and of land still belonging to the British Empire and its successor nation state. These internal borders increased dramatically and aggressively in the 1970s. This was, like the ability for the UK to retain bases on the island, facilitated by the US-backed decision for Cyprus to be supervised by three Guarantor Powers after ostensible decolonisation. These were Great Britain, Greece, and Turkey. While I have said much about the relationship between Cyprus and the UK, the other two powers have had similarly dominant influences over the island in ways which suggest a colonialist relationship between centre and periphery. Greek nationalism and Turkish nationalism are two ideological forces which have had significant impacts on Cypriots, before and after 1960. Many Cypriots who happen to speak Greek and/or Cypriot Greek view (or have viewed) Greece as the 'Motherland'. Similar sentiment can be said of Cypriots who happen to speak Turkish and/or Cypriot Turkish in relation to Turkey. While many citizens of the British Empire and then the Commonwealth of Nations (of which Cyprus is a member) have considered Britain a 'Motherland', or have been indoctrinated with the idea, Cypriots also (or instead) maintain this type of relationship with the nations centred around Athens and Ankara.

These nationalisms are not only theoretically fraught, but have had disastrous effects on islanders. So-called intercommunal conflict between Greek-speaking Christians and Turkish-speaking Muslims reached a head on the cusp of 1963 and 1964—stoked on by right-wing nationalists in Greece and Turkey, and embodying the divide-and-rule tactics of both British imperialism and Greek and Turkish irredentism. In this time, a permanent UN Peacekeeping Force was deployed and remains in place today. In the tragic summer of 1974, a *coup* organised by Athens' fascist government and a military invasion (or, self-styled intervention), lead by Ankara, resulted in the island became irreversibly partitioned. Around 250,000 Cypriots became refugees or internally-displaced persons, and thousands more lost their lives. Generally, speakers of Cypriot Turkish were forced to live only in the north (or move abroad), while speakers of Cypriot Greek, and the smaller communities who speak Cypriot Arabic and Armenian, were forced to live only in the south (or abroad). Many fled to the former British imperial metropolis of London. The partition is often referred to as the installation of an apartheid situation of ethnic segregation; the military events of 1974 were complicit in war crimes gesturing to ethnic cleansing. It remains unresolved.

The site of partition across what became known as the Green Line (or the Buffer Zone) remained impenetrably sealed for around thirty years until, in 2003, seven border crossings were opened to allow people to pass through, suffering the indignity of having to show their passports in order to visit 'the other side' of their home island and for refugees to return, as day visitors, to the homes they were forced to abandon three decades earlier. In 2018, two more crossings were opened. Despite these positive creeps forward in terms of progress, little else has changed and the sectarian division remains largely in place. Following failed interventions by the EU and the UN (including the Annan Plan and its unsuccessful 2004 referendum, named after the former UN Secretary-General), Cypriots have been moving further apart in recent years, despite the border openings. In the past decade, Cypriots have begun using two currencies (the Euro in the south and the Turkish Lira in the north) and are now, in summer time, living across two time zones (one shared with Greece, the other with Turkey). Several Cypriots in the south wave the flag of Greece alongside that of the Republic of Cyprus, with its still-intact copper island map gaining additional irony and poignancy. Meanwhile, several Cypriots in the north wave the flag of Turkey alongside that of the self-declared 'Turkish Republic of Northern Cyprus'. While the official languages of the southern part of the island are Greek and Turkish, public displays of text (like direction signs on a motorway) are typically written in Greek and English, showcasing both the linguistic divisions between islanders and the legacy of the colonial English tongue which remains on the island. It is the medium for intercommunal dialogue, the chief mode of expression in the tourism sector, and the official language of the British bases. Amidst these stark political differences, literary culture—often composed in English as an intercommunal, dialogical tool—remains one of the few spheres in which Cypriots are actively involved in close collaboration and exchange.

This unique confluence of factors demonstrates how Cyprus lives its postcolonial condition in ways which bear important echoes of other 'former' colonies of the British Empire, but which is also deeply particular to the specific issues impacting Cypriots. Nationalist forces on the island hold a neo-colonial stranglehold on islanders in ways which showcase the three, plural colonialisms which have claimed Cyprus and which prevent it from experiencing true independence or freedom (politically and culturally). The south relies heavily on Greece for goods, popular culture, and aspects of its identity formation, and the north relies on Turkey in similar ways. These relationships illustrate highly dependent centre-periphery models which resemble the colonial bondage between Britain and the island before 1960 and which complicate some of the expected dualistic discourse of postcolonial theory. Contemporary Cypriots are contesting colonialism(s) from multiple angles and not just from the residual British Empire. In fact, Greek nationalists often sing the praises of the Byzantine Empire while Turkish nationalists revere the Ottoman Empire from which the British wrestled the island in the nineteenth century. Categories like 'empire', 'nation', and 'dominant discourse' take new, multifaceted forms in Cyprus in ways which link to the rest of the decolonising world but which are also markedly distinct to this context.

For these reasons, I needed to formulate a new theoretical lens through which the culture of Cyprus could be understood and investigated, and I arrived on the concept of the *transportal* nature of Cyprus and, in particular, its literature. The majority of literature about, and composed in, Cyprus since 1878 has taken the form of travelogues or related genres. This, too, is unusual given the rise of the postcolonial novel across Africa and Asia in response to British imperialism. Forms of literature connected to travel writing offer a vital medium through which Cyprus can be represented due to the issues of movement which pertain to this insular space in specific ways. As an island, it floats precariously in the midst of the Levantine Sea where colonial powers have sought to use it as an intermediary to disperse through continents and to exert control over the rest of the Middle East. As such, Cyprus has long been a portal, or doorway, between 'East' and 'West', and has been appropriated as a 'strategic' hub for storing the transport facilities of maritime powers, from the Persians and Phoenicians to the Crusaders and the Venetians. Today, the island rocks between the shifting influences of Britain, Greece, and Turkey—as well as the EU, the United Staetes, and the UN—forcing it to move between geopolitical allegiances. It even moves between designations as part of 'Asia' or 'Europe'. All the while, Cypriots on the ground have long been unable to move across the Green Line; refugees were forced to transport their lives from one part of the island to another (or to leave their homeland altogether). What the island has opened up for the passage of empires has led to the closing down of free movement for its citizens.

British travel writers flocked to this exoticised space in the nineteenth century. The empire to which these writers were affiliated used Cypriot marinas as imperial ports for easy access to Suez and, in the following century, as the military headquarters of its Middle East Command. By the new millennium, the island had produced an entirely new landscape featuring an incongruous mixture of international tourists on both sides of the Green Line and of dispossessed Cypriots unable to cross the same frontier. Accordingly, Cypriot literature is laden with transportal images, including doorways between homes, openings between borders, and other liminal spaces across the island. These works have a generic specificity to island, hybridising conventional travelogues with elements of fictionality, reportage, and poeticism. This, combined with the recurring and often directly intertextual lexis of liminality, has produced what I call transportal literatures. The works I have selected to research for this book reveal these points of thematic and stylistic connection, through which they comparably grapple with the island's colonial, nationalist, and post-colonial experiences. Many respond to preceding works from this small context in urgent ways and account for my decision to include them. British women writers of the nineteenth century, for instance, put pressure on the misogynistic discourse of their contemporaries, while anti-colonial Cypriot writers of the 1950s and 1960s challenge British imperial writing in all its manifestations.

Today, Cypriot writers reject both the language of pre-1960s colonialism (including Lawrence Durrell's often-cited 1957 travelogue, *Bitter Lemons*) *and* the nationalist affiliations which were sometimes made uncritically during and after 1960. Their works are redolent with shared images of the empty refugee home and the doors into them, symbolising the open or closed doorways between north and south, freedom and confinement, or one ethnolinguistic community and another. Father figures (from the political figureheads of Atatürk and Venizelos, to Durrell as literary forebear) are often positioned as arbiters of these doors and architects of the arbitrary 'mother-fatherlands' in which Cypriots are forced to exist. These contemporary writers, including Aydın Mehmet Ali, Nora Nadjarian, and Yiannis Papadakis, create intertexts which knowingly engage with the political situation of Cyprus in order to transport discourse about the island into a postcolonial, or a *more* postcolonial, future.

These concerns, while largely unique to Cyprus, will also have major implications for other contexts of the decolonising world. I aim for this framework of transportal literatures to gain life beyond this book and to influence postcolonial theory in ways which allow for future application to contexts which grapple with plural and layered forms of colonialism(s), particularly for areas of the world considered liminal, both geographically and politically.

It has been vital that a roughly-equal number of Cypriot writers who are Greek-speaking and Turkish-speaking, and men and women, were included in this study. It was similarly important to feature the work of an Armenian-speaking Cypriot author (Nadjarian) as one primary case study for this research, to overcome the marginalisation of the island's smallest communities. No investigation of the cultural production of the island can be accurate if it does not attempt to represent its multiple ethnolinguistic communities and the varying experiences of Cypriotness lived according to the diverse linguistic, religious, and gendered backgrounds of Cypriots themselves. For the second chapter, there was comparable intention to resist the marginalisation of British women travel writers in studies of the genre.

The inspiration to research the topic of this book did not arise solely from academic motivations; it is a deeply personal project borne out of my own familial connection to Cyprus. In particular, my Cypriot maternal grandfather is an unending source of inspiration, personally and professionally. He lived with us in our family home for fifteen years until his death during the second year of my doctoral research. It was with him, and the rest of my close family, that I travelled to Cyprus yearly and it is because of his enduring life that I exist as I am today. As a Cypriot of the early twentieth century, my grandfather was born in the British Empire and he served in Egypt for the British military during the Second World War; he returned to the island to witness the rise in intercommunal conflict and faced colonial economic restrictions as a farmer. He, his siblings, and his widowed mother became refugees; he moved to the colonial heart of London while most of his family became internally-displaced peoples forced to cross over to the other side of what became the Buffer Zone. More than just a collection of historical stories, he was a hardworking, patient, and kind man. He helped teach me these values and he introduced me to the importance of story-telling. I would sit in awe of his accounts of the arid plains between Nicosia and Famagusta, or about the grim streets of post-war London. Central to his forgiving mindset was his inability to express anger towards the Cypriot 'Other'; he never participated in narratives which demonised Cypriots of different ethnolinguistic backgrounds or which homogenised people from Britain, Greece, or Turkey. On a partitioned island, and in a partitioned world, this is an invaluable quality. He died after being diagnosed with Alzheimer's, a disease which brings to the forefront the need to remember and to memorialise. Between 1974 and his death, he was never able to return to his childhood home on 'the other side' of the border. For over forty years, that home was little more than a memory, a memory which began to fade with illness. In fact, his childhood home no longer exists; it was demolished to make way for a byroad. Still, it was his new diasporic home in London—that odd place where his fig trees and vines still grow outside in the grey, smoggy air—that assumed a new centrality in his life. This book is dedicated to him—and to the rest of my immediate family who love him and remember him.

Drawing on my family background, therefore, I have always sought to answer important questions about what I had seen and heard in relation to Cyprus and Cypriotness. Why, as a child, would we drive past various internal borders and wave at an array of soldiers—Cypriot, British, Greek, Turkish, UN—stationed on this otherwise-quiet island? Why could we not cross that barbwire wall to see the specific villages where my ancestors were born and died? Why did some Cypriots call themselves 'Cypriots' and others called themselves 'Greeks' and 'Turks', or something else between? Why does one atlas place Cyprus in Asia and another in Europe? Is it in the Middle East? Why does one Cypriot identify as 'white' while another identifies as a person of colour? Why did I have great-uncles who died in prisoner of war camps *after* the Second World War? How is it that my grandfather was born somewhere on the fringes of the British Empire and then died nine decades later in Britain, yet both those places are thousands of miles apart? Why do all Cypriots seem to speak English fluently? What and where are the Republic of Cyprus, the 'Turkish Republic of Northern Cyprus', the British Bases, and the Buffer Zone? Where exactly is home?

Not all of these questions can be answered by this book alone. Yet, when I was first introduced to postcolonial theory during my time as an undergraduate, I began to find a model through which I could approach these long-held dilemmas. Reading Chinua Achebe, Benedict Anderson, Homi Bhabha, Elleke Boehmer, Frantz Fanon, Paul Gilroy, Stuart Hall, Jamaica Kincaid, Edward Said, Gayatri Spivak, and Robert Young—to mention but a few names—felt like a revelatory access into debates with which I had long wanted to engage but had lacked the tools to do so. I would sit for hours leafing through, annotating, and highlighting my hallowed copy of *The Post-Colonial Studies Reader*. I then learned that such a thing as literature from Cyprus existed. Beginning with Papadakis' groundbreaking *Echoes from the Dead Zone*, I gradually became aware of moving and captivating prose by Ali and Nadjarian, among many others. Researching this monograph has allowed me, with great personal and academic passion, to draw on these theorists and authors to perform research which I believe is vital for my family, for the wider Cypriot and British-Cypriot communities, and for the postcolonial discipline as a whole.

Oxford, UK
July 2020

Daniele Nunziata

Acknowledgements

I would like to acknowledge all the academics (arranged alphabetically) who have offered me invaluable assistance in approaching the questions considered in this book. From Queen Mary, University of London, I would like to thank all the lecturers who introduced me to postcolonialism and to the marvel of its study. These include Shahidha Bari, Rachael Gilmour, Bill Schwartz, and Andrew Van der Vlies. From the University of Oxford, I would like to thank all the lecturers who have shaped me into the scholar I am today, including all those involved in the MSt in World Literatures in English. These are Elleke Boehmer, Patrick Hayes, Michelle Kelly, Peter D. McDonald, Tiziana Morosetti, and Ankhi Mukherjee. In particular, I would like to enthusiastically thank my D.Phil. supervisor, Matthew Reynolds, without whom I would not be at this point in my academic career and whose support has been consistent, indispensable, and formative. As well as being a world-leading academic in the fields of comparative criticism and translation studies, his approachability and compassion enabled me to feel well-supported enough to complete my doctoral studies.

I must also thank my two doctoral examiners, Michelle Kelly and Robert Young, for their generous decision to assess my thesis and for their invaluable wisdom and advice. They made the viva process far less daunting than I feared and their meticulous observations on my work facilitated an intellectually-stimulating discussion which remains of great inspiration. I would like to thank St Hugh's College in which I was a postgraduate student and to all the administrative team who helped me in my years as a member there. My gratitude also goes to St Anne's College in which I have been a Lecturer in English Literature for the past three years and where I have been given amble support to grow in this role. At the College, I have thoroughly enjoyed teaching literature to new students. It has been an honour to create new courses on postcolonial literature for undergraduate, master's, and visiting students, and to observe their keen interest in the set reading to the extent that many of my students have chosen to continue this field of research through future postgraduate study on postcolonial writing. I couldn't ask for a greater sense of professional accomplishment.

I have had the most wonderful years in Oxford and am so grateful to everyone who has helped make this a time of abundant learning and growth. This includes current and former members of the Postcolonial Writing and Theory Seminar, of the Oxford Comparative Criticism and Translation (OCCT) group, and of the team behind *Writers Make Worlds*.

I would also like to thank the Cypriot writers I have had the privilege to meet and discuss ideas with. This includes Aydın Mehmet Ali, Christy Lefteri, and Yiannis Papadakis, all three of whom are significant inspirations to me as a scholar and as an activist. They have taught me that authorship and activism go hand in hand. Their prose is mesmerising.

My thanks also go to the entire team at Palgrave Macmillan. I am deeply appreciative of their decision to publish this book. I must thank Lina Aboujieb and Rebecca Hinsley for their dedicated work in bringing this project to life. I have been very well-supported throughout the process of adapting my words into a publication and have enjoyed these past few months of editing.

Finally, but most importantly, I want to express my unending gratitude to my loved ones: my family and my close friends. My grandparents, my parents, Rita and Giovanni, and my brothers, Antonio and Demitri, are infinite sources of influence, motivation, and guidance. There aren't enough words to adequately summarise my appreciation and indebtedness to you. Thank you and I love you. I could not have written this book without you. You are the wisest and most loyal people in my life. I hope I have made you proud.

Thanks to you all.

A Note on Terminology

As will become clear in the first chapter, I disagree with the concept that certain essentialised identities exist. Instead, I recognise that we each make identifications with a series of cultural discourses into which we are absorbed through processes of interpellation. As a consequence, I have decided not to make simple references to *ethnic identities* or *national identities*. In their place, I use the terms *ethnolinguistic identities* and *identifications* in relation to Cyprus. This draws on the notion that identifications made on the island can be associated with the language(s) a Cypriot happens to speak and not with a biological or transcendental essence. To this effect, I have chosen not to use the identity markers 'Greek Cypriot' and 'Turkish Cypriot' (or, indeed, to refer to Cypriot authors as 'Greeks' and 'Turks'). Where possible, I refer to Cypriots simply as Cypriots. Where there is a need to describe a Cypriot's linguistic or cultural background, I have chosen to use the terms 'Greek-speaking Cypriots' and 'Turkish-speaking Cypriots'. Again, I employ this terminology to stress the arbitrary linguistic difference between people inhabiting and/or from the island, rather than to draw on biological essentialism. This is not uncomplicated or unproblematic, and I do not suggest that other forms of identification are not acceptable. Nonetheless, this is the terminology I feel most comfortable with and which I feel best expresses my position that there is no essential or 'racial' difference between Cypriots who happen to speak different languages. These names are merely shorthand for describing something that cannot be easily reduced to one, two, or three words but which have been constructed through dominant and counter-dominant discourses over decades. I hope this book will elaborate how and why these identifications have emerged. There is also the issue that Cypriots speak languages other than Standard Modern Greek and Standard Modern Turkish, an important point addressed in the first chapter and throughout. In short, there is no unproblematic way to describe Cypriots who happen to live on one side of a barbwire partition or another.

Contents

About the Author

Dr. Daniele Nunziata is a Lecturer in English Literature at the University of Oxford. He teaches nineteenth-century and modern literature at St Anne's College. After finishing his undergraduate degree at Queen Mary, University of London, he was awarded a Violet Vaugh Morgan Studentship to read for an MSt in World Literatures in Oxford. He continued at the same university to complete a D.Phil., the research for which has informed the core material of this book. He has written widely on postcolonial literature, and his research has been published in *PMLA*, the *Journal of Postcolonial Writing*, *FORUM*, and *World Literature in Motion: Institution, Recognition, Location* (a book in the Columbia University Press series, *Studies in World Literature*). He is a contributor to the online postcolonial project *Writers Make Worlds*, has written for the Oxford Centre for Life-Writing and *Great Writers Inspire*, and has discussed his research live on BBC Radio. He has helped organise numerous conferences on world literature, such as *Translational Spaces* with the Oxford Comparative Criticism and Translation (OCCT) group, and has delivered research papers at multiple global institutions, including the University of Cambridge and Harvard University. As a poet, his words have been published in several journals. This is his first monograph.

Abbreviations

Commonwealth	Commonwealth of Nations
BOTs	British Overseas Territories
EOKA	*Ethniki Organosis Kyprion Agoniston* (National Organisation of Cypriot Fighters)
EU	European Union
NAM	Non-Aligned Movement
RoC	Republic of Cyprus
TMT	*Türk Mukavemet Teşkilatı* (Turkish Resistance Organisation)
'TRNC'	'Turkish Republic of Northern Cyprus'
SBA	Sovereign Base Areas of Akrotiri and Dhekelia
UN	United Nations
UNFICYP	United Nations Peacekeeping Force in Cyprus

CHAPTER 1

'The Key of Western Asia': An Introduction to Transportal Literatures

In January 2016, the American magazine *Foreign Affairs* published an article titled, 'Cyprus in the Middle: Nicosia Holds the Keys to Syria, the Migrant Crisis, and Gas in the Eastern Mediterranean'.[1] For centuries, most depictions of this island in the English-speaking media have emphasised its position in an important yet volatile geopolitical region, poised 'in the middle' of opposing ideological forces. In recent years, coverage has spanned from Britain's use of its Cypriot bases to send warplanes to Syria in December 2016 and April 2018, to renewed antagonism with Turkey over hydrocarbon treaties with Egypt, Greece, and Israel. Jonathan Gorvett in the aforementioned article paints the scene of an unstable and unpredictable locus in which competing governments parade their military power as the lingering residues, not only of the Cold War, but the Great Game before it: 'British warplanes… headed for Syria, just 100 miles away', 'Israeli warplanes', 'Russian warships', and a 'seismic research vessel, chartered by a U.S. company… shadowed by a Turkish frigate'.[2] All in one short paragraph, the vivid imagery suggests the inception of a third world war on the shores of the Eastern Mediterranean with Cyprus stranded, and fought over, 'in the middle'. Housing numerous foreign military powers, this 'far-flung Levantine outpost, is once again a Gordian knot of regional conflicts and conundrums'.[3]

If one were to trace the representation of the island across the preceding century, it would be evident that little has changed in the

D. Nunziata, *Colonial and Postcolonial Cyprus*,
https://doi.org/10.1007/978-3-030-58236-4_1

discourse that frames it.[4] Even following the same magazine's depiction of Cyprus during the most important years of its modern history is revealing of the discursive parallelism within which it is trapped. In July 1975, a little under a year after partition, 'The Mediterranean Crisis' was published, stressing that the Eastern 'Mediterranean today is the scene of serious local conflicts, of which those over Cyprus and over Palestine are the most intractable and the most dangerous [...] Add to this the continuing competition between the United States and Russia... and the uncertainty on all sides as to how far détente will be applied, if at all, in the Mediterranean and the Middle East'.[5] It is clear from the still enduring tension between American and Russian fleets, forty years later, that *détente* is far from being realised. While Gorvett speaks of 'gas trouble' in 2016, his forebear details the 'oil crisis' of 1975.

If we look back further to the year of Cyprus' independence from the British Empire, *Foreign Affairs* published one of the earliest commentaries on the twentieth century's most controversial neologism: 'Where is the Middle East?'. Writing in 1960, Roderic H. Davidson, one-time president of the Middle East Studies Association, argues that '[i]nternational crisis is one of the best teachers of geography. Among centers [*sic*] of crisis that have burst onto the American public's map in recent years are Suez, Cyprus, Baghdad, Algeria, the Lebanon and others commonly lumped together under the general label "Middle East"'.[6] Framing these events within 'the context of the cold war', he also stresses that 'no one knows where the Middle East is'.[7] In all three articles, the same textual figures recur. Paramount among them are the alliterative 'crisis', 'conflict', and 'cold war'. Importantly, Davidson indicates a tripartite relationship between politics, 'geography', and epistemology—a revision of Foucault's knowledge and power dialectic—rendered threatening when knowledge is found lacking. Perhaps the *Middle* East is deemed dangerous precisely because it is difficult to define—including the translingual and religiously-mixed Cyprus metonymic of this *Medi*terranean mediality.

Looking further back still, almost 140 years before the *Foreign Affairs* subtitle, 'Nicosia Holds the Keys to Syria', the British Prime Minister Benjamin Disraeli famously declared Cyprus 'the key of Western Asia' in his correspondence with Queen Victoria, in which he promises that the island will secure imperial hegemony across the continent and that her 'Majesty's Indian Empire [will be] immediately strengthened'.[8] The idiom has been repeated frequently by political commentators, travel writers, and novelists throughout the succeeding century. Imbricating political and literary discourses, the years succeeding the acquisition of the island, 1878, saw a sudden rise in published travelogues promoting the 'strategic' benefits of Cyprus to the colonial project. In 1879, the established travel writers Sir Samuel White Baker and William Hepworth Dixon both released their accounts: *Cyprus, As I Saw It in 1879* and *British Cyprus*, respectively. For the former, 'Cyprus is the key of a great position' as 'the missing link in the chain of our communications with… the Suez Canal and the subsequent route to India'.[9] For the latter, the island is 'the key of Egypt, Syria, and Asia Minor'.[10] Nearing the end of this generation of nineteenth-century travelogues, the polyglot and biblical scholar, Agnes Smith, who travelled twice to Cyprus with her sister, repeats this jingoistic imagery to herald the moment which 'induced the British lion to place his foot upon Cyprus, an island which, from its position, might easily be made the key to the Levant'.[11] These motifs echo into the twentieth century. The acclaimed novelist, Angela Carter, writing for *New Society* one year before the 1974 partition, reiterates aphoristically: 'He who holds Cyprus holds the key to the eastern Mediterranean'.[12]

For all, the image of keys positions Cyprus as a strategic gateway or *portal* through which military and cultural paradigms are exchanged. It is the limen between Europe and Asia, Christianity and Islam, West and East, America and Russia, Greece and Turkey, and the symbolic self and Other of the colonial imagination. Politically, holding these keys allows one to control the portal and extend one's hegemony over the other side. Controlling Cyprus has, for most of its history, allowed vast empires to cross continents and consolidate valuable resources. The portal becomes a dehumanised port in which the tools of imperialism have been, and continue to be, stationed north of Suez and east of Jerusalem. Colonisers, crusaders, and caliphs have fought for those keys since prehistory. In the words of Churchill, securing Cyprus in the Second World War meant 'the Levant thus came into a far more satisfactory condition. Our naval and air control over the Eastern end of the Mediterranean became effective, and we obtained… control of the pipe line and other resources'.[13] Even from these few examples, the intertextual repetition of discourse used to represent Cyprus from the late nineteenth century to the present is clear to see, as is the dependence of politics on literature to disseminate these claims.

The purpose of this book is to interrogate this diachronic literary tradition, particularly within the genre of travel writing. Investigating how cultural practitioners interpellate political landscapes into the textual imagining of space has long been an important facet of postcolonial studies, ever since Edward Said's influential theory of the Orientalist discourse used to construct ideological juxtapositions between 'East' and 'West' through 'imaginative geography'.[14] Nonetheless, the modern history and literatures of Cyprus have been infrequently featured within established postcolonial oeuvres. It is important, not only to bring the complex Cypriot context into the postcolonial field, but also to observe how Cyprus complicates established classifications of 'postcolonial' and 'world' literatures. How does its recent experiences of nationalist movements, partition, and enduring British military bases alter our understanding of the temporal colonial-postcolonial dichotomy? How does the island's position between multiple spheres of cultural influence challenge notions of 'worlds' and 'the world'? By asking these questions, I aim to showcase the centrality of travel writing for this overlooked region of the post/colonial planet and reveal how the travelogue form employed in the writing of Cyprus opens up a mode of *transportal* literatures and literary reading practices.

Historical, Linguistic, and Literary Background

For the majority of its history, the island of Cyprus has never not been under the administration of a foreign empire. Its earliest settlers sailed from the Neolithic Levantine mainland following the development of agriculture, beginning a long history of trade and transport between island and mainland. Thousands of years later, successive colonisations by regional powers took place, from Hittites, Egyptians, and Persians, to Mycenaeans, Phoenicians, and Neo-Assyrians. According to Herodotus, Cyprus belonged to the fifth satrapy of the Achaemenid Empire at around 400BC.[15] By 400AD, it had become part of Rome's Diocese of the East (*Dioecesis Orientis*). Both administrative regions stretched roughly from Anatolia to Egypt, including the entirety of the Levant. The two, therefore, represent the earliest subcontinental groupings to anticipate today's definition of 'the Middle East', or, as it was known from Roman times until recently, 'the Orient'.

Following Arab, English, and French occupations during the Crusades, the island came under Venetian rule which outlawed Orthodoxy and, through the creation of sugar plantations, implemented 'slave plantation agriculture'.[16] It was a colonial system to be 'transplanted to the New World three centuries later'.[17] Aside from a fleeting period of

Egyptian Mamluk intervention, the island remained Venetian until 1571 when it was ceded to the Ottoman Empire. This move from Christian to Islamic ownership becomes the paradigmatic source of terror at the heart of Shakespeare's *Othello* (c.1603). The Ottomans, as well as conveying Turkish-speaking settlers, removed both plantation slavery and the ban on Orthodox Christianity with the advent of its *millet* system of religious self-representation. By the nineteenth century, however, the Ottoman Porte was in decline and faced insurrection from increasingly-impoverished Cypriots and mainlanders, alike. Meanwhile, as the Great Game played out, Great Britain sought territorial expansion in the region between its allies and the Russian Empire. Consequently, in the same year as the onset of the Second Anglo-Afghan War, the Ottoman and British empires signed the 1878 Cyprus Convention, passing authority of the island from the former to latter, and guaranteeing British dominion over 'the future [of] the territories in Asia of His Imperial Majesty the Sultan'.[18] British rule was consolidated during the First World War. According to the Sykes-Picot Agreement (1916) dictating the borders of the modern Middle East, no-one but Britain may 'enter into negotiations for the cession of Cyprus to any third power'.[19] Following the Treaties of Sèvres and Lausanne, Cyprus became a Crown Colony in 1925. An integral part of the empire, especially during the Suez Crisis, it was selected as the new headquarters of the Middle East Command as Britain began losing control of Egypt. Once again, Cyprus functioned as political and military middle ground from which an empire could hold sway over the Eastern Mediterranean and beyond.

From 1955, however, Cypriots began protesting British rule. The Greek-speaking Cypriot military group EOKA employed guerrilla tactics against the empire and lobbied for *enosis*, or union, with Greece. The Turkish-speaking Cypriot group, TMT, opposed this and advocated *taksim*, or division, instead. This period was referred to by the British as the 'Cyprus Emergency', in parallel with coterminous *emergencies* in Kenya (from 1952) and Malaya (from 1948). All three ended in 1960, following the deaths of hundreds in Cyprus and the internment of dozens of EOKA fighters in camps. It resulted in Cyprus achieving independence from the British Empire that year. However, not only did Britain retain two military bases which remain to this day—the Sovereign Base Areas of Akrotiri and Dhekelia—but so-called independence came with the Treaty of Guarantee which established the UK, Greece, and Turkey as three Guarantor Powers with the right to intervene to 're-establish... the state of affairs' in case of political upheaval.[20] The nascent Republic of Cyprus was a child under the panoptic scrutiny of three mutually-distrustful parents.

The Republic divided the role of President and Vice President according to ethnolinguistic background: the former was to be Greek-speaking or Christian, the latter Turkish-speaking. The first two, almost echoing the religious representation of the *millet* system, were Archbishop Makarios III and Fazıl Küçük. Makarios, regularly viewed as a left-leaning threat by the United States, was a vocal spokesperson within the decolonising world. He attended the famous Bandung (or, Afro-Asian) Conference, alongside Nasser, Nehru, and Nkrumah, resulting in the Republic becoming a founding member of the Non-Aligned Movement in 1961. He attached the country to both the Commonwealth of Nations and the Afro-Asian People's Solidarity Organisation, and even hosted the latter's eighth Council Session in February 1967. Despite Makarios' charm on the world stage, his ability to maintain order on the island was ineffectual, and social and political tensions grew. Violence by, and between, nationalist organisations increased, including that of a new Greek-speaking paramilitary group, EOKA B, largely controlled by Georgios Grivas. In 1963, a massacre of Turkish-speaking Cypriots led to the deployment of a UN Peacekeeping Force early the following year. Extremist nationalists from both Greek- and Turkish-speaking communities not only promoted claims of ethnic opposition, but physically targeted Cypriots of different ethnolinguistic backgrounds as well as left-wing Cypriots of the same background.

The 'Cyprus problem' came to a head in 1974. On July 15, the fascist junta in Greece staged a *coup d'état* expelling Makarios with the desire to implement *enosis*. Makarios described it repeatedly as an 'invasion'.[21] Five days later, Turkey, acting on its guarantor status, responded with a military invasion (or, in its words, 'intervention') for the benefit of Turkish-speaking citizens. Violence continued until August 16 by which time Turkey had occupied the northern third of the island, including the northern third of the capital, Nicosia. Denounced by the UN Security Council Resolution 360, this division of territory is marked by a buffer zone that has since been named the 'Green Line'—not unlike the two Green Lines dividing nearby Jerusalem and Beirut. Patrolled by the UN, and following the deaths and dispossession of thousands, the line segregates Cypriots according to religious and ethnolinguistic identities as an act of partition. As it still stands, the island is divided into four administrative regions. As well as the British bases and UN Buffer Zone, most Cypriots who identify as speakers of Greek, Cypriot Arabic, or Armenian, the majority of whom are from Christian backgrounds, live in the southern de facto territory of the Republic of Cyprus. Turkish-speaking Cypriots, most of whom are either Sunni Muslim or irreligious, live in the northern part of the island which, in 1983, declared itself the 'Turkish Republic of Northern Cyprus' ('TRNC'), but has only been recognised by one UN member state, Turkey. Cypriots in the north have been joined by an undisclosed number of settlers from Turkey since this time. The stalemate has remained largely unchanged since August 1974, other than in April 2003 when seven openings were made in the Green Line, including one on Ledra Street in the middle of one of the world's last divided capitals. Cypriots were able to pass through the line of partition for the first time in almost thirty years. Talks for complete reunification have been unsuccessful and the partitioned island remains *home*, in some sense of the word, for over 200,000 internally-displaced persons, or roughly a quarter of its population.

While often reductively referred to as housing a 'Greek' and a 'Turkish' side, the languages of the island are more numerous. There is official English in the British Sovereign Base Areas, and the presence of small Cypriot communities who speak Armenian and Cypriot Arabic (or, Sanna, for Maronites), both afforded minority status in the south. The official languages of the Republic of Cyprus are Greek and Turkish, in the forms standardised in Athens and Ankara, respectively. It is these standard forms which prevail in education, politics, and the media.[22] The everyday vernaculars of Cypriots, however, are Kypriaka ('Cypriot Greek') and Kıbrıslıca (or, Kıbrıs Türkçesi; 'Cypriot Turkish')—both denied standardisation or official status, and both derided as rural *dialects* by nationalists who privilege the cultural forms of Greece or Turkey. On the other hand, for (predominately left-wing) Cypriots who advocate total independence, not only from British imperialism, but other manifestations of sociopolitical hegemony, these vernaculars are bestowed with greater cultural value and the potential to be standardised or even consecrated as languages. Standard Greek and Standard Turkish can be viewed as nationalist—and, indeed, neo-colonialist—interventions which estrange Cypriots from indigenous vernaculars in comparable ways to the introduction of English a century earlier. Of symbolic importance, the national anthem of the south is the same as that of Greece, and that of the north is the same as that of Turkey.

Most Cypriots are diglossic, speaking either Kypriaka and Greek, or Kıbrıslıca and Turkish, with equal fluency.[23] The majority also speak English with a high degree of proficiency. Cypriots from the smallest ethnolinguistic communities often speak three or four languages simultaneously, splicing words from one form into another, creating mixed languages through code-switching.[24] The Cypriot languages already exhibit significant degrees of lexical borrowing, with mutual loan words from Arabic, Greek, Turkish, and Western European languages.[25] As a consequence, linguistic identity is difficult to define for Cypriots who speak one (or two) language(s) privately—the vernaculars of the home—and another one or two publically—the official languages of the island's political structures and the omnipresent English of academia.

Many right-wing Cypriots identify with the dimorphic national(ist) categories of *Greeks* and *Turks* and as inheritors of the pure forms of the languages associated with those nations. By contrast, left-wing islanders increasingly espouse identifications *as Cypriots* with a collective cultural history in a translingual space home to many pre-colonial and pre-nationalist vernaculars. Many fall within this spectrum, classifying themselves as *Greek Cypriots*, *Turkish Cypriots*, *Maronite Cypriots*, and *Armenian Cypriots*, or using other markers of identity altogether. One of the most crucial theories to impact this monograph is Jacques Derrida's assessment that 'an identity is never given, received, or attained; only the interminable and indefinitely phantasmatic process of *identification* endures' (*emphasis mine*).[26]

In addition to history and language, Cyprus holds a confused position between the three continents which surround it. Geographically part of Asia, and nearer the continental coasts of both Asia and Africa than it is to Europe, the island fluctuates in its identifications with the *ideas* of continents. Despite being a member of the 'Group of Asia and the Pacific Small Island Developing States' at the UN General Assembly (and defined as part of 'Western Asia' by the UN), the Republic of Cyprus has nonetheless joined Europe-centred organisations, most notable of which is the European Union. Consequently, some atlases include the island in its maps of Asia, while others in those of Europe, illustrating how disciplines understood as objective or empirical in their study of the planet as a geographic or geological space are not immune from sociopolitical bias. For some geographers, the existence of a partly-Greek-speaking,

Christian-majority country in the Middle East threatens a neat delineation of culture across continental divides. It should be noted that, in addition to Cyprus, not every Middle Eastern state is Muslim-majority (Israel) or has Arabic as an official language (Turkey and Iran). The reality of ethnolinguistic diversity in this region between Europe and the rest of Asia is not conducive to stereotypes which present a monolithic and pejorative image of the oil-producing cradle of civilisation. Cyprus is emblematic of this *ambivalence*, situated on the limens of arbitrary classifications of East-West, Europe-Asia, and Christian-Muslim, threatening each dichotomy by presenting the failings of these long-held ideological oppositions. These oppositions, however, have been internalised by islanders themselves, culminating mostly violently in the erection of the Green Line. For some, this is the limit of continents, cultures, and civilisations. As the writer and academic Yiannis Papadakis has noted, Said's theory is integral to understanding both how Cyprus is represented by others and how Cypriots represent themselves.[27] The 'self and Other' of the colonial paradigm—British and 'native'—is reiterated as the 'self and Other' of Greek and Turk, or Christian and Muslim.[28] The partition of the globe into distinct spheres of influence has resulted in the psychological and geographic partition of Cypriots born on land which dangerously straddles 'Western' categories of friend and foe. According to tourist brochures, Cyprus is a sunny idyll in south-eastern Europe; for regional analysts, Cyprus is a Levantine ammunitions dump miles from Damascus and Baghdad. *Neither place is real* and both images elide the quotidian experiences of actual Cypriots attempting to manage the traumas of colonialism, nationalism, and partition.

Although Said wrote little on the representation of Cyprus, he alluded to the island many times in interviews and his monographs, often as a pertinent example of post/colonial partition, alongside Israel/Palestine, South Asia, and Ireland. In his desire to offer a mode of regional cultural production which moves away from Orientalism, he has advocated the need for Middle Eastern peoples to mobilise forms of 'social organization' which further the 'mutilation [of] the nation-state'. He describes this as a 'Mediterranean' structure, and one which would include Arabic-speaking and Jewish peoples, as well as Cypriots. Asked whether his idea would be specifically 'pan-Arab', he responded in an interview that it ought to be 'Mediterranean. Why should it not include Cyprus?'. In *Culture and Imperialism* (1993), he argues that 'the Middle East was linked internally by all sorts of ties', which included, not only European rule, but parallels between the actions of the Turkish government in Cyprus with Saddam Hussein in Kuwait.[29] For Said, the history of Cyprus was woven into the intertextual tapestry of the wider region, observing internal links between the forms of imperialism and sectarianism occurring across the post-Ottoman, post-Anglo-French 'Mediterranean'. While Orientalists would elide these complex similarities and differences, the task of those opposing this discourse is to tease out the intricate fabrics which have made this region, moving beyond national and ethnolinguistic partitions both on the ground and in academia.

Elsewhere in established postcolonial works, Cyprus is used as a byword for cultural transportation.[30] To quote W.E.B. Du Bois' anti-colonial world history, for instance, 'Africa appears as the Father of mankind, and the people who eventually settled there, wherever they have wandered before or since – along the Ganges, the Euphrates, and the Nile, in Cyprus and about the Mediterranean – form the largest… creators of human culture'.[31] Du Bois recalibrates Cyprus' position to the centre of, not simply an Afrocentric, but a postcolonial vision of the world as a diachronic nexus in which the former margins of the British Empire—much of Africa, India, Iraq, Egypt, and Cyprus—reclaim agency over that prized word of imperialists: civilisation. Importantly, it is an agency achieved through transcontinental connectivity.

Indeed, Cypriot intersections with the rest of the world, especially the Mediterranean, particularly through the medium of literature, date to the Bronze Age. It is the island's interstitiality which has fuelled, and complicated, literary renderings of it as a site of cultural inbetweenness. According to Jennifer Larson, ancient Cyprus was 'an intermediary for both goods and ideas travelling west' or east.[32] On the origins of world literature, David Damrosch notes that 'poet-singers were likely performing *Gilgamesh* in Syria and Cyprus during the period in which the Homeric epics were first being elaborated', with the former presenting a narratorial template for the latter.[33] The *Epic of Gilgamesh* represents the very first example of travel writing, both in terms of narrative content and its metatextual influence on succeeding literary practices overseas. Not only does it concern travel, but it too has travelled. Cyprus facilitated this transmission across forms and languages. As such, it marks the start of a long Cypriot tradition of developing mobile literatures which can be transported between continents, or of offering a metonymic context for works which narrate lives of transport. *Gilgamesh* impacted both Homeric and Biblical discourses with Cyprus midway between the ancient

Greek- and Semitic-speaking shores of the Mediterranean. The archetypal travel narrative of the New Testament, John's evangelising mission, frames Cyprus as his first destination beyond the Syro-Palestinian coast, and before he attempts to convert Asia Minor and Southern Europe. Cyprus arrives bombastically in English through the travelogue-laden register of Shakespeare's *Othello*. It is a play which borrows heavily from exoticist travel writing to present the island as a morally-dangerous space between Venice and Turkey, Europe and Asia, Christendom and Islam, black and white, and male and female. Travel becomes an embodiment of racialised and gendered fears at the very dawn of what would be the British Empire. Indeed, it was composed in the same year as the Union of England and Scotland Act 1603. This is not only the first major representation of Cyprus in English but the first piece of *British* colonial literature. England's former Crusader state, at this point Islamised, while Venetian slavery practices began being replicated in the 'New World', offers an early and acute example of colonial *ambivalence*. I would argue that the context and themes of this play were to be replicated in Shakespeare's last—his other play set on a dangerous island between continents, this time in the increasingly-important transatlantic, *The Tempest* (c.1610). Note the parallel storms which, in one case, carries Othello to Cyprus by ship and, in the other, directs European seafarers to the Atlantic island.

With this background, Cyprus became a focal point for colonial travel writers following its acquisition by the British Empire. A life of constant transportation, caused by the economic and political transactions of empire, was placed in juxtaposition with a space reputed for its transport of cultures. Illustrating Said's dialectical configuration of *culture and imperialism*, these works emerged as a direct response to colonialism, offering multifaceted forms of complicity and resistance to the ruling administration. British women travel writers, in particular, explored issues of race, gender, and sexuality in ways which allowed a life overseas to complicate their own domestic identities as 'Western' women. The confinement of imperialism abroad was placed alongside the gendered confinement of the Victorian metropolis, yet Cypriots were still objectified as exoticised, Orientalised, and racialised Others. Responding directly to these traditions, Cypriot writers of the 1960s and 1970s, including Taner Baybars and Costas Montis, composed counter-travelogues which denounced the violence of imperialism by 'writing-back' directly to this generic form and showcasing alternate approaches to understanding political space.[34] These writers also began questioning the impact of nationalism on their physical and cultural movements, but it was not until long after the rupturing inertia of partition that Cypriot counter-travelogues emerged fully formed as modes resisting British imperialism, Greco-Turkish nationalisms, partition, *and* gender inequality, simultaneously. As 1878 inspired a wave of colonial travel writing, the 2003 openings in the Green Line encouraged a new generation of anti-partition travel writers to question how people *move* across an island of refugees and concrete buffer zone s. Here, these are understood as *post-partition* writers, both temporally, as they compose after 1974 (and, indeed, after 2003), and ideologically, as they renounce the *status quo.* The tourists of nineteenth-century Britain seeking an exotic Levant are placed in contradistinction with the Cypriot refugees and their descendants using the same genre to explore the relationship between transport, literature, and politics.

In order to investigate this intertextual web of travel writing, the second chapter will begin by exploring the generic (and gendered) motifs of colonialist travelogues—from Baker's and Dixon's, to Lawrence Durrell's *Bitter Lemons* (1957)—before considering the engagement of British women travel writers with this tradition, examining Esmé Scott-Stevenson's *Our Home in Cyprus* and Annie Brassey's *Sunshine and Storm in the East* (both 1880), as well as the writings of Agnes Smith. Following this, the third chapter will examine anti-colonial Cypriot writers immediately after 1960, directly comparing the 'writings-back' of the Greek-speaking Montis' *Closed Doors: An Answer to* Bitter Lemons *by Lawrence Durrell* (1964) and the Turkish-speaking Baybars' *Plucked in a Far-Off Land* (1970). The fourth chapter will then analyse post-partition travelogues and their relationship with both colonialism and nationalisms, including the aforementioned Papadakis' *Echoes from the Dead Zone* (2005) and Aydın Mehmet Ali's *Forbidden Zone* (2013). From this, Ali's text will be reconsidered alongside Nora Nadjarian's *Ledra Street* (2006) and Neşe Yaşın's *Rose Falling into Night* (2017) in the final chapter to interrogate how gender impacts Cypriot travel literatures in the contemporary era. Each chapter, therefore, will query how these authors understand and re/define the paradigms of 'colonialism' and 'postcoloniality' according to their generation and their ethnolinguistic and gendered identifications.

The Problem of Cypriot Literatures and Postcolonialism

This book, however, does not aim simply to accomplish the intervention of Cyprus into postcolonial literary studies, but rather to use this context to complicate the parameters of the discipline itself, assessing its form, utility, and problems in the twenty-first century. One issue within postcolonialism, as it exists, is the prevailing reliance on the binaries of past/present and colony/postcolony. Although Stuart Hall long emphasised the condition of postcoloniality as a heterogeneous and polymorphous category,[35] greater scholarly sensitivity to *multiple*, overlapping, and coterminous forms of colonialisms is needed. What follows is my endeavour to unpack the meanings of the loaded signifiers of this book's subtitle: empire, nationalism, and partition.

Questions of identifying Cypriot literatures as 'postcolonial' are complicated by the ambiguous postcoloniality of the island and whether it has yet achieved the status of postcolony. This enquiry can be characterised in three ways: Cyprus' and Cypriots' relationship with (a) the UK, (b) Western Europe, and (c) the nationalisms associated with Greece and Turkey. It inhabits neither a totally colonial nor postcolonial position, but exists in the political limens between the two.

Cyprus and the UK

First, despite the Republic of Cyprus being a member of the UN and the Commonwealth, Britain's continued stationing of military bases illustrates how the island is neither physically, nor symbolically, free from British hegemony completely. The sanctioned persistence of military bases meets one of Kwame Nkrumah's rudimentary, albeit controversial, definitions of neo-colonialism.[36] However, Cyprus' *symbolic* relationship with Britain suggests a more complex legacy of the empire. British models of culture, education, and language are problematically venerated in ways which privilege the discourses of the London metropole as essentially superior and cosmopolitan, in dyadic contrast with the perceived parochialism of the 'pre-colonial' and local. Well over three-quarters of islanders speak English in addition to their primary tongues, rather than speaking the other official language, Greek or Turkish.[37] The desire and need to speak the international auxiliary language becomes a stumbling block—in addition to nationalist segregation policies—in the exchange of cultures across the Green Line. While English is studied at primary level on both sides, the official languages of Greek and Turkish are not taught as 'secondary' languages on the parts of the island where they are not spoken daily. Globalised English divides as much as it connects—although, such a summary does not put due emphasis on the island's nationalist institutions which seek to erase the language/s of the Cypriot Other, a point to which I shall promptly return. As Linda Colley has demonstrated, in the context of the UK, 'Britishness was superimposed over an array of differences in response to contact with [...and] conflict with the Other'.[38] Consequently, Greek and Turkish are similarly foreignised as the languages of 'the other side'.

More Cypriot higher education students study overseas than in their place of birth, with estimates suggesting that 'for every 1000 at home, there are 1380 enrolled abroad'.[39] The overwhelming majority leave the island to study—not in Greece or Turkey—but Britain. Despite nationalist affiliations with the respective 'motherlands', the metropole of the UK is, perhaps with some irony, privileged in matters of academic advancement. The pedagogical cultural capital associated with British models competes with, and in this case, trumps the nationalist cultural capital associated with Greece and Turkey.[40] The latter two are venerated as mythicised sites from which essentialist identifications are made regionally, but which are disavowed in favour of the globalist progress associated with the Anglophone 'world' as pedagogically, technologically, and artistically superior. Different drives to strengthen *the nation* compete: creating a skilled, British-educated local population is viewed more important than supporting the academies (and, by extension, economies) of 'motherland' Greece and Turkey. As is beginning to be evident, the tangled web of national, local, and global manifests itself in Cypriots' complex negotiation of insular identities in relation to *multiple* foreign stages.

According to 2011 data compiled in the south, approximately 40% of Cypriots have studied abroad,[41] while an earlier 2006 survey indicated that 98% of islanders believe their children need to learn English.[42] Yet, the language is not reserved solely for academic institutions. Having been internalised into daily life, a quarter of Cypriots use English weekly when reading books and newspapers—illustrating the pertinent link between this language and literary consumption—while 43% employ it at work and when communicating with friends.[43] Over half watch Anglophone films weekly.[44] More remarkably, 83% of Cypriots use English online, especially with friends, the highest figure for any EU state where English is not an official language.[45] It illustrates, not only the pervasiveness of the language on the island, but also its association with new technologies which are increasingly replacing print media and traditional forms of literary dissemination. English is becoming the monoglossic tongue of cultural forms of the future. These manifestations of neo-colonialism operate on a psychological level and, thus, obfuscate the choice of language for so-called postcolonial Cypriot literatures. Is writing in English an anti-nationalist literary tactic which, nonetheless, marginalises 'native' annunciation by creating 'mimic men'? Or, is speaking *standardised* Greek and Turkish an act of mimicry, too? I will explore both these questions below.

Cyprus and Western Europe

Second, Cyprus' relationship with an idealised 'Europe' as a geographically-Asian island seeking membership of the EU equally complicates its postcoloniality. Membership is a post-Orientalist strategy used to repudiate the yoke of Orientalism by asserting a counter *Occidental* identity. However, the island's political and cultural pro-Europeanism is complicit in reinscribing the colonialist binaries which suggest that power, progress, and modernity lie exclusively in 'the West' and that subjugation is an essential characteristic of 'the East' which, in turn, needs to be disavowed. Following this internalised neo-Orientalism, Cyprus was once part of 'the Orient' while—and because it was—colonised, but it has since *become* 'European' due to its formal independence, economic growth, and ascension to the European superpower. Colloquially, most Cypriots referred to EU membership as the moment the island 'joined Europe'. In other words, to disavow European subjugation of 'the East', including Cyprus, many Cypriots sought to sublimate the Eastern-ness of the island itself. Claiming an identification with the Western powers that formerly occupied the island—including Venetians, Genoese, Franks, and Byzantines, as well as the British—rather than other post-Crusader, post-Ottoman, and post-Anglo-French colonies of the Mediterranean, Cypriots participate in a wider project of deprovincialising Europe.[46] The equation of 'Europe' with global, and of whiteness with racial superiority, is a salient feature of a colonialist policing of modernity. As Robert Young has argued, 'implicit in the idea of "the other" is a distinction between the modern (the same) and the residue that is nonmodern (the other)', including 'people regarded as being outside modernity, or outside the West'.[47] The two axioms, modern and 'Western', become interchangeable.

Internalised by the margins of the erstwhile British Empire, many Cypriots chose to perform a Westernised or Europeanised identity, employing the proverbial 'white masks' described by Frantz Fanon. As *Black Skin, White Masks* (1952) has shown, identifications with the symbolic power denoted by images of whiteness, masculinity, and Europeanness are central to the psychological construction of sometimes-defensive 'postcolonial' identities across the planet.[48] They are, however, especially fraught within Cypriot political attempts to write the very island as a naturalised part of Europe, despite its geography and colonial history. A 'double consciousness' manifests itself in identities split between two continents, denying existence in the less powerful of the two. According to this colonial mentality, Cypriots are not simply *like* their former European rulers, they are essentially the same. This internalised Eurocentricity, *par excellence*, is an act of auto-Orientalism. In this regard, Cyprus shows parallels with the rest of the decolonising world as well as an important difference afforded by its unique and ambivalent geography. The closest parallels are to be found in political and cultural movements in Armenia, Azerbaijan, and Georgia—post-Ottoman and post-Soviet states predominately in Western Asia which largely renounce bilateral ties with Muslim, Arab-majority neighbours to the south in favour of joining the Council of Europe to the north. Like Cyprus, they choose to become 'European' because decades of European rule have enforced the impression that association with the continent is a marker of socio-economic progress. While geographically-Asian countries fight to be recognised as 'European', there is no opposing paradigm of a geographically-European state pushing to identify itself primarily with the ideas of 'Asia' or 'Africa'. Specifically to Cyprus, however, this process also relates to the Greek and Turkish nationalisms which are routinely framed in terms of European ancestry and the historical glory of Hellas and the Ottoman Porte as European powers, despite both being transcontinental entities spanning the Balkans and Asia Minor or Anatolia (itself the Greek word for 'Eastern').

Cyprus and Greco-Turkish Nationalisms

Third, and perhaps most importantly, the island's relationship with Greek (or, Pan-Hellenic) and Turkish (or, Pan-Turkic) nationalisms reveals how Cyprus' postcoloniality is uncertain as it remains under the cultural and militaristic hegemony of foreign (possibly 'European') agents. As noted already, the vernaculars of the island—'native' or 'subaltern' pre-colonial discursive forms—remain institutionally unrecognised and are reductively associated with the rural, parochial, and uneducated in antithesis with the externally-standardised Greek, Turkish, and English of pedagogy and politics. Crucially, these languages are *doubly* pre-colonial in the sense that they predate both the introduction of English in 1878 and the standardising of Greek and Turkish which began with the recruitment of so-called mainland teachers in the late nineteenth century and was consolidated by their official status in the 1960 Constitution. Ironically, while Cypriot Arabic and Armenian were recognised as minority languages in 2008, one of several cultural shifts following the opening of the border, the more frequently spoken Kypriaka and Kıbrıslıca remain without government acknowledgement or protection on either side of the Green Line. Neither has a standardised written form and, thus, remain orally-transmitted. These vernaculars are being gradually undermined and supplanted by the hegemony of Greek and Turkish. Even their frequent classification as 'dialects' rather than 'languages' reveals their intuitional subordination to the level of the subaltern. For the purpose of this book, I will consider the two as *languages* belonging to the same linguistic families as the forms spoken in Greece and Turkey, respectively.

Independence did not allow for the freedom of the vernaculars suppressed by less than a century of British imperialism. While many former British colonies formed national identities by consecrating pre-colonial languages to the status of the official, Greek and Turkish now perform the role that English played as the de facto externally-introduced language of education, politics, and urban infrastructure. In short, 'native' Cypriot languages remain under the yoke of other ('foreign' but naturalised) discourses.

In addition to language, many Cypriot political and literary narratives explicitly characterise Greek or Turkish foreign interventions as modes of *colonialism*. An interesting example can be found in *Lobby for Cyprus*, a series of Anglophone pamphlets produced by a Greek-speaking Cypriot organisation seeking an end to the Turkish military presence in the north. One from 2015 speaks of how 'Turkey invaded and ethnically cleansed the north of Cyprus' through policies of ethnic 'segregation' installing 'colonists from Turkey'. Earlier, it suggests that the divided capital 'was reminiscent of signs that existed in apartheid South Africa and the segregated USA'.[49] Lobby for Cyprus and many comparable organisations use the politically-charged analogy of apartheid to equate the racist and colonialist regime of South Africa with the perceived imperialist strategies of Turkey—a motif often also used in relation to neighbouring post-British Israel/Palestine. In an issue from the previous year, the pamphlet discusses the island's 'racially based' division in an article considering the lives and teachings of Nelson Mandela and Martin Luther King.[50] Compelling the reader to 'heed the example set by the' former, it suggests that the 'apartheid' situation of Cyprus is 'perpetuating the divisive Ottoman imperial concept of "bicommunalism", as well as the British colonial era policy of dividing along religious lines'.[51] It should be noted that no blame is attributed to any Greek-speaking individuals or entities for the current *status quo*. The publication goes on to produce a timeline of modern world history punctuated by the fourth year of every decade: 1944 and Nazism; 1954 and the US Supreme Court dismantling racial segregation (like 'racially-based and religiously-based segregation in Cyprus'); 1964 and Dr King's reception of the Nobel Peace Prize; 1974 and the partition of Cyprus; 1984 and the UN Security Council Resolution 550 condemning Turkey's actions in Cyprus; 1994 and Mandela's election; 2004 and the rejection of the unsuccessful 'Annan Plan' to reunite Cyprus.[52] Conveniently, this selective historiography overlooks the massacre of Turkish-speaking Cypriots in 1964.

Overall, many important ideas can be discerned. The ostensible 'imperial' strategies of the Ottoman Empire, the British Empire, and the Republic of Turkey are all analogised and deemed culpable for the partition of Cyprus. In turn, they are compared with the racist and colonial regimes of Nazi Germany, the segregated United States, and apartheid South Africa. The Anglophone form is chosen to disseminate this critique of 'Western' *and* neo-Ottoman colonial ideologies, to both Cypriots and wider English-speaking readers globally. It challenges the racism found in the 'Western' world and its perceived inaction over the events of 1974. In a rare break from pro-Europeanness, this Cypriot organisation uses the international auxiliary language to identify, and resist, the intersecting global network of racial segregation which has manifested itself for a century through colonialism and fascism. This is not achieved without controversy given its apparent absolving of any guilt from Greek-speakers. Nonetheless, it does powerfully illustrate how Cypriots understand and use the terms 'imperial' and 'colonist' in ways which necessarily relate to the rest of the decolonising world but are also highly specific to its immediate geopolitical context. For some Cypriots, parts (or all) of their island have simply been transferred from one empire to another.

Hence, as well as 'writing-back' to British colonialism—historical *and* contemporary—Cypriot writers contend with the colonialist structures of both *localised* nationalist movements and of the *foreign* interventions by neighbouring powers. These hegemons range from organisations like EOKA B and TMT, which were largely endemic to the island but supported by their respective 'motherlands', to the political, military, and cultural intercessions of Greece and Turkey, not only in 1974, but through more insidious forms today. To complicate this paradigm further, while some (mostly left-wing) Cypriots view all these interventions as *externally*-imported and colonialist in nature, other (mostly right-wing) islanders consider the nationalism to which they subscribe an *internal* tool for postcolonial identity formation. For the former, a postcolonial reality is always delayed by the presence of foreign interventionism; for the latter, a postcolonial Cyprus is in the process of being realised through the single nationalist ideology they approve—but hampered, of course, by the other ideology on the other side of the Green Line.

As Young's interrogation of the discipline has shown, 'postcolonialism has always been about the ongoing life of residues, living remains, lingering legacies', primary of which have been the nationalist constructs which reductively promote 'ethnic or cultural homogeneity' at the expense of difference.[53] Importantly, the field of postcolonialism in the twenty-first century 'is no longer a question of a formal colonizer-colonized relation'.[54] The paradigm must increasingly amplify itself to consider other colonialist intersections between, and within, former territories of European empires in order to examine the internalised colonial practices performed by nationalist denials of otherness, as well as the history of migration and globalisation which transform existing binaries of inside and outside. Fanon has famously demonstrated how nationalist elites of the decolonising world usurp the corrupt dominance of erstwhile imperial rulers. The foreign coloniser of yesteryear is replaced by the home-grown coloniser of today. He argues, for instance, that '[t]he national bourgeoisie turns its back more and more on the interior and on the real facts of its undeveloped country, and tends to look toward the former mother country and the foreign capitalists who count on its obliging compliance'.[55] Although Cyprus is no exception to this neocolonial inheritance of 'Western' political models in its androcentric and bourgeois performances of power—men in French suits and German cars achieving little at reunification talks—it is also radically different from other 'postcolonial' contexts. In Cyprus, while the power structures of the island are indebted to British templates, including the preservation of English Common Law, the nationalisms which help fuel partition emanate from another two 'mother countr[ies]', 'foreign capitalist' states which desire 'obliging compliance' in their creation of proxy empires. Unlike most Commonwealth members, Cyprus does not have simply one 'mother country' to negotiate with, but three, all of whom compete to maintain their dominance over the island. Cultural imperialism appears in multiple guises and Cypriot writers are forced to react to all three at once.

In short, nationalisms become forms of colonialism in and of themselves. As Papadakis illustrates, the self and Other of Orientalism has been internalised and re-written in Cyprus to characterise the national identifications on the other side of the Green Line as the new constitutive Other.[56] To paraphrase Young, the coloniser-colonised dichotomy is reiterated by nationalists as Greco-Turkish antagonism. It is indebted both to British colonialism and the coterminous nationalisms in Greece and Turkey which promote irredentist expansionism. Papadakis' interpretation of Said (to be shown in the fourth chapter) demonstrates the specific ways in which postcolonial theory must be adapted to the complex strata of the Cypriot context. For post-partition Cypriot writers, self and Other paradigms inherent in both British colonial policy and neo-colonial Greco-Turkish nationalisms must be read in parallel. As Young suggests, 'the most useful thing that Postcolonial Studies could do… would be to abandon the category of "the other" altogether'.[57] In Cyprus, the Other assumes many overlapping forms—the colonised Other; the Other on the other side of the partition; and even one's perception of one's own subcontinental self, internalising the Middle East through the lens of Orientalism as Other—all of which must be 'abandoned' in unison in order to possibly achieve an ultimate postcoloniality.

Overall, it is these *endo-colonialisms*, to quote Paul Gilroy, in addition to, or following, formal British rule, which uniquely affect the politics, cultures, and literatures of Cyprus as a distinct expression of post/colonialism.[58] With these concerns, it is salient to analyse the context in relation to Raymond Williams' models of *dominant, residual, and emergent*.[59] It is evident that Cypriot literature is still in a state of *emergence* as the island's very postcoloniality has yet to be fully actualised. The discourses which become mainstream and authoritative do so by interpolating into Anglocentric, Hellenocentric, or Turkocentric narrative forms and by employing the rigidly masculinist and even Orientalist strategies of nineteenth-century British representations of the island. Cyprus is a rare example of where anti-colonial nationalisms have come *almost entirely from the outside*. Nationalism as an ideology is a Western European construct of the eighteenth century which was imposed globally through the print cultures and pedagogical systems of various empires. It facilitates the dissemination of 'imagined communities', in Benedict Anderson's famous terminology, propagating an idealistic image of 'the nation' which is 'imagined as both inherently limited and sovereign'.[60] In addition to the European origins of this thinking, the multiple nationalisms co-opted by anti-colonial Cypriots are, like the Republic's official languages, codified in (European or Eurocentric) Greece and Turkey before reaching Cypriots. Many of the cultural and political *residues* (a motif used by both Williams and Young) of the three external Guarantor Powers, even after so-called independence, conform to simple definitions of colonialism. This indicates how nationalism can be used as a guise to support indirect modes of colonialism in the twentieth century. To paraphrase Anderson, Hellenocentric and Turkocentric ideologies actively reinforce discursive constructs of nation spaces which are *limited* in their exclusion of Cypriots from other linguistic backgrounds and which promote the *sovereign* authority of either Athens or Ankara over post-British Cyprus. As such, Greek and Turkish nationalisms are used to build images of circumscribed (ethnic or linguistic) *communities* to justify their colonial intentions over the island.

The model of metropole and colony—Britain and Cyprus—was not fully rescinded but reframed as the parallel paradigms of Greece–Cyprus or Turkey–Cyprus. Cypriots, in their desire for a national history with which to reject the need for British *paternalism*, sought identification with the monumentalised histories of the newly-created '*motherlands*' and their standardised languages. Ironically, despite claims of diametric opposition *within* these discourses, their narrative forms reveal important analogies as right-wing Cypriots make comparable claims but under different national labels. Both Greek- and Turkish-speaking nationalists stress the glory of the metropolis on the shores of the Bosporus. Yet, while, for the former, it is Constantinople, the erstwhile centre of the Orthodox Byzantine Empire, for the latter, it is the erstwhile centre of the Muslim Ottoman Empire. Cypriot events on October 28, Greek National Day, observe the history of Constantinople, while those on the following day, October 29, Turkish Republic Day, observe that of Istanbul. With a degree of paradox, and unlike most other movements in the decolonising world, Cypriot *anti-colonialists* drew on the imagery of other, historical, and partly-European empires to which the island once belonged in order to challenge continued ownership by their existing rulers. Rejecting the hegemony of the British Empire was performed through nationalisms which did not imagine the creation of a Cypriot nation—as was the case in India, Nigeria, and Ghana—but the symbolic re-absorption of the island into preceding empires which had long-ceased to exist. As a consequence of Cyprus having little in the way of an era of pre-colonial autonomy, tactics alluding to the pre-*colonial* could not be found and, hence, pre-*British—colonial* historical discourses were used instead.

According to this colonialist logic, culture comes *to* Cyprus, not *from* it. Increasingly, however, anti-nationalist Cypriot writers seek to put pressure on the identities of 'Greek' and 'Turkish' which are *residues* of both the British census and the irredentism of the Greek and Turkish republics. The *emergent* pro-Cypriot discourse is the first in the island's recent political history to fully reject the monumentalising of imperialism—British, Byzantine, and Ottoman, simultaneously—and, thus, marks the very onset of a cultural movement which can be described as 'postcolonial'.

It is worth offering, as a concluding bridge between these three categories, the official US response to Cypriot independence.[61] In 1960, the National Security Council, while nominally welcoming independence, listed its various concerns about the island, all of which emphasise the need to conserve Cyprus' strategic interests for the United States and to vigorously dissolve its association with territories outside Western Europe and North America, namely the Non-Aligned Movement. Their statement declares that '[t]he chief strategic importance of Cyprus to the West will continue to lie the in the British bases' from which the UK, and NATO by extension, will orchestrate their 'military operations in the Middle East and the Mediterranean'. These bases would not simply exist for British interests, but are poised as 'useful to the United States as a possible staging base for Middle East operations'. It goes on to detail the US radio communications already installed on the island, necessary for the global power's influence 'throughout the Middle East'. The statement goes on to strategise how this can be best maintained. One key approach is to foster improved relations between Cyprus and countries to its west, especially Britain, Greece, and Turkey. It is noted that many 'Cypriots are drawn toward the Afro-Asian community. Remembrance of support from within the Afro-Asian group for Cypriot self-determination in the United Nations' which, the US fears, 'will fortify Cypriot inclinations to fashion an independent foreign policy'. The proposed total *independence* of 1960 is a status the United States is actively attempting to dissuade and disrupt. By intervening to reduce the island's political independence through the encouraged intercession of the UK, Greece, and Turkey in future Cypriot affairs, the United States wants to safeguard its own 'useful' and 'strategic' interests in the Middle East by disempowering links between (non-'Western') states sympathetic to the ideals of the Non-Aligned Movement and 'to maintain a pro-Western outlook on Cyprus as a means of preserving present Free World interests on the island'. This remarkable document alone exposes US colonialist attitudes towards the island as an ostensible Middle Eastern military and communications hub. This manifests in an active encouragement of neo-colonial practices by *all three* Guarantor Powers and by imposing a 'pro-Western', Eurocentric agenda onto Cypriots with which to destabilise political networks of resistance between decolonising 'Afro-Asian' nations.

Cyprus is not only on the limens of geography, culture, and language, but between the temporalities of 'colonial' and 'postcolonial'. Literatures on Cyprus, to varying degrees, speak to this liminality by producing works that do not differentiate between a period of political oppression and a new era of autonomy either side of, say, 1960. Instead, *their postcoloniality is staggered, striated, and emergent*. In response to the male Orientalists of the nineteenth century, British women writers wrote-back in the same juncture to this gendered imperialism, before Cypriot male writers wrote-back from the 1960s onwards using the register of anti-colonial nation-building against both sets of imperialists. In the twenty-first century, Cypriot writers begin writing-back to this nationalism *in addition to* preceding, and lingering, British colonisation. Specifically, Cypriot women writers and LGBT Cypriots are responding to the assumptions, limitations, and lacunae of all these anterior discourses. Most, however, come from Greek-speaking and Turkish-speaking backgrounds, whereas Arabic-speaking, Maronite Cypriots and Armenian Cypriots have yet to publish as widely. The same is true of the difficulty experienced by LGBT Cypriots in having their voices recognised in mainstream media. Williams' notion of 'the emergent' may need to be recalibrated to mark multiple, and sometimes contradictory, *emergences* of counter-discursivity. Cyprus is *not quite* postcolonial, a status which invariably impacts writers' chosen linguistic and narrative forms.

Questions of Form: Travel and Transportal Literatures

Issues of genre, language, and audience feed crucially into the classification of Cypriot literatures. Most writings on Cyprus employ motifs of travel, from Victorian travelogues to post-partition refugee testimonies. As Said has shown, within the apparatus of Orientalism, travel writing performed a salient function in the interdependency of culture and imperialism.[62] In short, '[f]rom travellers' tales... colonies were created and *ethnocentric* perspectives secured' (*emphasis mine*).[63] What needs to be added to this, however, is that these 'ethnocentric perspectives' afforded by literatures of place and movement are problematically shared in both 'colonial' and 'postcolonial' junctures. Literatures of place cannot be divorced from a politics of the nation. As all geographies are imagined, including the Orient, then the geographies of Cyprus are discourses that are imagined before *and after* 1960. Post-independence literatures are not absolved of the reductive 'ethnocentric' policing of territory as ideological discourse. It is simply the specific ideological affiliation that changes over time.

Travel writing, in its broadest sense, performs a very specific function through the kinds of identification which can be made with movement. From the late nineteenth century onwards, maritime travellers like Durrell, with his transient associations between Britain, Ireland, and India, used representations of an unclassifiable insular space to echo an unclassifiable life of constant travel. It becomes a metonym of globalisation and of personal, or political, ambivalence towards it. Cyprus is not a precise place but a symbol, or penumbra, of the ontological views held by those depicting it. Cyprus is a literary *terra nullius*, an *empty space* only defined in relation to *other* spaces—Britain, Suez, Greece, and Turkey—becomes an empty conduit waiting to be filled by competing political agendas and cultural perspectives. Its status as an epistemic and ontological *empty space* means that it exists principally as a textual site of identity politics, rather than an independent geographic territory in and of itself. In other words, its independence is always deferred by those wanting to mark the island as an extension of the self.

It is interesting to briefly note that, in addition to the three Guarantor Powers, the island has been claimed by other regional geopolitical aspirations over the past century. Zionists like Davis Trietsch and Theodor Herzl proposed it as the site of a religious nation adjacent to the Holy

Land (before the creation of Israel in the 1940s). Pan-Syrian nationalists like Antoun Saadeh planned to incorporate the island as the star to the mainland Fertile Crescent of a proposed Greater Syrian nation. These two ideologies were grappling with the colonial history of the Middle East and the pressures to define national and religious borders in a post-Sykes-Picot Mediterranean. Neither plot was successful, but both illustrate (in Anderson's terms) how imaginings of ethnic and national identities are imposed onto land which is desired by those with power. The lucrative position of Cyprus between continents, and adjacent to symbolically important sites like Damascus and Jerusalem, cause it to be appropriated as a target for hypothetical or actual colonisation. The agency of its diverse inhabitants is denied; colonising forces use their print cultures to envisage the island as a vacant spot on the world map awaiting their occupation or protection.

In British colonial travel writing, the polymorphic island becomes a means of expressing Eurocentric fears towards transcontinental interstitiality—partly in order to externalise anxieties surrounding the writers' own interstitiality away from their metropolitan homes. In post-independence writings, Cyprus functions as a canvas to manifest concerns towards its relation to Greece, Turkey, or postcoloniality. While colonialists panic about the island's—and their own individual—status between a feminised Orient and a masculinised Occident (as will be shown in the second chapter), this is reinterpreted by Cypriot nationalists' comparable fears of how to ethnically define the space in relation to Greece and Turkey. Writers from both before and after 1960 are fixated with the question of whether Cyprus is Asian, European, or transcontinental, a question which travel writing can best mediate through its own transportationality. Cyprus is like travel writing itself: discursive forms always being constructed from the outside and about nowhere in particular. It is worth noting that the majority of texts considered in this monograph represent Cyprus but were first published in London.

As Cyprus is viewed as a symbolic *empty space*, it is routinely textualised mimetically through a genre similarly known for its liminality. Elizabeth Bohls, for instance, stresses that, from Behn's *Oroonoko* onwards, travel writing is unique in its 'generic and discursive hybridity'.[64] Comparatively, for Debbie Lisle, 'the vacillation between fact and fiction in travel writing was part of the colonial division of knowledge between academic and popular information'.[65] As I will show, colonial travelogues of the island fused elements of empirical observation with motifs from contemporary fictional genres. Such strategies render the texts more marketable, allowing important colonial knowledges to be more readily consumed. This meeting of travel and fiction is a central tenet of all colonial and postcolonial literary contexts. As Michel de Certeau has stressed, 'every story is a travel story'.[66] The paradigmatic fictions of British colonial discourse—from *Othello* to Joseph Conrad's *Heart of Darkness* (1899)—conglomerate the politicism of empire-building, the verisimilitude of travel guides, and the romance of tragic fiction. If travel writers are essentially homeless and if, for Georg Lukács, the novel is to be defined by its 'transcendental homelessness' as a condition of the alienating nature of modern global capital, then where do the genres of 'travel writing' and 'the novel' begin, end, and meet?[67] For Lukács, the protagonist of the novel experiences an 'estrangement… [their] self-made environment as a prison instead of as a parental home'.[68] Equally, for Sachidananda Mohanty, '[t]he traveller's deliberate denial of roots makes him a ceaseless wayfarer'.[69] The psychological motivations of the 'protagonist' and the 'traveller' are inextricably blurred in the limens between 'roots' and routes.[70]

For colonial travel writers, therefore, Cyprus becomes a space to mediate between British homes and a life estranged at sea. Travel writers identify with the island's own confused identity, belonging to neither one ontological category nor another. Similarly, in the discourse of Cypriot nationalists, *home* becomes an unending interchange between the fragmented local and the imagined, external 'roots' of Greece, Turkey, or another elsewhere. These are spaces which Salman Rushdie calls 'fictions, not actual cities or villages, but invisible ones, imaginary homelands', which, in South Asian literatures, manifest themselves through 'Indias of the mind'.[71] For post-partition Cypriot writers, some of whom are from refugee families, their narrators contend with personal identities across partition or between the homes of Cyprus and Britain. In other words, there is the ancestral home on the other side of the Green Line to which they cannot return; the home on the part of the island they are given the right to live in; and the home established as refugees, often in the UK. Added to this are Greece and Turkey as additional homes 'of the mind'. Travel between these sites of identification—*or, lack thereof*—is vital to the writing of Cypriot lives in the current century.

It needs to be stressed that one major departure of post-independence Cypriot literatures from other 'postcolonial' oeuvres is the paucity of the traditional novel form. While the literary field of postcolonialism is often characterised by its emergence through fictional novels like Chinua

Achebe's *Things Fall Apart* (1958) in English, or Tayeb Salih's *Season of Migration to the North* (1966) in Arabic, contemporaneous Cypriot writers from the 1960s typically use modes of travel writing to counter imperialist discourses. While many have noted the centrality of the conventional novel form to national 'writings-back',[72] travelogues, like Montis' *Closed Doors* and Baybars' *Plucked in a Far-Off Land*, perform this cultural resistance instead. As well as engaging with the genre's claims of manifesting authentic testimony—however difficult authenticity is to ascertain objectively—its elevation above the novel indicates the limitations of the latter for the Cypriot context. Even in the succeeding decades, 'postcolonial' travelogues like Papadakis' *Echoes from the Dead Zone* and Ali's *Forbidden Zones*, set across the two sides of the Green Line and published in London, typify this consistent literary imbrication of travel and quasi-fictionalisation. For Ali, this process is known as the creation of 'fictionalised realities'.[73] In many ways, their use of first-person narrators resembles—but puts pressure on—the conventions of the novel. Moreover, as the overwhelming majority of texts which Cypriots 'write-back' to belong to the tradition of travel writing, unlike the infamous novels of colonial India and sub-Saharan Africa, the response of Cypriot writers is to engage intertextually with this specific genre by reconstituting its constituent notions of literary and political movement. This island has seldom been successfully represented in, or adapted to, the novel. It, therefore, sits outside the typical modes of literary representation that postcolonial theory approaches.

Cypriot writers reject the novel because its claims of a focal everyperson character as a metonym of the nation cannot be realised for a context that has yet to fully realise its (national) independence and where one figure cannot represent the diversity of a polyphonic milieu. While Bakhtin understands the novel to be the site of heteroglossia *par excellence*,[74] Cypriot writers view the monoglossic novel—especially in the national(ist) languages of Greek and Turkish—as failing to manifest the island's cultural and linguistic heterogeneity. How can the novel synonymous with the nation be used for an island without a cohesive, singular national identity *but* which is home to multiple synchronic, but competing, nationalisms? It is travel writing that expresses the heteroglossic reality of the island more organically and without presupposing that a first-person protagonist could speak for—and, represent—Cypriots of all ethnolinguistic and political affiliations.

'Postcolonial' Travel Writing

The importance of travel writing for the Cypriot context is best exemplified by Said's definition of the genre from 1999. According to him, the narrator of the travelogue 'depends not on power, but on motion, on a willingness to go into different worlds, use different idioms, understand a variety of disguises, masks', as the narrative '*crosses over*, traverses territory, abandons fixed positions' (*emphasis in original*).[75] Within this, hugely influential concepts have been raised which will be elaborated on across this book, not least the notion that literatures can belong to 'different worlds' simultaneously, and the relationship between travel and the *crossing-over* denoted by translation's Latin etymology. In addition, through allusion to Foucault's knowledge and 'power' dialectic, travel writing is the generic form most attuned to the dualistic tension between metropole and periphery. In colonial travelogues of Cyprus, visiting the island and assuming the 'disguises' and 'masks' of either metropolitan authority or 'native' otherness is part of a complex performance of power: either consolidating imperial discipline or pushing against the restraints of Victorian London. In comparable ways, Cypriot travel writers also use the register of mobility to understand their own power, or powerlessness, as colonised peoples, either of British imperialism or nationalist hegemonies. In particular, anti-nationalist writers employ this form specifically to put pressure on 'fixed positions' and to seek greater understanding of fellow Cypriots trapped on the other side of the Green Line and treated, in ethnocentric discourses, as belonging to 'different worlds'. Ali, Papadakis, and their contemporaries enter into these 'different worlds', physically and textually, to transect and re-bridge the ostensible fixity of partition. The metropolis-periphery dichotomy is re-written, not as the division between global North and South, but as the partition between the northern and southern parts of the island, transforming and localising the poles of the genre in significant ways.

The category of 'postcolonial travel writing', or 'the postcolonial travelogue', is at an early stage of academic development. As Moroz and Sztachelska have noted, the study of travel writing alone as a legitimate field of literary analysis is extremely recent. Analogous to the study of Cypriot contexts, it is a relatively new and undervalued field of scholarship, and one marred by a lack of attention to 'travel writing texts written in languages other than English' or belonging to 'different literary traditions'.[76] The genre of postcolonial travel writing is important in its blurring of the figures of traveller, coloniser, migrant, and refugee. April Shemak has explored how '[r]efugee and asylum seeker narratives push the limits of travel writing', particularly given the tension between the first-person travel writer and the forced exoduses of refugees in groups.[77] There is a vast, insurmountable difference between voluntary travel (including mass tourism) and dispossession. As Graham Huggan observes in *Extreme Pursuits* (2009), 'travel writing continues to be haunted by its own imperial/colonial spectres', as well as the force of capitalism (or what he describes as globalism). This leads to queries as to whether travel can ever be uncoupled from colonialist and capitalist privilege, 'or are there other possibilities for travel writing: counternarratives of modernity; travel narratives "from below"? And *where* is the' traveller, if they inhabit a 'global space'?[78] These are the very questions which scholarship on the contemporary and future manifestations of this genre must address, particularly as global inequalities increase and the material differences between asylum seeker and privileged holidaymaker intensify.

For Robert Clarke, postcolonial travel writing is concerned primarily with a need to 'decolonize the genre' from within, eschewing 'emergent and renascent forms of colonialism and imperialism' by exhuming 'non-Anglophone and nonmetropolitan travel discourses'.[79] This is especially relevant for Cypriot writing given the numerous guises colonialism has assumed on the island, but it also raises the issue of how 'postcolonial' literatures can be both Anglophone and 'nonmetropolitan' simultaneously. Clarke argues, not unlike Moroz and Sztachelska, that there is 'a persistent bias towards Anglophone writing evident in much criticism on travel writing',[80] gesturing to a lacuna within this (already underrepresented) field of study. Nonetheless, composing Anglophone material is, itself, a 'nonmetropolitan' tactic for some Cypriots for whom the Greek and Turkish languages have assumed the status of metropolitan—an issue illustrating how postcolonial travel writing criss-crosses a global nexus of intersecting languages, forms, and politics despite emerging from a related stylistic and thematic source.

The postcolonial study of travel writing is interested in complicating the power structures bound up in how territories are represented, typically through models of centre and periphery. This is extremely urgent for the Cypriot context, demonstrating the need for a genre that acutely places the concerns of political positionality at the forefront of a landless and homeless form. Travel writing offers a literary mode that vocalises the concerns of postcolonial theory most vividly. However, following my own critique of the category of 'postcolonial', it is clear that these polemic drives are specific to each context. In a partitioned Cyprus with intimate ties to Greece, Turkey, and the UK, where does 'foreign' culture begin and end; how is the 'nation' conceived of; where are the poles of 'centre' and 'periphery' located? No two Cypriots would put forward the same answer to each question, nor would their responses directly echo those of other Commonwealth citizens.

Much of this discipline owes its origins to Mary Louise Pratt's *Imperial Eyes* (1992) and its theorising of the colonialist and gendered implications of literary travel. Tantamount to this is her use of the term *contact*. Developing Ron Carter's concept of 'contact literatures' for works 'written in European languages from outside Europe'—a useful category for Cypriot literatures in itself—Pratt observes how, in the study of travel writing, 'a "contact" perspective emphasizes how subjects get constituted in and by their relations to each other'.[81] This 'shifts the center of gravity' at 'the point at which their trajectories now intersect', as coloniser and colonised, self and Other, situated on the 'contact zone' or 'colonial frontier'.[82] Many of her ideas and idioms have influenced a range of scholars in related disciplines, from Huggan to Emily Apter. She stresses how 'western self-understanding functions only by inventing a projected other whose other is the European self', before showcasing how moments of contact throughout the history of travel writing, including Olaudah Equiano's famous narrative (1789), powerfully '*engage* western discourses of identity, community selfhood, and otherness' (*emphasis in original*).[83] This theory is crucial in understanding how British colonial writers understand their status on the 'colonial frontier' between Europe and Asia. However, it is also illuminates the necessity of the genre for Cypriot writers for whom it allows a revaluation of notions of 'selfhood, and otherness' in *contact*, not only with British imperialists, but with Cypriots of other ethnolinguistic backgrounds obscured by partition. Pratt repeatedly uses motifs of vision, exploring how 'exile rather than exploration situates the seeing-man and creates the otherness between the seer and the seen'.[84] Travel, and exile in particular, forces new ways of seeing one's own societal norms, and those of others, to emerge.

From this, Huggan and Patrick Holland have elaborated on the notion of 'countertravel'. For them, the writings of women, LGBT, and '(postcolonial) countertravellers' are those which 'locate themselves in opposition to conventional modes of travel, particularly tourism'.[85] This is especially evident in the work of Nadjarian, which not only explores her post/colonial and gendered identities, but also represents the island's commodification by the tourism industry through irony and bathos. Equally, as will be shown in the work of Ali, the hotel ubiquitous to tourist brochures becomes a site of violence in 1974, according to her refugee testimony. Cypriot travel writers imagine countertravels both to reverse the unequal flow of people caused by globalisation—the current of tourists going from North to South, in opposition to refugees forced from periphery to metropole—and to create counter-narratives against the inertia of partition.

For this reason, I understand the term transnationalism as failing for a series of authors who do not experience land through a simple definition of the nation. Is moving from the southern to the northern part of the island moving from one 'nation' to another? Does, for Greek nationalists, moving from one part of their Pan-Hellenic 'Greek nation' (the Hellenic Republic) to another (the Republic of Cyprus) constitute movement between 'nations'? Is the transit from one part of the British Empire to another, before 1960, a 'transnationalist' act? *Countertravel* allows authors to pick apart these arbitrary categories and to use moments of *contact* to reveal apertures in the Green Line capable of bridging-together individuals and communities. As a consequence, I turn to Bill Ashcroft's theory of the 'transnation', a space, physical or literary, which manifests itself through 'the rhizomic interplay of travelling subjects *within* as well as between nations' (*emphasis in original*).[86] It is 'a conjunction of dissolving borders', but specifically one which does not simply lie 'beyond the borders of the nation but also extending within' in order to 'paradoxically imagine a different world'.[87] This encapsulates the core of Cypriot travel writing which seeks a genre to unravel the dichotomy of nations and express modes of textual 'border'-passing to challenge both the dogmas of imperialism and nationalism, and the dualism inherent within the institutional study of transnationalism. The transnation is a space, if not every space, already and always intersectional, not something arrived at by moving from one dyad to another.

Ashcroft's essay concludes with a model for figuring 'a different world'. Doing so, he echoes Said's aforementioned description of travel as exposing 'different worlds' from over a decade earlier.[88] The relatively short history of postcolonial travel writing studies has shown how the genre exposes the limitations of existing discourse—from transnationalism to the 'world' of world literatures—as part of a discipline with as much mobility as the texts they analyse. For Cypriot writers, high literatures, including the novel, have failed to articulate a geopolitical position too complex to be contained within one 'nation' or another, or be defined simply as either 'colonial' or 'postcolonial'. Instead, countertravel and its resulting contact allows subversive movements *within* to expose the already-present existence of the transnation and to rip-apart the 'fixed positions' of all ideologues, from colonisers to academics.

In this respect, I am influenced by the model of the *planetarity* proposed by Gayatri Spivak. Across *Death of a Discipline* (2003), she illustrates the problems inherent within current institutional practices, from Area Studies to Comparative Literature. As she argues, while the former sought the sometimes-problematic study of 'foreign "areas"', the latter 'was made up of Western European "nations." This distinction, between "areas" and "nations," infected Comparative Literature from the start'.[89] The names of these disciplines indeed present an obvious problem for the Cypriot context. Not only is there the issue surrounding a nation-based paradigm, but it is difficult to determine the area to which the island belongs—it is not in the Balkans, but it is also the only Christian-majority country in the Levant or Middle East. The wider, multi-religious 'Mediterranean' which Said proposed has only recently begun being used in the scholarship of modern cultural production. In addition, Spivak highlights the problems of an Anglocentric set of academic practices, as many scholars of travel writing have similarly stressed, and the lack of language-skills offered and employed in the reading of works from outside the Anglo-American field. From this, the planet, which she sees as distinct from the technological, electronic, and capitalist globe of globalisation, reclaims an ecological character, to offer 'a paranational image that can substitute for international'.[90] A precursor to Ashcroft's 'transnation', Spivak presents an understanding of the planet which repudiates the national and the artificial. As such, she is 'outlining a politics of reading', particularly of texts beyond the nation state model and in a range of languages, not only English.[91]

Importantly for Cypriot travel writers, this kind of reading allows for the island to be observed in planetary terms by acknowledging, and moving away from, the constructivism of nations and partition. The island becomes a paranational terrain shared by all and from which texts can be read across the Green Line. It is no surprise that Spivak begins her first chapter, 'Crossing Borders', with an epigraph on the state of academia following the fall of the Berlin Wall.[92] The writers discussed in the final two chapters of this monograph represent the culmination of this thinking as post-partition writers who, after 2003, look beyond partition, politically *and academically*. It is also no coincidence that Cypriot travelogues are, as inheritors of Marx and Raymond Williams, interested in the division of city and country, counteracting the violent brutality of Ledra Street with topological images of family gardens or mountainous escapes. When Spivak explains that '[t]he globe is on our computers. No one lives there',[93] she offers a necessary idea for understanding the Cypriot context. Not only is Cyprus an *empty space* built by competing discourses, but nations themselves, as imagined and ideological constructs, are *spaces where no one lives*. Countertravel allows Cypriots to return to the planetary land in order to reconstruct existing identifications by physically experiencing, occupying, and inhabiting the land.

Nonetheless, it is possible to take exception to the idea that no one lives 'on our computers' in a generation where lives are increasingly performed online. Perhaps in the future, this assessment will be reversed to the point where *everyone* 'lives there'. For Cypriots, as stated earlier, much online dialogue is conducted in English. The internet itself may be a new digital empire, one that is more democratic but which risks supressing linguistic diversity. This also leads to further issues regarding language, now and in the future. Spivak seeks to resist 'the colonialism of European national language-based Comparative Literature'.[94] This is crucial when approaching Cypriot travel writing. However, the problems of colonialism and nationalism which Cypriots face not only emanate from Anglo-American academies, or even how those paradigms are replicated locally, but from the coterminous 'national language-based' paradigms imposed from Greece and Turkey. Spivak stresses the need for cultural production and reception to move beyond those which 'resemble metropolitan-language based work', engaging with 'nonhegmonic languages'.[95] I wholeheartedly agree that more work needs to be done in standardising and codifying Cyprus' 'nonhegemonic languages', including Kypriaka ('Cypriot Greek'), Kıbrıslıca ('Cypriot Turkish'), and Sanna ('Cypriot Arabic'), and subsequently using these in the formation of cultural materials. This can be facilitated by the rise of digital media invested in transcribing and recording language data. In the meantime, Cypriots face the problem of *three* competing metropolitan languages. How can Cypriots 'resist mere appropriation by the dominant' when it assumes multiple guises?[96] The predominance of Anglophone writing, which has been problematic across the planet, can sometimes be the least partisan for anti-partition and anti-nationalist writers in Cyprus. English will function as a cross-cultural *buffer* for as long as the *Buffer* Zone remains. While Spivak sees more 'language training' as necessary in revealing 'the irreducible hybridity of all languages',[97] this is something built into the Englishes of travelogues like Papadakis' where he uses the medium to ruminate on loanwords between Greek, Turkish, and other Mediterranean languages in the creation of a Levantine sprachbund ignored, or denied, by nationalism.[98] This remains invisible when libraries in the south fail to stock books about or from the north, and vice versa. English allows for a *distanced reading* to be performed in the present, rather than waiting for further changes to language preservation which are still at a nascent stage.[99]

Therefore, there are limitations to the planetarity model for the Cypriot context, including the heliocentric analogy for cultural production. Depending on the linguistic, political, and cultural affiliations of the individual writer, the 'planet' to which Cyprus belongs has different suns—Greece, Turkey, and the UK—upon which its existence depends. This does not include the pull of other forces, including the European Union or the very idea of 'Europe'. It would be better to suggest that Cypriot literatures represent constituent parts of a *satellite culture* balancing competing gravitational pulls and seeking to be absorbed into different definitions of the planetary. For a space where its postcoloniality is emergent and deferred, and where subaltern, 'nonhegemonic languages' remain unstandardised, any participation in planetary exchange, without recourse to mediating forces, is circumscribed. Cyprus is still 'in the middle'. But like a satellite, how does Cyprus impact its 'mother' planets, the way the moon impacts the earth's tides? How do Cypriot writers challenge prevailing political and linguistic paradigms? And, as moons in the solar system cannot be shared by different planets, how do Cypriots effectively satellite more than one cultural body, if at all? In this analogy, it would be best to understand Cyprus as an artificial satellite which, like spacecraft, can have its orbit forcibly rerouted but is constantly under the control of, and defined in relation to, other larger entities.

Transportal Literatures

From this, I propose that the travel writing of Cyprus be understood as *transportal literatures*. Moving beyond the confines of existing literary approaches, including even planetarity, a transportal reading of literature is one which understands texts and contexts to exist as portal-like structures, always on the limen of colonialism and postcoloniality, on the fringes of different nations or worlds, or between languages, continents, and religions, as Cyprus and its writers are. It is always an act of process and not arrival. In this vein, I interpret portals in their many etymological forms. They are doors (like the Greek *porta*), porches, or frames between internal and external. They are porous, like pores on the outside of the skin awaiting osmotic exchange. From this aqueous connotation comes the port, the reason for Cyprus' utility to the British Empire, north of Suez. From these ports, transport occurs, including the movement of goods emblematic of globalisation (and with specific colonial associations for continents like Australia). This wordplay extends to other languages as the Turkish for port, *liman*, relates to the Greek *limani* (port) and *limni* (lake), from which the English *limen* is derived. Liminality is metonymic of a transportal position.

All literatures on Cyprus look doubly, from one side of the doorframe to the other. Anglophone texts look to one set of publishing industries in the British metropole, while simultaneously facing the island post/colony. While colonialist travelogues speak between London and Cyprus, or Western Europe and the Levant, post-partition countertravelogues attempt to view the northern and southern parts of the island within one holistic text. Importantly, the image of *doors* recurs throughout this oeuvre. It is used candidly by Durrell to denote antagonism between Cypriots, but is appropriated more powerfully by Montis to write-back to the *closed doors* of British imperialism and its internment camps. For succeeding Cypriot travel writers, including Neşe Yaşın, this legacy of doors haunts their writing style as an example of aesthetics and politics feeding off one another. Doors can close or open at will. Portals can be sites of *contact*, as described by Pratt, and through which the dichotomy of artificial nations can be transected. They represent the moment one leaves or enters the 'different worlds' that Said suggests travel writing exposes.

Portals have an interesting history within literary studies. Georg Simmel analogises doors with bridges to conclude that the two represent how, 'in the physical as well as the intellectual sense, we are at any moment those who separate the connected and connect the separate', ultimately making '*one* cosmos out of all the individual elements' (*emphasis in original*).[100] Here, the motifs of both structures are employed to manifest oneness from fragmented parts. His use of the term 'cosmos', comparable with that of the world, demonstrates how heterogeneity is always a condition of worldliness and that this diversity can be *bridged* through expressions of connectivity. In many ways, this echoes Ngũgĩ's understanding of bridges as existing dialectically with borders, a paradigm he applies specifically to the meeting of cultures in post/colonial societies.[101] It is a transportal perspective that allows borders to be bridged.

Similarly, drawing on the liminality of contemporary cultural exchange, Gilroy notes how the 'special power' of transatlantic discourse 'derives from a doubleness, their unsteady location simultaneously inside and outside the conventions, assumptions, and aesthetic rules which distinguish and periodise modernity'.[102] This transcontinental model across dividing expanses of water not only offers a significant influence for understanding transmediterranean exports and imports between Africa, Asia, and Europe, but also demonstrates how portal-like structures offer a way of illustrating how all discourses exist 'simultaneously inside and outside' diverse traditions. Cyprus' comparable, but distinct, 'doubleness [...] being both inside and outside the West',[103] is one positioned precariously on the frame between political and literary paradigms—including, 'East and West' on the shores of the Mediterranean—and which manifests itself as criss-crossing lines of separation and transaction. Cyprus and its literatures become what the architectural theorist Alexander Gutzmer calls 'a medium' between states, 'to be inside and experience the outside at the same time', like motorised vehicles.[104]

Comparable to this is Kant's use of 'the metaphor of the *boundary* in order to fix the limits of reason' (*emphasis in translation*). For him, the boundary, on the edge of 'empty space', is one which 'belongs as much to what is within it as to the space lying outside a given totality, reason therefore, merely by expanding up to this boundary, partakes of a real, positive cognition'.[105] One learns about oneself and others up to, and at, the boundary—which is always both 'within' and without. Moving beyond this into 'empty space' does not allow one to experience real *noumena*, but to project onto that lacuna one's own values. Likewise, Cyprus is itself an empty springboard for various imperialisms which imagine it as the far limit of their cultural-political existence. How one approaches this limen and controls the meeting of self and Other is what Kant calls 'setting the boundary'.[106] Existing at this portal forces one to martial the real and imagined across an epistemic and ontological gateway.

From Kant's *parerga*, Derrida has constructed his own theory. Like a paratext, his *parergon* is a frame which supplements, surrounds, and is to the side of any given work. It is 'neither inside nor outside, neither above nor below' the work.[107] Similarly, Cyprus, at the fringes of academia, has routinely been exploited as a *parergon*. It is always to the side of larger textualities, never belonging to one precise institutional category or another, but frequently appropriated as the frame from which others explore their colonial or national identities. For post-partition travel writers, however, their unwitting position on this frame has forced them to ask questions of its existential character and to deprovincialise and recentre the limits of their subjecthood. Doing so, they reveal how every annunciation is one that speaks across a Kantian 'boundary'. Signification is always in transit. Meaning is never fully realised but inferred and deferred by constant movements between the constitutive 'inside and outside' of cultures: Europe and Asia, colonial and postcolonial, Greece and Turkey, north and south. Crucially, as I would add to Derrida's concept, there is no pure *work* separate from the *parergon*; all work is necessarily a *parergon* in and of itself. This status is best exemplified through the genre of travel writing, and the subject matter of Cyprus, which allow each other to reveal the intrinsically-transportal nature of every cultural act. All writing exists in, and as, a doorframe between writer and reader. Travel writing, especially from a site of ethnolinguistic partition, ruptures the ontological wall between self and Other through the manifestation of pores and portals through which the flows of culture become apparent, turning every ostensible *ergon* into *parergon*. In short, there are no works, only *frame*-works.

Throughout Derrida's oeuvre, there are recurring hints of the importance of the door. He stresses, for instance, that '[t]he welcome orients, it *turns* the *topos* of an opening of the door and of the threshold toward the other; it offers the other *as* the other'.[108] The door exposes the otherness inherent in the self as it attempts to move between states. Similarly, '[t]he open door… calls for the opening of an exteriority or of a transcendence of the idea of infinity'.[109] Through the open door, meaning is eternally moving, passing from the external to the internal, and vice versa. This door exists nowhere more powerfully than on the site of partition, and through the (literary) act of travel. Nonetheless, Derrida has dismissed the term *transport*. He asserts that, '[w]e will never have, and in fact have never had, to do with some "transport" of pure signifieds from one language to another'.[110] While I agree that what we are considering never involves any movement from a 'pure' form to another, I would suggest that the idea of the *transportal* offers the most lucid way of understanding how all culture sits in, and across, the doors of being and knowing which are erected to mark difference. It is the transportal literature of travel writing—and, especially, countertravel—which exposes these doors and allows their colonialist and nationalist frames to be remodelled.

Cyprus offers one of the most strikingly unique case studies for understanding how communities are imagined, precisely because of its complicated relationship with the ideas Anderson focuses on: nationhood, language, and print capitalism. The difficulty Cypriots experience in creating a singular print culture tied to one national language—given the constant pulls of Cypriot Greek, Cypriot Turkish, Greek, Turkish, and English—means that a sense of uniform national selfhood is stunted. Referrals, or deferrals, to other (imaged) nation states which are centred overseas are made instead. The project of even imaging a 'Cypriot nation' or a pan-Cypriot community—or putting forward the notion of 'Cypriotism' as a plausible mode of cultural and political identification—is only starting to gain any traction, over half a century after the British Empire claimed to give islanders independence. In fact, while Arjun Appadurai's theories of the 'postnational' are useful for thinking about how Cypriot writers publishing after 1974 are attempting to move beyond national(ist) affiliations with Greece and Turkey—and their respective print capitalist machineries—it might also be true to suggest that Cypriot writers are still *prenational* in not having quite created, or in not having the freedom to exist in, a Cypriot nation.[111] These writers, then, sit between these poles of the prenational and the postnational, attempting to mobilise forms which reject the nationalisms of elsewhere (a postnational gesture) while also considering what a truly local (Cypriot) national identity might be (a prenational desire). That is, if such an identification based on Cypriotism can ever exist without eventually becoming as hegemonic as the ideologies it would replace. How to reckon with this tension is the primary issue faced by Cypriot producers of culture. They sit in this liminal position between pre and post which is a direct consequence of the island's colonial history and its continuing state of flux between continued colonisation and a nascent postcoloniality. To return to the quoted article at the beginning of this chapter, Cyprus is 'in the middle', existing somewhat-uneasily on the doorway, the limen, or the portal between modes of being and becoming.

NOTES

1. Jonathan Gorvett, 'Cyprus in the Middle: Nicosia Holds the Keys to Syria, the Migrant Crisis, and Gas in the Eastern Mediterranean', *Foreign Affairs* (12 January 2016). https://www.foreignaffairs.com/articles/cyprus/2016-01-12/cyprus-middle [accessed 14 June 2018].
2. Ibid.
3. Ibid.
4. This historicist methodology is indebted to Raymond Williams' study of the apparent antonyms 'country' and 'city' and how, pushing back through junctures of English writing, 'certain images and associations persist… in relation to the historically varied experience'. He refers to this mode of criticism as assuming 'the escalator' of time, from which one can observe how that which is considered memory is in fact a matter of 'historical perspective'. Raymond Williams, *The Country and the City* (Oxford and New York: Oxford University Press, 1973), pp. 1–2, 10.
5. John C. Campbell, 'The Mediterranean Crisis', *Foreign Affairs* (1 July 1975). https://www.foreignaffairs.com/articles/cyprus/1975-07-01/mediterranean-crisis [accessed 14 June 2018].
6. Roderic H. Davidson, 'Where Is The Middle East?', *Foreign Affairs* (1 July 1960). https://www.foreignaffairs.com/articles/middle-east/1960-07-01/where-middle-east [accessed 14 June 2018].
7. Ibid.
8. Benjamin Disraeli, 5 May 1878, quoted in Anastasia Yiangou, *Cyprus in World War II: Politics and Conflict in the Eastern Mediterranean* (London: I.B. Tauris, 2010), p. 170.
9. Samuel W. Baker, *Cyprus, As I Saw It in 1879* (London: Echo Library, 2007), p. 89.
10. William Hepworth Dixon, *British Cyprus* (London: Chapman and Hall, 1879), p. 9.
11. Agnes Smith, *Through Cyprus* (London: Hurst and Blackett, 1887), p. 1.
12. Angela Carter, 'Triple Flavour', *New Society*, 25 (1973), 268–269 (p. 268).
13. Winston Churchill, *The War Speeches of the Rt. Hon. Winston S. Churchill: From June 25, 1941 to September 6, 1943* (Cambridge: The Riverside Press, 1953), p. 77.
14. Edward W. Said, *Reflections of Exile and Other Essays* (Cambridge, MA: Harvard University Press, 2001), p. 199.
15. Herodotus, *The History*, trans. by David Grene (Chicago: University of Chicago Press, 1987), p. 253.
16. Herbert S. Klein, *The Atlantic Slave Trade* (Cambridge: Cambridge University Press, 2010), p. 6.

17. Nayan Chanda, *Bound Together* (New Haven and London: Yale University Press, 2007), p. 219. For more on the 'colonial relationship [that] was established between the primary producing, cane-growing areas [in Cyprus] and the metropolitan, manufacturing and refining centers in Europe', and how 'sugar cane cultivation and slavery' in Cyprus related to nineteenth-century models, see J.H. Galloway, *The Sugar Cane Industry: An Historical Geography from its Origins to 1914* (Cambridge: Cambridge University Press, 1989), pp. 42–23.
18. 'Cyprus Convention', in Wikisource. http://en.wikisource.org/wiki/Cyprus_covention [accessed 11 August 2018].
19. 'The Sykes-Picot Agreement', in Wikisource. http://en.wikisource.org/wiki/The_Sykes-Picot_Agreement [accessed 11 August 2018].
20. 'Treaty of Guarantee', in Wikisource. http://en.wikisource.org/wiki/Treaty_of_Guarantee [accessed 11 August 2018].
21. Makarios told the UN in July 1974 that the *coup* facilitated a 'terrorist organisation' (EOKA B) and 'is an invasion, and from its consequences the whole people of Cyprus suffers, both Greeks and Turks'. Days earlier, he spoke on national radio to declare that 'the junta has decided to ruin Cyprus, to partition it'. Quoted in Kypros Tofallis, *The History of Cyprus: From the Ancient Times to the Present* (London: The Greek Institute, 2002), pp. 299, 293–294.
22. Xenia Hadjioannou, Stravoula Tsiplakou, and Matthias Kappler, 'Language Policy and Language Planning in Cyprus', *Current Issues in Language Planning*, 12 (2011), 503–569.
23. Amalia Arvaniti, 'Linguistic Practices in Cyprus and the Emergence of Cypriot Greek', *San Diego Linguistic Papers*, 2 (2006), 1–24.
24. Stavroula Tsiplakou, 'Code-Switching and Code-Mixing Between Related Varieties: Establishing the Blueprint', *International Journal of Humanities*, 6 (2006), 46–66.
25. V Ozan Gulle, 'Structural Borrowings in Cypriot Turkish from Cypriot Greek', *Mediterranean Language Review*, 18 (2011), 91–113.
26. Jacques Derrida, *Monolingualism of the Other; or, The Prosthesis of Origins*, trans. by Patrick Mensah (Stanford: Stanford University Press, 1998), p. 28.
27. As the dustjacket of the hardback edition sets out from the onset of his work, the travelling 'Papadakis, firmly planted in the Greek Cypriot world, sets out to discover "The Other"—the much maligned Turks'. Yiannis Papadakis, *Echoes from the Dead Zone: Across the Cyprus Divide* (London and New York: I.B. Tauris, 2005). Education is culpable in reiterating stereotypes through which 'Cypriot children construct notions of the ethnic self and other' which, alongside family stories, impact their conceptions of 'the other side' from an early age. Peter Stevens, *Ethnicity*

and Racism in Cyprus: National Pride and Prejudice? (London: Palgrave Macmillan, 2016), p. 13.

28. Diez notes how, in Cyprus, the partition helps 'reify the boundaries between self and other in both communities' self-construction [which] suppress[es] imagining a future together'. Thomas Diez, 'Introduction: Cyprus and the European Union as a Political and Theoretical Problem', in *The European Union and Cyprus: Modern Conflict, Postmodern Union*, ed. by Diez (Manchester: Manchester University Press, 2002), pp. 1–13 (p. 11).
29. Edward W. Said, *Culture and Imperialism* (London: Vintage Books, 1994), p. 358.
30. Note references to Cyprus in Rushdie's *The Satanic Verses*, for instance. Speaking of London, one character observes, 'African, Caribbean, Indian, Pakistani, Bangladeshi, Cypriot, Chinese, we are other than what we would have been had we not crossed the oceans... we shall also be the ones to remake this society'. Salman Rushdie, *The Satanic Verses* (London: Vintage Books, 1988), p. 414. The island also features in Salih's 'The Cypriot Man' (1973/1976) which revives characters from *Season of Migration to the North* (1966; 1991). Tayeb Salih, 'The Cypriot Man', in *Arabic Short Stories*, trans. by Denys Johnson-Davies, ed. by Roger Allen (Berkeley: University of California Press, 1994), pp. 75–83.
31. W.E.B. Du Bois, *A W.E.B. Du Bois Reader*, ed. by Andrew G. Paschal (New York: Collier Books, 1971), p. 203.
32. Jennifer Larson, 'Greece', in *The Cambridge Companion to Ancient Mediterranean Religions*, ed. by Barbette S. Spaeth (Cambridge: Cambridge University Press, 2013), pp. 136–156 (p. 138).
33. David Damrosch, *How to Read World Literature* (Oxford: Wiley-Blackwell, 2017), p. 43.
34. This alludes to 'writers, artists and social theorists who were actually engaging the power of imperial discourse – who were "writing-back"'. Bill Ashcroft, Gareth Griffiths, and Helen Tiffin, *The Empire Writes Back: Theory and Practice in Post-Colonial Literatures* (London and New York: Routledge, 1989), p. 198.
35. Stuart Hall, 'When was 'the Post-Colonial'?: Thinking at the Limit', in *The Post-Colonial Question*, ed. by Iain Chambers and Lidia Curti (London and New York: Routledge, 1996), pp. 242–260.
36. He cites the 'retention by the departing colonialist of various kinds of privileges which infringe our sovereignty [*sic*]: that of setting up military bases or stationing troops in former colonies'. Kwame Nkrumah, *Neo-Colonialism: The Last Stage of Imperialism* (New York: International Publishers, 1965), p. 246. Interestingly, this definition would also include the military presence of Greece and Turkey on the island as forms

of neo-colonialism. Perhaps, to modify Nkrumah's subtitle, Western European neo-colonialism is not always the very *last stage of imperialism* for states whose independence are repeatedly deferred. Briefly, it is worth noting that Nkrumah uses Cyprus, alongside Vietnam and Korea, as an example of contemporary 'military adventures' by neo-colonial powers (p. 228).

37. Boehmer observes how, in India and Ireland, '[t]he spread of the English language and of an English literary education… created the conditions of possibility for a cross-border transaction… to emerge', facilitating 'inter-discursive cross-over and mingling', spreading modes of anti-colonial resistance as well as reproducing the model of Western European nationalism. Elleke Boehmer, *Empire, the National, and the Postcolonial, 1890–1920: Resistance in Interaction* (Oxford: Oxford University Press, 2002), pp. 51, 57. Much has been studied on Indian English, Singapore English (and Singlish), and Nigerian English (and Nigerian Pidgin). See, Edgar W. Schneider, *Postcolonial Englishes: Varieties Across the World* (Cambridge: Cambridge University Press, 2007). There are many obvious parallels between the use of English, or English, in Cyprus and in India, Singapore, and Nigeria. It is worth noting some differences. In Cyprus, no form of English has official status (outside the British bases). The English spoken on the island is typically in its standardised, British variant, albeit modified slightly by code-switching and Greek/Turkish loanwords. In other words, no uniquely-Cypriot, English-based creole or pidgin exists. English has not become, politically or morphologically, 'an indigenized language' (Schneider, p. 1). Yet, this term then raises questions on the *indigeneity* of Greek and Turkish.
38. Linda Colley, *Britons: Forging the Nation, 1707–1837* (New Haven: Yale University Press, 1992), p. 6.
39. Bernd Wächter, 'Recent Trends in Student Mobility in Europe', in *Internationalisation of Higher Education and Global Mobility*, ed. by Bernhard Streitwieser (Oxford: Symposium Books, 2014), pp. 87–97 (p. 93).
40. Extremely influential to this monograph is Pierre Bourdieu's theory of economic, social, and cultural capital, and the ways that the three impact one another. See, Pierre Bourdieu, 'The Forms of Capital', trans. by Richard Nice, in *Handbook of Theory and Research*, ed. by John G. Richardson (New York: Greenwood Press, 1986), pp. 241–258.
41. European Commission, 'Youth on the Move: Analytical Report', Special Eurobarometer 319b (Brussels: The Gallup Organisation, 2011), p. 24.
42. European Commission, 'Europeans and their Languages: Summary', Special Eurobarometer 243 (Brussels: The Gallup Organisation, 2006), p. 9.

43. European Commission, 'Europeans and their Languages: Report', Special Eurobarometer 386 (Brussels: The Gallup Organisation, 2012), p. 52.
44. Ibid.
45. European Commission, 'User Language Preferences Online: Analytical Report', Special Eurobarometer 313 (Brussels: The Gallup Organisation, 2011), p. 16.
46. Dipesh Chakrabarty, *Provincializing Europe: Postcolonial Thought and Historical Difference* (Princeton, NJ: Princeton University Press, 2007).
47. Robert J.C. Young, 'Postcolonial Remains', *New Literary History*, 43 (2012), 19–42 (p. 36).
48. Frantz Fanon, *Black Skin/White Masks*, trans. by Charles Lam Markmann (London: Pluto Press, 1986). Fanon describes how, across the decolonising globe, 'there is clearly a wish to be white' and, according to him, 'this self-division is a direct result of colonialist subjugation' (pp. 17–18). His use of the concept of 'self-division' is particularly interesting for Cyprus, a (former) British colony which, not only struggles for cultural identifications among the residual *divisions* of continents and races (Europe and non-Europe) constructed in 'the West', but which internalises and territorialises this mentality though partition.
49. Lobby for Cyprus, 'Ankara Calls the Shots in Occupied Cyprus' and 'The True Face of Bizonalism', *Lobby For Cyprus News*, 28 (2015), 1–3 (pp. 1-3).
50. Lobby for Cyprus, 'The 10th Anniversary of the Annan Plan Referendum', *Lobby For Cyprus News*, 27 (2014), 2 (p. 2).
51. Ibid.
52. Lobby for Cyprus, 'A Call to End Impunity and Reject Segregation', *Lobby for Cyprus News*, 27 (2014), 2 (p. 2).
53. Young, 'Postcolonial Remains', pp. 20, 31.
54. Young, 'Postcolonial Remains', p. 27.
55. Frantz Fanon, *The Wretched of the Earth*, trans. by Constance Farrington (New York: Grove Press, 1968), p. 165.
56. Papadakis, pp. 1–2.
57. Young, 'Postcolonial Remains', p. 39.
58. Paul Gilroy, *Darker Than Blue: On the Moral Economies of Black Atlantic Culture* (Cambridge, MA: Harvard University Press, 2010), p. 135.
59. According to Williams, '[t]he complexity of culture is to be found... in the dynamic interrelations, at every point in the process, of historically varied and variable elements'. I use this to understand how forms of colonial ideology on the island are always 'variable', striated, and intersectional. They are to be usefully understood in terms of his '"epochal" analysis' observing how 'a cultural process is seized as a cultural system, with determinate dominant features'. One mode of cultural dualism

on the island functions as a reframing of another, earlier or coterminous, form. Williams defines 'emergent' as the formation of 'new meanings and values', although it is challenging to discern those 'which are substantially alternative or oppositional' to the dominant. Raymond Williams, *Marxism and Literature* (Oxford: Oxford University Press, 1977), p. 121.

60. Benedict Anderson, *Imagined Communities: Reflections on the Origin and Spread of Nationalism* (London and New York: Verso, 2006), p. 7.
61. 'Statement of U.S. Policy Toward Cyprus', National Security Council 6003, Department of State (9 February 1960). https://history.state.gov/historicaldocuments/frus1958-60v10p1/d347 [accessed 21 April 2020].
62. Edward W. Said, *Orientalism* (London: Penguin, 1995), p. 192.
63. Said, *Orientalism*, p. 117.
64. Elizabeth A. Bohls, 'Introduction', in *Travel Writing 1700–1830: An Anthology*, ed. by Bohls and Ian Ducan (Oxford: Oxford University Press, 2005), pp. xiii–xxvii (p. xxii).
65. Debbie Lisle, *The Global Politics of Contemporary Travel Writing* (Cambridge: Cambridge University Press, 2006), p. 28.
66. Michel de Certeau, *The Practice of Everyday Life*, trans. by Steven Rendall (Berkeley: University of California Press, 1984), p. 115.
67. Georg Lukács, *The Theory of the Novel: A Historico-Philosophical Essay on the Forms of Great Epic Literature*, trans. by Anna Bostock (Cambridge, MA: MIT Press, 1971), p. 41.
68. Ibid., p. 64.
69. Sachidananda Mohanty, 'Introduction: Beyond the Imperial Eye', in *Travel Writing and the Empire*, ed. by Mohanty (New Delhi: Katha, 2003), pp. ix–xxi (p. xi).
70. James Clifford, *Routes: Travel and Translation in the Late Twentieth Century* (Cambridge, MA: Harvard University Press, 1997). In his research, '*travel* emerged as an increasingly complex range of experiences: practices of crossing and interaction that troubled the localism of many common assumptions about culture' (p. 3).
71. Salman Rushdie, *Imaginary Homelands: Essays and Criticism, 1981–1991* (London: Granta Books, 1992), p. 10.
72. On the 'conception of the writer as pedagogue and nation-builder', *in English*, and often through the novel, see, Pascale Casanova, *The World Republic of Letters*, trans. by M.B. DeBevoise (Cambridge, MA: Harvard University Press, 2004), p. 196. See also, Homi K. Bhabha, 'Introduction: Narrating the Nation', in *Nation and Narration*, ed. by Bhabha (London and New York: Routledge, 1990), pp. 1–7.
73. Aydın Mehmet Ali, *Forbidden Zones: Short Stories & Others* (London: Fatal Publications, 2013), p. 5.

74. Mikhail Bakhtin, *The Dialogic Imagination: Four Essays*, trans. by Caryl Emerson and Michael Holquist (Austin, Texas: University of Texas Press, 2011), pp. 3–40. For Bakhtin, publishing in 1941, 'the novel is the sole genre that continues to develop, that is yet uncompleted', allowing it to reveal the heteroglossia of society (p. 3). Perhaps, in the decades since, the novel has attained a degree of *completeness* (within, and by, Euro-American institutions) which limits it from performing the roles it once did for Bakhtin in the pre- and inter-war years. In other words, the novel has, for 'postcolonial' writers, been previously *completed* by 'colonial' traditions. It is now travel writing which 'continues to develop', moved along by the dispossessions of the post-war, 'postcolonial' globe.
75. Edward W. Said, 'On The University', in *Edward Said and Critical Decolonization*, ed. by Ferial J. Ghazoul (Cairo and New York: The American University in Cairo Press, 2007), pp. 26–36 (p. 36).
76. Grzegorz Moroz and Jolanta Sztachelska, 'Preface', in *Metamorphoses of Travel Writing: Across Themes, Genres, Countries and Literary Traditions*, ed. by Moroz and Sztachelska (Newcastle upon Tyne: Cambridge Scholars Publishing, 2010), pp. ix–x (p. x).
77. April Shemak, 'Refugee and Asylum Seeker Narratives as Postcolonial Travel Writing', in *The Cambridge Companion to Postcolonial Life Writing*, ed. by Robert Clarke (Cambridge: Cambridge University Press, 2018), pp. 188–201 (p. 189).
78. Graham Huggan, *Extreme Pursuits: Travel/Writing in an Age of Globalization* (Ann Arbor: University of Michigan Press, 2009), pp. 8, 15.
79. Robert Clarke, 'Toward a Genealogy of Postcolonial Travel Writing: An Introduction', in *The Cambridge Companion to Postcolonial Life Writing*, ed. by Robert Clarke (Cambridge: Cambridge University Press, 2018), pp. 1–17 (pp. 6, 11).
80. Ibid., p. 6.
81. Mary Louise Pratt, *Imperial Eyes: Travel Writing and Transculturation* (Oxford and New York: Routledge, 1992), p. 8.
82. Ibid.
83. Ibid., pp. 248, 100.
84. Ibid., p. 180.
85. Patrick Holland and Graham Huggan, *Tourists with Typewriters: Critical Reflections on Contemporary Travel Writing* (Ann Arbor: The University of Michigan Press, 1998), p. 198.
86. Bill Ashcroft, 'Transnation', in *Re-routing the Postcolonial: New Dimensions for the New Millennium*, ed. by Janet Wilson, Cristina Sandru, and Sarah Lawson Welsh (Oxford and New York: Routledge, 2010), pp. 72–85 (p. 79).
87. Ibid., p. 84.

88. Said, 'On The University', p. 36.
89. Gayatri C. Spivak, *Death of a Discipline* (New York: Columbia University Press, 2003), p. 8.
90. Ibid., p. 95.
91. Ibid., p. 96.
92. Ibid., p. 1.
93. Spivak, *Death of a Discipline*, p. 72.
94. Ibid., pp. 10–11.
95. Ibid., p. 10.
96. Ibid., p. 11.
97. Ibid., p. 9.
98. In contrast to the English standardised in southern England, this is one of 'the various post-colonial englishes in use today', as defined by Ashcroft, Griffiths, and Tiffin, p. 8. Perhaps, this can be placed in conjunction with postcolonial Greeks, Turkishes, and Arabics in Cyprus.
99. Here, as I will elaborate on further in the book, I am alluding to Moretti's concept of 'distant reading' but in an extended sense. I see distance as a construct and therefore understand Cypriot writers as creating a consciously *distanced*, not essentially distant, set of reading practices. See, Franco Moretti, *Distant Reading* (London and New York: Verso, 2013). Note his view of world literatures as employing 'a compromise between a western formal influence (usually French or English) and local materials' (p. 50). For Cypriots, how one defines 'local', and whether Greek and Turkish 'influence[s]' perform similar roles to those of French and English elsewhere in the decolonising 'world', illustrate the complexities of this context beyond simple dichotomies of 'western'/non-'western' and foreign/'local'. Put simply, where and what is 'distant' and proximal?
100. Georg Simmel, 'Bridge and Door', *Theory, Culture & Society*, 7 (1994), 5–10 (p. 5).
101. Ngũgĩ wa Thiong'o, 'Borders and Bridges: Seeking Connections Between Things', in *The Pre-occupation of Postcolonial Studies*, ed. by Fawzia Afzal-Khan and Kalpana Seshadri-Crooks (Durham: Duke University Press, 2000), pp. 119–125.
102. Paul Gilroy, *The Black Atlantic: Modernity and Double Consciousness* (Cambridge, MA: Harvard University Press, 1993), p. 73.
103. Ibid., p. 30.
104. Alexander Gutzmer, *Brand-Driven City Building and the Virtualizing of Space* (Oxford and New York: Routledge, 2014), p. 63.
105. Immanuel Kant, *Theoretical Philosophy after 1781*, ed. by Henry Allison and Peter Heath, trans. by Gary Hatfield, Michael Friedman, Henry Allison, and Peter Heath (Cambridge: Cambridge University Press, 2004), p. 149.
106. Ibid., p. 150.

107. Jacques Derrida, *The Truth in Painting*, trans. by Geoffrey Bennington (Chicago: University of Chicago Press, 1987), p. 9.
108. Jacques Derrida, *Adieu to Emmanuel Levinas*, trans. by Pascale-Anne Brault and Michael Naas (Stanford: Stanford University Press, 1999), p. 54.
109. Ibid., p. 26.
110. Jacques Derrida, *Of Grammatology*, ed. by Judith Butler, trans. by Gayatri C. Spivak (Baltimore: John Hopkins University Press, 2016), p. 369.
111. Arjun Appadurai, *Modernity at Large: Cultural Dimensions of Globalization* (Minneapolis: University of Minnesota Press, 1996), p. 158ff.

CHAPTER 2

'A Business of Some Heat': Sexuality, Disease, and Gendered Orientalism on Venus' Island, 1878–1973

> Othello: What is the matter, think you?
> Cassio: Something from Cyprus, as I may divine. /It is a business of some heat.[1]
> (1.2.45–47)

From its earliest literary representations, Cyprus has been associated with imbricated anxieties towards race, gender, and sexuality. Notably, *Othello* appropriates the liminal setting as a space of uneasy female autonomy and as a locus of dangerous political and sexual activity orchestrated by men. Venus' island is, for Venice, a '*business* of some heat' (*emphasis mine*), a *commercial* hub degrading into a deathbed of intercultural, interfaith, and interracial sex. The play gradually transports the audience's frame of reference from the maritime city—a theatrical elsewhere with some cultural affinities to contemporary London—further along the Silk Road to the greater unknown of an island then under Islamic Ottoman rule and previously the eastern-most bastion of England's Crusading past. It is the last remnant of British dominion in the Levant, reimagined as a prototype for the imperial ventures beginning anew at the end of the sixteenth century.

Centuries later, to herald the British Empire's acquisition of its newest territorial possession, an August 1878 edition of the popular London periodical, *Punch*, featured an illustration of the salient colonial encounter replete with metonymic images of sexual exchange (Fig. 2.1). The monochrome print represents the martial figure of Sir Garnet Wolseley,

D. Nunziata, *Colonial and Postcolonial Cyprus*,
https://doi.org/10.1007/978-3-030-58236-4_2

Fig. 2.1 'Bien Venu Qui Apporte!' Cartoon by Linley Sambourne published in *Punch* on August 3, 1878, showing the island's High Commissioner, Sir Garnet Wolseley, wooing the Venus-like personification of Cyprus

the island's first High Commissioner, kissing the hand of a woman draped in the Union Flag and identified by a marker on her dress, 'CYPRUS'.[2] The woman is analogised with Venus, an inference furthered by the word-play in the French title, 'Bien Venu Qui Apporte!' In an empire governed by a queen, it is, nonetheless, a British man who personally embodies the conquest and penetration of gendered topographies. As in subsequent literary depictions of this moment, the illustration symbolically constructs the empire as a male-dominated, uniformed, chivalric enterprise—inheriting the courtly conventions of the nation's Crusader past—in its engagement with the effeminised otherness of its nascent colony who stoically welcomes, rather than rebuffs, the civilising advances of the 'Western' power. In the pastoral background, two doves are perched together in union: the wedding of coloniser and colonised is not only imagined as an amorous meeting of male self and female Other, but as one which precludes any of the political resistance to imperialism which emerges in the late nineteenth century and reaches its apex prior to independence.

As Anne McClintock has demonstrated, such imagery participates in a 'persistent gendering of the imperial unknown' in colonial discourses; she explicitly nuances Foucault's dialectic to express how 'women served as mediating and threshold figures by means of which men orientated themselves in space, as agents of power and agents of knowledge', in reference to the inevitable intersectionality of ethnicity and gender within the lexicons of empire.[3] Similarly, according to Nancy Leys Stepan, colonialist and nationalist theories of 'eugenics defined biological and cultural distinctions of gender and how race and gender intertwined to construct new images and social practices of the "fit" nation', within a body of discursive parallels between gender, race, and hygiene.[4] Indeed, if Cyprus, in particular, is characterised as a site of geographic, cultural, and *racial* inbetweenness—as well as being an *effeminised* space—then it is necessary to consider Young's summary, in his analysis of ambivalence towards 'hybridity', that '[n]ineteenth-century theories of race did not just consist of essentializing differentiations between self and other, they were also about a fascination with people having sex… illicit, inter-racial sex'.[5]

Cyprus, Degeneration, and Gendered Orientalism

This fetishising is repeated throughout Victorian men's travel writing and continues into the early twentieth century. Dixon, two paragraphs after alluding to the island as 'the connecting link of East and West' in the bodily 'throb and pulse of an imperial life', states that 'Cyprus has been at all times:- a dream and a desire of men… the embodiment of earthy loveliness… an object of abuse'.[6] Later, the misogynistic register is heightened to metaphorically analogise the military occupation with 'the rape of some fair mortal by one of the elder race of gods', implicating himself in this hierarchised act of violence by proclaiming that, 'We have taken Cyprus very much… as "marriage by force["]'.[7] His gendering and sexualising of the colonial mission is shared by his contemporary, Baker, who, more implicitly, introduces the Levant as 'this happily situated position [where] commerce was first cradled… by the interchange of ideas and natural productions'.[8] In addition to the politically-'strategical' site of the island between continents, as he refers to it elsewhere, the subtle sexual and reproductive connotations of 'commerce', 'cradled', 'interchange', and 'productions' all underscore an imbrication of imperial trade with sexuality. As Young emphasises, 'economic and sexual exchange were intimately bound up, coupled with each other, from the very first', notably through the dual 'meanings of the word "commerce"'.[9] For both Dixon and Baker, however, such 'commerce' was not always generative, but also a source of fear, disease, and infertility: the two describe Larnaca, the first coastal city they arrive at, as malaria-infested and 'barren', commencing a recurring theme throughout colonial literatures on Cyprus.[10] The former, for instance, dichotomises 'the barren hills of Larnaca' with jingoistic images of rural England, and accordingly, 'Cyprus is not green like Kent and Essex… Grass, the basis of our landscape beauty, is unknown', precisely because 'Cyprus is the East. You must not seek for pasture under palms'.[11] As well as juxtaposing the first-person habitus of his British readership with the climate of 'the East', the account expresses a preoccupation with fecundity and productivity before sententiously moralising against ('You must not…') the dangerously-sterilising cross-pollination of trade, agricultural technologies, and organic matter in the colonised Orient. Cyprus is less *virgin territory* and more the venereal site of multiple occupations by divergent imperial bodies.

In the succeeding century, these motifs are reiterated by the literary successors of nineteenth-century travel. The prominent travel writer Colin Thubron commences his work, *Journey into Cyprus* (1975), by describing the island as the liminal setting where 'Europe merges with Asia' producing 'half Asiatic lands', before echoing Dixon in his claim that they have been 'made with magic economy, and to them a man is always, inexplicitly, returning' as the land is 'much coveted, trodden by generations of peasants and soldiers... break[ing] the back of any plough or man'.[12] Alongside allusions to cultural pluralism, framing Cyprus as the miscegenated 'half' product of two parental spheres of influence, Thubron imagines colonisation as an androcentric saga of a 'man' in relation to global 'economy' and a 'coveted' sexual conquest: a masculinist, capitalist, and racialist individualism inherited from Daniel Defoe's *Robinson Crusoe*, if not Shakespeare's *The Tempest*.

Equally, in the introductory chapter of Durrell's travelogue, the narration describes his last moments in Venice, before departing for the island (recalling the metropolitan Italian and peripheral insular settings of both *Othello* and *The Tempest*), in which he sits with a Bolognese man discussing Cypriot women,

> "Very ugly," he said at last, in genuine regret. "Very ugly indeed." This was disheartening. We sat there in silence for a while until the steamer towering above us gave a loud lisp of steam *fffff*, while beaded bubbles of condensing steam trickled down the siren. It was time to say good-bye to Europe. ...The mist... quivered on the hills beyond Venice. With such associations how could I forget Catherine Cornaro, the last [Venetian] Queen of Cyprus.[13]

The scene commences his solo journey through the Orientalist anticipation of a 'quivering' sensuality, presenting Cypriot women, contemporary and historical, as exoticised objects of misogynistic study between European men. Through contrasting images, Cyprus is associated with a dying, defenceless matriarchy, and Venice with the potency of phallic symbols, 'the steamer towering' before its 'condensed steam trickled down' climactically (echoing the Classical narrative of Venus' maritime birth from the castrated and ejaculating genitals of a primal, patriarchal deity, Uranus). Most importantly, however, by denigrating the appearance of Cypriot women, Durrell, at the very beginning of both his expedition and his published narrative, forecloses the possibility—and threat—of sexual relations between a British man and 'native' women while still gesturing to his healthy desire for such a fantasy. He both defends his masculinist, heterosexual potency—aligning himself with the figure of 'the steamer'—*and* reassures readers of his sexual self-restraint and ethnic self-isolation before 'say[ing] good-bye to Europe' and the safety it guarantees. Ultimately, throughout *Bitter Lemons*, Durrell never converses with a woman of the same generation. The very title of the text, therefore, may be a warning of the unpalatable fruit of Europeans in the Orient, producing not only the 'emergency' of the 1950s, but other, unspeakably-'bitter' consequences of the marrying of 'East' and 'West'.

Across colonial travel writing, the vilifying of Cypriot women as incompatible with British men is a recurring trope. In his 1878 journal, Wolseley states that '[t]hey are a plain looking lot and do Venus no credit'.[14] Almost a century later, Thubron echoes this with the suggestion that '[d]espite their patron goddess, the women of Cyprus are not especially beautiful'.[15] Both are concerned with repudiating the literary relationship between the island and ancient goddesses of sexuality and prostitution—associations resulting in the archaic meaning of the euphemism *Cyprian* to denote prostitutes, or even the etymological corruption of *venereal* from 'Venus-like' to 'sexually-diseased'[16]—as a strategy which emphatically delimits interpersonal interactions between British men and Cypriot women in a culturally-porous space. Wolseley, Durrell, and Thubron construct what Sara Ahmed describes as a 'fantasy of distance premised on a refusal to encounter others' in the meeting of coloniser/colonised, male/female, Western/Oriental.[17] These writers' proleptic references allude to Cyprus as a gendered and morally-inferior locus outside a masculine, civilised Europe, before disavowing this motif in order to present their own moral quarantine averting a Kurtz-like assimilation. Indeed, Durrell's account of his nautical journey between 'Europe' and a British colony, mere paragraphs after his commentary on sexuality, outlines the ship in which he 'turned from the rail with a sigh, aware that the light was sifting quietly away into the darkness',[18] echoing the frame narrative of Conrad's novel and repeating the chiaroscuro motifs of 'light' and 'darkness' which dichotomise in the movement away from European metropolitanism.[19]

Durrell's attempts at demarcating safe binaries between 'Europe' and Cyprus, 'light' and 'darkness', and British men and 'native' women, relate to the figurative representation of Cyprus as sexually—as well as culturally—'hybrid' in Thubron's text. In an essentialist depiction of its inhabitants, Thubron argues that,

> Cypriots... were natural members of this dazzling hybrid, Byzantium. They, like it, lay midway between the classical and the oriental. Their softness and conservatism were not Hellenic. To them the character of

> the Greek mainland was unsympathetically masculine [in contrast to] Constantinople, which they felt to be their mother-city.[20]

The idioms 'hybrid' and 'midway' explicitly relate the interstitiality of the island between Greek and 'oriental' cultures, a cultural liminality of which its people become biologically, or 'natural[ly]', metonymic. In particular, however, this 'hybrid' essence is represented as an antagonism between, and mixture of, a 'masculine' Europe and effeminised spaces of the East (including the portrayal of Constantinople/Istanbul in modern Turkey as a 'mother-city'). In contradistinction to Durrell who emphatically repudiates the figuring of Byzantium as 'hybrid' within a polarised account of Greece and Turkey as dyadic opposites—'It was an entity *per say* [*sic*], not merely a colourful composite made up of assorted fragments of different cultures'[21]—Thubron offers a historiography which genders the Eastern Mediterranean and presents both the Byzantine Empire and Cyprus as the *intersex* products of masculine and feminine sources. Metaphoricity is a kind of literary transportation allowing him to play with definitions. As well as implicitly alluding to modern Greece and Turkey, the two major foci of 1960s nationalist movements, this relationship between Europe and Asia is frequently portrayed through images of ancient Greece and Phoenicia (two purported origins of some ancient Cypriots). For Thubron, 'these two civilizations constituted... the raw materials from which the Greek Cypriot race was hammered out... To the masculine Mycenaean world, the Phoenicians opposed a quicksilver people'.[22] Here, idioms of 'civilization' and 'race' are negotiated in relation to gender binaries, juxtaposing the 'masculine' with the effeminate. Later, a Cypriot man, Chambi, is claimed to have 'showed the hawk-nosed, delicate face of Phoenicia. His fingers were long and faintly effeminate',[23] appropriating anti-Levantine stereotypes to assess his physiognomy and present Chambi as a physical embodiment of the mixture of male and 'effeminate', and Greek and Phoenician, which characterises Cyprus for the author: a space 'between Europe and Asia [where t]he Semitic passions are tempered, the Greek pride blunted'.[24]

Notably, however, this motif reaches its apotheosis in the narrative's recurring fetishising of Aphrodite whose name appears in every chapter bar one. As a consequence of her religious eclecticism—having been absorbed by Hellenic cultures from a Babylonian mother goddess and Mesopotamian and Phoenician counterparts, Ishtar and Astarte, before being adopted by Rome as Venus—she is portrayed as the personified integration of 'the classical and the oriental' which Cyprus facilitates, as well as a symbol of its ostensibly-inherent effeminacy and sexuality. Repeating his own limited lexicon, Thubron asserts that 'in the masculine climate of Greece, Aphrodite was faintly suspect. Called "The Cyprian"… she never completely lived down her oriental birth [or her] licentiousness'.[25] Moreover, Cyprus is imagined as a cultural 'missing link', specifically in relation to gender: the translated, transmuted, 'many-faced Aphrodite—would keep the link unbroken between Neolithic embryo and modern man'; it is extended to cover 'the last human link, a link of vaguest memory' between Aphrodite and the Christo-Islamic Virgin Mary and the Islamic holy woman, Umm Haram, both venerated by contemporary Cypriots.[26] Here, matriarchy, mother-goddesses, and reproduction are associated with an antiquarian 'embryo' of an atavistic, feminine otherness, in contrast with the status of patriarchal, 'modern man', consequently positioning Cyprus—or, Cypriots—as a temporal, spatial, and gendered 'link' between binary states. Moreover, when he emphasises that ancient Cypriots often artistically depicted Aphrodite as a 'hermaphrodite and was worshipped by men and women in the dress of the opposite sex',[27] not only does he associate the goddess with the etymology of the word herm*aphrodite*, but expresses the cultural inbetweenness of a Greco-Phoenician deity through the imagery of transgender peoples.

If, as the same chapter suggests, Cyprus has a confused *ethno-cultural* identity—'Semitic or Mycenaean, even their style [of ancient art] is in dispute' by scholars[28]—then the narrative articulates this alongside a claim of a confused gendered identity. Similarly, Durrell earlier introduces this theme by describing 'the double-sexed Aphrodite… whose worshippers inverted their dress', causing him to meditate on 'whether the extraordinary number of hermaphrodites on Cyprus did not perhaps betoken some forgotten race, bred for the service of the temple'.[29] Essentialised idioms of 'race' and gender are inextricably coupled, presenting Cyprus as culturally, racially, *and sexually* in-between through a crude analogising of these colonialist categories, ultimately dehumanising both Cypriot and intersex peoples through the bestial connotations of 'bred'. Although these tropes are not uncommon across colonial discourses, they reach their apotheosis in representations of a context feared by travelling Western Europeans as home to an infamous interstitiality which contaminates all areas of its essence, including the 'race' and gender of its inhabitants. This threat of contamination risks the stability of their own identities as metropolitan men entering a transhistorical elsewhere between Classical and Oriental, both of which are understood as states between (temporal or spatial) familiarity and exoticism. The colonial travelogue is, therefore, employed to explore how colonial subjecthoods can survive when departing from the racial and gendered security of domestic British modernity.

The imagined relationship between the cultural 'hybrid' and intersex peoples is, as the term 'bred' suggests, articulated through pseudoscientific discourses of reproduction and infertility. Following the premise that 'hybrids' are biologically sterile, this imagery is used to stigmatise Cyprus' transcultural status as diseased, degenerate, and barren. Indeed, throughout both nineteenth- and twentieth-century travel writing on Ottoman and British Cyprus, the island is denigrated as a source of infection for otherwise-healthy Europeans. Even earlier, Defoe's fictional *A Journal of the Plague Year* (1722), in illustrating the threat of disease to the integrity of the commercial capital of London, posits that the 1664 outbreak 'was brought, some said from *Italy*, others from the [mainland] *Levant* among some Goods, which were brought home by their Turkey Fleet [the Levant Company]; others said it was brought from *Candia*; others from *Cyprus*'.[30] Charting the spread of the disease alongside the erstwhile movements of Venetian mercantile routes, and by placing specific emphasis on the Eastern Mediterranean, the narrative moralises against transcontinental trade and globalisation as sources of Orientalised contamination for Northern Europe. Defoe consequently advocates a greater rigidity for national borders in opposition with the growing porousness of the nascent imperial age.

Equally, Thubron's narrative repeats these motifs across his text while freighting idioms of trade and disease with those of sexuality. According to an account of the Ottoman occupation of the island, in the seventeenth century 'the flow of commerce was changing its bed'—repeating the erotic and economic dualism of the term 'commerce' which Young has emphasised—before stressing that 'Cyprus became a backwater... a dazed stagnation... the population had dwindled... [as] its air [was] so unhealthy', causing its very architecture, centuries later, to be forcibly destroyed in order to construct the Suez Canal from residual raw materials.[31] Like Defoe, transcontinental 'commerce', including Suez as a symbol of the hegemonic authority of the British Empire, is associated with local decline at the expense of globalised infrastructures. As well as a religiously-plural Ottoman *millet* Cyprus being framed as 'unhealthy', Thubron argues that the earlier Lusignan dynasty 'bequeathed nothing durable. It was impermeably alien, and died exotically in the soil which could not nourish it'.[32] The connotations of inheritance ('bequeathed') and topographic aridity portray the 'exotically'-mixed offspring of 'East' and 'West'—like the merging of Ottoman and Venetian cultures—as inherently barren and abortive. The preceding paragraph, an account of how Britain first occupied the island with Wolseley having 'landed two mules laden with newly minted sixpences',[33] correlates British commercial interests on the erstwhile-Ottoman island with the barrenness of the hybrid animal *par excellence*: the mule. Similarly, when describing the syncretised religious spaces of Famagusta (Catholic, Muslim, and Orthodox) 'whose names and even whose faith were sometimes unknown', the setting is embodied as 'a corpse withered' in 'decay' and 'ruins', wherein 'most of the ground lay barren', before explicitly analogising disease and cultural-eclecticism by summarising that, '[e]ven in ruin the town bears witness to a miasma of sects'.[34] Subsequently, he denigrates 'the marriage between Gothic and Byzantine' as creating juxtaposing images of 'the hybrid and the pure—like a belated lesson in integrity' failing.[35] As well as personifying the city and its cultural parentage, the narrative constructs a semantic taxonomy opposing the clean, healthy, European, and 'pure' with the polluted, diseased, intercultural, and 'hybrid' as the degenerate product of the 'marriage' between civilisations. Comparatively, when he argues that, in ancient art forms, '[c]onflicting sculptural traditions – Egyptian grandeur, Syrian force, Greek harmony – melt into a flaccid type',[36] the continuing parallel between culture and sexuality presents male impotence as a direct consequence of racially-'[im]pure' interactions, resulting in both barrenness and the emasculation of men. Indeed, in another account of the Lusignans, these motifs reach a climax. According to Thubron, 'the Lusignans had grown mellow with time and the sun. All the female trades of the East… flowed through their kingdom. The French nobles intermarried with the Greek and Armenian aristocracy… The style of living grew closer to that of a Syrian emir', before quoting a 1350 source which claims that Lusignan men *became* 'soft and effeminate… clad like women in soft robes', producing 'speeches, covered and bedecked with leaves, but with no fruit, like barren willow trees'.[37] Here, assimilation and 'intermarri[age]' are associated with Orientalist fears of racial and sexual degeneration in the Levant, portraying European men devolving into decadence, infertility, and 'effemina[cy]'.

Similarly, in William Mallock's 1892 travelogue, *In an Enchanted Isle*, the narrative fetishises an exoticist fantasy of gender transformativity in the Orient: 'my imagination would have been satisfied rather than surprised had there issued from any door some gorgeous crusading knight, grown effeminate in the East'.[38] Employing the same register as Thubron, including a Crusader subject, the sexual idioms 'satisfied' and 'issued' conjure a homo/eroticised account of the metamorphic influence of a sexually-fluid 'East'—in implicit contrast with the discipline of Victorian Britain—on the essential character of European masculinity. The 'door' here becomes a portal between racial and gendered identities in a gateway between times and places. The two writers express the complex ambivalence with which this motif is engaged with; while the psychic space of an 'imagined', Orientalist geography offers a freedom for Mallock's desires, in antithesis, Thubron repeats the same imagery to exhibit his own reservations. Not only is the latter's island a home for hermaphroditic Cypriots, it is also the liminal, transcultural setting where European men become dangerously androgynous and their cultural values are sterilised as a venereal consequence of acclimatising to the 'the East'. The island's unavoidable inbetweenness infects those who visit it even briefly. The association of the 'flows' of trade with 'intermarri[age]' and its *flows* of genetic material—or, more figuratively, blood—reveals, in Bourdieu's terms, a devaluation of commerce which frames the colonised habitus as ultimately 'fruit[less]' because of its threat to the symbolic capital of both nationalistic purity and 'Western' gender binaries.

These themes figure in the travel writing of Esmé Scott-Stevenson and Annie Brassey, both published in 1880, and reveal continuities and fissures in the discourse employed across these British perspectives. The two, travelling alongside their military spouses, view the island through a lens which is proximal to, and yet always distant from, formal political control. Consequently, the correlation of disease with emasculation is recontextualised in accounts of *contemporary* British military personnel and the implicit—yet unspeakably taboo—threat of sexuality on the colonial frontier. As William Greenslade has identified in his analysis of tropes of degeneration, much late nineteenth-century British literature articulates 'a prevailing sense that the nation's military incompetence is a symptom of a pervasive degeneracy at the heart of the Empire'.[39] Scott-Stevenson, as an instance of this, ascribes the prevalence of malaria among British soldiers to relative inactivity. She reflects, 'Is it any wonder that they got ill? They had no occupation, for it was too hot for parades; no recreation; nothing to do but to lie on their backs under the canvas… "going sick"'.[40] Notably, colonial disease is expressed through an idiomatic reconfiguration of theories of 'going native', interpenetrating assimilation into foreign, imperial spaces with the threat of degenerative infections—earlier in the chapter, she flippantly refers to the climate of the island as 'the tropical heat of Africa' in a homogenisation of colonial terrains.[41] Even the enumeration of slothfulness as symptomatic of military impotence echoes her ethnological report that 'Cypriotes are dull and lazy, they have no ambition',[42] presenting British soldiers as mimicking the alleged vices of the 'native' population. Moreover, in conspicuously omitting what the soldiers did when unoccupied, while freighting her discourse with eroticised images of men 'l[ying] on their backs' and with the generative connotations of 'recreation', Scott-Stevenson infers a tacit concern with sexual promiscuity away from the metropole. When she describes how, in Famagusta, 'no troops, whether English or foreign, can ever live in that perfect hotbed of fever',[43] the specific sexual motif and its echoes of *Othello*'s conclusion repeats the implicit association of disease with acts of lying down. Elsewhere, acknowledgement that 'married officers had been obliged to leave theirs [wives and families] at Malta, as there was no accommodation',[44] gestures to the disruption of normal domesticity which becomes an abstract suspended, even abandoned, on the southern fringes of Europe (Malta) in the movement to an Orientalised space as a gateway to 'tropical… Africa'.

Overall, the aphasias render it unclear whether degeneration, for Scott-Stevenson, is the consequence of either interracial, heterosexual liaisons—which also threaten the production of illegitimate, intercultural children—or illegal homosexual activity between soldiers, or, indeed, both. Subsequently, the narrative elucidates how, on the island, British 'men then deteriorate: the gossip of the clubs and at the garrison five o'clock teas is not of an elevating character', before juxtaposing the 'poisoned atmosphere' of Cyprus with 'a place like Aldershot' where ailments are 'reversed' and soldiers taught 'how to become a "thorough gentleman["]'.[45] Through a binary between centre and periphery, the text presents Cyprus as a miasmic locus which results in the decline of men in particular. Contrasts between Aldershot's regimes of producing a 'thorough gentleman' with the effeminate 'gossip' and 'teas' of an idle Cypriot routine express this devolution, like Thubron, as gendered, as well as cultural and medical: colonial lifestyles have a profound, pathogenic effect on the masculinity and sexual morality of British men.

While McClintock stresses how images of female sexuality in colonial men's writing are 'redolent not only of male megalomania and imperial aggression but also of male anxiety and paranoia', Scott-Stevenson's text reverses this paradigm by enunciating an inverted *female* 'anxiety and paranoia' towards the unreliable sexuality of men. For colonialist men, 'the boundary figures are female'; for Scott-Stevenson, men become the sources of ambivalent (racial and gender) 'boundary'-dissolution.[46] However, if as Bourdieu suggests, 'male domination… is constructed through the fundamental principle of division between the active male and the passive female',[47] then Scott-Stevenson's anxiety to British men being themselves dominated by sexual passions and disease also reiterates a misogynistic subject and object binary which seeks to consecrate (white) men—especially military figures—as 'active' subjects of power rather than lying in unhealthy, feminine, and Orientalised docility. In addition, Bourdieu's theory considers the 'active' and 'passive' dichotomy in homosexual acts, indicating, in conjunction with Scott-Stevenson's text, how the latter's concern with the instability of imperial power is articulated through imbricating discourses on racial, gendered, and sexual degeneration in British men overseas.

Brassey similarly appropriates the trope of colonial disease to figure apprehension towards colonial performances of gender. When she first alights at Larnaca, for instance, the writer observes how 'the flag of old England drooped languidly in the breezeless air', before describing the surrounding area as 'a barren spot, covered by the ruins' of classical, Christian, and Islamic architectures.[48] Like Thubron's description of so-called hybrid cultural artefacts as 'flaccid', the imagery of a limp flagpole offers a pathetic fallacy of the relationship between a stagnant colonial ennui and the impotence of a waning imperial masculinity incapable of fertilising 'barren' space. If colonialism is typically represented as the penetration of effeminised land by virile men (as evoked in the *Punch* illustration at the start of this chapter), then the occupation of Cyprus is perceived antithetically as a symbol of hegemonic decline. Subsequently, in an account of the diseases affecting British troops, Brassey focuses on one solider, Bonner, and her astonishment that 'so strong a man should have been taken suddenly ill',[49] revealing her surprise at the emasculating power of the Cypriot climate on an embodiment of British 'strong… man[lines]'. When she observes how '[h]e was placed on my long, cushioned basket-chair' to recover,[50] she presents him passively as an object being recontextualised to a feminine habitus by the disease (and on an article reminiscent of an Ottoman divan). Surrounded by effeminised Orientalist motifs, Bonner loses the position of grammatical subject in the discursive representation of the empire. Assimilation within the Orient reduces masculinist subjecthood. Interestingly, it allows the author and the object of her scrutiny to symbolically trade places as he occupies *her* furnishings. She, as a woman writer, assumes an agency over textuality usually reserved for men, while he is associated with the textiles of her luxurious couch. The alliteratively-named pair, Brassey and Bonner, become mirrors; she is the narrative's protagonist while he languishes in bed like Desdemona. Expressed ambivalently, it is an inversion which facilitates (temporary) power for Brassey as an otherwise-marginalised writer but which is nonetheless understood as a biological degeneracy threatening the stability of the British imperial body politic as a whole.

Similarly, an anecdote of how Bonner had once 'carried one woman seven miles across the burning sand', as an emblem of his erstwhile gendered heroism, is juxtaposed with his being contemporaneously 'carried by relays of ten of our men'.[51] It is a parallelism which symbolises the power of such an illness to invert his gendered identity from the active to the passive, from carrying to being 'carried'. In her analysis of the disease's origins, Brassey places some culpability with the huts used to shelter soldiers. She claims that they 'will not afford much protection against the cold [as…] the boards of which they are constructed do not fit well, the spaces between them rendering it [possible…] to see what is going on outside', before observing how Cypriot women would gather 'at a short distance from our huts, in order to see us'.[52] Not only does the poorly-constructed building, made from fragmented parts which 'do not fit well', offer a symbol of the incongruous cultural-heterogeneity of colonialism, but the porousness between inside and 'outside' which the edifice fails to contain represents the dangers associated with a borderless empire where the obfuscation between coloniser and colonised offers little 'protection' for the nationalist values of the patriarchal metropole. The building becomes an insignia of a Bhabha-esque *ambivalence* towards 'the spaces between'. Moreover, the specific emphasis on the proximity of Cypriot women and their powerful acts of returning the colonialist (and male) gaze mimics the soldiers being able 'to see' them while they 'see us'. The intimacy of the two genders across cultural lines, whereby institutional imperialism has failed to produce infrastructure to maintain segregation, is a threatening apotheosis of the deconstructed binary of 'us' and them which foreshadows, for Brassey, disease and degeneration.

Earlier, she outlines the prevalence of the illness on the fringes of Larnaca—near Hala Sultan Tekke and Stravrovouni—by describing the 'mosque, where the wet-nurse of the Prophet Mohammed is supposed to have been buried, and a Roman Catholic convent of Oros Stavro [*sic* where…] the sisters of mercy… have behaved like angels all through the recent times of sickness and misery'.[53] The account explicitly delimits an opposition between the 'angel[ic]' virginity of religious women—those whose 'behav[iour]' is morally appropriate and whose occupations involve charity and 'nurs[ing]'—and the frequency of disease, presenting these feminine figures as the only quarantined bodies in a contagious topography. Consequently, 'sickness' is sexualised as an unchaste pathogen for which (poorly-'behaved') colonising men are culpable for its spread. This view of the empire is, however, complicated by the paragraph's conclusion. An observation that the virginal landscape has 'not a trace of cultivation' is contrasted with a summary of how 'the Eastern Telegraph Company […is erecting] substantial iron posts' and offering a speedier form of telecommunication compared with 'heavily laden camels'.[54] The phallic imagery of 'iron posts' depicts the 'civilising' presence of imperialism as a masculinist authority which fertilises the (agri)culturally-barren terrain, according to the axioms of a pro-colonialist rhetoric. Brassey, therefore, as with Scott-Stevenson, presents an inherently *ambivalent* valuing of the androcentric empire. While she advocates the spread of British imperialism through the eroticised images of 'iron posts' generating pluralist Anglo-Cypriot technological offspring, she also fears the overdetermination of this paradigm in which the heterosexual intimacy of the colonial setting leads to ethnic desegregation, venereal disease, and a loss of the 'Western' gender dimorphism which underpins Victorian national identity. In Brassey's summary that 'fever seems to be very bad among both European and native residents',[55] disease is employed as a trope for the threatening deconstruction of racialised binaries and is implicitly associated with 'European[s]' *going* 'native'. Once again, it is Cyprus, the portal between Europe and non-Europe—or, Malta and 'tropical' Asia and Africa—that is used as an apotheosis for an anxiety which exists across the British Empire but which is especially threatening in the seemingly-borderless limen of the Christo-Islamic, 'herm*aphroditic*' Levant.

The Homosocial Segregation of Empire

One literary strategy offering protection from the ostensible menace of interracial, heterosexual coupling is the recurring depiction of interracial, homoerotic relationships throughout the oeuvre of male travel writing on Cyprus. Not only does it promote the exclusion of women from a homosocial imperialism, but in (re)directing sexual attention to non-reproductive interactions, the possibility of generating children is repudiated.

As Young has identified, 'hybridity as a cultural description will always carry with it an implicit politics of heterosexuality'; consequently, 'same-sex sex, though clearly locked into an identical same-but-different dialectic of racialized sexuality, posed no threat because it produced no children... remain[ing] silent, covert and unmarked'.[56] Indeed, despite contentious attitudes towards homosexuality in colonial Britain, Orientalist discourses of the nineteenth-century arbitrarily associated ethnic otherness with sexual difference by inferring, notably according to Richard Burton's theories of a 'sotadic zone', the universality of homoeroticism from across the Mediterranean to Southeast Asia.[57] The 1922 autobiography of T.E. Lawrence, when privileging homosexual relationships between British military personnel over unions with 'Arab' women, echoes many of the motifs of venereal sexuality appropriated in existing representations of Cyprus. According to Lawrence, 'Arab... women... have been nothing... even had their raddled meat been palatable to a man of healthy parts. In horror of such sordid commerce our youths began indifferently to slake one another's few needs in their own clean bodies... some began to justify this sterile process... [displaying] a savage pride in degrading the body'.[58] The narrative employs sensual idioms of appetite; reiterates the sexual-economic doubleness of 'commerce'; and creates a binary between the 'healthy', 'clean', 'pure', and 'sterile' and the threats of disease and 'miscegenation' in the sexual-economic frontiers of imperial conquest. Overall, Lawrence exhibits an ambivalence to this convention. While same-sex relationships are denigrated as 'savage'—discursively intersecting the degenerate otherness associated with both (domestic) homosexuality and non-European colonised peoples—this self-conscious alternative to interracial heterosexuality is conceived of as a 'sterile' means of preserving racial 'pur[ity]' and dominance.

Baker, Dixon, and Mallock all offer comparative fantasies of colonial domination in their hierarchical relationships with eroticised serving-men,

Georgi, Hassan, and 'Scotty', respectively. Through intertextual parallels with the power dynamic of Crusoe and Friday, these portrayals both safely marginalise Cypriot women from their experiences while symbolising the (sexualised) authority of the colonising man over the colonised 'Oriental'. Baker, for instance, objectifies his twenty-one years old servant as 'the innocent-minded, broad-shouldered, herculean Georgi', having employed him because he 'liked his face'.[59] In his efforts to assist the impoverished figure, Baker expresses a concern that '[i]t is dangerous to pick up a "waif and stray," as such objects of philanthropy frequently disappear',[60] rendering him a dehumanised model for a personalised 'civilising mission' to be enacted on. This subject and object binary (itself a reconfiguration of active/passive and male/female) is furthered when he claims that 'Georgi was a handsome and exceedingly powerful man... but the truth must be told, he was stupid [and...] a slave' to higher reasoning, summarising that, he, 'poor fellow, had all in bone and muscle, and not in brain'.[61] Georgi, who is defined according to his physicality, becomes a constitutive mirror reflecting the inferior bodily sensuality of the Other in antithesis with the superior intellect of the British self. According to this Orientalist fancy, Georgi is docile, 'handsome', and 'slave'-like, while the enslaving coloniser is the 'brain' who inspires cultural improvement. Inconsistencies in his characterisation, moreover, indicate that Georgi is less a depiction of a real figure and more an imagined ideal of imperial power politics. Initially, 'he was short, thickset', and thus vertically diminutive; subsequently, however, he is 'upwards of six feet high'.[62] Baker's narrative suspends the realism of the travel writing form by choosing to elevate literary fictionality over the accurate portrayal of an actual person or relationship. The claim that 'Georgi was transformed into a respectable-looking servant' is redolent of the civilising, 'transform[ational]' influence of imperialism on the 'native' and occurs two paragraphs after an account that the nascent road between Larnaca and Nicosia, the first of its kind on the island, 'represented the new birth of British enterprise'.[63] The homosocial interaction between Baker and Georgi embodies the interpersonal interactions of an empire which gives 'birth' to new infrastructures alone and emphatically *not* to Anglo-Cypriot offspring.

These homoerotic vignettes are more explicitly fantastic in Dixon's and Mallock's texts. In these scenes chosen, or created, for the sake of martialling heterosexual segregation, fictionality presses more obviously on the claimed verisimilitude of the travelogue. The former describes his encounter with a servant, Hassan, while suffering from a mild fever. Describing his dehydration, Dixon claims to be

> thinking about Zem-zem; longing for the water of that peerless spring… I want not only water, but a nurse. […] A tall, dark figure glides through the half-open door… [with] a voice like that of a Sister of Mercy… "Will the Effendi please…" Something in his accent takes me, and I feel that I am going to like this man. […] Cooled by the draught, I doze again; dreaming… of men in parti-coloured shawls, and of a strange hadge [*sic*] with a phial in his hand… In dreams I blend that figure with the servant in my room. […] only when I wish him to speak, he speaks. […] I look my thanks; though not a word is said… I seize his hand and give him a hearty shake. Again he understands, a weird and beautiful fire lighting up in his oriental eyes. […] He seems a clean good fellow…[64]

The narrative intersects imagination with reality in a dialectic of 'oriental' desires and actual experience. Not only is Hassan associated with 'dreaming', but the allusion to the 'Zem-zem' of *The Arabian Nights* emphasises the imagined, intertextual nature of this exoticised depiction of a 'dark figure'. Occurring in the intimate setting of a bedroom, recurring references to the unspoken or ineffable gestures to the relationship as taboo and presents the unspeakability of homosexuality in Victorian society: even Dixon's ambivalence to Hassan's eroticised eyes which are simultaneously 'weird and beautiful' indicates his own uncertainty about their proximity. Standing in a 'half-open' gateway, Hassan symbolises the liminality of Dixon's sentiments caught between anxiety and attraction. In addition, Dixon's authority over Hassan's speech emphasises his (discursive) power over Hassan as colonial writer. When he refers to the other as 'Effendi', or lord, Hassan's speech is co-opted to articulate his subordination, affirming Dixon's masculinist dominance *through* an effeminised 'voice' (itself paralleled with that of 'a Sister of Mercy'). The active/passive binary of patriarchal discourses is appropriated in this relationship in order to figure Dixon as the masculine subject and Hassan as the 'oriental' object, while firmly excluding women from this project of colonial subject formation. Even the allusion to chaste nuns, as with Brassey's own depiction of Cyprus' Catholic convent, presents the relationship as having a higher spirituality than heterosexual fornication, with Dixon's emphasis that Hassan is 'clean' contrasting the couple with the threat of disease associated with heterosexuality or with women in particular. While Brassey's text figures men as sources of contagion, Dixon's misogyny characterises male homoeroticism, like T.E. Lawrence, as a 'clean' alternative to interactions with 'native' women.

Mallock's representation of his relationship with the interpreter Abdullah 'Scotty' engages with related themes and motifs. The latter's name and occupation between languages, alongside the reported malapropisms used in stating that, 'This coat, these trousers, I get him both from Glasgow',[65] presents the heterogeneous textuality of his performed identity as a polyglot figure personifying the island's own ostensible pluralism. As Scotty is revealed to be 'an Arab from Syria', the relationship instrumentalises Cyprus as a neutral limen accommodating a fantasy of the encounter between Westerner and 'Arab', due to its recurring manifestation '[a]s an island of the imagination in the world of fable and history'.[66] Within this Orientalist 'imagination', the pair are emblematised as courtly lovers, with Scotty assuming the role of subordinate in an unequal union. Mallock describes with homoerotic nuance how, at their first meeting, he observed 'a red fez cap at the window, and a brown bearded face, courting my attention with a plaintive, enquiring smile'.[67] The image of a 'window' is employed to articulate—as with the 'half-open door' in Dixon's narrative—the meeting of East and West across the portal which Cyprus symbolises. Subsequently, in an account reminiscent of both Dixon's 'dark' Hassan and of Baker's description of Georgi as a 'waif and stray', Mallock claims that 'his face, handsome in feature and dark in colour, had the curious expression of appeal and devotion like that of a faithful dog'.[68] The hierarchical register dehumanises Scotty through a colonialist gaze, co-opting the discourses of eroticism in order to signify the objectifying dominance of the imperial master over a docile subject. When Mallock claims that Scotty would appear 'in response to my voice, with such promptness, that I seemed to have created him myself out of some block of masonry',[69] he privileges the power of his voice over the silence of the subaltern while commodifying Scotty as an object of physicality in contrast with the reasoned eloquence of the author's speech. Furthermore, by echoing the classical myth of King Pygmalion and Galatea set in Cyprus, the narrative frames Scotty as an erotic monolith for the services of a powerful man, while elevating the patriarchal ethos of the original narrative by fully excluding women from the subject and object binary of masculine domination.

Elsewhere, following this binary, Mallock claims that Scotty's 'nerves were far more delicate than my own',[70] effeminising the latter in the construction of a gendered mirror juxtaposing the essential rationality of

'Western' men over the sentimentality of 'Arab' men (and, by implication, other peoples considered 'delicate' in, and for, the British metropole). The relationship reaches its climax during Mallock's departure from the island, in which themes of unspeakability, halfness, and physical contact recur from the meeting of Dixon and Hassan: 'He looked at me with eyes full of disproportionate thanks, seized my hand, kissed it, and hurried out of the door. I followed him, and found him motionless half way up the stairs… crying into the sleeve of his coat… I did not wish to disturb him'.[71] Unlike Dixon, however, Mallock registers the 'disproportionate', or unequal, nature of their economic relationship. When Mallock commences the succeeding chapter with his welcome 'restoration to civilisation' in London,[72] his erotic narrative is reduced to a mere textual device for exploring methods of fleetingly 'going native' among the racial and sexual non-'civilisation' of the 'sotadic zone' (and, especially, on an island portrayed as a topos of the literary imagination). Indeed, his partial relish at removing the superficial epidermis of an adventure with Scotty correlates with Gail Ching-Liang Low's theory that within colonial desires to assume the dress and manners of 'natives'—as typified by Rudyard Kipling's *Kim* (1901)—the final removal of such pretences, especially on return to Europe, marks the relief of a conspicuously enacted rearticulation of essential cultural difference.[73] Hence, an Orientalist figuring of homoeroticism as a transient and disposable performance suitable for travels to 'the East' demonstrates how categories of alterity are arbitrarily associated in the creation of fantasies of 'Western' men departing from the safety of heteronormative Europe—but only briefly, and only if children remain unproduced. Like Durrell who 'say[s] good-bye to Europe' by swearing his separation from Cypriot women, Mallock sails back 'to civilisation' by discarding his homoerotic desires as transitory Orientalist fancies and without transporting threatening surplus—disease, children, a new sexual identity—into the metropolis.

Moving several decades later, homoeroticism is similarly appropriated as a political strategy in Durrell's travelogue in which his intimacy with Panos, a Cypriot academic eventually murdered by an EOKA A supporter, is used to personify the relationship between colonial Cyprus and a philhellenic Britain through the register of tragic love. In the penultimate chapter, Durrell describes with relish spending his last day with his companion, two days before Panos is fatally shot, in the pastoral setting of the anemone and cyclamen groves of the Kyrenia mountain range. As a guide, 'Panos had his own favourite nooks… just as a lover will have favourite places in which to plant an expected kiss – the nape of the neck, or the curve of a pectoral muscle'.[74] The erotic discourse analogises the pair's movements in the landscape with the actions of a 'lover' towards an explicitly-*male* body. Not only does the dual-meaning of 'plant' compare kissing with botany—a form of fertilisation in the absence of women—but the account of 'the curve of a pectoral muscle' is echoed in a subsequent reference to the 'bearded curves of lowland'[75] in an embodied representation of the surrounding terrain. The figurative bodies of place and nation, including Cyprus in particular, are etched onto the actual bodies of Durrell and Panos.

Ultimately, the imagery used throughout this vignette associates the pair with Venus and Adonis, with specific allusion to Shakespeare's poem. Despite Vangelis Calotychos' analysis of the ways in which Durrell 'portrays the pre-EOKA days as edenic and somewhat outside history',[76] such a reading of the biblical resonances in the narrative can be extended to consider the influence of Ovidian myth. While Michael Given suggests that '[n]owhere in *Bitter Lemons* is Cyprus allowed to participate in hellenic or classical civilisation',[77] it is apparent that subtle references to the Cypriot goddess and her semi-divine lover, albeit filtered through Shakespearean revision, is dramatically reserved for the text's compelling climax. Indeed, the depiction of Panos as having 'thrust out his hands until his fingers were buried in the dense clumps of anemones'[78] foreshadows his eventual death through images of the flowers symbolically associated with the tragic demise of Adonis. Equally, an ominous reference to how 'the Karpass threw up its snouts of stone' echoes the physiology of the murderous boar of the classical narrative, while the suggestion that flowers 'wished to pull us down into the Underworld from which they had sprung, nourished by the tears and wounds of the immortals'[79] engages with Greco-Roman idioms associated both with mythological geographies and with Adonis' kidnap by Persephone, a chthonic deity. After Durrell analyses the 'haunting trace of Aphrodite's name' in Modern Greek, his succeeding sentence summarises how he had 'told Panos that I would go and bathe while he did his tour of inspection',[80] associating himself with Aphrodite/Venus, a goddess represented in antiquity as emerging from the sea and 'bath[ing]' in Cypriot waters. Moreover, the recurring use of the colour 'violet' throughout the chapter—sexualised as 'that throbbing dark mauve which inhabits the heart of a violet'; 'the violet sky'; and 'the violet evening'[81]—is an analogue of the opening stanza of *Venus and Adonis* and the rise of 'the sun with purple-colour'd face'.[82] When Panos describes the bundle of flowers they had picked as creating an attraction 'like a village marriage', drawing parallels between their affection and that of a married couple, Durrell's response that they return to 'our thrones of granite' and commence a picnic presents the pair as consecrated beings, reiterating Shakespeare's depiction of Adonis as 'a king perplexèd in his throne'.[83]

The meticulous construction of this allegory is used to powerfully articulate the iconoclasm of Panos' death in the narrative and, by association, the dissolution of the relationship between Britain and Cyprus which Durrell privileges and eroticises. The narrative suggests that 'the image – the mythopoeic image of the Englishman which every Greek carried… was… dashed into a thousand pieces' by contemporary political events.[84] Not only does this allude to an abstract 'image' of nations entertained by propaganda but, more implicitly, to 'the mythopoeic image[ry]' used to convey Anglo-Cypriot relations in Durrell's imagining of the island. Earlier, Panos is depicted 'toasting a dying affection which might never be revived – one of those bright dreams of… an England and Greece which are bondsmen in the spirit'.[85] The speech's content resonates with the death of the speaker and, in turn, with the figurative death of the colonial bond between Britain and Greek-speaking Cypriots which Durrell mourns as an instance of what Gilroy terms 'postimperial and postcolonial melancholia'.[86] In a blatant disregard for the socio-economic and racial inequalities of British imperialism, Panos' voice is co-opted to ruminate, 'what does it all matter? Nationality, language, race?', before pronouncing the 'tastes of lemons, of lemon-blossom' in this idyllic meeting of coloniser and colonised in a quasi-imagined topos.[87] The reference to 'lemons' marks a salient peripeteia in the text in which the 'lemon-blossom' of a romanticised empire is dramatically abased to the bitterness of the work's title. The death of Panos by EOKA violence symbolises the termination of Durrell's hitherto-idealistic appraisals of both imperialism and philhellenism; at the beginning of this scene, Durrell stresses that growing insurgence had meant that 'we had all become – bitter'.[88] Homoeroticism, therefore, is appropriated as a device in Durrell's attempts to counter anti-colonial sentiment with classical and Shakespearean fantasies of philhellenic harmony. The choice of Panos as object of Durrell's tragic love—to the extent that he effeminises himself through association with the Cypriot goddess—excludes women from the male homosociality of the British Empire as an overseas expansion of the patriarchal Classical education of domestic Britain. Furthermore, by appropriating a childless union between two men, the narrative reductively figures homosexuality as a trope for expressing the barrenness of British and Greek-speaking peoples in a contemporary juncture where political urgencies override the simplicity of a classical idealism which Durrell naively wishes to see reproduced. It is also important to note that while 'Panos' was based on a real person Durrell encountered, the actual Panos did not die during Durrell's stay and was not attacked by EOKA sympathisers.[89] Like the inconsistencies in Baker's narrative, elements of fictionality, in addition to the intertextual substrata of poetic allusion, impede on the quasi-empiricism of the travelogue.

The character of 'Panos' and his death are both fictions appropriated to malign anti-colonialism. This propaganda for the continuance of British rule is performed through distance, using erotic images which ambivalently desire the union of coloniser and colonised while fearing the unspeakable threat of 'miscegenation'. It is always, and only, a half-hearted commitment to transcontinental exchange. As Abdul JanMohamed has identified in relation to the 'unconscious desire' towards, and 'fetishization of[,] the Other', most 'imaginary' colonialist narratives 'end with the elimination of the offending natives'.[90] It is an enduring and unescapable motif beginning in *Othello*. Employing it, Durrell is able to safely extricate himself from any responsibilities towards the colony upon his return *to civilisation* (like Mallock), purging himself of any sexual or racial deviance associated with his neoclassical fantasies before re-assimilation into urban, modern, heteronormative 'Europe'.

Ultimately, the themes of hermaphroditism, degeneration, and homoeroticism employed across this corpus of travel writing are compounded in Baker's succinct denigration of women in his 1878 travelogue:

> Cyprus was the supposed birthplace of Venus, and... was at one time celebrated for the beauty of women and immorality: the change has been radical, as I believe no women are... less attractive, than the Cypriotes of the present time. They... are hardly treated by the men, as they perform most of the rough work in the cultivation of the ground... the men, on the contrary, are usually good-looking and far more attentive to their personal appearance.[91]

Not only does the allusion to Venus participate in the tradition of (under)valuing Cypriot women as objects of a disavowed sexuality, but the explicit juxtaposition between classical idealism and contemporary realism figures this transition as a cataclysmic 'change' symbolic of diachronic biological deterioration. The assessment of Cypriot men as 'good-looking' displaces a heterosexual, interracial interest in 'native' women in favour of a homoerotic (or, homosexual) alternative. It simultaneously expresses an unease towards the gendered subject and object binaries of the island which invert 'Western' parallels: Cypriot women are economic agents as the subjects of 'work', producing agricultural 'cultivation' distinct from the 'cultivation' of offspring, while Cypriot men are the fair objects of an eroticised gaze. Similarly, when travelling with Georgi, he claims to have met 'the only Venus that I have seen in Cyprus, his wife; but even that pretty Venus was ruined by high boots and baggy trousers'.[92] The particular emphasis on the unisex attire shared by men and women reveals a concern towards the perceived *androgyny* of Cypriot women and their subversion of British gender dimorphism which challenges nineteenth-century gender theories through the reality of cultural relativism. His use of the architecturally-inflected 'ruined' portrays such a performance of gendered identity as dangerously deconstructive and even implies that Cypriot women are in need of the forms of the civilising influence which patriarchal colonialism typically extends to infrastructure.

Earlier in the same paragraph, he observes that '[t]he energy of English ladies rather astonishes the people of this country, where inertia is considered to be happiness'.[93] The account parallels cultural and gendered binaries by articulating discrete dichotomies between 'English ladies' and both their English male and Cypriot female equivalents. The focus on 'energy' and 'inertia', moreover, contextualised according to nineteenth-century notions of women's 'hysteria', interrelates his anxiety towards 'ruined', degenerated Cypriot women with a description of English women according to a scientific register of entropy. The possibility of entropy is a menace to the domestic gender conventions which the colonial encounter—and the androgyny of Cyprus-as-limen—threatens. While Bhabha's theory of ambivalence exposes the fear towards cultural pluralism in colonialist discourses, Baker's text indicates a specific, yet related, unease towards forms of gender inbetweeness, inversion, or mimicry which occurs outside patriarchal Europe or when European women—like Shakespeare's Desdemona and Celia—supersede the limits of centre/periphery in a conventionally male-dominated empire.

Ironically, while Baker is accompanied on his travels by his wife, she is only introduced through a fleeting, imprecise allusion in the third chapter and remains unnamed and uncharacterised throughout the text.[94] By excluding his own spouse from the colonial narrative, Baker acts to marginalise and disempower the role of British women on the imperial stage—while simultaneously denigrating 'native' women as symbols of alterity. Indeed, when he describes the maritime journey to the island from Alexandria, he claims that the ships are 'small and uncomfortable steamers, which are by no means suitable for ladies or invalids',[95] delimiting the kinds of peoples 'suitable' for engaging with naval technology, transcontinental movement, and imperialism. The text's colonialist rhetoric in advocating the 'civilising mission'—'[t]he Cypriote has never been accustomed to unrestricted freedom [and thus] requires a certain amount of control, and his energies must be directed by a driver or a ruler'[96]—especially in his echo of the 'energy' of a healthy body (politic), suggests a correlation between the racist rule of the empire with the patriarchal rule of domestic women. Baker, therefore, desires to restrain the threateningly-increasing 'freedom' of both politically-conscious colonised subjects (men and women alike) *and* spatially-mobile British women who, following his idiom, ought not to become the autonomous 'driver[s]' of colonial machinery. Cyprus not only weakens the cultural binaries of East/West or Asia/Europe, but, as a topos associated with the inbetweenness of androgyny and hermaphroditism, dangerously facilitates the disintegration of domestic gender conventions both as a psychic space outside the bounds of British moral codes and as a physical destination for travelling women.

In short, my prevailing conclusion is that the literary motifs of homoeroticism are appropriated by male travel writers who espouse heteronormative identifications in the British metropole in order to express a misogynistic and racialist segregation from Orientalised women abroad—all at the expense of effacing and misrepresenting the voices of (Cypriot and British) figures who might be (anachronistically) understood as 'queer'. However, there is room within this assessment to examine a slightly greater complexity. While Baker, Dixon, and Durrell all married, Mallock remained a lifelong bachelor. For the latter in particular, but perhaps also for the other three, travel to an island famed for its suppression of binary thinking and perceived sexual ambiguity may allow for literary, or personal, freedom from the restraints of Victorian Britain in which homosexuality was unquestionably illegal. Nonetheless, it remains problematic to impose twenty-first-century identifications onto these authors and, if this literary strategy has any veracity, it is performed at the expense of colonised Cypriots, including those who would have been arrested under *British-imposed* anti-sodomy laws. A British middle-class (and male-dominated) liberty to depart from British moral codes, however briefly, is a luxury denied to most nineteenth-century Cypriots—and, indeed, many contemporary British women.

'I Am Bound to Speak': British Women's Responses to Orientalism

In reaction to Baker's androcentric discourse, women's travel writing on Cyprus emerged in the late nineteenth century and articulated a political resistance to the prevailing gendering of empire. In particular, Agnes Smith frames her 1887 narrative, *Through Cyprus*, by explicitly opposing the spatial and literary movements which have preceded her. The text itself is the product of a *female* homosocial journey to Egypt and Cyprus commenced with her sister, Margaret Dunlop Gibson (under the pseudonym 'Violet'); both were renowned Presbyterian biblical scholars and polyglots. In her introductory peritext, Smith references the publishing industries within which she consciously situates her work, identifying how '[w]ithin eighteen months after the cession, several excellent books on the subject were published'. She subsequently claims that '[i]t savours somewhat of presumption for anyone to venture upon ground trodden by an experienced observer like Sir Samuel Baker… But several years have elapsed since [his] works saw the light… and it is just possible that the eyes of two lady travellers may have been able to discern something new and worth telling'.[97] In an account which autoexoticises her gender as one 'of two lady travellers', Smith's intertextuality juxtaposes Baker's *Cyprus, As I Saw It In 1879*, as a paradigm of men's travel writing, with the renewed 'eyes' of women who 'saw' the island less than a decade later. The recurring images of observation reverse the male gaze of both British imperialism and the literatures used to consolidate it. Rhetorically praising Baker's proficiency while simultaneously undermining the accuracy of his now-dated depiction of Cyprus, Smith values the cultural 'worth' of her work—playing with the economic connotations of the word—according to the relative novelty of her perspective as a woman traveller. This unique subject position is presented as reigniting the waning 'light' of a narrowly-male project of imperial enlightenment.

Throughout the text, Smith's aptitude in Arabic and Greek is articulated as a measure of her linguistic authenticity and is frequently figured through an intimate knowledge of the heteroglossia of Cypriot cultural and religious pluralism. She describes, for instance, how her 'Greek [Orthodox] muleteers caught up [Islamic] expressions from the Arabs, and [one] advised me seriously to say, "Allah ma'ak[" *glossed as* 'God be with thee']' before riding.[98] In addition to her translations between languages and religions, Smith's introduction mounts her writing as a *translation* of Baker's patriarchal discourse into the autonomous product of independent women academics. Indeed, it is in the symbolic locus of a linguistically-plural Cyprus which transcends—or, transgresses—stable 'Western' categories of East/West and Islam/Christianity that Smith seeks to overcome the limitations of Victorian gender dimorphism. Indeed, as a woman writer she appropriates the subaltern speech of 'native' languages, counter to the dominant discursive register of male contemporaries, to associate the otherness of her gendered perspective with alternative modes of linguistic knowledge which she claims to use in order to intimately, and authentically, access the imperial unknown. The text suspends any further reference to Baker and, in the final chapters, political meditations on nationalism, religion, and the legal structures of imperial rule are, instead, expressed through a rebuttal of the pro-Turkish sentiments of 'Mrs. Scott Stevenson [*sic*]', including specific reference to an episode 'on page 198 of her narrative'.[99] Smith creates a work which self-consciously positions itself as subversively female-generated and as one in intertextual discussion with the extant discourses of British *women* on Cyprus.

The activism of her expedition and her resultant writing is illustrated more explicitly in her earlier narrative, *Eastern Pilgrims: The Travels of Three Ladies* (1870), in which she, Margaret, and their tutor, Grace Blyth (or, 'Edith'), journey across the Middle East, including Cyprus, Egypt, and the Holy Land. The work commences with a commentary on the social and institutional contexts of Smith's literary output,

> The Holy Land seems to be considered quite the tour for a gentleman. "And a strong lady may accompany her husband," says Dr. Macleod. So when my two friends and myself resolved, in the summer of 1868, to absent ourselves for a year for the purposes of visiting scenes endeared to us by so many hallowed associations, great was the consternation expressed by our friends at the idea of three ladies venturing on so lengthened a pilgrimage alone. "Do you think they will ever come back? They are going amongst Mohammedans and barbarians," said some, who know of our intention.[100]

The reported speech expresses how, following Bourdieu's conceptualisation, 'the simple *repetition* of a work from the past in a radically transformed field of compossibles produces an entirely automatic *effect of parody*'.[101] In her critique of patriarchal ideology, Smith satirises both the misogynistic opinions of those resistant to women's travel—the quoted 'consternation' repeated retrospectively with bathos as meaningless counterpoints to her successful expedition—and the genre of travel writing within which she participates. In other words, she radically departs from 'the gendered division of labor around travel and writing'.[102] Emphasis on her status as one 'of three ladies', in an echo of the published title, conspicuously markets the work according to the gendered identities of its subjects as a signifier of the lucrative difference—or *exoticism*—of the project. Not only does the text recount journeys to an Orientalised Mediterranean in the juncture of Richard Burton's translation of *The Arabian Nights* (1885), but as a member of the rare oeuvre of women's travel writing, the work is doubly novel in its access, for metropolitan male readers, to the lives and experiences of peoples analogised as Others in nineteenth-century Britain.[103] The consequent possibilities of commercial gain, tacitly marked here and in *Through Cyprus*, demonstrate the socio-economic potential of the work in promoting Smith and her partners as economic agents.

As Virginia Woolf has suggested, from the late eighteenth century, '[t]he extreme activity of mind… among women… was founded on the solid fact that women could make money by writing'.[104] When Woolf stresses that such a juncture symbolises a movement 'of greater importance than the Crusades',[105] it is notable that Smith's 'pilgrimage' to the Levant, mimicking the expedition of male Crusades centuries earlier, repeats, in order to reinscribe, the historical record within which she is both incorporated and marginalised. Hence, Smith reveals her express desire to subvert gender expectations by treading spaces—physical and symbolic, geographic and literary—typically delimited 'for a gentlemen' (including the corpus of Romantic works denoted by the evocative term 'tour'). By choosing to observe places which have acquired familiar 'associations' from afar, Smith attempts to transgress the hegemony of male-dominated cultural authorities on the monumentalised Orient in favour of direct, personal experience. In particular, as a biblical scholar, her engagements with an androcentric discipline studying the works of Abrahamic patriarchs promotes an independent relationship, as a woman, with scriptural history, reducing the mediation of male intercessors between the ancient 'Holy Land' and her occupations in contemporary Britain.

Across *Through Cyprus*, she attempts to extend this intimacy of women with writing by challenging the gendered economic divisions of pedagogy on the island. As well as communicating with Cypriot women that they 'will remain poor if you don't learn' and maintain only domestic instruction on 'how to cook well', she utilises the Gospels as a symbol of power with which each individual should engage: 'it would be far better if each of us could read the story of His life and His teaching for ourselves, without anyone's help', in reference to male clerical oration.[106] Despite the irony of offering a mode of missionary intervention which diminishes the independence of colonised subjects—while problematically *translating* expectations of 'Western' feminism onto non-European cultural traditions—her desire to see 'native' women autonomously read the Bible offers an antithesis to Bhabha's seminal concept of the (male) colonial ambivalence towards the appropriation of religious texts as 'signs taken for wonders' and 'insignia[s] of colonial authority... and discipline'.[107] For Smith, the freedom she experiences as a woman abroad is a status she attempts to replicate in her sympathy towards Cypriot women, even donating funds to a school in the village of Kampos.[108]

However, such empathy is limited ethnocentrically and her subject position is problematically biased by her religious and socio-economic background. Despite attempting to defend the patriarchal register of biblical narratives—accordingly, 'the Creator intended woman to be man's help-meet not his plaything nor his slave',[109] in a nuanced reading of the inequalities of Adam's and Eve's creations in Genesis—she denigrates the Islamic textual parallel. She claims that '[m]any of the precepts of the [Koran] are excellent; but we have to bring against that book the charge not only of degrading women, but of... limiting human progress'.[110] When she concludes her text aphoristically by suggesting that, '[w]ithout freedom there can be no thorough education', and vice versa, she delimits any 'freedom' and 'education' as purely Christocentric—as evidenced by her limited discourse with Muslim women throughout the text—before *repeating*, without satire, the colonialist mantra that 'Cyprus, I think, we ought to keep'.[111] While she challenges the gendered limits of imperialism, she nonetheless supports the evangelising colonial mission as a whole; despite mimicking the misogyny of opponents to her journey, the racist fears towards 'Mohammedans and barbarians' articulated by her peers in *Eastern Pilgrims* is a charge she is less emphatic about questioning.

Furthermore, when she elaborates, in the same work, that 'our education [will] enable us to protect ourselves from the influence of… dangerous opinions',[112] her expounding on 'education' through a Foucauldian dialectic of knowledge and power reveals how an ability to transcend gender limits is achieved through the parochial advantages of her socio-economic status. In this confluence of gender, class, and ethnicity—as a middle-class British heiress—she is capable of movements denied to impoverished British and colonised Cypriot women alike. The opening chapters of both her texts concern performances of conspicuous consumption—'[e]ach traveller buys a pair of mackintosh sheets; they cost a guinea, and will be invaluable…'[113]—as a signifier of the 'invaluable' commodity excess which both challenges the economic inequalities of gender in Britain *and* rearticulates the economic disparities between metropole and colony. In trading translated representations of *Eastern* women (and men) for the commercial benefit gleaned in London's publishing institutions, Smith's work is culpable of a 'reification of people and places into exchangeable aesthetic objects', according to Huggan, as '[t]ourism, like exoticism, betrays a privilege of movement' between centre and periphery which is here subverted only slightly.[114] In a description of an Easter church service, for instance, Smith elaborates on how the space is segregated: 'the men and boys being all in front, and the women behind' while she 'however, was directed into a side-stall, with a moveable seat'.[115] The power of her ethnicity and class to transcend the reductive gender demarcations of Cypriot society, symbolised by the spatial mobility of her 'moveable' position, demonstrates how her economic status as colonial traveller offers her fundamental rights denied to Cypriot women—an inequality which, in this scene, she wilfully ignores or chooses not to critique. Through this work, Smith is able to use travel (and travel writing) in order to *transport* her identity away from the constraints of British metropolitan life, yet it is a mode of existential *transportation* denied to less-privileged women. As Spivak has warned, 'much so-called cross-cultural disciplinary practice, even when "feminist," reproduces and forecloses colonialist structures: sanctioned ignorance, and a refusal of subject-status and therefore human-ness' of non-European women.[116]

Indeed, in her fleeting depiction of Cyprus in *Eastern Pilgrims*, Smith pronounces anti-Islamic rhetoric while also dramatising inequalities between British and Cypriot women, both Muslim and Orthodox.

The narrative commences with a jingoistic appraisal that '[o]ur Northern skies are certainly more favourable… for such barren hills we never before beheld',[117] associating the island with the motifs of (female) infertility commonplace in the succeeding works of Baker and his contemporaries through binaries of North and South. As the party alight from the ship, the following dialogue is recounted: '"How many Turks there are!" said Mrs. Horn "They seem to have nothing to do but smoke and stare at us. Are there no women here?" "They are all indoors," said Herr Karl'.[118] It represents the focus of a colonialist gaze and its fear of being reversed by the eyes of 'natives', while generalising on the public and private structures of gender expected of Muslim women according to Western European stereotypes. Smith repeats this gendered voyeurism in describing a 'veil[ed]' woman, of indeterminate religion, who causes her to exclaim, 'Oh! what a crowd of women live here!' as the objects of an exoticist curiosity.[119] Subsequently, when a fellow traveller marvels, 'Here is something stranger', in allusion to a train of camels, the account frames Cypriot women, not only as 'strange' commodities to view and be written about, but also as dehumanised figures in clausal parallel with bestial wonders: 'the crowd of [veiled] women' and '[a] number of camels' become interchangeable—and for the purposes of the published work, exchangeable—Orientalist penumbra.[120] As camels carry freight for people, so too do Cypriot women carry the burden of being imagined for the economic gain of British writers. Following Spivak's theory, these subaltern women, who are denied voice across this text, have their subjectivity and humanity repudiated.

When her sister comically falls from one of these camels, Smith reproves how '[h]undreds of Greek women rushed out to witness the strange spectacle, which doubtless afforded food for a month to the Larnaca gossips, even if it was not inscribed in the town's annals'.[121] Notably, Smith momentarily assumes the subject position of Cypriot women, particularly through the reiteration of the adjective 'strange', in a vignette which marks exoticism as culturally-relative. However, her idioms regarding consumption (or, 'food') and production (or, 'inscribed… annals') gesture to, without critique, the economic inequalities between impoverished Cypriot women and her own commercial stability as an 'inscribed', published writer. The figurative 'food' Smith gains from the reportage of this same anecdote is substantially more (in economic terms) than a 'month' of local attention. The account, therefore, blurs between British and Cypriot perspectives, not as a relinquishing of voyeuristic power to a 'native' subjectivity, but to firmly juxtapose Smith's privileged status as an erudite, economic agent with the literary silence of oral 'gossips'. The complex engagement with gender in Smith's works illustrates how her resistance to imperial patriarchy is enacted *at the expense* of interpellating herself into an axiomatic defence of empire which constructs misogynistic portrayals of Cypriot women as the exoticised, Orientalised 'Other' in order to promote her own racialised superiority as a 'Western', capitalist individualist through binary difference.

Within her expression of gendered freedom, the aforementioned introduction to *Eastern Pilgrims* also offers an implicit critique of the *married* woman traveller who, through reported discourse, 'may accompany her husband' as the only method of global movement, unlike Smith and her companions.[122] Brassey and Scott-Stevenson both journey with their spouses—and, in the case of Brassey, their three children—on colonial expeditions. While Scott-Stevenson and her husband, Captain Andrew, are based in Kyrenia for his temporary position as the district's Civil Commissioner, Brassey alights briefly on the island during naval missions in the Mediterranean on the Sunbeam. Contemporary reception of these authors was frequently unfavourable, partially due to misogynistic attitudes towards women's writing in general. *The Saturday Review* essentialises Scott-Stevenson's work through a negative comparison with the same male contemporary writer Smith resists association with: 'the origin of the two books was entirely different, and so is their character. Mrs. Scott-Stevenson admires Cyprus as it is; Sir Samuel Baker admires Cyprus as it might be. Mrs. Scott-Stevenson is the wife of Captain Scott-Stevenson…'.[123] Using similar discourse, Edward Bunbury's review, published in *The Academy* on the same day, suggests that '[t]he book of Mrs. Scott-Stevenson is one of a very different character' from Baker's travelogue.[124] While the former 'records the personal experiences and impressions of the author', the latter, composed by 'the more sober and calm-judging Sir S. Baker', is deemed to be 'by far the most valuable contribution [for…] form[ing] an impartial estimate of the… future prospects of our new acquisition'.[125] A series of juxtapositions dichotomise the two works as emblems of gendered difference. While one is the 'impartial' forward-thinking account of a knighted 'Sir', the other—or, indeed, Other—is the irrational and sentimental narrative of a 'Mrs' defined in relation to her husband. The former is appraised as a product of a masculinist ascendancy and, consequently, as one of greater provenance and political 'valu[e]' than the output of a travelling housewife. Even advertising by Scott-Stevenson's publisher, Chapman and Hall, printed in the back-pages of their other works, summarises that 'Mrs. Scott-Stevenson tells her story with delightful *naïveté* and womanly simplicity',[126] echoing a contemporary colonialist register used to infantilise colonised peoples as 'simpl[e]' and atavistic. The text is tacitly marketed, therefore, as a means for British male readers to access the double '*naïveté*' of an infantilised woman describing implicitly-infantile colonial subjects.[127] While Smith offers a powerful resistance to this recurring theme—explicitly disassociating *Through Cyprus* from a paradigmatic, yet outmoded, Baker—the inaugural sentences of her earlier *Eastern Pilgrims* reveals the pervasiveness of women writers being denigrated for their marital status in nineteenth-century publishing industries.

Nonetheless, Brassey and Scott-Stevenson frame their narratives as literary artefacts in conjunction with, and in support of, the political activities of their husbands, displacing the androcentric homosociality of empire and its textual dissemination by constructing a symbolic marriage of—in Said's terms—*culture and imperialism* within which they are inextricable agents. Both writers bestow their introductory dedications to the men of the British Empire. While Scott-Stevenson explicitly 'dedicate[s] this book to my husband, Captain Andrew Scott-Stevenson, Forty-Second royal Highlanders',[128] Brassey commits her work '[t]o the brave true-hearted sailors of England', a category into which her husband could be included, before quoting, as an epigram, Walter Colton's poetic line, 'I love the sailor: his eventful life'.[129] In the two peritexts, imperialism becomes a marital or heterosexual exchange between the military and the cultural, articulating the mutually-consolidating roles of British husband and wife in the colonial project through a simplistically-dimorphic gendering of warfare as masculine and cultural expression as feminine. Following the sexualised political idioms of *Othello*, the marital bed and the martial stage become indistinguishable; a strategy which places women at the forefront of empire, in contradistinction with the marginalised figure of Baker's unnamed wife fleetingly mentioned in his travelogue. The maps, temperature charts, and illustrations compiled in these works are figured as salient ephemera in the (cultural) regulation of the island. Brassey, in particular, intersects her text into an extant corpus of maritime activities, supporting the ethos of Britain's growing naval power, while implicitly categorising her own 'eventful life' and experiences as a pioneering woman 'sailor'-of-sorts into this otherwise-androcentric tradition. She stresses the innovation of her position by expounding on how she and her daughters are 'the first ladies to pass a night in the [military] camp' near Nicosia.[130] Equally, Scott-Stevenson claims to be 'the first English lady seen in these parts; and for miles… the men [were] too astounded even to call out', before autoexoticising herself through the perspective of Cypriot *women*, suggesting that 'the sight of an English lady in European costume was one to be remembered for all time'.[131]

In fetishising the difference of their gender from the predominately-male colonising authorities, *and* of their ethnicity and culture from Cypriots, the narratives denote an ambivalent liminal status between English male rulers and the ruled Cypriot masses. As Oyèrónké Oyěwùmí has demonstrated in southern African contexts, 'in the colonial situation, there was a hierarchy of four, not two categories. Beginning at the top these were: men (European), women (European), native (African men), and Other (African women)'.[132] Drawing on this, Scott-Stevenson sporadically forges transient identifications with Cypriots also under British male rule. As Boehmer queries, 'did [British] women see the colonized differently, in more nuanced and identified ways?'.[133] For instance, Scott-Stevenson explicitly articulates how, 'I, myself, like the heathens, as some people are audacious enough to call the Mahommedans, far better than the Cypriote Christians'.[134] Her association with colonised peoples of a distinct religious identity to her own reveals an allocentric perspective which transcends a selected sympathy with the island's Christian majority. Subsequently, the travelogue elaborates on Scott-Stevenson's demarcation from, and parody of, the island's power (infra)structures. Despite the promise of domestic naturalisation claimed by the work's title, *Our Home in Cyprus*, the narrative represents the courthouse in which her husband is occupied as a symbolic space from which Scott-Stevenson, as wife, is firmly excluded, complicating the ostensible equality of their experiences as colonial settlers denoted by the title's first-person plural pronoun. She expounds on how '[t]he Court was forbidden ground; but one day, knowing the Commissioner was away and that my husband was sitting with his back to the light, I summoned the courage to peep in at the window'.[135] The intertextual allusion to Eve and her gendered segregation from modes of 'forbidden' knowledge—as well as the haram or 'forbidden' gender spaces of the Islamic harem—contextualises this marginalisation as paradigmatic of the delimited freedom of women and wives spanning from the ancient to the contemporary Levant. The borders between inside and outside, as with those of imperial centre and periphery, demonstrate her spatialised barring from the administrative authority enacted by her husband within. Nonetheless, her decision to 'peep in at the' penumbral, porous structures on the limits of public and private emphasises, not only her comic disregard for nineteenth-century gender conventions, but also how her status as neither an English man nor a Cypriot 'native' permanently situates her in an undefinable middle space between power and subordination.

She consequently reports how she 'was so fascinated watching the... curious performance that' she 'only became aware of my position by seeing the keen eye of Sucri, the zaptieh corporal, fixed on me with a stern look'.[136] The esoteric knowledge shared by the alliteratively-named Scott-Stevenson and Sucri demonstrates her active identification with a Muslim Cypriot—following her earlier claims of sympathy—illustrating how her liminal social 'position' is symbolised by an interpersonal interaction with a 'native' manoeuvring across the borders of colonial power. Notably, however, such an association is only with a Cypriot *man*—and one who assumes localised power as a zaptieh (or Ottoman-style police officer)—rather than with a subaltern Cypriot woman. Indeed, even the role of zaptieh is one which symbolises his, and the island's, liminality between Ottoman (Muslim) and British (Christian) rule and which is appropriated as metonym of Scott-Stevenson's existential inbetweenness. The two, therefore, occupy Oyěwùmí's theoretical taxonomies between European man and 'native' woman as liminal figures of social stratification who fill neither category of colonising self nor the lowest stratum of colonised Other. Despite this, the power of their eyes in sharing a subject 'position' outside the panopticism of the colonialist, male gaze reveals how the relationship destabilises the typical structures of imperial power. Describing the internal action as a 'performance' to be watched by a woman—denigrated subsequently as 'the ludicrously punctilious performance of their duties'[137]—the account reduces the perceived essentialism of gender to its performative state allowing Scott-Stevenson to dissolve the integrity of the gender structures which the building-as-stage attempts to consecrate. Content to have 'seen what I wanted to see',[138] in metatextual allusion to the episode's utility as a repeatable anecdote, Scott-Stevenson departs from the court having acquired power both through observed knowledge of the arcane world of male politicians and, ultimately, through the cultural and economic capital acquired from the autonomous publication she foresees.[139]

This carnivalesque of gender performativity, despite its critique of the ideology which seeks to arbitrarily extricate (European) women from positions of power, is, nonetheless, a singular episode in a narrative which otherwise seeks to reinforce the racial-gender hierarchies of empire. Following the counter-discursive description of the courtroom scene, Scott-Stevenson immediately relishes the *performance* of race which her husband symbolises as an essentialised monolith of imperial whiteness, modernity, and masculinist power: 'I had noticed the striking contrast between… his cool well-made English clothes and… clear blue eyes, and the wizened Turks and dirty Greeks… he had the commanding air of one accustomed to be obeyed'.[140] The binary difference of costume and physiognomy is notable here for its context within a scene which parodies gender 'performance' yet seeks to consolidate displays of racial and cultural difference without the same satirical register.

Indeed, the travelogue as a whole manifests pleasure from the forms of colonial power Scott-Stevenson experiences as the British wife of an influential Commissioner, especially in her hierarchical status above Cypriot women figured as inescapably Other. During her first weeks in Kyrenia, she marvels at her 'curious feeling of freedom. I felt for once in my life that I was queen of all I surveyed – that we were absolutely our own master and mistress, with no one to have to obey'. Identified as 'the only English people in Kyrenia', she 'took of my liberty to go [...to the f]orbidden ground' of a former military camp.[141] The reiteration of 'forbidden' spaces articulates her unprecedented 'freedom' as a British woman in a colonial habitus where the rigid regulations of the Victorian metropole are not only undervalued but are policed solely by her husband and his inferiors. The emphasis on the singularity of their *ethnicity* explicitly reveals how her autonomy emanates from the essentialised superiority she assumes over colonised subjects who, socially and politically, must 'obey' *her* as a member of the minority ruling class. While the aforementioned account of Andrew as a subject 'to be obeyed' may imply an association between her loyalty to her husband with the loyalty of colonial subjects to the British Crown (of which he and his court are metonymic), her use of the same verb here to include herself as one *obeyed* and not *obeying* illustrates how his ethnic status as colonial 'master' is one she interpellates herself into as co-regent 'mistress'. Even the canonising of her position as 'queen' symbolically correlates her with Victoria, the newly-crowned Empress of India, figuring the kinds of relative empowerment the colonial setting affords British women at the expense, however, of politically-subjugated colonised peoples. When Scott-Stevenson parades through rural settlements, Cypriot women are voiced shouting 'Viva Victoria!'; she subsequently remarks, 'Poor creatures! they had never left their villages' until she, 'an English lady', is exhibited before them, a 'still primitive people'.[142] While demonstrating the reductive commodification of Scott-Stevenson as a mere effigy of a racialised ideal, the repeated reference to Victoria and the (mistaken) identification of the author with the monarch—firmly repudiating a possible identification with 'native' women instead—transform the scene into a projection of Scott-Stevenson's fantasy of stratified colonial power as a venerated and exoticised British woman over 'primitive' female subjects.

This racist and misogynistic denigration of Cypriot women is more explicit elsewhere. Scott-Stevenson claims, early in the narrative, that 'it is yet impossible to look upon them as a substitute for the society of one's own sex at home. Habits of life... cause their notions to be entirely different to those of an English lady, as, in truth, might naturally be expected'.[143] Her commentary on 'Cypriote female society', strategically positioned in the first chapter, immediately forecloses any association on the basis of gender, revealing how a 'natural', or essentialised, conjunction of *race and gender* is appropriated to firmly demarcate a partition between European and Orientalised women. This strategy articulates what Low terms 'the contemporary segregationist politics of temporal distancing' in the discursive construction and performance of colonialist binaries of self and Other.[144] By isolating '[h]abits of life' as the cause of this symbolic *distancing*, the account frames Cypriot cultural values as irrevocably different from British alternatives in an Orientalist binary opposing the familiar, domestic, and habitual from the vulgar inferiority of the encountered Other. Despite the title of the work, *Our Home in Cyprus*, it is clear that the types of local integration she enacts are layered throughout the text as her British 'home' of fellow-European women is idealised and privileged above a temporary and resisted assimilation with 'natives'. While Simone de Beauvoir suggests that 'women lack concrete means for organising themselves into a unit which stand face to face with the correlative unit' of patriarchy,[145] here colonialist categories of race and culture are compounded with 'Western' gender conventions to further facilitate a socio-political division of women.

Subsequently, Scott-Stevenson appropriates colonialist axioms in the description of a curious, young Muslim girl, Mariehou, whose 'weird...

beauty'—like Hassan's 'weird and beautiful eyes' for Dixon—becomes a recurring exoticised object for her colonialist gaze.[146]

> One day,... she could not resist the temptation of peeping in at the door. In a moment I had caught her: how she kicked and struggled! But I would not let her go till I had fairly dragged her inside, and shutting the door, stood with my back to it. We were both out of breath... and I saw the big blue eyes gazing round with a startled look, like a wild animal caught in a trap.[147]

The eroticised imagery marks a female parallel to the homoerotic relationships of Baker's, Dixon's, and Mallock's contemporaneous narratives. Scott-Stevenson constructs a fantasy of her (quasi-sexual) power over the dehumanised Other through a mirror of reflected eyes. Notably, the repetition of idioms employed to describe the courtroom episode—whereby, here, it is the 'native' woman who is 'peeping' into the forbidden site of colonial settlement and authority—reverses the dynamics of power, allowing Scott-Stevenson to assume the physical agency of colonial jailer in opposition with a voiceless, immobilised Cypriot woman. The urge to capture Mariehou initially emanates from the intermingled fear and desire Scott-Stevenson experiences towards her ethnic features. As a paradigm of colonial ambivalence, Scott-Stevenson is fixated on her 'big blue eyes', chiefly because '[t]he contrast with the brown skin was as charming as it was rare',[148] a commodified figure of arresting exoticism in anticipation of the iconic June 1985 *National Geographic* cover of the green-eyed 'Afghan girl', Sharbat Gula, shot by Steve McCurry.[149] Scott-Stevenson's narrative, therefore, seeks to physically express her racialised power over the Cypriot Other, while attempting to regulate the movements of a figure whose ethnically-ambiguous features disturbs her (physiologically and erotically), co-opting the discourse and anxieties of male Orientalists to do so. Again, the fear of 'miscegenation' returns. Comparatively, Brassey's text, which marginalises and objectifies Cypriot women throughout, intertextually echoes male contemporaries by asserting that 'Venus certainly has not left behind her much of her beauty as a legacy to this her favourite isle'.[150] It also consistently employs racial stereotypes, generalising, for instance, that 'the Armenians are, as a rule, a money-getting race'.[151]

Scholarship by Lisa Lowe and Reina Lewis has developed Said's original thesis of Orientalism by elucidating on the complex gendered heterogeneity of the discourse which is capable of disrupting it *from the inside*. While Lowe has discerned 'junctures at which narratives of gendered... differences complicate and interrupt the narratives of orientalism', notably through motifs of 'minority coalitions [which] thematize... a heterogeneity of counterhegemonic interests'[152]; Lewis comparatively assesses how 'women's differential, gendered access to the positionalities of imperial discourse produced a gaze on the Orient and the Orientalized 'other' that registered difference less pejoratively' than male Orientalists.[153] This strategy is most apparent in British women writers' brief moments of partial, autoexotic identification with 'native' subjects as expressions of (gendered) differentiation from a masculinist colonial elite. However, the discourse employed by Brassey, Scott-Stevenson, and Smith ultimately reiterates the conventions of an Orientalist ideology which seeks to disavow an association with the Cypriot woman-as-Other, notably *despite* potent critiques against the gendered limitations of imperial administration. As Meyda Yeğenoğlu has crucially observed, nineteenth-century women writers' 'apparently dissenting and critical distance from Orientalism,... through the rhetoric of identification, does not prevent [them] from exercising the imperialist and masculinist act of cultural *translation* and subject constitution' (*emphasis mine*).[154] Indeed, although Smith transiently assumes and subsumes the subject position of Larnaca 'gossips', and Scott-Stevenson shares a subversive gaze with a (male) zaptieh, both appropriate these relatively-uncharacterised individuals as objects with which to *translate* their own subjectivity of difference rather than to articulate substantiated bonds of anti-colonial solidarity. Following Oyěwùmí's theory of colonial hierarchies of race and gender, Smith seeks to manifest her difference from both male authorities writing about Cyprus *and* Cypriot women whose oral narratives are inferiorised of lesser (cultural and economic) value. Equally, Scott-Stevenson's recurring identifications with Victoria and with 'one's own sex at home' over and above primitivised and exoticised 'native' women (in the colonial *Home* of her work's title) reveals how moments of association with the otherness of colonised peoples give way to firmer expressions of racial difference and superiority. Both dehumanise Cypriot women; for Scott-Stevenson, Mariehou is merely 'a wild animal caught' in a colonial habitus, while Smith syntactically analogises veiled women with camels as comparatively-'strange' commodities of literary curiosity.

Ultimately, it is the layered and heterogeneous hierarchies of colonial power that afford British women—in positions between British men and 'native' subjects—a space to linguistically and metaphorically *translate* (to employ Yeğenoğlu's idiom) Cypriot women for a largely-male contemporary readership. The polyglot Smith converses with Orientalised women in Arabic and Greek in order to construct a text which commercially rivals Baker's. In conscious contrast with the antecedent 'guide-books and... official reports' of an androcentric governing body, Smith formulates a work which 'observe[s] not only the temper of the Cypriots themselves, but that of several nationalities to which they are closely related', having briefly described Egypt and Lebanon before Cyprus, in order to gauge the socio-economic 'capabilities of the island'.[155] Smith's evangelising agenda routinely denigrates Islam as the sole cause of female subjugation in Cyprus and, accordingly, Orthodox women's reticence is 'evidently the result of Turkish discipline', despite having exposed, in the same chapter, the fact that the male Orthodox clerical elite and the British colonial regime have made little provision for women's formal education.[156] Smith *translates* this pro-feminist yet colonialist and anti-Islamic perspective in the composition of a pro-imperial work through which '[a] new chapter has to be written', in English, which proves that, economically, Cyprus 'will form... that bridge which connects the severed ports of our great empire', and, socially, '[t]he Turkish portion of her people will enjoy more rights under our rule' and 'Cypriot Greeks will find that, as British subjects, they can do infinitely more for their own race than they could by giving their allegiance to Athens'.[157] It is a racialised defence of colonial 'paternalism' and Protestant missionary ideology *par excellence*, and one which uses her *transportal* position to promote 'bridges' which sustain imperialism globally rather than between British and Orientalised women specifically.

Consequently, the 'dark page' of Ottoman Cyprus is re-written by the pro-colonialist historiography of a white writer in defence of the occupation of a resource-laden strategic site in the Levant.[158] Such a relegation of misogyny as simply (or predominately) an Islamic practice which British imperialism can counter annunciates Joyce Zonana's influential theory of a 'feminist Orientalism' which conceptualises how European women writers utilise Orientalised contexts to symbolically juxtapose the individualist agency which Europe, Britain, or Western Christianity potentially offers.[159] Similarly, Scott-Stevenson promises her readers that the island will 'become one of the richest of the smaller English colonies' and that Britain will civilise 'these wild people'.[160] Through a hierarchy of gender, ethnicity, and religion, and with discourse similar to Smith, she pronounces a diatribe of disassociation from the *wildest* of these people: 'I have no sympathy with Turkish ladies. They are as utterly devoid of intelligence as they are uneducated, and it is impossible to converse without an interpreter, who, of course, is inadmissible' to women's spaces.[161] When she does interact with groups of Cypriot women, she personally affects the role of 'interpreter' or translator—literally between languages and figuratively between the poles of male colonial power and female 'native' subordination. She describes how, with 'their faces carefully covered over by a yashmak or white veil', they would exclaim, '"Hanoum! Madama! Madama!" or in Greek, "Kokona! Kokna! Keria!" (lady! lady!)',[162] translating their translingual discourses while co-opting their voices to ventriloquise her own hierarchical ladyship. In Orientalist scenes of harem-like gender spaces where Levantine women are tantalisingly sexualised as 'gradually unveiling themselves and displaying their undergarments of Cyprus cotton and coats of Manchester stuff', as objects of transcontinental cultural consumption, Scott-Stevenson 'got by degrees to know... and learn all about them'.[163] This act of Foucauldian surveillance from a position of intimacy denied for male colonists *translates* esoteric moments for British readers, desacralising the privacy of these spaces by realising fantasies of quasi-nude harem or hamam practices 'only done before other women'.[164] Through her narrative, male readers are welcomed into this exoticising and eroticising gaze which exposes the 'unveil[ed]' Orientalised woman. If, for Fanon, the veil potentially 'protects, reassures, isolates' women from a male, colonial gaze,[165] then the power of the veil as textile is sublimated in favour of colonial men who access textual representations of veils causing the women underneath to become knowable objects for voyeuristic, even pornographic, observation. Elsewhere in the narrative, the recurring trope of her spouse being referred to as 'the great English pasha' forms an autoexotic association with pre-British (Ottoman) customs, discourse, and imagery as a *translation* of power and knowledge from the ground.[166] Captain Andrew Scott-Stevenson mimics a Levantine title of authority to locally express his superiority in Cypriot terms. As in Kipling's *Kim*, fleeting masquerades as 'native' allow colonisers to assume the authority of surveillance which never fully relinquishes essentialised racial difference or power: Scott-Stevenson is not a member of a harem, her husband is not a pasha, but both are fantasies of performed Orientalist identification which can be used to intimately acquire epistemic wealth on 'natives' which can be transcribed and translated as part of imperialism's written project.

In the twentieth century, the dissemination of women's travelogues on Cyprus diminishes. Nonetheless, similar motifs of the exoticising and eroticising gaze are evident in the *New Society* article by Angela Carter, a writer typically renowned for her ('Western') feminism. In an echo of Scott-Stevenson's relationship with Mariehou, Carter travels to the pre-partition island on which '[e]verybody has trampled on her', before directing the focus of the reader to a Muslim girl.

> ...beyond the United Nation's lookout post and the tangle of barbed wire, you can see, for example, a young girl with the perfect oval face of an Ingres odalisque. Her black hair is parted at the centre, a striped silk handkerchief is tied round the low chignon. She is all complete, sitting at an open window like an invention of the romantic imagination, or a sign that says: "The Levant".[167]

Published only a few years before *Orientalism*, the narrative vividly anticipates Said's analysis of the psychic space as 'almost a European invention'.[168] For Carter, the 'black hair[ed]', veiled girl becomes a metonym for the effeminised island as a mere 'odalisque', 'invention', 'sign', or textual monolith which can be read as an uncomplicated, unhuman figure of the Orient. Situated through the frame of 'on open window', the 'romantic' imagery is reduced to a voyeuristic symbol of the picturesque and one associated with the limen of an island between cultural spheres. The direct address to the reader, moreover, correlates what she/he 'can see' with the lines of sight occupied by the UN 'lookout post', comparing a neo-colonial, exoticising gaze towards the people of a war-torn post/colony with the panopticism of global power structures. Even the parallel between 'the tangle of barbed wire', portrayed idiomatically as hair, with the girl's physiology utilises the latter as an embodiment of a Levantine setting dominated by conflict and division within which she is not a political agent but a silent, powerless subaltern defined by corporeal aesthetics alone. In this vaguely-erotic fantasy of the volatile Middle East, the article instrumentalises Orientalised femininity in order to cater to institutional market trends for a voyeuristic insight into the wars outside, or on cusp of, a masculinised Europe. In antithesis with the majority of Carter's literary oeuvre, the objectification of this Muslim girl offers a paradigm of Zonana's 'feminist Orientalism' by demonstrating how the writer's authoritative feminist critiques of patriarchal ideology fall short of challenging the axioms of imperialism and its misogynistic representations of non-European women as exoticised Others. By comparison, British novelist Sadie Jones, author of a fictional portrayal of the 1950s 'Emergency', *Small Wars* (2009), claimed that the Cypriot context, with which she was previously unfamiliar, was chosen as contemporaneous photographs of the conflict had caused the author to observe 'similarities between' it and the British army's activities in Afghanistan, asserting that 'perhaps Cyprus could be a vehicle for me to say what I wanted about what's happening now [in the war in Afghanistan] and the difficulties soldiers face'.[169] Such a strategy, obfuscating one Orientalised post/colony with another as deindividuated sites of alterity for the commercial gain of publication within a post-9/11 industry seeking marketable products concerning the Middle East, reveals how the island is diachronically appropriated according to varying agendas which seek to foreclose it as a 'vehicle' for elaborating on wider geopolitical concerns regarding Britain's relationship with its gendered, erstwhile empire. Ultimately, Carter's image of a 'native' woman marked as a passive symbol of 'The Levant' echoes, reiterates, and consolidates the illustration of a woman, 'CYPRUS', printed almost a century earlier in *Punch* as a metropolitan publication's figuring of the land-as-woman subordinately conceding the advance of an active, British, male agent.

Conclusions

Representations of Cyprus in colonial travel writing engage with a gendered Orientalism which seeks to present the island as an effeminised topos in need of a masculinist, imperialist penetration. The resulting product of the colonial mission is a threateningly hermaphroditic space symbolic of the in-between of a masculinised Europe and an effeminised Asia. As a consequence of the resulting ambivalence towards the (cultural and gendered) liminality of the island, narratives of disease and barrenness are employed which figure the dangers of this heterosexual cultural fertilising of non-European topography by neo-Crusaders. Baker, Dixon, Durrell, and Mallock all counter this recurring fear with the depiction of homosocial encounters between the male coloniser and the male colonised which both marginalises women from political and literary arenas and appropriates homoeroticism in order to foreclose the possibility of cross-cultural children born of illegitimate heterosexuality in the colonial setting. Women's writings of Cyprus, including the counter-discursive works of Smith in resistance to Baker, offer important departures from the oeuvre of men's colonial writing by challenging the androcentricity of an empire attempting to restrict the independence of British women and by articulating 'voices that... contest and to varying extents transform the power relations of hegemonic discourse'.[170] These 'extents' which Lewis identifies, however, gesture to the limitations of this discourse which, despite its radical writing-back to reductive male textualities, ultimately repeats, rather than destabilises, the racialised construction of Cypriots—and, in particular, Cypriot women—as commodified and Orientalised exotics. Discourses of gender, therefore, are crucially imbricated in notions of race and are co-opted to figure Cyprus as a space where 'Western' norms concerning gender and sexuality are—in the ambivalent limen between threat and freedom—reformed. For male writers, a non-masculine, androgynous Cyprus *produces* venereal pathogens and menacingly mobile women travellers; for women writers, Venus' island is the inspiration for autonomous cultural *production*. Both corpuses, however, reductively disavow the voices of Cypriots themselves in their marking of the island as site of *British* anxieties or freedoms. If Brassey, Carter, Scott-Stevenson, and Smith, like Shakespeare's Celia, are 'bound to speak' against patriarchy, they choose not to share such speech with the Cypriots they encounter and describe for economic gain.[171] These writers exist in the layers between metropolitan and nonmetropolitan, or hegemonic and nonhegemonic, and ultimately appropriate this ambivalent inbetweenness, in line with the liminality associated with the island setting itself, to manifest their power over peoples (especially women) hierarchised as racially inferior.

Notes

1. William Shakespeare, *The Oxford Shakespeare: Othello*, ed. by Michael Neil (Oxford: Oxford University Press, 2006), p. 211.
2. Linley Sambourne, 'Bien Venu Qui Apporte!' *Punch Magazine*, 3 August 1878.
3. Anne McClintock, *Imperial Leather* (London and New York: Routledge, 1995), p. 24.
4. Nancy Leys Stepan, *The Hour of Eugenics: Race, Gender, and Nation in Latin America* (New York: Cornell University Press, 1991), p. 18. Similarly, Laura Brown has identified 'the contemporaneity of issues of race

and gender in the context of a particular stage in the history of British capitalism associated broadly with commodity exchange and colonialist exploitation'. Laura Brown, *Ends of Empire: Women and Ideology in Early Eighteenth-Century English Literature* (New York: Cornell University Press, 1993), p. 34.

5. Robert J.C. Young, *Colonial Desire: Hybridity in Theory, Culture and Race* (London and New York: Routledge, 1995), p. 171. Comparative is Bhabha's 'insistence that power must be thought in the hybridity of race and sexuality' (Homi K. Bhabha, *The Location of Culture* [London and New York: Routledge, 1994], p. 122).
6. Dixon, pp. 10–11.
7. Dixon, p. 49.
8. Baker, p. 2.
9. Young, *Colonial Desire*, p. 172.
10. Dixon, p. 13; Baker, p. 7.
11. Dixon, pp. 13–14.
12. Colin Thubron, *Journey into Cyprus* (London: Vintage, 2012), p. 1.
13. Lawrence Durrell, *Bitter Lemons of Cyprus* (London: Faber and Faber, 2000), p. 4.
14. Wolseley, p. 18.
15. Thubron, p. 19.
16. In a source near-contemporaneous with Cyprus' occupation by Britain, 'Cyprian' is defined solely as 'Prostitute, courtesan, harlot, whore…'. Richard Soule, *A Dictionary of English Synonyms* (Boston: Little, Brown, and Company, 1871), p. 99. On the etymology of 'venereal', see, William S. Haubrich, *Medical Meanings: A Glossary of Word Origins* (Philadelphia, PA: American College of Physicians, 2003), p. 19.
17. Sara Ahmed, *Strange Encounters: Embodied Others in Post-coloniality* (Oxford and New York: Routledge, 2000), p. 144.
18. Durrell, p. 5.
19. In the novel's conclusion, the protagonist, Marlow, recalls having heard 'a light sigh' in his meeting with Kurtz's widow, before the vessel he is travelling on 'seemed to lead into the heart of an immense darkness' in his racist representation of colonial Western and Central Africa (p. 111). Even his vivid depiction of the Ottoman occupation, and how 'the drums beat' (p. 5) in proclamation, echoes the haunting 'beat of the drum… like the beating of a heart – the heart of a conquering darkness' throughout Conrad's novel (p. 105). Later, Durrell describes 'the darkness which Turkey brought upon the world she inherited' (p. 125). Joseph Conrad, *Heart of Darkness* (London: Penguin, 1994).
20. Thubron, p. 156.
21. Durrell, p. 123.
22. Thubron, pp. 29–30.

23. Thubron, pp. 85–86.
24. Thubron, p. 13.
25. Thubron, p. 93.
26. Thubron, pp. 7, 17.
27. Thubron, p. 14.
28. Thubron, p. 14.
29. Durrell, p. 101.
30. Daniel Defoe, *A Journal of the Plague Year* (New York: Dover, 2001), p. 1.
31. Thubron, pp. 330–331.
32. Thubron, p. 332.
33. Thubron, p. 331.
34. Thubron, pp. 312–313.
35. Thubron, p. 313.
36. Thubron, p. 92.
37. Thubron, p. 239.
38. William Hurrell Mallock, *In an Enchanted Isle, Or, A Winter's Retreat in Cyprus* (London: Richard Bentley & Son, 1892), p. 85.
39. William Greenslade, *Degeneration, Culture, and the Novel, 1880–1940* (Cambridge: Cambridge University Press, 1994), p. 191.
40. Mrs [Esmé] Scott-Stevenson, *Our Home in Cyprus* (London: Chapman and Hall, 1880), p. 40.
41. Scott-Stevenson, p. 39.
42. Scott-Stevenson, p. 300
43. Scott-Stevenson, p. 65.
44. Scott-Stevenson, p. 138.
45. Scott-Stevenson, p. 68.
46. McClintock, p. 26.
47. Pierre Bourdieu, *Masculine Domination*, trans. by Richard Nice (Stanford: Stanford University Press, 2001), p. 21.
48. Mrs [Annie] Brassey, *Sunshine and Storm in the East: Or, Cruises to Cyprus and Constantinople* (London: Longmans, Green, and Co., 1880), p. 253.
49. Brassey, p. 283.
50. Brassey, p. 282.
51. Brassey, p. 283.
52. Brassey, p. 271.
53. Brassey, p. 262.
54. Brassey, p. 263.
55. Brassey, p. 259.
56. Young, *Colonial Desire*, p. 24.
57. Anjali Arondekar, *For the Record: On Sexuality and the Colonial Archive in India* (Durham, NC: Duke University Press, 2009), pp. 45-46.

58. T.E. Lawrence, *Seven Pillars of Wisdom: A Triumph* (New York: Anchor Books, 1991), p. 30.
59. Baker, pp. 80, 16.
60. Baker, p. 16.
61. Baker, pp. 21–22.
62. Baker, pp. 16, 21.
63. Baker, p. 15.
64. Dixon, pp. 91–95.
65. Mallock, p. 56.
66. Mallock, pp. 53, 49.
67. Mallock, p. 52.
68. Mallock, p. 53.
69. Mallock, p. 301.
70. Mallock, p. 326.
71. Mallock, pp. 385–386.
72. Mallock, p. 387.
73. Gail Ching-Liang Low, *White Skin/Black Masks: Representation and Colonialism* (London: Routledge, 1996). Low evaluates 'the fantasy of disguise' (188) central to colonialist representations of transcultural attire. She suggests, in her analysis of Kipling's novel, that, '[a]t the end of their escapades, London and Kim are able to cast off their costumes and return to their original identities. Some object guarantees the integrity of their identities during the metamorphosis' (215). Similarly, Mallock reassures his readers that both he and heteronormative London have remained essentially unchanged upon his readmission 'to civilisation'.
74. Durrell, p. 233.
75. Durrell, p. 237.
76. Vangelis Calotychos, '"Lawrence Durrell, the Bitterest Lemon?": Cyprus and Brits Loving Each Other to Death in Cyprus, 1953–57', in *Lawrence Durrell and the Greek World*, ed. by Anna Lillios (Selinsgrove: Susquehanna University Press, 2004), pp. 169–187 (p. 180).
77. Michael Given, '"Father of his Landscape": Lawrence Durrell's Creation of Landscape and Character in Cyprus', *Deus Loci: The Lawrence Durrell Journal*, 5 (1997), 55–65 (p. 58). Also quoted in Calotychos, p. 174.
78. Durrell, p. 239.
79. Durrell, p. 237.
80. Durrell, p. 252.
81. Durrell, pp. 254, 258, 260.
82. William Shakespeare, 'Venus and Adonis', in *The Oxford Shakespeare: The Complete Sonnets and Poems*, ed. by Colin Burrow (Oxford: Oxford University Press, 2002), pp. 175–236 (p. 175).
83. Ibid., p. 229.

84. Durrell, p. 260.
85. Durrell, p. 237.
86. Paul Gilroy, *Postcolonial Melancholia* (New York: Columbia University Press, 2005), p. 102.
87. Durrell, p. 240.
88. Durrell, p. 231.
89. Buzard summarises this as an 'entirely invented plot twist'. James Buzard, 'Postcolonial Valediction: Durrell's *Bitter Lemons of Cyprus* and the Legacies of the Grand Tour', in *The Legacy of the Grand Tour: New Essays on Travel, Literature, and Culture*, ed. by Lisa Colletta (Lanham, Maryland: Fairleigh Dickinson University Press), pp. 115–131 (p. 121).
90. Abdul JanMohamed, 'The Economy of the Manichean Allegory: The Function of Racial Difference in Colonialist Literature', *Critical Inquiry*, 12 (1985), 59–87 (p. 67).
91. Baker, p. 29.
92. Baker, p. 95.
93. Baker, p. 95.
94. Baker, p. 27. With an incidental tone, he describes how 'women threw orange-flower water over my wife and myself… to avert the "evil-eye"'.
95. Baker, p. 229.
96. Baker, p. 228.
97. Smith, *Through Cyprus*, pp. 1–2.
98. Smith, *Through Cyprus*, p. 193.
99. Smith, *Through Cyprus*, pp. 321, 310.
100. Agnes Smith, *Eastern Pilgrims: The Travels of Three Ladies* (London: Hurst and Blackett, 1870), p. 1.
101. Pierre Bourdieu, 'The Field of Cultural Production, or: The Economic World Reversed', trans. by Richard Nice, in *The Field of Cultural Production: Essays on Art and Literature*, ed. by Randal Johnson (Cambridge: Polity Press, 1993), pp. 29–73 (p. 31).
102. Pratt, p. 104.
103. According to Said, 'The Oriental was linked thus to elements in Western society (delinquents, the insane, women, the poor) having in common an identity best described as lamentably alien'. *Orientalism*, p. 207.
104. Virginia Woolf, *A Room of One's Own* (Toronto: Broadway Press, 2001), p. 78.
105. Woolf, p. 78.
106. Smith, *Through Cyprus*, pp. 129, 201.
107. Bhabha, *The Location of Culture*, p. 146.
108. Smith, *Through Cyprus*, p. 184.
109. Smith, *Through Cyprus*, p. 129.
110. Smith, *Through Cyprus*, pp. 321–322.
111. Smith, *Through Cyprus*, p. 340.

112. Smith, *Eastern Pilgrims*, p. 2.
113. Smith, *Eastern Pilgrims*, p. 3.
114. Graham Huggan, *The Postcolonial Exotic: Marketing the Margins* (London and New York: Routledge, 2001), pp. 19, 207.
115. Smith, *Through Cyprus*, p. 108.
116. Gayatri Chakravorty Spivak, *Toward a History of the Vanishing Present* (Cambridge, Massachusetts: Harvard University Press, 1999), p. 167.
117. Smith, *Eastern Pilgrims*, p. 69.
118. Smith, *Eastern Pilgrims*, p. 69.
119. Smith, *Eastern Pilgrims*, p. 70.
120. Smith, *Eastern Pilgrims*, p. 70.
121. Smith, *Eastern Pilgrims*, p. 71.
122. Smith, *Eastern Pilgrims*, p. 1.
123. 'More About Cyprus', *The Saturday Review*, 6 December 1879, pp. 701–702 (p. 701).
124. E.H. Bunbury, 'Cyprus', *The Academy*, 6 December 1879, pp. 402–403 (p. 402).
125. Bunbury, p. 402.
126. See, Frances Ellen Colenso, *History of the Zulu War and its Origins* (London: Chapman and Hall, 1880), p. 505.
127. On reading habits of the time, Cunningham notes that '[m]en, until the late nineteenth century, had a higher rate of literacy than women, and they may have had easier access to literature'. H. Cunningham, 'Leisure and Culture', in *The Cambridge Social History of Britain, 1750–1950, Volume 2: People and their Environment*, ed. by F.M.L. Thompson (Cambridge: Cambridge University Press, 1990), pp. 279–340 (p. 308).
128. Scott-Stevenson, p. v.
129. Brassey, p. v. See also, Walter Colton, *Ship or Shore; or, Leaves from the Journal of a Cruise to the Levant* (New York: Leavitt, Lord & Co., 1835), pp. 280–281. Note parallels in the titles of Brassey's and Colton's works, especially the repetition of *Cruise/s* and the geographic markers of *the East* and *the Levant*, respectively. This suggests an attempt to frame and market Brassey's narrative as a successor to, and perhaps revision of, a male forebear's literary output.
130. Brassey, p. 267.
131. Scott-Stevenson, pp. 13, 57.
132. Oyèrónkẹ́ Oyěwùmí, *The Invention of Women: Making an African Sense of Western Gender Discourses* (Minneapolis: Minnesota University Press, 1997), p. 122.
133. Elleke Boehmer, *Empire Writing: An Anthology of Colonial Literature, 1870–1918* (Oxford: Oxford University Press, 2009), p. xxviii.
134. Scott-Stevenson, pp. xi-xii.
135. Scott-Stevenson, p. 119.

136. Scott-Stevenson, p. 120.
137. Scott-Stevenson, p. 121.
138. Scott-Stevenson, p. 121.
139. Such a representation of gender performativity and repetition correlates with the salient theories of Judith Butler: 'This is not an appropriation of dominant culture in order to remain subordinated by its terms, but an appropriation that seeks to make over the terms of domination, a making over which is itself a kind of agency, a power in and as discourse, in and as performance, which repeats in order to remake and sometimes succeeds'. Judith Butler, *Bodies That Matter: On The Discursive Limits of "Sex"* (Oxford and New York: Routledge, 1993), p. 137. Scott-Stevenson therefore achieves 'power' (and economic 'agency' as writer) through her counter-discursive repetition of the display of male, colonial power which reduces its (esoteric) conventions by exposing it as an ideological 'performance'.
140. Scott-Stevenson, p. 121.
141. Scott-Stevenson, p. 69.
142. Scott-Stevenson, pp. 57–58.
143. Scott-Stevenson, p. 5.
144. Low, p. 72.
145. Simone de Beauvoir, *The Second Sex*, trans. and ed. by H.M. Parshley (London: Vintage, 1997), p. 19.
146. Scott-Stevenson, p. 87. Compare with Dixon, p. 94.
147. Scott-Stevenson, p. 88.
148. Scott-Stevenson, p. 87.
149. Dinah Zeiger, 'That (Afghan) Girl! Ideology Unveiled in *National Geographic*', in *The Veil: Women Writers on its History, Lore, and Politics*, ed. by Jennifer Heath (Berkeley and Los Angeles: University of California Press, 2008), pp. 266–280.
150. Brassey, p. 297.
151. Brassey, p. 276.
152. Lisa Lowe, *Critical Terrains: French and British Orientalisms* (New York: Cornell University Press, 1994), pp. 5, 197.
153. Reina Lewis, *Gendering Orientalism: Race, Femininity and Representation* (London and New York: Routledge, 1996), p. 4.
154. Meyda Yeğenoğlu, *Colonial Fantasises: Towards a Feminist Reading of Orientalism* (Cambridge: Cambridge University Press, 1998), p. 85.
155. Smith, *Through Cyprus*, p. 313.
156. Smith, *Through Cyprus*, p. 129.
157. Smith, *Through Cyprus*, pp. 310–311.
158. Smith, *Through Cyprus*, p. 310.
159. Joyce Zonana, 'The Sultan and the Slave: Feminist Orientalism and the Structures of *Jane Eyre*', *Signs*, 18 (1993), 592–617.

160. Scott-Stevenson, pp. 230, 235.
161. Scott-Stevenson, p. 173.
162. Scott-Stevenson, p. 82.
163. Scott-Stevenson, pp. 82–83.
164. Scott-Stevenson, p. 83.
165. Frantz Fanon, *A Dying Colonialism*, trans. by Haakon Chevalier (New York: Grove Press, 1967), p. 59.
166. Scott-Stevenson, p. 311.
167. Carter, pp. 208–209.
168. Said, *Orientalism*, p. 1.
169. Eva Wiseman, 'Small Wars by Sadie Jones', *The Guardian*, 22 August 2009, www.theguardian.com/books/2009/aug/23/jones-soldier-small-wars [accessed 14 December 2014]. See also, Sadie Jones, *Small Wars* (London: Chatto and Windus, 2009).
170. Lewis, p. 4.
171. Shakespeare, *Othello*, p. 385.

CHAPTER 3

Re-imagining the Cypriot Nation: Writing-Back to the Colonial Travelogue, 1964–1974

> [T]he Cypriots have no history; they are mere servants, more or less willing, in the strong hands of those who hold their country. We have little to write about them; we can tell only what foreigners did with their island. ...the history of Cyprus can scarcely be called the history of the Cypriots. [...] A new chapter has to be written... They have a sure place in the heart of Great Britain.[1]
>
> In an inconceivable moment we saw before us once again the Greek Revolution [of the 1820s], no longer lifeless in print with beautiful, colored pictures... [but] the most breathtaking repetition of history one could possibly imagine. [...] It was the worst time possible time to read heroic tales of other people, other places. The stories seemed irrelevant, incapable of any relation to our present...[2]
>
> In our history classes we were constantly reminded of the important part Cyprus played in the shaping of ancient history. It... had absorbed the blood and culture of numerous civilisations... The glory of the island... was never apparent to me, not until I escaped from it severing my roots. Going back there now I would behave like a tourist, visit the historical spots, read about them in a travel book, take photographs.[3]

The first of these three quotations is from the colonial writing of Agnes Smith in the late nineteenth century, while the succeeding two were composed by two Cypriot authors, Costas Montis and Taner Baybars, in the decade leading up to the 1974 partition. Parallels between the three extracts expose how interrelated motifs of historiography, travel writing, and illustration pervade these otherwise-divergent representations of the

D. Nunziata, *Colonial and Postcolonial Cyprus*,
https://doi.org/10.1007/978-3-030-58236-4_3

history of Cyprus. For Agnes Smith, Cypriots are merely docile bodies requiring the paternalism of succeeding imperial hegemons to control their subjectivity. Idiomatically echoing Hegel's infamously ethnocentric and racist axiom—'Africa… is no historical part of the World; it has no movement or development to exhibit'[4]—Smith positions herself as an agent of transcontinental *movement* using her status as colonial writer to ethnocentrically define civilisation and to offer the sociopolitical *development* of the Great British 'heart' for a culturally-juvenile and essentially-subservient people. Smith foreshadows how Cypriot history is one 'to be written' in the succeeding century, but anticipates that this 'new chapter' will only be composed by colonisers—the eventual Orientalist reportage of Durrell and Thubron—without calling for the autonomous voices of Cypriots themselves.

Decades later, however, Taner Baybars and Costas Montis began constructing resistant subject positions through literature. For these two notable writers of the so-called Cypriot Renaissance publishing in the juncture between the Second World War and the island's partition, any understanding of the history and culture of Cyprus must actively re-read and re-write extant dominant narratives which categorise, or explicitly disavow, 'Cypriotism'. As well as the 'travel book' which Baybars re-reads through an autoexotic, touristic gaze from a position of exile, both he and Montis are equally concerned with the textual and pictorial images disseminated by pedagogical structures, each seeking to put pressure on the respective conceits of pro-Turkish and pro-Greek education systems. As demonstrated in the preceding chapters, British colonial policy (and the literatures which consolidated it) selectively instrumentalised theories of either a hybridised Cypriot identification, or of essentialised differences in monolithic 'Greek' and 'Turkish' identities, to marshal anti-colonial national subjectivities. In particular, exocentric education played a significant role in the rise of division on the island; discrete teaching bodies for Greek-speakers and Turkish-speakers (as well as Maronite Arabic-speakers and Armenian-speakers) was culpable 'more than any other single factor for the assimilation of notions of Greek versus Turkish nationality among the populace'.[5]

Indeed, colonial travelogues are entrenched in commentaries on pedagogy, not least Durrell's fluctuating accounts of teaching Greek-speakers with a mixture of neoclassical zeal and vehement anti-Hellenism. Similarly, Baker's divide-and-rule theses, including the notion that '[t]here can be no better soldier than the Turk under British officers', also campaigns that 'schools should be established throughout the island for the instruction of... English... [to] assimilate [Cypriots] with our customs and ideas' (itself quoted in full by Smith).[6] While his journal reveals High Commissioner Wolseley's firm rejection to making Greek a national language in August 1878,[7] Smith's lengthy rumination on education concludes that effective colonial rule ought to 'acknowledge that three-fourths of the Cypriots are Greeks' and should be taught in the (biblical) language. It is a summary formed following her assessment, five paragraphs earlier, that 'Greeks and Moslems get on pleasantly enough', leading to her ambivalently-expressed concerns towards to the pervasiveness of religious conversions.[8] In 1881, Secretary of State for the Colonies, the Earl of Kimberley, began enacting this transition from Anglocentric schooling to a system which lauded ancient Greek literatures as models for Westernisation.[9] For these writers and legislators, historiography, education, and language are tools of imperial regulation manifested through deeply politicised acts of denying or co-opting the history of the island. Reviewing the potential cultural capital of pedagogy, Baybars describes colonial Cyprus as 'that education-crazy island' vying between the metropolitan disseminations of London, Athens, and Ankara.[10]

In the early twentieth century, Cypriot literatures emerged which sought to resist the assumptions of colonial travel writing. In the same juncture as Al-Nahda (*the renaissance*) in neighbouring Arab-majority regions of the Levant, the 'Cypriot Renaissance' between the 1940s and 1970s sought to revise Orientalising ethnologies of the island through the agency of self-representation. Poetic and prose narratives of Cypriot topographies and personhood in many ways typify the anti-colonial (and postcolonial) 'literary activity of self-making and nation-building... the ways in which writing – in particular perhaps the novel – was used to project autonomous identity, to re-create traditional, communal relationships'.[11] This impulse actively participates in the interplay of nation and narration which exemplifies the project of re/writing imagined national spaces in the wake of imperial rule and (pending) decolonisation. In short, writers of this period contest the notion that 'Cypriots have no history' or culture. This is achieved, in part, through 'writing-back' to earlier colonialist discourses through the creation of subversive literary genres which hybridise the forms of the travelogue as well as Cypriot oral poetry.

However, if anti-colonial writing practices are to be understood as negotiating a double consciousness within corporeal, psychological, and socio-economic spheres, then the Fanonian theory of the colonial 'inferiority complex [as] the outcome of a double process' between centre and periphery[12] is more complex in a space peripheral to *multiple* imagined sites of metropolitan superiority, national affiliation, and educational capital. The 'Cypriot Renaissance' which developed through multiple literary and linguistic forms—English, Greek, and Turkish—is a polyphonic movement (or, series of smaller constituent movements) within which Cypriot authors wrest with concepts of colonialism and nationalism, manoeuvring across the ostensible doubleness which ruptures Cypriot history, culture, and identifications, not only between paradigms of coloniser/colonised, but of Greek/Turkish. By reclaiming history, Cypriots like Baybars and Montis attempt to showcase the existence of an historical past *and present* which differs from the historiographies constructed through colonialist discourses.

One fundamental issue with this is the degree to which anti-colonial narratives depend on a construction of the nation. Cypriots, therefore, mediate between manifestations of Cyprus as a national space and of the established, consecrated nations of Greece and Turkey (and, occasionally, Lebanon and Armenia) as the 'imaginary homelands' of dispersed peoples seeking a wider, pan-national 'imagined community'. This depends on the extent to which these writers see themselves as either 'Cypriots', or as 'Greeks' and 'Turks', or both; it is the extent to which they express themselves as one nation or as a series of national diasporas. The ways in which these existential concerns have lent themselves to social division and bi-communal violence—during the same juncture in which the 'Cypriot Renaissance' writers were being published—demonstrate the issues inherent in attempting to resist colonial discourses while also *internalising* its dualism to construct a constituent Cypriot Other when defining the independent self. The so-called '*feeling* of foreignness, of alienation from themselves' that Durrell briefly discusses,[13] and which colonial politicians instrumentalised to maintain British rule, is part of the cultural and existential polymorphism which surrounds anti-colonial nationalisms on the island.

These tensions are bound up in what Anderson calls 'the discontinuity-in-connectedness between print-languages, national consciousness, and nation states'.[14] These contradictions have additional complexity for the Cypriot context in which allegiances according to (print) language and national identifications are always slipping and uncertain, with Cypriot writers moving between local, regional, and global forms in order to imagine an anti-colonial 'national consciousness'. As Appadurai reminds us, 'the nation-state has often created, revitalized, or fractured ethnic identities that were previously fluid, negotiable, or nascent'. Nationalism frequently appropriates existing 'ethnic categories that in turn drive others to construct counterethnicities' in response to 'ethnonationalist' violence.[15] In mid-twentieth-century Cyprus, islanders were grappling with the nationalist ideologies which used, transformed, and concretised pre-colonial cultural identities in ways which veered to violent extremes. Nationalism offered a possible antidote to British colonialism while also raising newer existential and sectarian problems. Centres of print capitalism outside the island (in English, Greek, and Turkish) were employed to fix cultural identities in order to erase the flexibility of earlier (or subversive) imaginings of Cypriot selfhood. The notion of a 'fluid, negotiable, or nascent' Cypriot identity, or pan-Cypriot community, was threatening to all hegemonic agents attempting to control the island from either London, Athens, or Ankara. What follows is the difficult task of attempting to form 'counterethnicities' to those offered by both colonialism and nationalism. For writers, this has involved careful revisions of the past which re-examine historical moments and cultural forms outside the print interventions of English censuses and literature, *and* Greek and Turkish propaganda.

Most early Cypriot literary compositions during the British colonial period were oral and most, excluding those transformed as proverbs, have been lost. These were routinely performed through the related poetry recitations and duals of *tsiattistá* in Kypriaka ('Cypriot Greek') and *mâni* in Kıbrıslıca ('Cypriot Turkish'), as well as shared musical traditions and the socially-reflexive shadow puppet shows of protagonist Karagiozis/Karagöz.[16] While these oral forms are denigrated as unsophisticated by Durrell, particularly for their expression 'in such pure *patois* that I couldn't follow' them as a speaker of Standard Modern Greek,[17] both *tsiattistá* and Karagöz have since been recognised as UNESCO Intangible Cultural Heritages. In addition to parallel forms, Cypriot records from the late nineteenth century reveal intercommunal public spaces of cultural production, including an 1889 article for the *Foni tis Kyprou* ('Voice of Cyprus') which describes how, unlike those frequenting coffeehouses, '[t]he high social class spends its time mostly in a Greek-Armenian-Turkish theatre'.[18]

One of the few explicitly anti-colonial oral narratives which has been preserved is that concerning the folk hero, Hasanpouli(a), a Robin Hood-like outlaw lauded by Cypriots of all linguistic backgrounds and based on a real figure who challenged the colonial establishment in the late nineteenth century (long before the paramilitary groups EOKA and TMT). As recorded by Costas Constantinou, one extant poem extols the figure as, 'Hasanpoulia, flying like birds,/Dressed in different clothes everyday,/Greek today and Turkish tomorrow'.[19] The name, a translingual portmanteau of the Turkish (or, Muslim) Hasan and the Greek for bird, *pouli*, echoes the character's dual manifestation in both Kypriaka and Kıbrıslıca poems in which his alterations in costume, appearance, and language are used to evade colonial panopticism and arrest. Some accounts suggest he used women's attire as disguise and emphasise that he was sheltered by both Greek-speakers and Turkish-speakers across the island. As well as transgressing British law, the exilic figure deconstructs hierarchies of ethnicity, gender, and even species (through his association with birds). By parodying a colonial fear of miscategorisation, the narratives present these identities as performative, arbitrary, and colonialist in origin. Hasanpouli is an embodiment of cultural pluralism. Consequently, by figuring him as one who resists both British legal codes *and* codes of ethnic identification, the poems infer a link between anti-colonialism and anti-nationalism.

The colonial 'outlaw' on the fringes of organised society has long been one 'mixed in hybrid forms which confuse the rule of Law'.[20] Indeed, the historical figure was responsible for the introduction of the 1895 Outlaw's Proclamation Act in the years following the first census, and his crimes, according to Graham Seal, 'were widely interpreted by both Greek and Turkish Cypriots at the time as being directed against the British'.[21] Such accounts use much the same celebratory discourse as literatures and popular histories representing EOKA in the 1950s. Yet, in this pre-1955 period, it exists within *a shared, pan-Cypriot narration* framing the overcoming of colonialism as a united—and uniting—Cypriot endeavour. Notably, the folk hero became the subject of a Greek-language biopic, *Hasaboulia tis Kyprou* ('Hasaboulia of Cyprus', a title explicitly claiming the figure as Cypriot), filmed and released in 1974. Despite this, allusions to him, especially among Greek-speakers, became sparse following the Second World War and the rise of both anti-colonial and bi-communal violence. The growth of pro-Hellenic and pro-Turkic nationalisms rendered the cultural-plurality of Hasanpouli problematic for their ideologies. As Constantinou suggests, what 'ethnocentricists do not accept – and indeed may find most abhorrent – is the Hasanpoulia dimension of Cypriotness'.[22]

From the 1950s onwards, many anti-colonial narratives within the 'Cypriot Renaissance', following the linguistic divisions of education, increasingly rejected motifs of cultural pluralism or 'Cypriotism' in favour of claims of ethnic purity in association with the nationalisms of Greece (Venizelism and the *Megali Idea*) and Turkey (Kemalism). When resisting the colonialist axiom that 'Cypriots have no history', their literary reactions involve interpellating Cypriots into the wider, celebrated histories of the respective 'homelands'. Greek-speaking writers seeking political *enosis* with Greece, for instance, sought a coterminous cultural union of the Hellenophone literatures of Cyprus and Greece. Writers from Greece during this period constructed narratives sympathising with Cypriot anti-colonialism by representing the island as a surviving bastion of ancient Hellenism.

Notably, Nikos Kazantzakis, in his predominately-Levantine travelogue, *Journeying: Travels in Italy, Egypt, Sinai, Palestine, and Cyprus* (1927, translated in 1975), describes the last as 'indeed the native land of Aphrodite. I've never looked upon a more feminine island, or breathed an air so saturated with voluptuous and dangerous suggestions. I feel elevated. ...my soul capsizes and gives up, like Aphrodite, the holy prostitute. You become deeply permeated here by a sweetness like the scent of jasmine'.[23] The account frames Cyprus Hellenocentrically as the purported birthplace of a Greek goddess, while simultaneously echoing the Orientalist register of British travel writing by effeminising, exoticising, and mythically dehistoricising the contemporary island. It shares, for instance, the effeminising legacy of Aphrodite posited by Thubron. While colonial travel writing is invested in Orientalising Cyprus in order to justify the need for its absorption into a larger political hegemon, Kazantzakis' writing performs a similar function in support of Greek cultural imperialism. Even claims of Greek sovereignty based on ancient Greek colonisation echo nineteenth-century British claims of restaging the earlier English Crusades.

Cyprus, here, is associated with both self and Other, a site of alterity which widens the Greek map into exotic terrain, fetishising the very moment of maritime conquest by contemporary man. Similarly, the Nobel laureate Giorgos Seferis repeatedly refers to Cyprus in conjunction with both Classical Greek histories and modern personal discovery. As quoted in *A Levant Journal* (composed 1941–1944), he cites his 'First impression: from here one feels Greece (suddenly) to be more spacious, broader. The sense that there exists a world of people speaking Greek, a Greek world'.[24] Elsewhere, he describes dancing in Beirut having its 'root… in Aphrodite, in the sensual body… the erotic',[25] echoing the exoticising objectification of Levantine female corporeality in both Kazantzakis and Thubron. The same travelogue, nonetheless, also reveals an ambivalence towards the *Megali Idea*, wanting 'not to do harm to that world, trying to make it better, without turning it into a province of the Greek mainland, like Corfu'.[26] Mediating on the relationship between metropole and 'province', Seferis offers brief concern for how political unity will function practically, if realised.

Nonetheless, the choice of genre employed by both Greek writers reveals important stylistic and political links with contemporary British travelogues. During this juncture—following the collapse of the Ottoman Empire, the population exchanges between Greece and Turkey, and the Second World War—the authors use travel writing to explore their fluctuating identities in an unstable Mediterranean. As the borders of those two powers changed and, with them, the symbolic limits of Europe and Asia, writers in Greece and Turkey employed the genre of movement *par excellence* to understand the changing demarcations of their cultural and national identities. Cyprus becomes the apotheosis of land which is both foreign and familiar, much like their new identities as post-Ottoman citizens of the relatively-nascent Hellenic and Turkish republics. It is this legacy, of competing metropolitan discourses co-opting the island as a marker of politicised identities, which is then internalised by Cypriots themselves.

Indeed, Greek-speaking Cypriot writers likewise composed works drawing on Classical literary traditions as markers of national/ist identification. Panos Ioannides' short story 'Cinyras' (1972) constructs an antiquarian narrative of political leadership on the ancient island (and during the Trojan War), tacitly comparing the bearded eponymous king with Cyprus' contemporary, bearded leader, Makarios, during the advent of a new conflict on the border of Asia and Europe. Emblematic of Greek nationalism in Cypriot literatures, one character is voiced aphoristically extolling Hellenism during a speech on war: 'in the final analysis a Cypriot soldier is a Greek soldier. Cyprus is part of Greece. Loyalty to Cyprus is less Greek loyalty than loyalty to Greece itself'.[27] Although the monologue is framed as that of an ancient figure, it could equally be recontextualised as part of a slogan or pamphlet for EOKA in which support for the Greek 'Motherland', as it is explicitly identified in the text, supersedes any allegiance to the local.

The *Anthology of Cypriot Poetry (From Ancient Times Until Today)* (1965; 1973), edited by Montis and Andreas Christofides, despite its name, features no poetry from Cypriots writing in a language other than Greek. Instead, it emphasises in its introductory peritext that '[t]he Cypriot poetic tradition – purely Greek in character and content – goes far back in time', an antiquarian and essentialist historiography that excludes the ostensibly non-'Greek' from Cypriot history while interpellating contemporary Cypriot writing into a broader category alongside that 'from other provinces of Greece'.[28] Among Turkish-speaking Cypriots, parallel projects of cultural nationalism and division occurred simultaneously. Poet Özker Yaşın, father of Mehmet and Neşe, not only volunteered for TMT in 1963, but a recurring theme of his verse is the monumentalising of Atatürk: an interchange of politics and literature characteristic of works from this period. The majority of these texts were composed in the standard modern forms of Greek and Turkish, rather than Cypriot vernaculars, revealing a binary opposition between written and oral in which the Western European printed form privileges the standardised languages of metropolitan centres: English, Greek, and Turkish, not pre-colonial and pre-nationalist Kypriaka or Kıbrıslıca. To return to the importance of nationalist education, most leaders of Cypriot anti-colonial political movements, like the writers of Al-Nahda, were members of the nascent 'intelligentsia' educated *separately* in standardised languages, and galvanising support from non-'professionals'.[29] Montis, indeed, was closely affiliated with EOKA throughout the 1950s, just as Özker Yaşın was with TMT the following decade.

Although this survey of (male) writers is far from exhaustive, it gestures towards common tropes of Greek and Turkish nationalisms within the literary activities of this midway juncture. Motifs of exocentric national affiliation challenge the continuing claims of Britain over the island while simultaneously anticipating the erection of partitions—cultural and physical—between Greek-speaking and Turkish-speaking Cypriots.

'Postcolonial' Tactics: Costas Montis' *Closed Doors* and Taner Baybars' *Plucked in a Far-Off Land*

The 'Cypriot Renaissance' generation of writers, therefore, struggle between constructing anti-colonial literary modes and developing a coherent cultural identity as Cypriots. They manoeuvre between the models of resistance suggested by vernacular Hasanpouli traditions, on the one hand, and Greek or Turkish nationalisms, on the other. The case study of this chapter will investigate these tensions through a comparison of the Greek-speaking Montis and the Turkish-speaking Baybars, both poets and prose writers, whose self-reflexive prose works—*Closed Doors: An Answer to* Bitter Lemons *by Lawrence Durrell* (1964) and *Plucked in a Far-Off Land: Images in Self Biography* (1970)—were first published in the period between independence and partition.

The majority of Montis' texts are composed in Standard Modern Greek, while Baybars' oeuvre, since 1963, has been predominately in English and first published in London (including translations of contemporaries like Mehmet Yaşın). Each, to varying degrees, consider identifications with the hegemons of Greece and Turkey and both are—although perhaps Montis more so—interpellated into the broad, delineating categories of 'Greek literary production' and 'Turkish literary production' consecrated in Athens and Ankara, respectively. However, despite differences in linguistic form, parallels in both their early lives and their literary compositions suggest that, beyond the expected polarising of culture from this period, these two writers share related narrative tactics as constituent parts of a *pan-Cypriot* and 'postcolonial' literary movement. The two texts are semi-fictional, first-person *bildungsromane* integrating elements of travel writing and prose poetry and concerning the lives of adolescent narrators: for Montis, the brother of an EOKA volunteer eventually killed in combat; for Baybars, an aspiring poet in the years preceding his emigration to the UK. They draw on the writers' individual experiences in the colony yet, like Durrell's work, are compounded with elements of fictionality. Notably, Montis names the brother after his own, Nikos, who also died prematurely but of leukaemia, not in war. Also important are the comparable afterlives of the two works. The opening of the border heralded an increase in their readerships as *Closed Doors* was first translated into English in 2004, and *Plucked in a Far-Off Land* was republished in the Republic of Cyprus the following year.

Like Makarios and Denktaş (and other political figures of the decolonising world, including Gandhi), both writers studied law. The two emigrated in their youths to read law abroad: Montis in Athens and Baybars in England. However, for different reasons, neither eventually practised as lawyers. When he returned to colonial Cyprus, Montis was banned from doing so because of the non-British provenance of his degree. Baybars abandoned his studies part-way through and remained in the UK as a full-time writer and translator. Experiences of exile and overseas degrees in law indicate the imbrication of the legal, political, pedagogical, and literary within their planetary worldviews—although the different metropolitan centres in which they were based accounts for the emergence of their distinct linguistic modes. During an historical moment where forms of anti-colonial violence categorised variously as 'liberation', 'paramilitary', and 'terrorist' competed with the sanctioned violence of the colonial administration, early Cypriot writing is consciously concerned with the legal parameters of how imperialism can be challenged and usurped.

As Stephen Morton has demonstrated in his research on colonial 'emergencies' of the mid-twentieth century, albeit without specific reference to Cypriot contexts, there exists an important 'relationship between law, state violence and colonial sovereignty' which anti-colonial and postcolonial writers attempt to navigate.[30] For Michel de Certeau, whose theoretical contrast of *strategy* and *tactic* elucidates the dichotomy of the authorised and resistant, '[f]rom birth to mourning after death, law "takes hold of" bodies in order to make them its "text"'.[31]

For anti-colonial writers, including those depicting the transcultural outlaw Hasanpouli, the colonised Cypriot body is textualised and regulated by a series of literary and legal discourses. While comparisons have been made between colonial Cyprus and other 'emergencies' in Algeria, Kenya, and Malaya, the former offers a unique set of legal factors in that most anti-colonial political movements were generated, not towards the creation of a new nation state, but a legalised re-administration of the island by Greece or Turkey, instead. As to be shown, Baybars' narrative, not written in one of the two national languages rendered official in 1960, strays further from representations of, and allegiance with, nationalist violence than Montis' account of the youth fighters of EOKA, an organisation he was personally involved with. Nonetheless, the two engage, through similar generic forms, in the projects of *simultaneously* writing-back to the colonial travelogue and reflecting on the contemporary rise of nationalisms in cultural and political fields.

The two are set before independence (Montis' between 1955 and 1960; Baybars' between 1938 and the late 1940s), and yet they gesture equally to the politics of the post-independence era in which they were published. Baybars, for instance, intertextually ends his narrative (as Durrell does) with a poem penned 'in a whirlwind of emotions during 1963', the year Özker Yaşın joined TMT, and months before both Montis' publication and the deployment of the UN Peacekeeping Force.[32] This temporal doubleness indicates the dual politics of Cypriot narratives which mediate the sanctioned ideologies of *colonialism and nationalisms concurrently*.

The full title of Montis' text, *Closed Doors: An Answer to* Bitter Lemons *by Lawrence Durrell*, signals a direct writing-back to the British writer. Montis achieves this by pressing on the *closed doors* of internment camps established by the British Empire to confine anti-colonial insurgents. His text is equally invested, however, in considering the national and cultural identities of Cypriots resisting British rule and the extent to which Hellenism is a valid anti-colonial identification. The same concerns, from the perspective of a Turkish-speaker mediating the fall of British imperialism and the rise of Turkish nationalism within his familial habitus, pervade Baybars' work. Both writers portray countertravels across the island to offer *transportal* modes which re-write and dismantle the various hegemonic pulls on Cyprus from both inside and outside. They re-imagine the gateways of identity, from the doors of prisons to homes. It is, therefore, necessary to consider these writers' chosen linguistic and textual interventions into the existing narratives of imperialism and nationalism.

Intersecting Genres

It is within the confluence of legal and historical discourses that both Baybars and Montis employ generic forms between travel writing and the *bildungsroman* to reclaim the first-person pronoun from the colonial travelogue and express the agency of (male) Cypriots. They stage acts of political testimony which privilege the personal and mundane as historic. As Saree Makdisi suggests of modern Arabic literature, 'the possibility of a return to a mythic past is rejected' in favour of 'a highly unstable and contradictory present, one that defies the convenient and false reassurances of new and old political, religious, and literary dogmatisms'.[33]

Although both writers allude, often in significant ways, to earlier historical moments, the monumentalist dimensions of both imperial historiography and nationalist epics are forfeited in favour of the individual experiences of the authors in the twentieth century. If colonialists like Smith suggest Cypriots have no history in order to justify British rule, then the nationalist traditions born in Greece and Turkey similarly posit that Cypriots have no history *without, or before, these nationalist bodies*. In response to the weight of a nullified historical consciousness, the present-as-historical articulates Fanon's assertion that '[i]n no way should I dedicate myself to the revival of an unjustly unrecognized Negro civilization. I will not make myself the man of any past. I do not want to exalt the past at the expense of my present and of my future'.[34]

Events recounted in these texts are intimately familiar to Cypriot readers and shifts between the first-person singular and plural—occasionally in the present tense in *Closed Doors* where '[i]n our story, I have no name'[35]—construct a subject position identifiable for readers as the (attempted) collective voice of the nameless Cypriot every-person. (Inevitably, empathy is here circumscribed as the every-person is often an every*man* which does not necessarily include women, illiterate people, or Cypriots who do not speak the chosen language of the text.) When the family of Montis' narrator becomes implicated in the 'emergency', he reflects on how they 'thought we had great public responsibilities, that our house was involved in the making of history'.[36] The domestic is rendered historiographic through ruptures of personal and 'public' whereby the plural refers to the history of one (perhaps representative) family unit, rather than an amorphous people: although the text is occasionally depicted as a commentary on EOKA, its focus is on the psychological lives of select individuals, rather than an ethnological survey or a hagiographic tribute to famous figures.

As Shemak notes of refugee narratives and 'postcolonial travel writing', these genres 'disrupt the idea of individual travel, since [the refugee] experience often includes mass migration'.[37] Doing so puts pressure on the conventional individualism of colonial travelogues. However, in a context where nationalist narratives seek to speak for the collective consciousness, Baybars and Montis manoeuvre cautiously and ambivalently between the communal and individual. Both, for instance, use the plural pronoun to commence each of their second paragraphs. The former describes how 'Our house [in Vassilia between the hills and the sea] was on a slope, tucked beyond the mosque without a minaret'[38]; the latter states that 'We lived in Ayios Dometios, a suburb of Nicosia, which due to its proximity to the airport, had seen the largest share of the city's sudden growth'.[39] The two, therefore, commence their works, structurally and thematically, with parallel motifs of adolescence in Cypriot communities, using the pronoun to interpellate contemporary readers leading comparable lives. They envision the house of the impoverished Cypriot, not the port of the colonial traveller.

Yet, the two narratives stress the specificity of their *own* individual experiences. Neither village is nameless but precise. Indeed, the Muslim 'minaret' proximal to Baybars' home, and the Christian name of Montis' 'suburb', the Greek for Saint Dometios, stresses differences in cultural identity (regardless of, say, Baybars' scenes of irreligiousness within the text and actual conversion to Catholicism without).

Nonetheless, both texts stress liminality. Adolescence, symbolised by the absence of the erect phallic image of the 'minaret' and by the coterminous social 'growth' of the island, represents a *temporal* transition from 'colonial' to 'postcolonial' which the accounts of an in-between 'slope' and a suburban 'airport' signify as *spatial*. Both Vassilia and Ayios D(h)ometios were 'mixed' villages—and the latter, coincidentally, has become of the seven checkpoints between the partitioned north and south since 2003. Specifically, Baybars chooses to use the Greek name of the village to identify his home while Montis draws on the name of a Persian saint uncommon to Orthodox worship. These shifts in nomenclature, alongside motifs of interstitiality, complicate the political identity movements *growing* multifariously during this period. The first-person of both texts exists between the individual and collective, and, while explicitly associated with imagined concepts of Turkey/Islam or Greece/Orthodoxy, it tacitly resists categorisation.

Repeatedly, Montis' narrator parenthetically stresses that '(I'm only speaking about Nicosia of course)',[40] and, while overwhelmingly sympathetic of EOKA, he is never actively absorbed by the organisation as a fighter—like Montis himself. The emphasis on the parochial repudiates an attempt to become—or, to be instrumentalised as—a representative of all (Greek-speaking) Cypriots, avowing a limited, localised perspective on the fringes of a paramilitary group, at the gateway, or 'suburb', of a specific city. It is a consciously *decentred* subjectivity in a colonised periphery.

This sense of existential *inbetweenness* is reflected in the related generic styles of both works, synthesising the travelogue with the semi-fictional *bildungsroman*. Notably, as composers of prose and verse, the authors' texts are structured by short sections or vignettes—described as 'Images' by Baybars and 'chapters' by Montis—which function as prose poetry.[41] By intermixing oral poetic expression with written European prose traditions, the texts, following Franco Moretti's theory, coalesce 'foreign form, local material – *and local form*', assimilating the written with 'local *narrative voice*'.[42] This *shared* composite genre stages an embodied integration of cultural modes—oral and print—within anti-colonial textual corpuses mimicking the transformational body of Hasanpouli. These works perform what Said describes as a 'conscious effort to enter into the discourse of Europe and the West, to mix with it, transform it, make it acknowledge marginalized or suppressed or forgotten histories',[43] including the history of the recent past. Within this, their distinctly postmodern use of translingualism, intertextuality, unreliable narrators, and moments of temporal and spatial discontinuity, all unravel the unities of action, time, and place expected of the 'Western' travelogue—*and* the Aristotelian unities of Classical Greek drama.

One vignette near the end of *Plucked in a Far-Off Land*, entitled 'Reflections on images', performs self-reflexive theorising of writing practices between more conventional 'images' of Cypriot life. Questioning his own reliability, the narrator reveals that, 'In my memory… images are all fused into one year… memorable through various smells [recalled…] in the London summer… and within a few seconds [I] let the computation of memory sort out, classify and bring back those small moments which I cannot recapture in verse or prose'.[44] The account, with its ruptures in time and space between colonial centre and periphery, alongside representations of synaesthesia, emphasises the ineffability of individual experience which evades confinement by either 'verse or prose'. It metatextually highlights the importance of the work's composite form, itself between centre and periphery, which expresses subjectivity through a narrative transcending, by combining, 'verse [and] prose'. The scientific images of 'computation' and classification are implicitly contrasted with more naturalistic modes of self-expression. It consequently dismantles the stability of generic demarcations from within, during a time when the borders between linguistic and discursive identities were strengthening on the island.

Elsewhere, reality and fiction merge through representations of dream sequences. In one, the narrator suggests that 'my dreams became a coagulation of nightly fear and daily joy… Poppies. Bees. A honeycomb for breakfast. But it was still March… and to a child a day is long'.[45] Indicative of the text's disjointed, poetically-inflected discourse, the description sutures times, emotions, and dreams through a textual melange framed by motifs of paradox and liminality. Earlier in the same 'image', the narrator's closest friend, Ibrahim, whose development as a visual artist parallels the quasi-*künstlerroman* of the writer, is depicted drawing 'marvellous scenes of our mosque, always adding a minaret it'. Meanwhile, the narrator's mother recites a story: 'the image of a newly married couple [from] A village in Anatolia'.[46] The narrator, however, pays more attention to the picture than the story. Here, forms of artistic production are compared, and the addition of the fictive (the unreal minaret) to the actual (the mosque) demonstrates the imbrication of the real and imagined within modes of self-representation. Importantly, the juxtaposition of the illustration of their ('our') Cypriot village with a discursive 'image' of a 'village in Anatolia', alongside the religious symbolism of the mosque, introduces the concept that 'image[s]'—metatextually including Baybars'—of national, cultural, and religious signifiers are frequently unreliable: the *imaginary homeland* of the 'Anatolia' constructed through narrative has its fictionality explicitly rendered, and 'image[s]' of the two 'village[s]' exist incongruously as the products of artistic desire rather than fact.

Emblematic of the text as a whole, the scene reduces the authority of both the Anglophone written form *and* the symbols, visual and textual, of religious and national belonging employed by some Turkish-speaking Cypriots. Even the narrator's 'image' of his 'village' is rendered suspect by association, critiquing the credibility of all representations of self and place. Nonetheless, influenced by Ibrahim, the narrator goes on to 'draw something with [crayons]: the carob tree, the tangerine-covered table and the hurricane lamps'.[47] In parallel with the text's opening paragraphs—'this gigantic carob tree opposite the mosque. Two hurricane lamps… a tangerine'[48]—both creative acts privilege the mundane, familiar, and local. The products of both Baybars-the-author and Baybars-the-character-within-the-text overcome an identification with the global or pan-national, unlike colonial travellers and nationalistic propaganda, whereby only the immediacy of selfhood in relation to native land is treated with any authenticity.

Describing the illiterate all-women audience listening to his mother's Turkish recitation, the narrator claims 'it must have sounded real, although they could themselves tell much more interesting tales than those printed in books [through] the magic of the printed word'.[49] In this *mise en abyme*, the verisimilitude of writing is undermined and the ostensible 'magic' properties of modern publishing industries reduced. Not only is the apparent superiority of the written over the oral diminished, but the life stories of impoverished, uneducated Cypriot women—a subaltern group without voice in dominant discourses—is elevated to greater importance than print narratives. The account challenges the limited 'real[ism]' of colonial reports of orature—the Cypriot women gossips in Scott-Stevenson's and Smith's travelogues or, according to Durrell, the 'oral tradition and common gossip' of 'communities which do not read'[50]—while also privileging the local over the pan-national (and even religious). The 'magic of the printed' colonial book, religious text, and nationalist pamphlet are all repudiated in a narrative which consciously complicates conventions of printed prose literature. To complicate Moretti's triangular formulation, Baybars mediates between the *foreign* forms of Britain *and* Turkey and the *local* materials of Cypriot oral narratives. This is achieved by his destabilising definitions of the foreign: not only does he render the otherness of Turkish cultures and places, but the gendered divisions of story-telling in this scene reveals layers of esotericism inherent in the production of cultural self-representation.

Comparable postmodern devices appear in *Closed Doors*, signposted early in Montis' defence of style in his preface, 'An Explanation'. In allusion to contemporary conflict, Montis reveals that '[a] life of trials, worries, and disappointments shattered my sense of continuity', resulting in an 'elliptical poetry, which shared its chats with silence', 'half-finished stories, sketches', and 'fragmented thoughts' with 'many parentheses... doubts... and the lacunae that are not explained'.[51] Justifying the narrative's form as the product of its environment, its discontinuities are metonymic of the sporadic violence of post/colonial Cyprus, through which, in Derridean terms, 'the limits, the borders, and the distinctions have been shaken by an earthquake from which no classificational concept... can be sheltered. Order is no longer assured'.[52] In a text representing the violence of colonial and anti-colonial bodies, the writing itself performs a parallel iconoclasm against the corporeal structure of the written form.

For Montis, the de-ordering of fiction echoes the destruction of civil order which EOKA performs against the colonial cityscape. By emphasising how 'the Revolution came to take control and concentrate my fragmented thoughts',[53] he envisions the re-ordering of disparate pieces of text as a political act against the *status quo*. Elsewhere, the narrator stresses the unreliability of the work through second-person parentheses directly addressing the reader: '(do you expect now an inconsistency in each phrase? very well, then, expect an inconsistency)'.[54] Equally, approaching the conclusion, the narrator suggests that '[t]he chapters have become smaller… and ruin and betray your plan for the book', doubting whether 'I have set everything in the right chronological order… I must also have left many things out of my account… I cannot promise to fill these lacunae'.[55] Breaking the distinction between writer and reader, the aporia reduces the authority of the narrative while celebrating the destruction of the 'order' and 'plan' expected of the prose form by readers. Similarly, in the preface, Montis asserts that, regarding the theme of *Closed Doors*, 'the subject must be dealt with at some length… some means must be found… no longer merely… utilizing the same white paper and pencil'. Explicitly aiming to respond, with urgency, to colonial misrepresentations of the island by adding testimony to imperial violence, the 'means' he employs is one which explicitly revises Durrell's work while challenging the form he, Durrell, uses. The colonial page, 'white' in both its textual and racial connotations, is being abandoned in favour of new textualities.

As will be demonstrated later, the Greek language and symbols of Greek nationalism predominate as the chosen tactic in responding to the hegemony of English discourse and British rule. Nonetheless, moments of doubt towards the textualities of nationalism, including the narrator's repudiation of 'comparisons or analogies'—themselves figures of speech—with the Greek War of Independence, suggest how disavowing 'the same white paper and pencil', through a disjointed and 'fragmented' form, facilitates a dual unpacking of colonial *and* nationalist textualities.

Crucially, both Baybars and Montis re-iterate the discourse of travel writing as means of restructuring the genre and their relationships with it. When the former's narrator first approaches the neighbouring village of Değirmenlik, he observes how, in contrast with Vassilia, '[t]he whole village seemed years ahead', home to the 'smell of petrol, alien… Pressure-lamps ready to be lit. Bicycles everywhere' (in opposition with the aforementioned hurricane lamps of his home).[56] The account presents a reverse migration from economic margins to centre, in which, unlike Tayeb Salih's novel on migrating from Sudan to Britain, *both* poles are situated as proximal Cypriot villages, rather than international dimorphs. Within this inversion, 'Western' cultural paraphernalia is, for an Anglophone reader, estranged and exoticised as 'alien' commodities perused by the colonised 'native'. Nicosia, framed from the perspective of Vassilia, becomes 'that distant city' of 'unthinkable distance', through binary oppositions between his 'cool' village and the 'sweltering noons of Nicosia… holiday[s]'.[57] The city is a quasi-fantastic site of the imagination encountered through migrations which usurp those from the 'cool' UK to the 'heat' of the Mediterranean and which, in turn, trivialises Baybars' emigration from Cyprus to a Britain which remains unrepresented. Stylistically, it echoes V.S. Naipaul's *Miguel Street* (1959) in which the author-narrator gestures to migration to Britain at the end of the text without fully describing it.

Comparatively, Montis not only depicts Nicosia as a re-inhabited space, but breaks from the continuity of the narrative on Cyprus to describe his real journey to Ireland as a brief frame-narrative counter-travelogue. This chapter—the one which consciously 'ruin[s] and betray[s] your plan for the book'—defamiliarises the genre. Juxtaposing his movement outward with the movement of an Irish soldier, Daniel, to the island, Montis' narrator uses the parallelism to suggest similarities in Cypriot and Irish anti-colonial histories, alleging that 'I live your struggle just as intensely as I live ours', aligning the alliterative names of Kyrenia and Killiney, and quoting the proclamation of Easter Monday 1916 as he had the EOKA Oath earlier.[58] Exoticising the Irish landscape while autoexoticising his own otherness in Northern Europe, he describes lakes that 'surely are not part of this world' which 'observe the foreign visitors (even from Cyprus, imagine that)',[59] thereby redefining the expectations of global travel from south to north. In particular, however, these comparisons are appropriated in order to show confusion towards Daniel's participation in the British army; he asks the dead soldier personally, 'how could you have come to kill us?'.[60] As well as commentary against British military conscripts, one which nonetheless sympathises with the economic incentives of the position, the alliterative similarities—like those of the aforementioned town names—suggest that the figure of Daniel is a sublimated form of Durrell himself. Durrell, who was of partial Irish ancestry, has his participation in the colonial project questioned, equating the ostensible epistemic violence of his works with the actual violence of the

British military. By engaging with motifs of travel, Montis' text contests the political affiliations of the literary form and, like Baybars, does so by re-defining the geographic dichotomy of centre and periphery which defines it.

Writing-Back to the British Colonial Book

The two narratives write-back to colonial literary representations of the island by offering 'counter-discursive strategies to the dominant discourse',[61] in order 'to provid[e] a voice to previously silenced individuals'.[62] In many ways, they offer a resistance to the colonial 'quest voyage motif' which parallels Said's reading of Tayeb Salih's near-contemporaneous *The Season of Migration to the North*: 'Conrad's first-person British narrative style and European protagonists are in a sense reversed, first through the use of Arabic; second in that Salih's novel concerns the northward voyage… to Europe; and third, because the narrator speaks from a Sudanese village'.[63]

Montis explicitly positions his text, *An Answer to* Bitter Lemons *by Lawrence Durrell*, as an intertextual response to the thematic, as well as structural, conceits of the earlier travelogue. Throughout *Bitter Lemons*, images of doors recur as signifiers of colonial division. For Durrell, discussions on independence 'constituted a firmly closed door – closed as irrevocably as the Cyprus question was in the minds of our mandarins in London – and only to be abruptly opened by the crash of dynamite'.[64] Drawing on this metaphor throughout his work, Montis portrays the advent of EOKA's anti-colonial violence as the *dynamite* deconstructing, in this revisionist history, the 'doors of the [concentration] camps' at Kokkinotrimithia, Mammari, and Pyla.[65] If, as Calotychos identifies of Durrell's literary output, the colonial writer 'does not mention the armed struggle being waged… and the torture chambers' used by the British military,[66] then Montis' text seeks to expose and fill these lacunae in contemporary historiography: the 'helmets, shields, clubs, tear gas' placed at odds with mythicised, exoticised images of the island as a tourist destination.[67] In doing so, the text uses personal testimony to revise the events of Durrell's narrative. Both commence their accounts of the 'emergency' with the same event—the seizing of the *Saint George* caique delivering contraband weaponry—but from opposing ideological and stylistic perspectives. For Durrell, it is a source of 'human comedy', derived from the involved Cypriots' attempts at learning the colonial language from 'an English grammar'[68]; for Montis, composing in Greek, the caique emblematises the beginning of a *tragedy* in which violence is a dual source of death and hope, and the destructive weaponry 'moored itself in our thoughts' as the promise of decolonisation.[69]

While *Plucked in a Far-Off Land* does not explicitly represent the conflict of this period, it nonetheless exposes the oppression of the colonialist-capitalist nexus by revising the tropes of British travel writing. Notably, throughout Baybars' oeuvre, solar imagery is employed to figure impending imperial decline, reimagining the emblems of the Empire's red map over which 'the sun never sets'. *Bitter Lemons*, for instance, commences at 'dawn' on a ship travelling to Cyprus,[70] while Mallock similarly describes how 'London… had had brighter sunshine than usual, and… the evening skies flushed redder' in anticipation of his voyage to a Levantine sky where '[b]ars of crimson and purple were brightening over unseen Palestine'.[71] Baybars' narrative, commenced on land and at sunset, vividly inverts the spatial and temporal positioning of colonial literatures on Cyprus, including Durrell's dawn motif. Early in the text, the narrator observes how 'the sun vanished. I rushed out to the mosque yard and from under the carob tree I could see… the sun prematurely set… shooting lights as fire after fire was lit… Whether we believed it or not the sun was still shining on the other side of the Five Fingers [Kyrenia mountain range]… My wish was to… see what it looked like on the other side'.[72] Drawing on the primacy of land expressed both here and in *Closed Doors*, the narrator offers the nuanced perspective of a Turkish-speaking, Muslim colonised subject—he who views the world from 'the mosque yard' near his home—observing the last moments of the imperial sun as it figuratively 'set[s]' on the island. The suggestion, however, that the sun continues to shine in refracted, insidious ways foreshadows the neo-colonial legacies of imperialism addressed subsequently. The oppressive politics of the colonial administration are reformed as the politics of nationalist organisations constructing new sources of violent light—the 'fire[s]' after sunset—which divide the island into 'other side[s]' marshalled into sects. Like Montis' text, where the hopeful promise of independence is tempered by a history of recent warfare, the optimism of Baybars' 'vanished' sun is offset by its reiterations in the independent Cypriot state. Despite this, his narrator attempts to see Cyprus from more than one 'side', offering a metaphor of his resistance against both the divisiveness of imperialism and the anti-imperial nationalisms it inspired.

Within their counter-travelogues of the island, both narratives are set in locations frequented by Durrell, revising the colonialist's ethnological survey of the north-eastern region. Each describes childhood or ancestral movements from the rural villages near Kyrenia to the (sub)urban spaces of Nicosia, employing themes of landlessness to re-view the unequal movements of post/colonial travel. Montis' text, although set almost entirely in the latter, nonetheless offers an external analepsis to earlier moments across Lapithos, one of the sites of Durrell's journey. Of 'the village of my father's youth', the narrator recalls from his own 'memories' that Lapithos is 'a place half-sea and half-mountain, with one foot in the sand… and the other in the water mills of Kephalovriso where the Nereids still dwell'.[73] Recounting a familial migration from rural to urban, the text recalibrates the axis of centre and periphery to, not only re-centre Cyprus in this narrative, but to deconstruct the binary by excluding the British metropole as an arbiter of geographic reference. The imagery associates the land with liminality, a place of 'half'-ness, *through* which an imaginary homeland of purely-Greek identification is constructed: his paternal village is defined by the Classical Greek literary heritage denoted by 'Nereids'. In the present, however, Lapithos becomes the site where 'five villagers had been buried alive in the sand during interrogation' and is thus a place symbolic of both pre-colonial and anti-colonial histories, now re-written onto the pastoral, idyllic village of Durrell's account. Antithetical to Durrell's idealism, *land* in Montis' text is not only denied to Cypriots politically but is physically employed against them: the 'sand' of the narrator's ancestral home suffocates interned EOKA fights.

While the reason for his father's displacement remains obscure, the first chapter stresses that in their new suburban home near the (now-defunct) airport, 'we just managed to make ends meet… in a time of uncontrolled escalation in rents, especially in our suburb that had experienced the greatest influx of English families'.[74] The representation of 'Western'-controlled capitalism on the island indicates, in Young's words, 'the closure of land and the resulting enforced movement of its inhabitants to the only available… work in the cities'.[75] This is before both Montis' and Baybars' emigrations and the displacement of Cypriot refugees commencing in the year of the former's publication (1963/1964). The juxtaposition between the transcontinental movement of 'English families' facilitated by the airport and the dislocation of impoverished Cypriots reveals the economic inequalities of a globalised world.

An 'influx' of British travellers, colonial personnel, and expatriates is marked in opposition with a corresponding efflux of Cypriots themselves.

In the text, adolescent maturation is used to embody the colony's social, economic, and literary development—the fifteen-year-old narrator's symbolic 'deepening of the voice' is placed in parallel with 'the city's sudden growth', 'rapid expansion', and 'escalation in rents'. This personal development, however, is always stunted in a colonial system preventing social progress. Childhood is rarely completed. The ending, despite depicting scenes of jubilation at the promise of impending independence, is marred by the sanctioned killing of Nikos, the narrator's guerrilla brother, and the implied deaths of his father and sister, Stalo. In reference to his mother's mourning, the narrator pleads with the reader, 'don't tell her I will not return, don't let her know I am gone as well. Don't let her grope at my books'.[76] The anaphoric statements allude to Montis' (temporary) exile from the island, based on his real emigration following his brother's and father's deaths, demonstrating how pedagogy—and the cultural and economic capital it facilitates—is firmly located outside the island. Despite the re-centring of Cyprus by the narrative, it remains a margin in the field of global capital. His 'books' can only be produced through displacement from the land, a figurative demise paralleled with the actual deaths caused during the 'emergency'. A reclaiming of the land which anti-colonial politics aspires towards, and which independence promises, is unfulfilled in a population beleaguered with premature deaths and emigrations.

Indeed, throughout the text, the narrator utilises motifs of childhood to emblematise this unrealised growth. For him, 'all of the Greeks were just like children' under the pseudo-paternalism of an empire whose literature routinely infantilised its subjects,[77] and yet it is the actual youth of Cyprus who form the core of the anti-colonial resistance. This, however, leads to a perverse progression towards 'militant maturity' in which individuals are 'cut off from parents, siblings, friends, in short, from the entire world of normal childhood'.[78] As the ending infers, the narrator is 'cut off', not only from his family, but from the island itself. Unlike colonial discourses which present degeneration and docility as essential characteristics of Cypriots, Montis frames social stagnation as a condition of colonial rule which can only be countered by exile—a lone displacement from native land in opposition with the socio-economically privileged movements of colonial British writers and their intact 'families'.

Baybars' narrative uses comparable motifs of land and landlessness in a text set similarly in Nicosia and the Kyrenia villages of Lapithos, Değirmenlik (the Turkish name of the village near the Kephalovriso area described by Montis), and Vassilia. Its numerous journeys across the island revisit the spaces of Durrell's travelogue, culminating in an allusion to viewing 'the house on top of a hill which father told us was occupied by a very unusual Englishman'.[79] The account which marginalises the identity of the figure—as indeed are the identities of 'Englishm[e]n' throughout this text and that of Montis[80]—reduces Durrell to a spectre of 'unusual' exoticism and otherness. The verb 'occupied', given its militaristic connotations, presents the colonial writer's presence as a political invasion of native land.

In opposition to the Englishman's autonomous 'hill', the site of Baybars' earliest 'images', Vassilia, is described as a liminal space 'between the hills and the sea',[81] echoing the 'half-sea and half-mountain' of Montis' ancestral Lapithos. The opening words of the text, introducing Vassilia through the interstitiality of '[a]n early spring evening', identifies the narrator with a setting defined as both temporally and spatially in-between: a 'mixed village'[82] with a Greek name, prominent mosque, recounted during the waning twilight of the British Empire. Moreover, the name of the village, meaning ***kingdom***, re-centres these colonised margins as the core of an Anglophone text usurping the metropole of the UK from which most colonial writers commence their travelogues. A Cypriot writer looks out from the land to the shore, rather than a British writer observing the land while docking at a port. His description of 'Our house… on a slope' reclaims the *Our Home in Cyprus* of Scott-Stevenson's narrative, also located in the Kyrenia mountain range. Accounts of Cypriot women's intellectual spaces—his home becomes the space where his former-'schoolmistress' mother 'read ten or twenty pages of a book' to other Turkish-speaking women every evening[83]—challenge both the racist-misogynistic assumptions of Scott-Stevenson's work and the objectifying images of harems in Orientalist narratives as a whole.

Cyprus is here presented as a place of self-generating progress; both parents read and teach, and his polylingual father frequents the village coffeehouse which 'couldn't afford a wireless' to read-aloud print news (English, Greek, and Turkish) as '[a]lmost all of them [the patrons] couldn't read'. In a globalised world where rural colonised subjects are denied the privileges of the 'wireless' as a symbol of transcontinental interchange—ironically Cyprus has been home to the British East

Mediterranean Relay Station since 1957—local orality provides cultural and educational capital instead. Notably, the early descriptions of '[m]y father, the schoolmaster' whose classroom was connected to their living quarters through 'a communicating door'[84] present a figure who usurps the authority of Durrell, the Greek-speaking colonial schoolteacher. In this writing-back, an educated, Turkish-speaking Cypriot is the individual controlling pedagogy, rather than the pseudo-paternal imperial system. Their liminal home allows for the easy transfusion of the educational into the domestic through a porous 'communicating door' in contrast with the *closed doors* of imperialism which Montis seeks to challenge in similar ways. Likewise, the father in Montis' text, described as a model student in his youth, would translate and 'read [newspaper reports of the conflict] aloud at home so that we children could listen'.[85]

In *Plucked in a Far-Off Land*, as its intertextual title suggests, the *land* of colonised natives is de-marginalised and de-exoticised. In contrast with colonialist accounts of Cyprus as infertile, Vassilia, *away from the centre of colonial administration in cities*, becomes a place of productivity, replete with portrayals of agricultural fecundity. When the narrator depicts their 'enormous garden, trees, mainly olive, wild pears, cherries which never gave fruit… [a] gigantic carob tree',[86] it is not only a scene of fertility, but the non-native cherry is framed as the only source of sterility. As aforementioned, the narrator's first artistic product is a visual rendering of this carob tree, and his poetic juvenilia is concerned with representing nature. His summary of the 'satisfying world around me, food, tales, gardens and trees, Ibrahim's crayons'[87] constructs a habitus which correlates agricultural and artistic modes of production, forming a dialectic of native land and self-narration. Indeed, the '[s]mell of baking bread' pervades the text as a constant in his development as a writer.[88] As Adolfo Gilly affirms in his introduction to Fanon, '[t]he essence of revolution is not the struggle for bread; it is the struggle for human dignity. Certainly this includes bread [and other basic] economic conditions'.[89] Baybars' narrator stresses that during the Second World War, '[t]he only serious impact… was the rationing of flour… obliged by law'.[90] By altering familial recipes, it represents the symbolic violence enacted by British and global politics on the island's agri/cultural productivity.

However, much like the father in Montis' text, Baybars' narrator recounts how his family was forced to move between villages, before eventually settling in Nicosia, due the difficulties his father experienced in finding teaching work. Upon leaving Vassilia, Baybars' narrator describes feeling 'homeless' for the first time, his 'first intimation of impermanence',[91] in this *internal* economic migration preceding the author's eventual exile from the island. Emphasising how the decision had been made on his father's behalf by 'those people in Nicosia, my father's bosses',[92] the narrative frames these unwilling movements as the externally-generated actions of faceless people in metropolitan spaces: explicitly local administration in the capital, implicitly also political centres outside the island. Cypriots are presented with little control over their relationship with the land, despite the text's attempt to re-centre, not simply the island as a whole, but the rural *kingdom* of Baybars' childhood.

Regardless of the agricultural productivity of his village, artistic production can only be achieved through mediation with Britain. Topographic imagery is subsequently employed to articulate how, since he 'had been removed from Vassilia', he 'had suffered the shock of an uprooted plant'. He goes on to stress that 'my whole future was going to be a constant awareness of my roots' now 'planted out on the English soil, my name (as if it were *Turcofolia Cypriotii*) makes so many people think… I am hypothetical… Although I feel strong as a tree, I am looked upon as a *bonsai*'.[93] The diachronic connections between each movement—from Vassilia to Nicosia; from Cyprus to the UK—illustrate how forced movements between poles of centre and periphery define his lifelong relationship with identity and literature. The socio-economic problems of a youth spent in various colonial margins (rural/urban and colony/metropole) force the narrator-author to leave Cyprus in order to become an autonomous writer, resulting in an irreconcilable rupture from his 'roots', both physical and cultural. Like his father, he is compelled into exile to find work but, in this generation, growing economic and political pressures force him overseas. Unlike Durrell, finding a literary voice through travel is not a position achieved with much agency.

The Latin classification idiom reveals how, in a post-enlightenment London, his identity is commodified, exoticised, and diminished; it is reduced to the status of a distinctly non-European '*bonsai*'. As with the aforementioned tension between scientific and phenomenological registers, the narrator stresses the limitations of metropolitan discourses when codifying human experience. Not only are people dehumanised by a discursive system craving taxonomic order, but he is personally confined by markers of otherness as a colonial migrant. Regardless of attempts to naturalise—to use a term appropriate for horticulture, linguistic culture, and peoples—he is always defined as alien and Other. Despite how he defines himself (a 'strong… tree'), he cannot escape how others categorise him.

Moreover, the metatextual commentary on writing practices in the colonial metropole reveals a ubiquitous concern with 'roots'. His literature, including this very text, is relentlessly preoccupied with reclaiming the connection with the eponymous *Land* he has lost. He exemplifies 'the issue of home, belonging, and identity' which Avtar Brah notes as the central concern of diaspora literatures, offering not simply an imaginary *homeland* but an imagining of a specific *home* of the past: 'an image of "home" as the site of everyday lived experience… a discourse of locality… rootedness… [and] the mundane'.[94] More than this, however, is his awareness that as an *exoticised* writer living in London, he is compelled to author works which conform to publishing industries' expectations of his producing *exoticist* texts. He is always defined as one from a *Far-Off Land* and it is to this context which his work is concentrically compelled to return. Nonetheless, by drawing on what Brah calls 'the mundane', Baybars attempts to reroute these institutional pressure from the inside. By re-imagining a 'mundane' version of his home, he de-exoticises the conventions of travel writing while also allowing him a cathartic return to his birthplace through an act of literary homecoming. He redefines 'home' in a work first published in London in which 'home', for him, is the uninteresting, ordinary, and 'mundane' place under a carob tree and minaret. He destabilises what is, and is not, foreign, homely, or exotic. As he is transported into London, like an adorned bonsai paraded at The Great Exhibition, so too he *transports* the spatial and literary frames expected of Anglophone literatures. It almost goes without saying that these references to grafted roots are conscious allusions to the hybridising cultural practices feared by colonialist and nationalist purists alike.

Languages as/and Cutting Instruments

Echoing Montis' narrator being 'cut off' from family and home, Baybars' narrative employs the theme of *cutting* which recurs throughout. It also mirrors the cutting of 'an uprooted plant', or, the 'flower of chance, the quixotic irrational love of England' in Durrell's travelogue.[95] Baybars' final paragraph, which references his composing poetry abroad in 1963, describes the cutting involved in his circumcision—a symbol of culturally-defined maturation—reflecting on how, 'childhood is over. The paradise is lost', creating 'a certain dividing line in my life'.[96] Like Montis' text, youth is used to represent both personal and social (anti-)development, and cutting is employed to mark an abrupt end to 'childhood' as the post-lapsarian loss of 'innocence' in the face of conflict and migration. If, as Calotychos suggests, Durrell 'portrays the pre-EOKA days as edenic',[97] then Baybars re-iterates this topos to stress the idealism of an era, if not pre-colonial, then less-mediated by imperialist and capitalist interventions. The emphasis on the year of poetry composition indicates that colonialism not only *cuts* Baybars off from his native home but is complicit in the construction of lacerations across Cypriot communities, including the 'dividing line' emerging between Greek-speaking and Turkish-speaking residents in 1963/1964.

Earlier, he refers to his dual identity between multiple nexuses of centre and periphery—Vassilia/Nicosia, Cyprus/Britain, English/Turkish—as the 'duplicity' of one 'transMutated' and 'translocated'.[98] His 'urge to return, to migrate'—explicitly to Vassilia in the narrative, implicitly also to Cyprus itself as a denaturalised adult—'was not to be fulfilled'.[99] Notably, Baybars' descriptions of unwilling *transmutation* appear in the same 'image' in which he first learns English. The language produces a 'duplicity' in his cultural life: on the one hand, it is the medium through which he composes his (anti-colonial, anti-nationalist) works, and yet, on the other, its elevation in the globalised post/colony creates ruptures both between colonial and 'native' cultures, and Turkish-speaking and Greek-speaking Cypriots who learn English more readily than the island's pre-colonial vernaculars. The narrator, for instance, describes his experience of 'English words gradually *cutting* into my tongue' at school, as a form of epistemic violence *cutting* him off from his "native" Kıbrıslıca and/or Turkish, before depicting Hollywood cinematic imports as 'American heavies… with the[ir] ugly charm… mov[ing] across the white screen like a pair of *scissors*' (*emphases mine*).[100] Comparable with 'the same white paper and pencil' Montis attempts to reject, English, British, and American cultural imperialisms are framed as dominant discourses which perform irreparable divisions in the identities and cultures of the post/colonial world. Similarly, he alludes elsewhere to the 'teeth of modernism' as a symbol of the striations caused by westernisation and global capitalist consumption.[101]

Although a common trope of 'postcolonial' literatures, Baybars' narrative extends it further to demonstrate its specific impact on the already-polyglot island. Learning English, elevated for its exotic appeal as a foreign, global language, is 'a new wonderful experience, more so than learning Greek words because I had not seen a Greek textbook, had only heard and spoken the few odd words'.[102] Recounted in the same 'image' as his description of English 'cutting into my [mother-]tongue', the proximity suggests that the dominance of the language in colonial education policy, whereby English books replace 'Greek textbook[s]' as 'second language' texts, facilitates the social division of Cypriots. Unlike his father, uncles, and their friends who are frequently depicted as speakers of both Turkish and Greek (as will addressed later in the chapter), Baybars' generation, on the receiving end of colonial pedagogical reforms and American commodity excess, are increasingly *cut off* from one another—if not by migration then by linguistic division—resulting in a loss of the 'paradise' of the symbolically pre-colonial as a time of greater pan-Cypriot unity.

Ironically, however, it is only *through* English that a Cypriot narration can disseminate across all socio-linguistic communities due to the preponderance of English-speakers on the island. As Jamaica Kincaid asserts in her counter-travelogue of the postcolonial island of Antigua, 'the only language that I have in which to speak of this crime [of imperialism] is the language of the criminal who committed the crime'.[103] Following the description of his severed 'roots', Baybars' relocation to a xenophobic London is part of a series of coerced travels, literary practices, and social identifications over which he has limited control. Nonetheless, he is forced to choose between this experience as an Anglophone writer *cut-off* from other Cypriots and that of remaining in a linguistically-divided island in which Greek- and Turkish-speakers lack common literary ground, even before the formal partition of 1974. In both paradigms, the English language is partially culpable—especially with his taxonomic divisions of peoples into pseudoscientific categories—but it is also a hypothetical cultural mediator, as will be shown. He gestures to alternate ways of consuming culture, counter to the imperialist-capitalist 'teeth of modernism' introduced by British and American hegemons.

In less coded terms, Montis' narrative similarly assigns blame to colonialism for trans-communal strife. The narrator, for instance, argues that 'the English… created a force of local Turks called the "auxiliary police," whom they incited with fears… to manufacture such feelings' of separateness, before asking, 'hadn't they done so in similar circumstances in India and other places in their empire?'.[104] Later described as 'the game of divide and rule',[105] the reflection on colonial policy posits a relationship with other contexts across the British Empire, including the partitioned Indian subcontinent, as a trans-colonial issue. Like the account of Ireland, sympathetic intersections of literary anti-colonialism are sought, while simultaneously framing social division as an import from outside the island, rather than an essence of indigenous cultural identities. The use of the terms 'created', 'incited', and 'manufacture' depicts these antagonisms as artificial products of political manipulation and coercion. This representation, therefore, infers parallels between colonialism and sectarian fanaticism as externally-generated constructs.

Indeed, the narrative participates in a reaction against the ostensible discursivity of colonial warfare throughout. In *Bitter Lemons*, acts of literary production and of violent destruction are frequently compared. After quoting the EOKA Oath, Durrell metaphorically describes how nights were 'punctuated by… grenades' as part 'the tragicomic landscape of the Near East'.[106] In opposition to 'a series of attacks by Athens radio', Sir John Martin 'was armed… with a copy of the *Iliad*'.[107] Analogous to his own anti-colonial testimony, Montis' narrator similarly textualises the conflict by suggesting that Cypriot guerrillas 'had to rise up and face their special end… to write their own story very real on the rock'.[108] Like the project of a realist writing-back to colonial literatures, violence is depicted as a reinscriptive process which alters the physical landscape of the island—its foundational '[bed]rock'—and challenges the perceived inauthenticity, and '[un]real[ness]', of colonial literary and political discourses. Earlier, violence is presented in both its actual and imaginative capacity as EOKA's first shipment of weaponry on the island is conceived of as a source of public morale: 'Arms?… What was this word that echoed (exploded really) upon our slumbering servitude…?'.[109] Arms are held in the same hands as writing instruments. Here, the anticipation of violence has as great an impact on the imagination and discourse as it does on the political structures of imperialism; the very 'word… exploded' *before* the actual weapons.

Moreover, in conjunction with the dissemination of EOKA pamphlets, the narrator describes how '[t]here was also a war against the English language – against English road signs… The war was to completely eliminate their language from our lives'.[110] Demonstrating the epistemic dimensions of warfare, he is invested in a campaign to target the cultural imports of the empire, beginning with an iconoclastic destruction of Anglophone edifices, physical and symbolic, across the island. Supplemented by boycotts against British goods, demanding '"Nothing English"… in that… Cypriot voice', the narrator substitutes British textiles for 'native' 'alajia'.[111] This is a reaction against textual Englishness in which the textualities of fabric and paper are implicitly analogised. Crucially, the anti-colonial avowal—in a rare moment of departure from images of reactionary Greek nationalism—is a pre-colonial *and* pre-nationalist 'Cypriot voice', mimetically represented by 'alajia', a Cypriot word of Turkish etymology (*alaca*) denoting a local, pan-Cypriot material based on Syrian designs. Indeed, the consonant *j/tz* is markedly uncommon (if not absent) in Standard Modern Greek. A pan-Cypriot mode of textuality as a marker of the local, the non-standardised, and the oral assumes the forefront of anti-colonial resistance, rather than the discourses of Greece (or Turkey). The metropole is challenged by that which is doubly marginal—or, subaltern—in both the colonialist paradigms of Britain/Cyprus and Greece-Turkey/Cyprus.

This resistance to English, which echoes Baybars' depiction of the language as a *cutting* instrument, is metatextually manifested through acts of counter-consumption and -production. The father's translations of English newspapers, like those of Baybars' father character, accommodate 'new ways of seeing', while the radio (featuring transmissions from Britain, Cyprus, and Greece), in opposition to Durrell's fear of the device, is described as a beacon that the family 'laid siege to'.[112] Furthermore, the heteroglossic narrative imbricates English words to present the otherness of both their cultural signification and Latin form in a Hellenophone work. He states, in one chapter, '*curfews* (I use the English word because it is weighed down in such pain… [without] equivalent… in Greek.)', after having repudiated '[e]xpressions from a foggy northern country, political spin with no relation to our lives'.[113] Unlike Baybars' choice of linguistic form, Montis' work rejects the language as politically, culturally, and geographically Other, viewing it as insidiously harbouring an essential violence which cannot be translated into another language. An act of resistance to British imperialism, for Montis and his narrator, involves the need to actively re-read and re-write its dominant discourses. The latter, understood as inherently engaged in the 'political spin' and violence of the empire it represents, can only be countered by an expulsion of the English language itself from Cyprus and its 'postcolonial' literary endeavours.

Despite the reference to *alajia*, a single, pan-Cypriot vernacular does not exist to replace English, accounting for Baybars' reluctant use of the Anglophone form to challenge the *divide and rule* associated with British epistemic violence. While Montis' work is invested in repealing colonialism, it does not address, as fully, the *linguistic* divisions of anti-colonial nationalisms which his text, nonetheless, posits as the very product of imperial machination. The word *alajia* appears fleetingly; it never returns in the text and the narrator never explicitly explains its Turkish etymology or its symbolic potential as an emblem of translingual cultural unity. Ultimately, while the word foreignises his Greek corpus for readers in Greece, illustrating Cyprus' cultural specificity, the work as a whole (first published in Athens, and not translated until the following century) cannot be read in the original by the overwhelming majority of Turkish-speaking Cypriots. It is this literary divisiveness that Baybars wishes to overcome. He simultaneously laments and welcomes English as creating borders *and* bridges between the Greek and Turkish languages on the island. For Montis, the borders—or, *closed doors*—imposed by English need to be destroyed at all costs, leaving, in their wake, the potential absence of a linguistic bridge between Greek- and Turkish-speakers. Baybars seeks to open these Anglophone doors rather than remove their frame(work)s completely.

Writing-Back to Nationalisms

Elaborating on these imbrications between British imperialism and 'post-colonial' nationalisms, the two narratives consider the complex relationship national identities have with literature, history, and anti-colonial politics. *Plucked in a Far-Off Land*, like much of Baybars' works, mounts a comprehensive resistance to all nationalisms, possibly with more vehemence than his contestations against British rule. On the other hand, *Closed Doors* offers a more ambivalent stance which gradually develops from appropriating Greek symbols as part of an essentialist identity in opposition with British colonialism, at the beginning of the text, to a greater consideration of a uniquely Cypriot—albeit, perhaps, a specifically *Greek-speaking* Cypriot—historical consciousness by the end.

In 1998, Baybars discussed his sense of internal conflict living 'under the nationalist oppression on a small island. Poets are always forced to accept prevailing ethics and social roles to become a part of the collective national struggle of a minority community'.[114] Accounting for both his migration away from the 'small island' and his use of English as a non-'national' literary language, his resulting oeuvre puts pressure on the restrictive discourses of nationalist identification through specific, self-reflexive commentaries on his relationship with Turkey and its standardised language. He chooses this approach rather than critiquing the so-called Cypriot 'Other' (Greek-speakers and/or Greek nationalists). For the writer, anti-nationalism begins with an evaluation of the self and one's own cultural identifications and biases.

This is evident across his published poetry collections. In 'Letter to Homeland', a poetic correspondence from London to his father, the first-person speaker describes himself as one with an 'alien past', alleging that 'I've never had a home', before and after his exile from the island.[115] He is both homeless as a colonial immigrant, and devoid of historical continuity as the native of a space without a straightforward pre-colonial past. Comparably, 'Summer Incident', one of the few third-person poems in the same anthology, describes a silent man found deserted on a beach. A crowd congregate asking, 'Who was this mysterious man?/Why did he never speak? Why the colour/of the cresset was white instead of red?/So they whipped him […] And his lips never told'.[116] The use of the symbolic colours, 'red' and 'white', demonstrates how the man espouses an identity which struggles to fit into established and expected categories but which tacitly associates itself with the whiteness of the newly-designed Cypriot flag, in contrast with the redness of the Turkish alternative. His political subversion leads to physical violence as well as an epistemic silencing. Withholding and self-censorship—which may include the disavowal of a linguistic form, and in Baybars' case, the Turkish language—are marked as modes of resistance. Yet, in this poem, he lacks the subjecthood to espouse the first-person mode. In 'Two Cases of Identity', which, as the title suggests, discusses a dual identification between Cyprus and Britain, the speaker infers that his identity has always been fragmented, ruptured, and unconventional, asking in one line, 'Why am I outcast? I'm myself as always been. It hurts'.[117] He is doubly an 'outcast' as an ethnic minority in 1960s London, and as a counter-nationalist writer from post-independence Cyprus. It is an alienness conveyed metonymically by his broken syntax which foreignises the Anglophone form and represents his repudiation against linguistic standardisation. Across these poems, the rhetorical questions suggest an ongoing interrogation of cultural identity which, nonetheless, evades simple solutions. He does, however, *transport* both discursive identities across various sites of belonging (metropolitan and marginal) and the semiotic systems (linguistic, vexillogical, corporeal) used to *convey* them. Doing so, Baybars' work offers one of the earliest literary traditions which engage with, and tacitly promote, notions of 'Cypriotism'. It is, however, a category in development, like the liminal progress of his adolescent prose narrator, without a fully-formed set of parameters.

In *Plucked in a Far-Off Land*, as well as demonstrating how the sectarian politics of the British Empire culminated in the neo-colonial construction of 'a certain dividing line' between Cypriots by 1963,[118] the text simultaneously reveals the complicity of nationalist cultural movements in this process, ones which the narrator, as a child poet, participates in. Crucially, the *bildungsroman* and *künstlerroman* elements of the text symbolise a progression from childhood affiliations with (Turkish) nationalism to an adult, post-nationalist worldview, and the impact of this paradigm shift on literary production. In one description of a Turkish National Day (either April 23 or May 19), the narrator publically recites Turkish poetry, verses from *National Poems for Turkish Children*, to mark the event at the behest of his cousin Hazim. He recalls how,

> father and mother… were both pleased and disturbed… I remember how my feelings towards the Greek and Armenian neighbour children suddenly changed as I rehearsed the poems standing on the window sill. I ceased to be a Cypriot. The language was the only tie between me and Turkey whose history I was learning as a matter of course. A record of a conquering past. […] such legends were constantly inoculated upon our minds, us children. It is not conjectural to add that similar stories were circulating among the Greeks but only on National Days would we feel that there was a ditch between the two communities. […] Uncle Hasan often told me to hear [the Armenian neighbour, Hamparsum] carefully so I could appreciate the beauty of our pure language. He [Hasan] didn't much care for the Turkish Cypriot dialect.[119]

The transportal limen of the 'window sill' from which he performs and the dialectical imbrication of past and present in nationalist discourse gesture to the inherent paradox of the nation state given its 'objective modernity' in antithesis with its 'subjective antiquity in the eyes of nationalists'.[120] It is here complicated further by an investment in the nascent Turkish nation through reference to an Ottoman past at odds with the contemporary, secular, post-imperial Republic, recounted here outside Turkey's territorial borders. As well as the 'disjunctive temporality of the nation', the account's emphasis on the relationship between historiographic education and public display realises Bhabha's theory of 'the contest of narrative authority between the pedagogical and the performative' within the dissemi*nation* of national identities.[121] It is through participation in nationalism and theories of 'pure'—in tacit opposition with pluralist—languages, histories, and identities that social divisions occur between Cypriot socio-linguistic groups. Indeed, the narrator stresses that it is 'only' during such performances of nationalism, such as this civic expression of literature and flags on a day honouring Turkish history, that ruptures emerge between Cypriots. As a consequence, he 'ceased to be a Cypriot', repudiating this intercommunal identification, viewing Greek- and Armenian-speakers through a xenophobic and elitist lens. Identity is here a conscious choice and, in the face of colonialist claims of Cypriot non-history, an interpellation into 'a conquering past' of an *established* nation—here Ottoman Turkey (perhaps itself an oxymoron), elsewhere Classical Greece or Greater Armenia—becomes the chosen tactic of existential resistance.

However, the account complicates this simple identification with an imagined Turkey, not least framed by his parents' ambivalent response, both 'pleased and disturbed', as members of a translingual generation raised before both Atatürk's birthing of the Turkish state and the conflicts of the 1950s and 1960s. His parents are not metonyms of the so-called mother-fatherland of Turkey.[122] Ironically, one of the narrator's few encounters with spoken Standard Modern Turkish in its ostensibly 'pure' form is that spoken by an *Armenian* 'refugee' neighbour. By contrast, the actual vernacular of the narrator, Kıbrıslıca, implicitly a pidgin-like alternative, is at a distance from 'pure' Turkish cultural forms and is one denigrated and marginalised by Turkish nationalists like Hasan. The actual components of their everyday cultural lives are abandoned in nationalist discourses in favour of imports from outside the island. If English is a foreign, hegemonic language which *cuts* Cyprus, then the hegemonic cultures of the nationalist 'mother-fatherlands' perform similar roles in dividing Cypriots from each other *and* from their indigenous so-called dialect[s].

Related to this is the concept that Greek-speakers (or, Kypriaka-speakers) had 'similar stories... *but* only on National Days would' they perceive sociocultural differences (*emphasis mine*). Through the use of the conjunction 'but', the narrator stresses that such nationalist performances—ubiquitous across the island's linguistic groups—is one that *unifies* Cypriots as a parallel phenomenon of contemporary culture that accounts for a greater similarity than the divisive moments nationalist poetry is able to construct. In other words, nationalism is not unique to one discrete socio-linguistic group but a pan-Cypriot issue through which colonialist axioms of purity and pluralism compete. All nationalists in Cyprus reiterate comparable 'stories' of grand, imperial ancestry, the only significant difference is the erstwhile empire onto which they project their selfhood: typically either the Ottoman or Byzantine.

In a subsequent account of one May 19 celebration, performances—'on public platforms, nationalist speeches, poems... flags to the tunes of military marches'—tend towards sectarian violence. In a dialectic of culture and warfare, 'Blood and words run high. Anti-Greek sentiment too. How the Turks had fought to get rid of the *Megalo Idea*'.[123] These ideologies are internalised by an attending 'juvenile group', including the reluctant narrator, headed by his schoolmate Ozkul. After having kidnapped a Greek-speaking peer, Andrikko, 'the son of my father's friend', Ozkul attempts to 'take revenge on those who killed our brothers on Turkish soil'; the narrator, however, retaliates by speaking to Andrikko 'in my limited Greek vocabulary: Don't be afraid, my friend', and his father eventually finds and punishes the group, in free-indirect speech: 'I'll teach them what it is to take the entire history into their own hands. I had never seen him so sincerely upset and... I harboured no resentment' for the reprimand.[124]

The account articulates varying engagements with historiography. It illustrates the opposition between the father's 'sincere' resistance to trans-communal conflict and a nationalism which is associated with both childhood ignorance and the nascence of the anti-colonial generation. The maturation towards an independent island is conceived of as conterminous with the rise of violent nationalism. The young Ozkul represents an investment in antiquarian histories *reiterating* past Greco-Turkish binaries; the older father, Halil, warns against misappropriations of an 'entire history' in the present and symbolises an established—perhaps *historical*—union of Greek and Turkish influences embodied by his relationship with a Greek-speaking 'friend'. The narrator, in the limens of these opposing generational ideologies, hesitantly assimilates into Ozkul's (pseudo-political) group while, nonetheless, breaking linguistic divisions by using Greek to identify Andrikkos as 'my friend' in a *reiteration* of his father. Moreover, the name Ozkul bears homophonic echoes of Özker Yaşın, suggesting that this 'image' represents the author's own literary ambivalence towards the politics of Özker's poetic oeuvre valorising Atatürk in the 1960s. Baybars, therefore, commences a project of writing-back, not only to Durrell and other British colonial narratives, but also to the nationalist models of select anti-colonialists. In this habitus of socio-linguistic dichotomies of self and Other, the ideologies used to counter British rule become (neo-)colonialist themselves.

Describing the education of Cypriots, the narrator reports sardonically on how a man's arranged marriage with an affluent 'marriageable daughter' would be the 'greatest reward for all that brainwashing in London and Ankara'.[125] Exposing the gendered inequalities of pedagogy, the account intersects the epistemic violence of capitalism, patriarchy, colonialism, and nationalism as mutually-consolidating phenomena of social division. For him, the hegemonic indoctrination of Britain's education system is equal to that of Turkey. The text seeks to challenge both the colonial metropole and the nationalist 'Motherland'—here, Ankara, but elsewhere, Istanbul—as comparable proselytising centres.[126]

Earlier, in a scene set during the Second World War, the narrator describes an elderly man, Mustafa, 'one of the few people left in Nicosia who religiously wore a fez. He was against Atatürk, against Churchill and against Hitler. He didn't like children much and we reciprocated'.[127] Mustafa's political stance, although not explicitly shared by the narrator, analogises the hegemons of nationalist Turkey, colonialist Britain, and fascist Germany, all led by men iconised and lauded by their subjects. The man's wearing of the fez, in conjunction with the adverb 'religiously', indicates his engagement with symbols outlawed by sectarian Kemalism, including the wearing of the fez by men and the hijab by women. Like Halil, and as emphasised by Mustafa's age and distrust of the youngest generation of Cypriots, the elderly man represents an active continuation of pre-colonial *and pre-nationalist* cultural artefacts in resistance to the homogenising of cultural identities performed by imperialist, nationalist, and fascist states. Even Hasan, the uncle privileging 'pure' Turkish over 'dialect' struggles with 'Atatürk's reforms': 'the new Language Movement' which replaces Osmanlıca with Modern/Istanbul Turkish (by exorcising loanwords from Arabic, Persian, and Greek, while usurping the Arabic alphabet with the Latin) causes Hasan to believe 'no one would be able to write a single sentence of intelligible Turkish' and the narrator to understand only 'very little' Osmanlıca.[128] Three vernaculars grouped under the category of Turkish—Osmanlıca, Kıbrıslıca, Modern/Istanbul Turkish—all compete in the construction of a seemingly-homogenous linguistic identity through fraught mediations on tradition and modernity. Paradoxically, it is in *Modern* Turkish that 'nationalist poems… about the Huns' and the Ottoman period are composed.[129]

Critiquing the import of cultural modes from Kemalist Istanbul—the *imaginary homeland* 'as much part of a Turkish Cypriot's dream as Mecca was a fervent Moslem's'[130] (and also a Greek-speaker's in its guise as Constantinople)—the narrator repeatedly depicts their otherness or inauthenticity in contemporary Cyprus. In one 'image', he 'began to speak with an Istanbul accent in order to win [his Turkish-educated cousin] Aydin's admiration'. His accent, however, 'became so affected' that it produced 'a mixture of parroting and nightingaling' which exposes to his peers that he 'had never been to Turkey', leading to 'the demolition of all those stories' to the contrary.[131] Comparable to his *mimicry*, in Bhabha's terms, of colonialist English, the idiolect is framed as an inauthentic performance of his identity, invested in the creation of an imagined association with Turkey in order to profit from the cultural and educational capital of Istanbul as an artistic centre. The margin's borrowing of the culture of *a* centre is perceived as mere 'parroting' which creates narratives, or 'stories', of belonging in tension with one's specific local identity.

Similarly, he considers earlier how a village 'play, like most cultural material, had come from Turkey. The events took place in an Anatolian village. The setting, names and even the idiom had affinities [...but some terms, like *jandarma*] were alien'.[132] The play represents acts akin to glocalisation whereby the pan-national is appropriated as a metonym for local identity through local re-production. Even the subsequent description of how villagers began 'calling the village bobby *jandarma*' demonstrates how a translation of cultural values is used to construct an identity *between* periphery and multiple cultural centres, and, specifically, how Istanbul motifs are employed to challenge the Anglophone discourses of the colonial administration. The very embodiment of parochial colonial authority, the bobby, is re-written and recast by Turkish-speakers with 'an unselfconscious air of knowing' beyond the colonial axis of knowledge and power. However, the simultaneous emphasis on the play's alterity as partly-'alien' echoes the description at the very start of the text of his mother's fantastic stories set 'in an Anatolian village' in contrast with both Ibrahim's quasi-realist illustration of Vassilia's mosque and, metatextually, the narrator-author's verisimilitude depicting a specific *Cypriot* village. It puts pressure on a performance of local culture which relies entirely on external textualities. Like Baybars' use of the word to describe his 'alien past' in the poem 'Letter to Homeland', conveying his alienation in Britain and within the English language, its repetition here also signifies the unhomely character of Istanbul Turkish and the 'homeland' its cultural products offer. As Dennis Lee argues of English, '[t]he language was drenched with our nonbelonging', instigating a conscious expunging of select words; consequently, '[t]he first necessity for the colonial writer... is to start writing of what he knows. His imagination must come home', away from 'the imperial centre you've dreamt about'.[133] Within this process, complicated by Cyprus' specific relationship between various colonial and nationalist metropoles, Baybars selectively departs from Turkish as his literary language, engaging with a foreignised English to write his Cypriot *home* in lieu of the *imaginary homeland* of Turkey. In the works of his contemporaries, that homeland is also Greece, Lebanon, or Armenia. For Cypriots, there is not simply one, but many, 'imperial centre[s they have] dreamt' of, including London, Athens, Ankara, and the doubly-inscribed Istanbul/Constantinople.

As the narrator asks of Cyprus' literary traditions, 'Why did people flock to the theatres when a Turkish troupe from Istanbul was on the island and yet there was no drive to establish an indigenous Cypriot repertoire?'[134] This opposition between the pan-nationalist and the local emblematises Baybars' ongoing project of developing 'an indigenous Cypriot' literature with emphasis on the 'native', alongside the struggle to find a readership which values the local as greatly as metropolitan imports. Even the earliest theatres established in Cyprus, including Montis' Lyriko Theatre, were largely monolingualist, highlighting linguistic problems in the construction of an island-wide, 'indigenous' form. As a child, the narrator attempts to learn at least one Greek word daily. In one 'image', when he is sent to a Greek-speaking baker, he returns with half a loaf. Consequently, his parents 'laughed. How bad I was at learning the language of my neighbours. Why half? They hadn't taught me that word! But somehow I must have picked it up'.[135] Despite attempts at bridging linguistic oppositions in Cyprus—learning the Greek or Kypriaka of his 'neighbours' long before his introduction to both Osmanlıca and English—he still fails to overcome the divisiveness, the 'half[ness]', which osmotically and insidiously enters into the Cypriot discourses produced and consumed like bread.

Nonetheless, the Cypriot home he envisions throughout the text draws on its linguistic and cultural pluralism, transcending the monolithic purism of nationalist ideologies. In this counter-toponymy of Nicosia, '[i]t was always called the Town, *Şeher*. *Şehir* in Turkish Turkish',[136] a label which re-writes the city from a local perspective in opposition, not only to colonialist maps inscribing Cypriot places with English names (Nicosia, not Lefkosia or Lefkoşa), but to the 'Turkish Turkish' discourses which valorise Istanbul as '*the* City'. It re-centres the map of the Eastern Mediterranean to focus the capital of Cyprus at its heart. In antithesis with national days, the narrator subsequently imagines public, intercommunal festivals. Although his family did not observe Christmas religiously, 'we enjoyed the holiday. Our Christian neighbours, the Greeks and Armenians, did [observe it], in a non-European way... But the New Year's Eve was a common festivity among the Turks, the Greeks, the Armenians and the Maronites'.[137] Inclusive of the cultural heterogeneity of the island—referencing the Armenian-speakers and Arabic-speaking Maronites often elided in nationalist narratives—the account expresses, if not metatextually *celebrates*, the intercommunal similarities and points of contact present in religiously-mixed spaces before the period of violent nationalist conflicts and in contrast with the ethno-religious differences textualised by both the Ottoman *millet* system and the British census. Even the emphasis on Eastern, 'non-European' forms of Christian worship disavows an association of Cypriot Christians with evangelising colonisers, framing these festivities as pre-colonial (and pre-nationalist) traditions which have long-facilitated social integration and intercultural exchange.

Earlier, when the narrator asks why his father does not drink wine like his Greek-speaking friends, Kara Kosta and Kostari, one of his father's superiors informs him that 'Turks are Moslems. In Islam wine is *haram*'.[138] This simple categorisation of ethnicity and religion appears as dramatic irony within a scene which complicates dimorphic cultural identities—beginning with Kara Kosta's linguistically-mixed name (*kara* is Turkish for black), and echoed later with the character Kochino Mustafa (*kochino* is Kypriaka, but not Standard Greek, for red).[139] The father of his friend, Alptekin (a schoolmate often dichotomised with the anti-Greek Ozkul), '[a]lthough he was a Turkish Cypriot[, ...] spoke better Greek than Turkish and... drank quantities of wine'.[140] This idiom repeats elsewhere. He suggests that Paphiot 'Turkish Cypriots' were 'difficult to understand [...as t]hey generally spoke better Greek than Turkish'.[141] The Paphiot Hamida is said to speak 'half-Greek, half-Turkish' as a metonym of the south-western villages where, he surmises, 'the Turks could not speak Turkish at all. In their mosques they prayed in Greek. They even wanted to have Atatürk's monumental speech... translated into Greek so that they might be able to hear it'.[142] Deconstructing the binaries surrounding linguistic, ethnic, and religious affiliations, Cypriots are embodied with heteroglossic identities which, just like Hasanpouli, amalgamate various interpretations of established discourses in their constructions of selfhood. Some Islamic spaces become Greek-speaking, while some Muslims become secular. Cypriot vernaculars are 'half'-indebted to standardised forms and 'half' intersect with adjacent languages. Most notably, Atatürk's dialogue on the purifying of the Turkish language, culture, and nation is ironically 'translated' for its reception by people nonetheless identifying (or, forcibly identified) as 'Turks'. All these depictions stage a resistance to nationalist identifications which repudiate heterogeneity. Cultural difference is composed of imbricating shades rather than discrete oppositions. Similarly, both Greek-speaking Kara Kosta and Kostari are imagined as translingual family friends, and the latter is depicted performing music with Halil in a pastoral scene echoing Durrell's cross-cultural picnic with Panos.[143] Their related names (Kosta and Kostari) may even suggest that Baybars' recurring motifs of intercommunal solidarity not only write-back to the rejection of Cypriot intercultural pluralism by Turkish nationalists, but also engage intertextually with the Hellenophone oeuvre of *Costas* Montis.

The earliest chapters of *Closed Doors* ostensibly reiterate the nationalist sentiments of EOKA members, using an identification with Greece and an endorsement of *enosis* to challenge the persistence of British rule. Comparable to the national days of Baybars' narrative, Montis' text is replete with images of nationalist Greek fervour. One scene, for instance, depicts how crowds would 'sing hymns... in front of the Archbishop's Palace and... the Consulate (for us there was only one consulate—the Greek). Then we marched with Greek flags... cry[ing] for "Enosis," a demand for liberation that echoed from time to time [...in] every Greek territory outside the borders of the free motherland. In school, we wrote enthusiastic essays about freedom'.[144] Like Baybars' representation of Turkish nationalism, it is in the confluence of the performative and pedagogical—public displays consolidating selective education—that nationalist identities are constructed and, subsequently, distributed through the textualities of music, 'flags', and 'essays'. The ideologies of 'freedom' taught in schools are then repeated as a call for 'liberation' in public spaces. In this chapter, however, postcolonial emancipation can only be conceived of as a purely Greek and Eastern Orthodox enterprise; neither an independent Cypriot identification is espoused, nor are intercommunal modes of resistance with Turkish-speakers imagined, to combat the 'foreign yoke' of British imperialism.[145] Ironically, it is the culture of the Greek metropolis, itself beyond existing territorial 'borders', which is instrumentalised to counter the non-nativism of the British Empire. In this monolithic interpretation of Cypriot society, all culture is homogenously Greek: 'there was only one consulate', according to a worldview in which the diplomatic mission of a *foreign* political body is naturalised as local—much like the language of the text, Standard Modern Greek, itself.

Similarly, in a juncture before the conception of Cypriot national symbols, references to 'the flag' refer simply to the Greek model, causing the narrator to rhetorically ask: 'Is it still necessary to say "Greek" flag?'.[146] In his youthful enthusiasm as a student, Hellenism becomes a metonym for all areas of social, historical, and political consciousness for the Greek-speaking Cypriot narrator. Indeed, the allusion to the *Megali Idea* as temporally and spatially fluid—one which transcends the delineations of time and geographic 'territory'—commences a recurring depiction of essentialist, antiquarian histories throughout most of the text. Within an explicitly discursive historiography, he goes on to unravel 'the "links" and "threads" with the past'. For him, in EOKA, 'we saw before us once again the Greek Revolution, no longer in lifeless print with beautiful, colored pictures', it is now 'the most breathtaking repetition of history'.[147] Citing male figures of the Greek resistance to Ottoman rule, including Kolokotronis and Dhiakos, this androcentric history uses elements of an ethnocentric education system to restage the Cypriot conflict of the 1950s, not even as a 'repetition' of an era of Cypriot history under Greek rule, but of the history of Greece itself. Given the didactic tone of the narrative, such 'threads' may also metatextually suggest parallels with the contemporary violence of 1963 and 1964. An imagined opposition between Greeks and Ottomans in the nineteenth century can be used to interpret echoes, not only of the conflict between (Greek-speaking) Cypriots and the British army *within* the text, but also the emerging—or, to reiterate the idiom of this historiography, *re*-emerging—antagonism between peoples defined without geographic or temporal specificity as homogenous 'Greeks' and 'Turks'.

Indeed, when the narrator's father recites 'ancient stories from' the 'collective memory of the October Uprising of 1931' for their contextual importance in the 1950s,[148] the motif of paternal story-telling may posit a link with Montis' narration of the 1950s for its perceived pertinence in relation to the post-independence clashes of the 1960s. While the father figure reads from newspapers, in addition to recounting personal anecdotes, Montis formerly edited the Hellenophone newspapers *Eleftheri*

Foni (*Free Voice*) and *Ethnos* (*Nation*). These nationalistic representations of history are not only a source of imagined identification, but are instruments which tend towards the propagation of actual violence.

Nonetheless, in a narrative of individual growth, internal textual revisions and diachronic changes in the narrator's attitude towards Hellenism reveal a gradual complicating of national identities. In short, the narrator repeats—before then questioning—established tactics of pro-Greek interpellation. Allusions to his early stance on anti-colonial warfare are explicitly grounded, like his participation on national days, 'in our childish excitement',[149] suggesting that maturation involves, like that for Baybars' narrator, a movement away from the naïveté of nationalist violence as an underdeveloped mode of resistance. In one of the few representations of Turkish-speaking Cypriots, one of the final chapters begins with a Saidian dichotomy of self and Other to describe the emergence of transcommunal conflict, before putting pressure on the absoluteness of this apparent opposition.

> As soon as darkness fell the Turks stirred from the depths of Asia, from the depths of centuries past, armed with knives and axes… Their flag bearers… were smeared with the blood of an ox. So began a story, where and when it would end no one could tell… (Who in Greece would pay the price for this? Who in Turkey, or in England, or in the rest of the world? Those responsible must be found and brought to account… because we lived for hundreds of years with these people. But the Turks we saw now were not the ones we had known earlier. Who had changed them? …"Don't let the English win the game of divide and rule"). In the end, that strategy proved impossible and a civil war blazed. […] We hid pickaxes and… trained ourselves… with a knife. Every day our side had deaths, and so did theirs: men, women, and children. […] You could not tell in the street if a person was a Greek or a Turk… Don't even use the city's name [Nicosia]. It did not even know itself.[150]

Nationalism here is the discursive reiteration of colonialist binaries: the oppositions of Europe/'Asia' and lightness/'darkness' are reappropriated to denigrate cultural differences. This Orientalist schism associates Turkish-speakers with an essential, timeless violence which threatens the stability of the island. However, the repetition of the instruments of conflict used by 'Turks' and 'Greeks'—the 'knives and axes' of the former become the 'pickaxes [and] knife' of the latter—imbricates parallels between the two groupings, like the shared figure of the nationalist 'flag bearer', to deconstruct absolute difference. Indeed, counter to racialist concepts of physiognomic characteristics including those constructed by colonialist ethnologists, the physical, cultural, and social identities of 'a Greek or a Turk' cannot be visually differentiated by the narrator. Instead, he creates a subject position which sympathises with the *mutual* experiences of mourning across the island, regardless of linguistic 'sides'.

Breaking from Hellenistic historical narratives, he stresses that the modern history of the island involves centuries of intercommunal cohesion, one which, having been ruptured, distorts the intrinsic *identity* of Nicosia itself. Framing these 'change[s]' as the product of a colonial 'divide and rule' policy, the account gestures metatextually to the changing structures of the increasingly-divided Nicosia of the 1960s (foreshadowing the climax of 1974), in opposition with pre-colonial unity described here and in Baybars' text. In addition to imperialism, however, the allusion to all three Guarantor Powers—Britain, Greece, and Turkey—distributes culpability among all three metropoles. Commencing with Greece, the monumentalised centres are re-written as sources, not only of culture, but sectarian politics. Nationalism and nationalist division are framed as a discursive 'story' reshaping history, society, and urban infrastructures for their agendas—a 'story' here repeated, but then revised, in the narrator's writing-back to political interventions by both the British Empire and the equally-expansionist bodies of Greece and Turkey.

A preceding description of Nicosia presents it, like Baybars, as an essentially-pluralistic space 'with Greek, Turkish, and Frankish quarters' within its Venetian walls. Stressing that '[w]ithin a few steps of one another were churches, mosques, covered Venetian balconies, the square of Serai where the Turkish Pasha's palace had stood…',[151] the narrative imagines a transcultural city where religious buildings of different denominations exist peacefully and the last structure, the 'Pasha's palace', is recognised as an alternative to the Orthodox 'Archbishop's Palace' detailed in the Hellenocentric first chapter. While the narrator initially argues that outside 'the walls the new city of Nicosia began, free from the memory of conquerors, completely Greek', as part of a nationalist, anti-colonial restructuring of the space in response to Western European modernity, he revises this summary in the chapter's conclusion to suggest that '[t]he new city did not break from the past… it had been built on the same foundation of history'.[152] The closing refers ambivalently to how both British imperialism has failed to be fully repudiated and how Nicosia's layered, pluralistic 'past' cannot be elided by purist nationalisms.

Indeed, in the final chapters of the work, almost all references to Greece and Hellenism are suspended. The final allusion appears during a depiction of the parades celebrating the advent of independence. Through textual parallelism marking direct contrast with the Greek national days described in the first chapter, the narrator asserts that '[i]t was a real parade, not like the ones on the 25th of March [Greece's Independence Day] or the 28th of October [Greece's National Day]'.[153] The fulfilment of decolonisation performs a celebration of the Cypriot nation which usurps the erstwhile observation of dates honouring events of Greece's history (its independence from Ottoman and Italian occupations).

Wanting to re-write Cypriot public spaces, the narrator implores the reader to '[p]aint all of Nicosia in one embrace, clinging tightly and crying... And paint the city throwing its school cap into the air... Call out its name a thousand times. It knows its name again'.[154] Here, the city as a discursive structure, without any reference to specific socio-linguistic groups, is manifested as an embodiment of social unity. Decolonisation is viewed as the fulfilment of adolescent maturation, a graduation in which one's (nationalist) 'school' education is completed, if not rejected, in the search for a future identity. This identity, one of a unified Nicosia, reclaims the 'name' it had lost as a result of nationalist anti-colonial violence spilling into trans-communal conflict. It revives the pluralist past the narrator had previously lauded without explicit association with Hellenism.

This tacit correlation of anti-colonialism with anti-nationalism also appears in the representation of EOKA's first attacks. In its wake, a 'diverse crowd suddenly fill[s] the street, half asleep, half dressed, wandering aimlessly', with images of 'half'-ness metonymic of its heterogeneous 'divers[ity]'. For the narrator, 'space had so shrunk that all of Nicosia seemed without sections or neighborhoods... You had the sense that the explosions had... banged on your door and asked you to come outside'.[155] In one of the first allusions to 'doors' in the text, the relationship between the violence against the *closed doors* of imperialism and the destruction of divisive urban structures suggests a theorising of anti-colonialism as actively involved in the deconstruction of physical and psychic borders between Cyprus' 'diverse' socio-linguistic groups. The violence brings Cypriots together into urban spaces—rather than simply Greek-speakers on Greek national days, for instance—and eradicates the demarcations of 'ethnic' 'neighborhoods'. As Elias Canetti argues, a crowd's 'destruction of representational images is the destruction of a hierarchy which is no longer recognized'.[156] Like iconoclastic epistemic violence against the English language depicted throughout the narrative, this scene of the crowd demonstrates how counter-colonial movements are involved in a 'destruction of [the ethnic] hierarchy' which the British Empire inscribes onto the colony through its census and education reforms. Divide-and-rule is combated in these representations of Nicosia through tropes of unity wherein no character is marked as 'Greek' or 'Turk', identifiers conspicuous by their absence in these chapters. Counter to Canetti's theory of humans' intrinsic fear of being touched by strangers,[157] it is a Nicosian population which enthusiastically 'embrace[s]' each other—and perhaps *the* Other—that best challenges the strictures of colonial curfews and segregation.

Elsewhere, Montis' text decentres Greek nationalism and its textual dissemination, inferring that it, in conjunction with British imperialism, is responsible for the marginalisation of (pan-)Cypriot identifications. In response to the perceived heroism of anti-colonial guerrillas, the narrator repudiates his earlier equivalence with moments from Greek history 'books' by asserting that '[i]t was the worst possible time to read heroic tales of other people, other places… our struggle was so blind that it would admit of no comparisons or analogies… even with such beloved names as Thermopylae or Maniaki'.[158] The discourse of these pedagogical texts is disavowed in the face of creating a new historiography valorising (Greek-speaking) Cypriots as identifiable idols, expunging the cultural 'analogies' made earlier with Greece, now re-written as a site of alterity and the source of textualities *belonging* to 'other people, other places' foreign to the Cypriot present. In doing so, the narrator creates a counter-narrative within which (Greek-speaking) Cypriots can stage a sense of immediate identification and belonging.

As he states earlier, upon discovering that Grivas was Cyprus-born, 'however much we came to admire the Greeks from our readings in school. We wanted those who took up arms to be Cypriots… How could we envision those arms in the hands of others?'.[159] The account uses similar motifs of resisting the conventions of Hellenocentric education by creating a distinctly 'Cypriot' political and historical consciousness which marks 'Greeks' as a separate category of 'others'. Even the image of 'hands', in addition to holding ammunition, suggests that Montis' writing is a mode of self-representation which reclaims Cypriot literary agency from depictions of the island composed by the 'hands' of Greeks—those writing, uninvited, 'in our own name'.[160] As well as writing-back to Durrell, the text participates in a representation of Cyprus independent from the (equally Orientalist) travelogues of Kazantzakis and Seferis. Notably in 1959, the Greek writer Rodis Roufos first published a response to Durrell entitled 'Sour Grapes', anthologised in *The Age of Bronze* (translated for Heinemann in 1960). It follows a Cypriot protagonist as he zealously joins EOKA. Half a decade later, Montis' work becomes the first published narrative to write the pre-independence era from an autonomous Cypriot perspective. This transition closely follows Fanon's *The Wretched of the Earth*, an urtext of anti-colonialism: 'The native intellectual accepted the cogency of [the West]... ready to defend the Greco-Latin pedestal. Now it so happens that during the struggle for liberation, at the moment that the native intellectual comes into touch again with his people, this artificial sentinel is turned into dust. All the [northern] Mediterranean values... become lifeless... dead words'.[161] Counter to these 'dead words' is the revived toponym, Nicosia, which 'knows it name again'.

Ultimately, in reaction to centralised Hellenism, the narrator performs an iconoclasm of the mythos surrounding Eleftherios Venizelos, the Greek leader whose support for the *Megali Idea* often saw him compared to the similarly-nationalistic Atatürk. While Venizelos initially appears as a literal and figurative icon in the family home, after his inaction relative to Cyprus' anti-colonial movements, '[h]is portrait in the living room was knocked a bit off-centre... After the first hangings we came to hate him... The house deserted him. We never let him back in'.[162] The domestic space of the Cypriot home is represented abandoning both the politician and the Venizelism he symbolised, de-'centr[ing]' his authority in the colony. If anti-colonial violence opens 'doors' between Cypriots, then in the same period, it leads to the closing-off of forms of Greek nationalism blind to the sanctioned violence of the British Empire. Venizelos is depicted as 'a stalwart friend of the English', above and before his relationship with Cypriots. As the narrator grows, the Cypriot home becomes a symbolic site in the establishment of an independent identity and one which consciously rejects the selective expansionist politics of Venizelism—a hegemon seeking to interpellate the island into its nation with limited concern for the welfare of its citizens.

Comparably, and in contrast with nationalist poets like Özker Yaşın, Baybars' opening 'image' in *Plucked in a Far-Off Land* trivialises the death of Atatürk. Bluntly informing his parents, the young narrator states, 'Atatürk is dead… Let's eat… You mustn't be sad, you've got me. I'll be a great man when I grow up'.[163] In a narrative of diachronic textual progress, its focal character attempts to usurp the authority of the former Turkish leader with his own future career as a writer from, and of, *Cyprus*. The domestic space, and the narrative which surrounds it, does not mourn the loss of the iconic nationalist or herald the legacy of Kemalism. They both instead privilege the consumption of local products, in this case, Cypriot village food. Both narratives are inevitably complicated by form—Baybars' English departs from the local, while Montis' Standard Modern Greek creates a Cypriot history with a bias towards its Greek-speaking population. Neither are endemic Cypriot vernaculars. Nonetheless, these forms, rupturing extant historiographic models and integrating the heteroglossia of subversive counter-perspectives within shared portrayals of nationalist parades, challenge the simplicity of nationalist epics which, structurally and thematically, espouse purity and conformity.

This process is especially fraught for this context, compared to other 'postcolonial' literatures, given the writers' constant need to manoeuvre between multiple sites variously considered 'local' and 'foreign', or 'native' and 'colonial'. The *doors* surrounding their pastoral homes have to mediate the frontiers of identity as they imbricate between Britain, Greece, Turkey, and a gradually-decolonising Cyprus. For Montis, while Venizelos is once internalised as a figure of domestic identification, he is later repudiated in a text which also puts pressure on the confinement of British imperialism, from the *closed doors* of internment camps to the epistemic violence of its literary discourse. Both he and Baybars examine equally the colonialism and nationalisms introduced from outside the island. Using countertravel across Cyprus, and between it and multiple metropoles (physical or imagined), they re-appropriate the travelogue to showcase their personal development from infantilised subjects indoctrinated by various dominant discourses to mature, critical thinkers willing to *move-away* from the hegemonies permeating their childhood homes. These are not celebratory texts of independence; they are marred by foreshadowing of racialised violence and partition. They demonstrate how identities are ever-changing categories of 'the home' which can be co-opted by competing ideological state apparatuses. Attempting to *transport* these groupings away from divisive political structures, they illustrate the culpability of multiple institutions—education, religion, newspapers, nationalist parades, and the colonial book—in reiterating the divide-and-rule of all (neo-)colonialist bodies, be they British, Greek, Turkish, or even Cypriot in origin.

Conclusions

Counter to the prevailing view that Cypriot writers, particularly from the 1955 to 1974 generation, can be simply segregated into the categories of 'Greek literary production' and 'Turkish literary production', parallels in the works of Taner Baybars and Costas Montis reveal how they respond to the same context through related narrative tactics—creating comparable polymorphic counter-travelogues to write-back to British imperialism while simultaneously complicating nationalist discourses—suggesting a (conscious or otherwise) participation in a uniquely Cypriot, or pan-Cypriot, literary movement.

Alongside form, analogies in the content of *Closed Doors* and *Plucked in a Far-Off Land* correlate the two as intertextual commentaries on contemporary political identity movements. They respond equally to Durrell's travelogue through re-viewings of Nicosia and the north-eastern villages of his earlier stay, offering potent critiques of the epistemic violence committed by the English language and its constituent literatures. The two works incorporate elements of the first-person *bildungsroman* genre. Replete with images of reading, writing, and oral story-telling, the texts appropriate figures of young men as metonyms for the social development of the newly-independent island and its nascent literary oeuvre. For both, however, the endings gesture hopelessly to migrations out, presenting social growth as stunted and the cause of ruptures within familial and communal lives. Nonetheless, the figure of the father is important in both texts and associated with story-telling, translation, and pedagogy—Baybars' father, for instance, as a school-master—presenting characters who usurp the pseudo-paternal authority of both Durrell the teacher and the British Empire as purported civiliser. In scenes of youth education, the student generation of Durrell's journey write-back against him.

Through depictions of the island's topology and urban spaces, the texts destabilise imperial mappings and recalibrate centre-and-periphery models in their elevation of Nicosia as the metropole to which characters gravitate. Allusions to Northern Europe on the margins of the text, including chronological breaks referencing Baybars' future residency in London and Montis' voyage to Ireland, mimic the travelogue genre by repositioning the British Isles as peripheral sites of otherness alien to the Cypriot villages and cities re-represented without the Orientalist tropes of British travel writing. While anticipating the end of imperialism, the two texts also put pressure on the conceits of succeeding nationalist hegemonies and the education systems which support them. Adolescent growth is used to symbolise changes in nationalist affiliation which move from naïve participations in national days to matured reflections on the appropriateness of be interpellated into established nationalist politics. As well as the culpability of imperial divide-and-rule policies, nationalisms and their cultural forms are presented *cutting* Cypriot communities and *closing doors* between them. For both narrators, the Cypriot home becomes the domestic space which usurps the residencies of colonialists and, within which, critiques of Atatürk and Venizelos are staged through the marginalising of Turkey and Greece in favour of images of the locally Cypriot.

Having published almost exclusively in Standard Modern Greek, Montis has been routinely interpellated into epitextual narratives of 'Greek literature' by agencies in both Greece and Cyprus. In 1995, for instance, while being bestowed the Republic of Cyprus' Award for Excellence in Letters and the Arts, Montis was lauded as 'not simply a great Cypriot poet. He is the leading, living Greek poet'.[164] The rhetorical epistrophe repeats Montis' profession to elevate the status conferred as a 'Greek poet' over the provincialised role of a mere 'Cypriot poet'.

In contrast, Baybars' Anglophone publications and vehemently anti-nationalist content see him identified differently. His biography in *Contemporary Poets of the English Language* (1974) describes him as 'British. Born in Nicosia, Cyprus… Came to England to study law'[165]; while the succeeding *Contemporary Poets* (1991), four years before Montis' award, elaborates that 'Taner Baybars is a Cypriot whose first book of poems, written in Turkish, was published [...before c]oming to England'.[166] Consolidating his identities as Cypriot and British, Mehmet Yaşın argues that he 'is the only Cypriot poet who has established his reputation as a "British" poet',[167] and Baybars has similarly stressed his status as a British poet who happens to be from a (Turkish-speaking) Cypriot, and not simply a Turkish, background.

Interestingly, it is in 2004, *months after the border between north and south began opening*, within an *English* translation of his prose, that

Montis is explicitly framed by his translator as 'a Cypriot', 'Cyprus's greatest poet', and a composer of 'Cypriot literature'. David Roessel even goes as far as to quote Roufos' Greek counter-discourse to Durrell, *The Age of Bronze* (a 'book was needed to fill in the gaps, to give the Greek view'), *after* stressing that *Closed Doors* offers 'a relentless... Cypriot point of view'.[168] Montis' 'Cypriotism' is not only emphasised, but it is tacitly viewed as oppositional to the Greek narratives on Cyprus disseminated by his overseas contemporaries. The year of publication—almost half a century after the start of the 'emergency'; forty years after the deployment of the UN Peacekeeping Force; and the year of Montis' death—symbolises the changes in the island anticipating the partial dissolution of the Green Line, the fulfilment of the opening of doors closed by colonialism and nationalisms. Language is here used as a metonym for the increased movement of goods, peoples, and cultures across the Buffer Zone. The following year, Baybars was republished by Moufflon Publications in the Republic of Cyprus. As will be seen in the post-2003 Anglophone literatures of Cypriots, it is within this form that 'Cypriotism' as a discrete ideological construct is able to emerge. It is the only language shared by the majority of contemporary Cypriots following decades of education marginalising the teaching of Greek (in the north) and Turkish (in the south) as 'secondary' tongues.

For Montis, whose text involves copious references to resisting English textualities, writing in a nationalist language realises his most-privileged concern of contesting British imperialism. For Baybars, on the other hand, the pertinence he places on revising nationalism results in him appropriating the colonialist, but non-nationalist, language. His English allows for cultural networks to form between Cypriot readers, if not also wider Mediterranean and 'postcolonial' audiences. Notably, in his poem 'Journey of a Cyclist', he describes: 'That city... unwillingly hated./I rushed to sea and climbed hills/hoping to find quiescence'.[169] The words have intertextual echoes, not only of the opening 'image' of his prose work, but of Khalil Gibran's prose-poetry *The Prophet* (1923) as shared Anglophone Levantine commentaries on post/colonial identities: Almustafa 'climbed the hill without the city walls and looked seaward', awaiting a return, like Baybars, 'to the isle of his birth'.[170]

In *Plucked in a Far-Off Land*, Baybars, investigating his relationship with Cypriot history while composing in London, responds both to Smith's non-history and to purist national historiographies by embracing the cultural polymorphism of an 'important' island having 'absorbed the blood and cultures of numerous civilisations'. Crucially, however, such a perspective could not emerge 'until I escaped from it severing my roots'. The syntax renders it unclear what the pronoun refers to, but it implies that only by 'escap[ing]' Cyprus, and disavowing Turkish as a literary language, that the colonialist and nationalist projects of *cutting* Cypriots off from a rich, diverse, and heteroglossic set of 'roots' can be challenged. In contrast with both 'our history classes' and British 'travel book[s]', it is through a *distanced reading* of Cyprus as an emigrant that he views the past in terms of 'Cypriotism'.[171] Following Moretti's theory of '*the distance from the text*: the more ambitious the project, the greater the distance must be', distant reading 'allows you to focus on units that are… much larger than the text: devices, themes, tropes – or genres and systems'.[172] It is through a methodology partially informed by distant reading that this chapter has performed a comparison of the 'genres and systems' employed by Baybars and Montis. But it is also a distanced reading which Baybars performs in his review of Cypriot historical remains from London, and which he consequently encourages by using the international auxiliary language of English as a tool for communication between, and across, socio-linguistic communities. The much larger 'system' of pan-Cypriot writing, transcending Greek and Turkish subcategories or 'worlds', is elaborated through this distance above *all* borders.

Baybars and Montis, therefore, manifest radical, iconoclastic revisions of nationalist discourses, disavowing the pan-national in favour of the *transcultural*. For Bond and Rapson, transculturalism involves 'a threat to distinct forms of identity, catalysing a reassertion of bounded notions of past histories and identities'.[173] In contrast with the *dividing line* crystallising in 1963 (if not earlier), the promise of the 'postnational', as defined by Appadurai, ensures that concepts of nationhood and ethnicity are 'forever slipping in and through the cracks between states and borders', both physical and imagined.[174] If these forms of historiography, which involve the remembering of transcultural unity in the *present*, are at an early stage of development in Baybars' and Montis' works, then they re-emerge fully-formed in the Cypriot literatures of the twenty-first century, around the time of the first English translation of *Closed Doors* and the first Republic of Cyprus edition of *Plucked in a Far-Off Land*. Of the two, perhaps, it is Baybars who, writing for a transcultural readership, is 'an example of a poet [and travel writer] who did not fit his times' as a forerunner of Ali, Nadjarian, and Papadakis.[175] He is as much a post-nationalist as he is a postcolonialist. His work is a *transportal* rejection of all cultural partitions.

Notes

1. Smith, *Through Cyprus*, pp. 293, 304, 310.
2. Costas Montis, *Closed Doors: An Answer to* Bitter Lemons *by Lawrence Durrell*, trans. by David Roessel and Soterios G. Stavrou (Minneapolis, MI: Nostos, 2004), pp. 6, 37.
3. Taner Baybars, *Plucked in a Far-Off Land: Images of Self-Biography* (Nicosia: Moufflon Publications, 2005), pp. 166–167.
4. Georg Wilhelm Friedrich Hegel, *The Philosophy of History*, trans. by J. Sibree (Mineola, New York: Dover Publications, 2004), p. 99.
5. Adamantia Pollis, 'Intergroup Conflict and British Colonial Policy: The Case of Cyprus', *Comparative Politics*, 5 (1973), 575–599 (p. 589). Also quoted in Costas M. Constantinou, 'Cyprus, Violent Cartography and the Distribution of Ethnic Identity', in *The New Violent Cartography: Geo-Analysis After the Aesthetic Turn*, ed. by Samson Opondo and Michael J. Shapiro (Oxford: Routledge, 2012), pp. 195–213 (p. 207).
6. Baker, pp. 226, 221. Smith, p. 330.
7. Wolseley, p. 40.
8. Smith, *Through Cyprus*, pp. 339–340.
9. Tabitha Morgan, *Sweet and Bitter Island: A History of the British in Cyprus* (London and New York: I.B. Tauris), p. 38.
10. Baybars, *Plucked*, p. 216.
11. Elleke Boehmer, *Colonial and Postcolonial Literature: Migrant Metaphors*, 2nd edn (Oxford: Oxford University Press, 2005), p. 164.
12. Fanon, *Black Skin, White Masks*, p. 13.
13. Durrell, p. 139.
14. Anderson, p. 48.
15. Appadurai, p. 162.
16. For further analysis of Cypriot 'folk poetry' and other musical traditions, see, *Music in Cyprus*, ed. by Nicoletta Demetriou and Jim Samson (Surrey: Ashgate, 2015).
17. Durrell, p. 79.
18. From *Foni tis Kyprou*, 11 June 1889, quoted in Anastasia Hasikou, 'The Emergence of European Music', in *Music in Cyprus*, pp. 103–127 (p. 110). Similarly, on how, in the 1920s, Turkish-speaking theatre sporadically included 'some Armenian and Greek Cypriot women' due to the exclusion of Muslim women for religious reasons, see, Ahmet An, 'The Cypriot Armenian Minority and their Cultural Relationship with

the Turkish Cypriots', in *The Minorities of Cyprus: Development Patterns and the Identity of the Internal-Exclusion*, ed. by Andrekos Varnaca, Nicholas Coureas and Marina Elia (Newcastle upon Tyne: Cambridge Scholars, 2009), pp. 282–298 (p. 291).
19. Constantinou, p. 195.
20. Gillian Whitlock, 'Outlaws of the Text: Women's Bodies and the Organisation of Gender in Imperial Space', in *The Post-Colonial Studies Reader*, ed. by Bill Ashcroft, Gareth Griffiths, and Helen Tiffin (London and New York: Routledge, 1995), pp. 306–308 (p. 306).
21. Graham Seal, *Outlaw Heroes in Myth and History* (London: Anthem Press, 2011), p. 54.
22. Constantinou, p. 197.
23. Quoted in Helen Kazantzakis, *Nikos Kazantzakis: A Biography Based on His Letters*, trans. by Amy Mims (New York: Simon & Schuster, 1968), p. 136.
24. George Seferis, *A Levant Journal*, ed. and trans. by Roderick Beaton (Jerusalem: Ibis, 2007), p. 113.
25. Seferis, *Levant*, p. 131.
26. Seferis, *Levant*, p. 113.
27. Panos Ioannides, 'Cinyras', in *Gregory and Other Stories*, trans. by David Bailey (Nicosia: Armida, 2009), pp. 82–133 (p. 111).
28. Costas Montis and Andreas Christofides, 'Introductory Remarks', in *Anthology of Cypriot Poetry (From Ancient Times Until Today)*, ed. by Montis and Christofides (Nicosia: Cultural Service of the Ministry of Education, 1974), pp. i–v (p. i).
29. Matthew Lange, *Educations in Ethnic Violence: Identity, Educational Bubbles, and Resource Mobilization* (Cambridge: Cambridge University Press, 2012), pp. 92–93: 'From the beginning, doctors, lawyers, journalists, teachers, church officials, and other professionals played a vital role publicizing the enosis movement and inspiring other Greek Cypriots to pursue it'.
30. Stephen Morton, *States of Emergency: Colonialism, Literature and Law* (Liverpool: Liverpool University Press, 2013), p. 2.
31. de Certeau, p. 139.
32. Baybars, *Plucked*, p. 222. The poem, 'Circumcision Just Before Puberty', was anthologised in *Narcissus in a Dry Pool* (London: Sidgwick & Jackson Limited, 1978), p. 28.
33. Saree Makdisi, 'Postcolonial Literature in a Neocolonial World: Modern Arabic Culture and the End of Modernity', in *The Pre-occupation of Postcolonial Studies*, ed. by Fawzia Afkal-Khan and Kalpana Seshadri-Crooks (Durham, NC: Duke University Press, 2000), pp. 266–291 (p. 275).
34. Fanon, *Black Skin, White Masks*, p. 169.
35. Montis, *Closed*, p. 83.
36. Montis, *Closed*, p. 85.

37. Shemak, p. 189.
38. Baybars, *Plucked*, p. 11.
39. Montis, *Closed*, p. 3.
40. Montis, *Closed*, p. 67. See also, p. 49.
41. As Roessel identifies in his introduction of Montis, the latter employs 'a series of vignettes that resemble prose poetry' (Montis, *Closed*, p. xiv). Kappler describes how Baybars 'makes extensive use of multicultural and multilingual rhetorical devices in form, expression, and language'. Matthias Kappler, 'Remembering a Childhood in Cyprus: Taner Baybars' "Smellscape" and Multiculturalism in His Autobiography, *Plucked in a Far-Off Land*', in *Turkish Literature and Cultural Memory: "Multiculturalism" as a Literary Theme After 1980*, ed. by Catharina Dufft (Wiesbaden: Harrassowitz Verlag, 2009), pp. 207–224 (p. 207).
42. Franco Moretti, 'Conjectures on World Literature', *New Left Review*, 1 (2000), 54–68 (p. 65).
43. Said, *Culture and Imperialism*, p. 260.
44. Baybars, *Plucked*, pp. 206–207.
45. Baybars, *Plucked*, p. 15.
46. Baybars, *Plucked*, p. 13.
47. Baybars, *Plucked*, p. 14.
48. Baybars, *Plucked*, p. 11.
49. Baybars, *Plucked*, p. 12.
50. Durrell, p. 43.
51. Montis, *Closed*, p. 1.
52. Jacques Derrida, *Archive Fever: A Freudian Impression*, trans. by Eric Prenowitz (Chicago and London: University of Chicago Press, 1996), p. 5.
53. Montis, *Closed*, p. 1.
54. Montis, *Closed*, p. 4.
55. Montis, *Closed*, p. 113.
56. Baybars, *Plucked*, pp. 86–87.
57. Baybars, *Plucked*, pp. 29, 12, 47.
58. Montis, *Closed*, p. 110.
59. Montis, *Closed*, p. 108.
60. Montis, *Closed*, p. 110.
61. Helen Tiffin, 'Post-Colonial Literatures and Counter-Discourse', *Kunapipi*, 9 (1987), 17–34 (p. 18).
62. Marvin Carlson, *Performance: A Critical Introduction*, 2nd edn (London and New York: Routledge, 1996), p. 179.
63. Said, *Culture and Imperialism*, p. 255.
64. Durrell, p. 143.
65. Montis, *Closed*, p. 116. See also, pp. 43–45.
66. Calotychos, p. 175.
67. Montis, *Closed*, p. 38.

68. Durrell, p. 187.
69. Montis, *Closed*, p. 6.
70. Durrell, p. 1.
71. Mallock, pp. 30, 48.
72. Baybars, *Plucked*, p. 18.
73. Montis, *Closed*, p. 28.
74. Montis, *Closed*, p. 3.
75. Robert J.C. Young, *Postcolonialism: A Very Short Introduction* (Oxford: Oxford University Press, 2003), p. 45.
76. Montis, *Closed*, p. 117.
77. Montis, *Closed*, p. 11.
78. Montis, *Closed*, pp. 12–13.
79. Baybars, *Plucked*, p. 57.
80. It is worth noting that the only British Army soldiers Montis characterises in detail are Irish and Welsh.
81. Baybars, *Plucked*, p. 11.
82. Baybars, *Plucked*, p. 24.
83. Baybars, *Plucked*, p. 12.
84. Baybars, *Plucked*, p. 11.
85. Montis, *Closed*, p. 11.
86. Baybars, *Plucked*, p. 11.
87. Baybars, *Plucked*, pp. 21–22.
88. Baybars, *Plucked*, p. 16.
89. Fanon, *A Dying Colonialism*, p. 12.
90. Baybars, *Plucked*, p. 91.
91. Baybars, *Plucked*, p. 79.
92. Baybars, *Plucked*, p. 84.
93. Baybars, *Plucked*, p. 101.
94. Avtar Brah, *Cartographies of Diaspora: Contesting Identities* (London and New York: Routledge, 1996), pp. 2, 4.
95. Durrell, p. 130.
96. Baybars, *Plucked*, p. 222.
97. Calotychos, p. 180.
98. Baybars, *Plucked*, pp. 191, 194.
99. Baybars, *Plucked*, p. 191.
100. Baybars, *Plucked*, pp. 192, 215.
101. Baybars, *Plucked*, p. 153.
102. Baybars, *Plucked*, p. 195.
103. Jamaica Kincaid, *A Small Place* (New York: Farrar, Straus and Giroux, 1988), p. 31.
104. Montis, *Closed*, p. 24.
105. Montis, *Closed*, p. 113.
106. Durrell, pp. 195, 186.
107. Durrell, pp. 210, 206.

108. Montis, *Closed*, p. 14.
109. Montis, *Closed*, p. 6.
110. Montis, *Closed*, p. 36.
111. Montis, *Closed*, p. 88.
112. Montis, *Closed*, pp. 8, 25.
113. Montis, *Closed*, pp. 67, 29.
114. Taner Baybars, 1998, quoted in, Susan Pattie, 'Imagining Homelands: Poetics and Performance among Cypriot Armenians', in *Cyprus and the Politics of Memory: History, Community and Conflict*, ed. by Rebecca Bryant and Yiannis Papadakis (London and New York: I.B. Tauris, 2012), pp. 140–167 (p. 159).
115. Taner Baybars, *To Catch a Falling Man* (London: Scorpion Press, 1963), p. 19.
116. Baybars, *Falling Man*, p. 24.
117. Baybars, *Falling Man*, p. 58.
118. Baybars, *Plucked*, p. 222.
119. Baybars, *Plucked*, pp. 116–117.
120. Anderson, p. 5.
121. Bhabha, *The Location of Culture*, p. 212.
122. Papadakis, pp. 25–29.
123. Baybars, *Plucked*, p. 140.
124. Baybars, *Plucked*, pp. 141–143.
125. Baybars, *Plucked*, p. 216.
126. Baybars, *Plucked*, p. 128.
127. Baybars, *Plucked*, p. 62.
128. Baybars, *Plucked*, p. 171.
129. Baybars, *Plucked*, p. 178.
130. Baybars, *Plucked*, p. 107.
131. Baybars, *Plucked*, p. 212.
132. Baybars, *Plucked*, p. 144.
133. Dennis Lee, *Body Music* (Toronto: Anansi, 1998), p. 18.
134. Baybars, *Plucked*, p. 99.
135. Baybars, *Plucked*, p. 28.
136. Baybars, *Plucked*, p. 90.
137. Baybars, *Plucked*, p. 115.
138. Baybars, *Plucked*, p. 76.
139. Baybars, *Plucked*, p. 203.
140. Baybars, *Plucked*, pp. 106–107.
141. Baybars, *Plucked*, p. 62.
142. Baybars, *Plucked*, p. 152.
143. Baybars, *Plucked*, p. 56.
144. Montis, *Closed*, pp. 3–4.
145. Montis, *Closed*, p. 3.

146. Montis, *Closed*, p. 89.
147. Montis, *Closed*, p. 6.
148. Montis, *Closed*, pp. 4–5.
149. Montis, *Closed*, p. 38.
150. Montis, *Closed*, p. 113.
151. Montis, *Closed*, p. 74.
152. Montis, *Closed*, p. 76.
153. Montis, *Closed*, p. 115.
154. Montis, *Closed*, p. 115.
155. Montis, *Closed*, pp. 15–16.
156. Elias Canetti, *Crowds and Power*, trans. by Carol Stewart (London: Phoenix Press, 1962), p. 19.
157. Canetti, p. 15.
158. Montis, *Closed*, p. 37.
159. Montis, *Closed*, p. 22.
160. Montis, *Closed*, p. 22.
161. Fanon, *The Wretched of the Earth*, pp. 37–38.
162. Montis, *Closed*, p. 56.
163. Baybars, *Plucked*, p. 13.
164. Claire Angelidou, quoted on 'Arts in Cyprus'. www.kypros.org/Cyprus Panel/cyprus/arts.html [accessed 13 October, 2016].
165. *Contemporary Poets of the English Language*, ed. by Rosalie Murphy (Chicago and London: St James Press, 1974), p. 59.
166. *Contemporary Poets*, ed. by Tracy Chevalier (Chicago and London: St James Press, 1991), p. 45.
167. *Step-Mothertongue: From Nationalism to Multiculturalism: Literatures of Cyprus*, ed. by Mehmet Yashin [*sic*] (London: Middlesex University Press, 2000), p. xiii.
168. Montis, *Closed*, pp. ix–xii. Compare with an earlier 1996 commentary on Roufos in which the editors of *The Lawrence Durrell Journal* also stipulate that the 'author of *The Age of Bronze*, was Greek, not Cypriot'. Ian S. MacNiven and Carol Peirce, 'From the Editors', *Deus Loci: The Lawrence Durrell Journal*, 4 (1996), vi–vii (p. vii).
169. Baybars, *Falling Man*, p. 13.
170. Kahlil Gibran, *The Prophet* (Hertfordshire: Wordsworth Editions Limited, 1996), p. 1.
171. Baybars, *Plucked*, pp. 166–167.
172. Moretti, p. 57.
173. Lucy Bond and Jessica Rapson, 'Introduction', in *The Transcultural Turn: Interrogating Memory Between and Beyond Borders*, ed. by Bond and Rapson (Berlin: De Gruyter, 2014), pp. 1–26 (p. 19).
174. Appadurai, p. 41.
175. Pattie, p. 159.

CHAPTER 4

Travelling Across the Buffer Zone: Intersections in Language, Genre, and Identity, 2000–2013

After almost thirty years of formal partition, and forty years after the UN Peacekeeping Force was first deployed, the Buffer Zone was partially opened in April 2003. This moment was an act of iconoclasm against the decades-old symbols of division. As thousands of Cypriots passed through the capital's now-porous Ledra Street, an unprecedented new juncture in the island's political and cultural history had begun. In response, Cypriot writers, many of whom had previously been involved in intercommunal projects held in both Cyprus and London, began developing works which engaged with the deconstruction of all borders: linguistic and cultural, as well as territorial. While literary representations of Cyprus from the earlier two generations—colonial and post-independence—were similarly informed by the genre of travel writing, for this post-partition generation, the topos of free movement becomes a more loaded signifier. There is an important paradigmatic shift in which the conventions of the colonial travelogue and its reported *global* movements across the empire are appropriated subversively to express *internal* trans-partition journeying.

This generation of writing is *post*-partition in the senses of being both temporally after 2003 and ideologically against ethnic segregation in Cyprus. In the years following the border-opening, similarly-titled prose works with related themes began to be published in English, often as revisions or anthologies of earlier compositions. In 2005, the Greek-speaking Cypriot Yiannis Papadakis released *Echoes from the Dead Zone*, a collection of travelogues set in Cyprus and Turkey based on research for a PhD in

D. Nunziata, *Colonial and Postcolonial Cyprus*,
https://doi.org/10.1007/978-3-030-58236-4_4

Social Anthropology at the University of Cambridge. The following year, the Armenian-speaking Cypriot Nora Nadjarian published *Ledra Street*, succeeded by the work of the Turkish-speaking Cypriot Aydın Mehmet Ali, *Forbidden Zones*, in 2013. Both are anthologies of short stories written throughout their careers, including Ali's near-eponymous story, 'Forbidden Zone', first published in the postcolonial journal *Kunapipi* in 2011.[1] All three draw on the personal travels of their respective authors and share the same emphasis on the politics of positionality, questioning the ways in which their narrators situate themselves in relation to the 'Dead Zone' or 'Forbidden Zone' across Ledra Street. Narratorial self-positioning has long been a concern of travel writers mediating their relationship with the cultural inbetweenness of the island. However, there is a greater sensitivity and self-awareness for Cypriot countertravellers exploring their movements, or inaction, in relation to the problem of partition and the hope raised by its partial dissolution.

Moreover, the border-opening fuelled an urgent search by publishers to disseminate material on an event of historical importance for the Middle East, Europe, and the postcolonial 'world'. Much like the literary rush following Cyprus' absorption into the British Empire, mass publication responding to a political theme is marketed, in part, to a touristic gaze.[2] However, while Papadakis' work was first published by the London-based I.B. Tauris, known for its emphasis on texts concerning the Middle East, Ali's was published jointly in London and Nicosia, and Nadjarian's in Nicosia alone. These are narratives with a complex double vision between Cyprus and the Anglophone 'world', composed in Englishes directed partly to Cypriot readers already familiar with the context, and partly to a global, Anglophone audience curious to political upheaval in the Levant.

These planetary works of three Cypriots who all lived and studied in the UK employ motifs of *travel* and the *home* to illustrate the stunted movements which prevent refugees from returning to the houses of their birth, having been dispossessed either abroad or to the other side of the previously-impenetrable Buffer Zone. In a post-9/11 era, this act of trans-border movement powerfully reinscribes the tradition of travel writing by probing and loosening the limits of nation, language, and selfhood at a time in which the planet is rendered smaller by globalisation online and yet remains fragmented by sectarianism on the ground. Ali, Nadjarian, and Papadakis seek to deconstruct the sociocultural categories of 'Cypriot', 'Turkish', 'Armenian', 'Greek', and 'English' through complicity in the break-down of physical walls by composing *transportal* Anglophone texts which, like their authors, travel across national/ist borders. In doing so, they challenge and transect the dominant discourses of both British imperialism and hegemonic nationalisms, Greek and Turkish, which have advocated division as the *status quo*. They speak from, and across, the limens of a disjointed society, re/constructing a Cypriot selfhood which, while honouring the historic dead, imagines a future of intercommunal solidarity free from ideological barriers.

Re-writing the Limits of Nationalist Partitions

The primary case studies of this chapter will be Ali's *Forbidden Zones* and Papadakis' *Echoes from the Dead Zone*. The narrators of the two works are presented moving across borders, both the physical demarcation of the Buffer Zone and the internalised delineations of nationalist collective consciousness. Challenging their assumptions about identity, the two aim to understand the ongoing Cyprus problem from multiple sides, giving voice to Turkish-speaking victims of 1963 as much as Greek-speaking victims of 1974. While Papadakis concludes his text with a postface representing the 2013 border-opening, much of his research was conducted during the 1990s when he performed ethnological fieldwork in both southern and northern Nicosia, in Istanbul, and in one of the few remaining 'mixed' villages in Cyprus, Pyla or Pile.[3] Attesting to personal changes in his perspective on Cypriot history, Papadakis' text is invested in uncovering testimony of individual experience to expose the truth of the conflicts previously concealed by nationalist historiography and pedagogy—a comparable theme to Baybars' and Montis' own challenges to their childhood educations. Mirroring the process of a truth and reconciliation commission, like that of post-apartheid South Africa, Papadakis' movements across the segregating Buffer Zone—an act denied to the majority of Cypriots before 2003—allows him to transcend psychological borders as a necessary step towards deconstructing the legacies of partition. As an interviewed Cypriot woman stresses to him, 'I know, I lived it myself'.[4]

Discovering the truth of history through individual experience is similarly at the core of Ali's work. In her preface, she describes her anthology as 'a rescue operation for' narratives frozen 'over the last thirty-five years'.[5] Her idiom presents the urgency of this anti-partition writing as an act of humanitarian work. If imperialist writers posit a relationship between the representation of land and its subsequent political colonisation, then Ali and Papadakis compose works no less political, but conversely engaged with a decolonisation of the island from the hegemonies of empire, nationalism, and segregation. Ali's emphasis on time, dating her stories to the 1970s, demonstrates the inextricable links between writing and politics, and how the border-opening not only facilitates a freer movement of people but ideas. Overcoming the threat of sanctioned censorship, the two writers challenge the neo-colonial and nationalist binary of 'Greek' and 'Turk'—sometimes, Christian and Muslim—by actively demystifying the Other. Comparing the two travel writers reveals important intersections in their thematic and linguistic forms. The two share parallel concerns with post-war testimony and the reconstruction of identities as Cypriots in the present. The latter is embodied through the motif of walking across the border, by revealing the pluralist heterogeneity of culture and language beyond nationalist standardisations, and by engaging with issues of land rights by imagining the former homes of exiles.

Papadakis' preface begins by explicitly framing his counter-travelogue as planetary and postcolonial. Following an epigram from the Indian poet Suniti Namjoshi, the prose begins with an image of the Great Wall of China as the 'largest single human-made structure'.[6] Symbolically, the narrative assumes a global perspective which dislodges the limits of the individual or local. As well as engaging with world literatures, the use of the gender-neutral 'human' renounces androcentric discourse in its commitment to humanist ideals. Assuming the power gained from a position of verticality, Papadakis views the world from above. In the Cypriot context, he observes both sides of the wall simultaneously, transcending the divisions which mark the land through dichotomies of 'one side' and 'the other'. Doing so, he alludes directly to Said's *Orientalism*, a paradigm of dualistic alterity which 'sounded so familiar. Just like Greeks and Turks'.[7] While appropriating the colonialist form of the travelogue to re-write space, his interrogation of nationalism exposes its discursive structuring as a neo-colonial usurpation of pre-1960 ideology. He challenges ethnocentricity by using the methodological tools of the Anglo-American academy, aligning himself with a postcolonial framework to revise nationalist histories of Cyprus.

The recurring emphasis on how he 'was marked by [his] birth in 1964' relates to the premise of Salman Rushdie's *Midnight's Children*

(1981) in which the partition of the South Asian subcontinent has a numinous bearing on the consciousness of those born during the inception of India and Pakistan.[8] Accordingly, 'I was born at the same time as the Dead Zone, under the same circumstances', much like the children given the Turkish name Savaş, or War, illustrating the totalising impact of the conflict on an individual's selfhood and cultural identity.[9] Also comparable to Rushdie's novel is Papadakis' motif of schizophrenia when he 'beg[ins] to hear voices'—those of Greek patriotism competing with Cypriot intercommunal sentiment.[10] In a fragmented text set in multiple cities following an Anglophone Greek-speaking Cypriot learning Turkish, the multiplicity of voices, both within his mind and of his interviewees, represents the heterogeneity of perspectives used to contest the monolithic conceits of nationalism. In the preface, following the description of China's Great Wall, he returns to the Buffer Zone, revealing that, beneath the surface, '[o]nly the excrement in the sewers [...] has gained the unquestionable right of free movement'. He stresses how 'the dead have been left underground [...] unburied [...] A place inhabited by the phantoms of lost people' to which he must travel.[11] In addition to the bathos which reduces nationalist borders to the scatological, the shift from above to below denotes the doubleness of his standpoint. Images of death express his movement across the limens of space, time, and states of being, exploring Nicosia as a *layered city* in need of archaeological excavation.[12] His own excavation is performed through interviews which question existing historiography and give voice to those, including left-wing Cypriots, whose views have been elided; the faint *echoes* of dissent now given textual sustenance. He concludes the work with promise for the future, wanting Cyprus to become a symbol 'of hope in this post-9/11 era that has witnessed boundaries turning into iron lines of division, as dangerous and difficult to cross as our own barbed wire line'.[13] Cyprus has long been co-opted as a metonym of these global and (neo-)colonial 'lines' of separation, dividing civilisations between 'Eastern' and 'Western'. For Papadakis, this is a Blakean world where people are mechanised in a violent habitus of 'iron' and 'barbed wire', the inheritance of imperialism, the Cold War, and the War on Terror. In nationalist imagery, '[m]en and machines blended into each other [...] the guns became part of the body [...] like robots'.[14] Papadakis seeks to overcome these ideological practices which dehumanise the individual, reduce free thought, and sterilise culture, offering quiet encouragement from the model of his pre-2001 crossings across places and languages.

These 'lines of division', re-crystallised after 9/11, are visually represented on the cover and chapter title pages of *Forbidden Zones* as four transecting lines which pass through the text, including Ali's name and back-cover photograph. As well as the divisions of global power, the lines represent the sectarianism which cuts and punctures Cypriot voices—perhaps, one for the island and the remaining three for the Guarantor Powers. This printing style is metonymic of the fragmented structure of the collection as a whole, repudiating a holistic narrative in favour of representing the discontinuities, ruptures, and internal divisions which characterise Cypriot selfhoods in the twenty-first century. Moreover, the range of stories is planetary, teasing out connections between experiences of marginality across the modern world; while the majority concern Cypriot lives, others depict Jamaican, Jewish, and Anatolian women in London. The preface stresses that they are all 'fictionalised realities…', illustrating their origins as autofictional products of a planetary life: 'Some [stories] are still travelling with me across time-zones, barriers and locations'.[15] As with Papadakis, the topos of travel is vital to the work and is characterised as the subversive movements of a Cypriot refugee surmounting political hurdles through unrestrained words. Mirroring Papadakis' postface, Ali's preface is signed from 'Nicosia'. Left unclear as to whether she is referring to north or south, the author sets her subject position in the porous reopened city of 2013 which is neither the divided Lefkosia nor the divided Lefkoşa of the 1963–2003 period. Comparably, for Papadakis, three succeeding chapters of his work are titled 'Lefkosia', 'Lefkosha', and 'Lefkosha/Lefkosia', demonstrating how the identities of both him and the city have transformed during his travels, ultimately experiencing three different places all claimed as the Cypriot capital.

In *Forbidden Zones*, the first story, 'Forbidden Zone', uses third-person narration to blur between memories from various times, comparing the experiences of exile, rape, and murder endured by a Greek-speaking family in July 1974 with the testimony of a Turkish-speaking former soldier in the present. In 'Finding Maro' and 'The Midwife', however, the first-person is used to present Ali's reunions with Greek-speaking Cypriot women after the border is opened. While the generic form of these 'fictionalised realities' differs slightly from Papadakis' text—particularly in the way the latter partially presents itself as research—Ali has similarly published academic works in which the first-person presses on the expected objective register of theory. In *Turkish Speaking Communities and Education* (2001), she recounts having to 'seek refuge from a war' by moving to London, selecting a career inspired by the 'similar stories of others who had to leave home' for the colonial centre.[16] Ultimately, '[t]he essence of my work' is 'giving voices to the silenced',[17] including individual experiences which mirror her own, allowing Ali to construct a new '*home*' within research and publishing. Indeed, in *Turkish Cypriot Identity in Literature* (1990), she asserts that 'Cypriot intellectuals have still to define themselves in relation to their "motherland"' but are attempting to assert 'their own will-power against this destiny'.[18] The same idiom is used in *Echoes from the Dead Zone* to imagine 'a kind of destiny' which haunts Cypriot history.[19] It is a nationalist 'destiny' within which individuals are trapped but which both authors understand as being weakened by the act of writing.

The two not only contest nationalism with their works but formulate their own theoretical models which function alongside, without deferring to the authority of, the Anglo-American academy. For Ali, '[e]veryone is talking and yet only the Cypriot says nothing',[20] anticipating a postcolonial reclaiming of autonomous Cypriot voices from British, Greek, and Turkish dominant discourses. In particular, Ali has repudiated the commonly-used identity markers 'Greek Cypriot' and 'Turkish Cypriot' and, throughout her works, uses the terms 'Cypriotgreek' and 'Cypriotturkish'. Not only is this a more literal translation of the Turkish equivalents, *Kıbrıs Rumları* and *Kıbrıs Türkleri*, re-calibrating the Anglophone conventions of colonially-inherited categories, but the merging of the nouns places an individual's relationship with Cyprus before the idealised sites of Greece or Turkey which remain lowercase and secondary.

Using comparable discourse to Papadakis, the narrator of 'Forbidden Zone' describes contemporary Cyprus, for a former soldier, as a 'schizophrenic society of cowards his children and grandchildren now inhabited'.[21] Interested in the importance of remembering, she stresses that '[w]henever they dug the ruins of the past… skeletons emerged with the recent excavations […] emerged to tell half the story, the other half still a secret', safeguarded by 'Shame? Guilt?'.[22] The motif of schizophrenia is again appropriated to express the heterogeneity of identities as Cypriots where a single consciousness is the site of plural, sometimes opposing, ideologies. In this island of ostensible doubleness, only 'half' a historiographic narrative is ever evident; the perspective of 'the other half'—or, in Papadakis' words, 'the other side'—is effaced. The layers of what it means to be Cypriot, from one's cultural identity to the physical levels of mass graves, require excavation to expose the realities of the conflict, including the suffering of Cypriots of different ethnolinguistic backgrounds. Notably, in this story, Ali chooses to depict a Greek-speaking Cypriot family to represent the victimisation of Cypriot domestic units.

Shame, valued highly in many Eastern Mediterranean communities, is depicted as an inhibitor of honesty. Likewise, Papadakis comments: 'Shame. This was the emotional equivalent of the Dead Zone in space', revealing the internalisation of social trauma on the mind.[23] For him, shame needs to be bypassed in order for truth-telling to emerge within intercommunal dialogue so one can 'meet people from the other side, talk to each other *and hear what they ha[ve] to say*' (*emphasis mine*), as the first step towards 'conciliation'.[24] For Ali, any 'silence' surrounding institutionalised violence amounts to complicity: a former soldier's 'silence for over thirty-four years? He colluded. He was complicit in the creation of this history'.[25] Notably, this period of time is parallel to that of Ali's personal history of writing mentioned previously in the preface (one of 'thirty-five years')[26]; it is her work which defies this pervasive epistemic silencing in Cyprus across this juncture.

Following from the importance of testimony—from Papadakis' interviewees to the interviewed ex-soldier in Ali's 'Forbidden Zone', all wrestling with shame—is its impact on identity. Papadakis draws on his university training to turn the academic gaze inwards and evaluate how he and his fellow Cypriots construct their ethnic and national identifications. Throughout the work, he intertextually reiterates nationalist historiographies—including those disseminated by schools—before challenging the biases of these received authorities in favour of individual experience. Describing the aphasias created by nationalism, he argues that contemporary Cypriots were 'tast[ing] the bitter harvest of not daring to act humanely, the consequences of keeping silent'.[27] Earlier, in describing Cypriot history, he lists, 'Arabs, Venetians, Byzantines, Ottomans, British, Greeks and Turks, all outsiders who used us for their own satisfaction… then abandoned us to bear the bitter fruits of our encounters'.[28] The recurring allusion to the title of Durrell's travelogue, as well as the nineteenth-century motif of hybrid 'fruits', re-writes the idiomatic conventions of colonial literature in its diatribe against occupation. However, by tacitly linking British imperialism with the Byzantine and Ottoman empires, as well as contemporary Greek and Turkish nationalisms, he reveals how the latter usurp the 'bitter' legacy of British colonial violence through selective misremembering.

The nationalist *silences* represented in both Papadakis' and Ali's texts are here rendered forms of neo-colonial repression, reflecting Tom Nairn's thesis that '"nationalism" is the pathology of modern developmental history' allowing 'for descent into dementia'.[29] Contrary to pro-Hellenic or pro-Turkic narratives of self, both Greeks and Turks, as well as their medieval empires, are *othered* as 'outsiders', foreign to the collective 'us' of all Cypriots. In this totalising critique of all nationalist discourses—or, 'the tyranny of school maps'[30]—Papadakis compares institutional spaces in both northern and southern Cyprus, as well as Greece and Turkey, to illustrate the ironic mirroring of strategies used to endorse difference. Recalling his childhood in southern Cyprus, he states that he 'had learned at school [... h]ow the Turks had attacked our glorious, civilized, tolerant and cosmopolitan Byzantine Empire reducing it to the current small Greek state' as the result of an Ottoman 'expansionism' culminating (anachronistically) in the events of 1974.[31] While visiting Istanbul, however, he discovers that Turkish citizens are conversely taught that the Ottomans 'had created a cosmopolitan, multi-ethnic, tolerant state' which 'liberated and civilized' before being 'reduced [...] to the small state of Turkey' following Greece's 'expansionist policy', culminating in its impact on Cyprus in 1974.[32] The parallelism not only compares the discourse of the two, revealing paradoxical similarities in their constructions of an historicised self, but the use of 'Western' colonialist idioms of civilisation demonstrates how this language of dualistic otherness is an inheritance, and internalisation, of British imperial ideology. While in other postcolonial societies the 'pre-colonial' is understood as a juncture of pre-'Western' independence, in Cyprus, the history of successive imperial occupations complicates this paradigm. Cypriots, therefore, arbitrarily assign a period of pre-British history, either Ottoman or Byzantine/Classic Greek, with a quixotic image of 'glorious' freedom by projecting back the jingoist ethos of the British Empire onto an equally-oppressive antecedent regime. Cypriot 'anti-colonialist' discourse, ironically, becomes a narrative which contests one form of colonialism while valorising another, leading to the acceptance of nationalist hegemonies from abroad. Elsewhere in the text, Papadakis visits an Istanbul museum viewing *echoes* in their exhibits: their cartography 'was the opposite of our normal maps' and, in its depiction of the violence of Cypriot history, 'the accusation was reversed'.[33] These mirrorings continue in the museums on either side of the Buffer Zone, elucidating how each 'passionately disagreed speaking the same language and in the same tone of voice'.[34] Crucially, this not only demonstrates the limitations of nationalist 'language'—*the only common 'language', other than English, which all Cypriots speak*—but shows that its writing of modern history, especially the conflicts between 1963 and 1974, are problematically invested in a dualism absolving the culpability of the self by placing all blame on an historicised Other. It also demonstrates how difficult it is to describe a collective 'us' of all Cypriots separate from Greek and Turkish affiliations, and especially without the Anglophone medium.

Ali, in 'Finding Maro', similarly describes her own viewpoint on history, observing, adjacent to 'barbed wire, six flags representing… what? Nation statehoods of foreign lands… of invaders… of ex-colonial powers in new roles as global rulers?'.[35] These are the flags of the Republic of Cyprus, the 'TRNC', Greece, Turkey, the UK, and the United Nations. Here, British cultural imperialism over the globe is elided with Greek and Turkish hegemonies over the island, framing the three as equally 'foreign' and symptomatic of occupation from the outside. Disavowing the flags and turning away from them, Ali states 'I don't want the mental pollution… Indelibly scratched on everything I look at […including t]he old yellow-stone houses' of the north once constructed by now-exiled Greek-speaking Cypriots.[36] The use of the ecological term illustrates how Cypriot consciousness has been colonised by nationalism in parallel with the damaged land. It is a colonisation which writes itself onto every section of society, defacing the former domestic spaces of refugees, now a relic of the 'yellow' symbolism of an independent Cyprus.

Repudiating this insidious contaminant, she strictly does not 'want to pollute the images of a past life together' in intercommunal peace, *recollecting* the coexistence before nationalist conflict and erasure.[37] Even the coffee she drinks, a signifier of the quotidian, suffers from 'a multiple-identity syndrome', like much of Cypriot culture, being variously named 'Cypriot', 'Turkish', or 'Greek' coffee according to the speaker's political agenda.[38] Repeating this theme of nationalism as a miasmic contagion—or, pathogen, in Nairn's idiom—Ali, in her foreword to *Turkish Cypriot Identity in Literature*, describes Cyprus as an island with 'a recent history covered in smoke and dust', forcing intellectuals to 'create dust storms'.[39] The same metaphor recurs in 'Forbidden Zone' in scenes depicting the July 1974 war: 'Clouds of dust descend. […] Dust covered bodies try out slow ghostly movements […] An imperceptible silence'.[40] The paratactic structure realises the intensity of conflict, one which introduces epistemic 'silence' to the island while dehumanising civilians. People lose their agency and become either depersonalised 'bodies' or penumbral 'ghost[s]', an ethereal image present in both Papadakis' account of the 'Dead Zone' and, as to be discussed, Mehmet Yaşın's poetry. In particular, if 'dust' represents the debris of nationalism which 'seep' into all aspects of Cypriot lives, it is here an ideological 'dust' rained down alongside bombs, osmotically permeating individuals' minds and 'bodies'.

Like Papadakis' depiction of robotised soldiers, in Ali's narrative, everyone is a victim of this social conditioning. In the ex-soldier's testimony, he describes the actions preceding the rape of a woman by a fellow soldier: 'A light elegant little thing she was. Like a bird. Young, barely in her mid-twenties. I heard him shout like a wounded animal'.[41] Far from a defence of his actions, the mirroring of 'bird' and 'animal' nonetheless illustrates the ways in which nationalist politics reduces all humans to a bestial state. Stripped of their humanity, they become mere vacuoles of ideology, preying on the weakest members of society. The third-person narrator, early in the story, describes the signs stating 'Forbidden Zone' as 'Black letters with black soldiers gun in hand tangled in barbed wire guard the empty hotels'.[42] The confusing syntax with no punctuation to divide clauses is metonymic of this 'tangled' mess of nationalism. It is unclear where words, spaces, weapons, people, and borders begin or end. Spaces are 'written' by jingoist 'hand[s]' also carrying ammunition, while soldiers themselves become dehumanised cyphers of nationalist identity, posted on the landscape like words on a signboard. The stylistic energy is reminiscent of Montis' own chaotic prose on (para-)military lives. Do the soldiers perform the 'guard[ing]' or is it the 'letters' of nationalism which ultimately police contested territory?

Both writers, therefore, stage explicit rejections of Greek and Turkish nationalist identifications and the historiographies which consolidate them. Commencing her academic 'Foreword', Ali asks, 'When does the history of [Cyprus] begin',[43] in relation to a given identity. Alluding to its inherent selectivity, she questions the narratorial starting points of a historicised feeling of belonging, anticipating Papadakis' conclusion that '[b]eginnings... happened much later'.[44] According to both, nationalist history is a constructivist and politicised category which depends on the disavowal of unpleasant truths which curtails the accuracy of its conceits. Moreover, it is culpable of physical and symbolic violence. For Ali, the 'pages of history have been written in blood',[45] while for Papadakis, those words have been applied to the writing of national spaces, including the Buffer Zone which 'became a savagely fought-over boundary, as it was drenched in blood'.[46] In addition to the actual consequence of war, 'blood' has a double meaning in its nationalist connotations of ethnic essence. Hence, history is written in the discourse of a racialised essentialism, the symbolic marking of a 'boundary' between ethnic groups, which is then violently manifested in the construction of bordered spaces. As a consequence, Ali argues, Cypriots 'have always been forced to be someone else'.[47] Cypriots are interpellated into fixed neo/colonial categories, within which their individualism is reduced and intersections between the various Cypriot communities are denied. Equally, Papadakis reveals the ways in which others attempt 'to impose a different identity on me'.[48] This includes, not only nationalist institutions in Cyprus enforcing a Greek identity onto him, but also Eurocentric pressures to assume a Greek identification 'in order to be favourably accepted in the West'.[49] The Greek identity is both a yielding to a nationalist narrative *and* a postcolonial, Fanonian 'white mask' which eschews the Orientalism of the British imperial imagination in favour of a performance of Westernisation.

As Nadjarian queries in her depiction of a Cypriot museum, 'aren't we nearly Europeans? [...] does [EU membership] necessarily make us Europeans? [...] I know deep down, it does not, we are not. Not really'.[50] This is a Bhabha-esque commentary on being 'not quite/not white'.[51] The colonialist debate subsequently leaches into existential questions on being *not quite* Cypriot, or Greek, or Turkish, and the ways in which monocentric continental, national, and ethnic identifications are policed by institutions as varied as museum and military installations. All three authors, therefore, grapple with the need to create literary and linguistic forms which can transport culture and identities beyond the neo-colonial, nationalist dichotomies which dissect all areas of Cypriot society, from the political and academic to the quotidian. It is the motif of (counter)travel that is chosen to accomplish this.

Counter-Travelling the Buffer Zone

Papadakis' counter-travelogue showcases encounters with Cypriots who deny either identities as Cypriots or their geographic position in Western Asia. The existence of many 'Cypriot[s] who... did not want to be one' are placed in parallel with Kemalists in Turkey who valorise Atatürk's blue eyes and assert themselves, through racialised historiography, as 'a white, Aryan people'.[52] Nonetheless, it is his travels which facilitate a *bildungsroman*-like personal development in his sense of selfhood. He states at the very onset of the work that he 'changed so much on the way': in Istanbul, learning Turkish became a mode of 'self-revelation', rather than the study of an Othered culture; flying back to Cyprus, he 'felt different', rendering 'it impossible for me to remain a Greek'.[53] In this existential voyage, and revealed in liminal spaces like the *empty space* of the airplane, Papadakis understands identity as fragmented, transformational, and multi-layered, disavowing the essentialism of a purely 'Greek' subjecthood in favour of one which, like the movements of an airplane, is transcultural and in flux.

Similarly, in 'The Midwife', Ali depicts reuniting with her mother's former Greek-speaking colleague, Yiannoulla (notably also rendered as Γιαννούλλα), as an existential 'journey' of mutual self-discovery, shifting from 'stranger' to friend.[54] In 'Finding Maro', she describes how she and the eponymous character, a Greek-speaking childhood friend separated by the Buffer Zone, no longer 'know these women each has become'.[55] *The erection of the border altered identities into dyadic opposites; the reopening of this dividing line allows for changes in subjecthood once again.* Both writers invariably struggle with this process and the two use the terms *traitor*, *betrayal* and *spy* across their oeuvres to denote the responses from those who view efforts towards intercommunal peace as disloyalty to a 'national cause'.[56] Ultimately, as Gilroy suggests, 'modes of belonging articulated through appeals to the power of sovereign territory and the bonds of rooted, exclusive national cultures, are contrasted with the different translocal solidarities that have been constituted by diaspora dispersal and estrangement'.[57]

In this context, the translocal positioning of the writers is uniquely manifold: both publish from London, both have travelled to the national 'motherlands' of Greece and Turkey, and both surmount the limits of the local by travelling across the Buffer Zone. The 'estrangement' in this case, especially for Ali, is that of being made a refugee, a transcultural self without a specific sense of the local. Their works transcend nationalist confines through movements in language, space, and subject position which decentre the expectations of an unmovable national isolationism. This is emblematised by the portrayal of walking across borders in both *Echoes from the Dead Zone* and *Forbidden Zones*. In 'Finding Maro', the action of walking allows Ali to reunite with her childhood friend, culminating in her arrival at Maro's new home in southern Nicosia while being followed by a film crew. Ali describes, with the vivid intensity of paratactic present tense, how, 'I come up to her garden wall. [...] A simple gate. [...] I am now in her world. No one else exists. [...] I reach the closed front door. I put my hand on the wall and lean on it for a second. [...] A few moments later a woman opens the door'.[58] This account realises a personal crossing counter to the detached register of journalistic or statistical accounts of political change, including that of the film crew who attempt to coerce her experience into their narrative. The imagery commences the recurring motifs of surmounting closed barriers throughout her stories. While Montis was concerned with the *closed doors* of British imperialism, in the post-partition generation of Cypriot writers, it is the doors closed between families and acquaintances as a consequence of war, exile, and segregation that need to be reopened.

In this scene, Ali re-enters the intimate 'world' of a dear friend, moving away from the sterile political in-between spaces which dehumanise Cypriots. While embracing, Ali stresses that her 'eyes are closed. The moment is ours [...] I open my eyes... as though waking up from a dream [...] We are holding hands not as fifty-five-year-olds but as ten-year-old little girls'.[59] Repeating the motif of 'closed' spaces, it is here that the internalised borders of the mind have reopened, allowing the pair to recapture an ineffable sensation outside the confines of time and space. This is 'a timeless zone', transcending the politically-sanctioned habitus of the divided city.[60] Moreover, their meeting allows for the free movement of cultural artefacts, as Ali shares with Maro a story she wrote in London about their friendship. This metafictional paradigm demonstrates how subversive writing, *in English*, is a medium through which intercommunal reunification can be achieved as narratives are transported across international borders and, now, exchanged between northern and southern Nicosia. More importantly, *this textual interaction which could once only occur in London can now be experienced in post-2003 Nicosia as a space newly made culturally-plural*. Indeed, people and places in Nicosia have altered. For instance, Ali anthropomorphises how its 'Ottoman Kiosks... with courtyards *nuzzle up* to Venetian yellow stone arched houses'; she subsequently passes Maro's own courtyard before the latter '*snuggles up* and we begin to read [the story] together' (*emphases mine*).[61] Their unity realises the inherent cultural pluralism of the city which nationalism had denied it, reclaiming an intimacy which enables mutual access to a shared, trans-communal culture.

As Ali states in 'The Midwife'—a story which spans from describing Greek-speaking Cypriot friends in North London to her visiting a Maronite village in the north—it is a 'fact that Cyprus was always multicultural'.[62] It is a 'fact' evidenced by the 'multicultural' Cypriot community of London *and experienced anew* in the Cyprus altering in the wake of the border-opening. Idiomatically echoing the preceding story ('Finding Maro'), Ali describes how she is reunited with her mother's former colleague, the titular midwife, Yiannoulla. Sitting in parallel gardens, Yiannoulla realises who Ali is, and, having 'located me in her past, that we had shared spaces and a life together, she wanted to come closer'. To do so, she must overcome the garden 'wall lined with cactus pots... in between', causing Ali 'to open the blue courtyard gate', as 'golden brown [leaves] kept falling around us', before Yiannoulla begins singing in Turkish.[63]

Set in the south-western city of Paphos, Yiannoulla goes on to telephone Ali's mother in the north, mirroring how, in 'Finding Maro', Ali telephones Maro from the north to arrange a meeting in the south. The intertextual porousness reflects how cultural discourse (including music) is able to dislodge conventional boundaries of place and culture. The scene is allegorical of the border-opening, with the sharp cacti symbolising the precarious dangers of the Buffer Zone dissecting Cypriots. However, Ali repudiates the generic form of objective political commentary, instead cultivating a personalised account of how larger political events are experienced by individuals. Instead, the stylistic mode of travel writing is subversively used to represent, not intercontinental movements across the planet, but the movements of individuals across the physically small, but symbolically vast, portal between two Cypriot homes occupied by a Greek-speaker and a Turkish-speaker.

The two share a psychic space of the past, recreating and reforming their pre-1963 lives, once frozen, in the gradually-altering island. The borders of space and time dissolve; the 'blue courtyard gate' metonymic of Greek nationalism no longer blocks their path; and the 'golden brown' signifiers of Cypriot independence rains over their translingual dialogue. If gardens represent edenic spaces, then this marks a new genesis for Cypriot intercommunality. Doing so, the allegory breaks temporal unities by imagining an idealised future for Cyprus which harks back to the more peaceful era of Ali's birth.

Indeed, Yiannoulla tells Ali a story of her career as a midwife which the latter repeats as a third-person, analeptic frame narrative. Within it, a Turkish-speaking Cypriot, during the conflict of the 1960s, walks from his village to implore Yiannoulla to attend to his wife's pregnancy. Hearing a knock on her front door, unaware of his 'identity', he introduces himself as 'Χασάνης' (Hasanis); as Ali states, 'he has added *–is* to *Hasan* to accommodate Greek grammar, a common device for bilingual people switching between languages'.[64] Situated at the porous limen of the door, the wind—like words or the aforementioned dust in 'Forbidden Zone'—is depicted '[s]eeping in through the cracks of the door'.[65] In short, the object of division is overcome by dialogue between the two. It is facilitated by self-translation, not only of discourse, but one's own 'identity'. Hasan transforms his name to mirror the common suffix of masculine Greek names as a marker of familiarity. She eventually delivers the baby, resulting in Hasan's temporary imprisonment for liaising with someone outside his linguistic community. As Ali stresses, he was detained from 'the door of the house' he lived in for being a 'traitor'.[66] In this instance, *doors* symbolise the borders imposed by nationalist self-segregation, the domestic home being forced to disavow the Other outside. Yet, Hasan, in his rage, commences a diatribe against the TMT: '"*I pezevengi*!" he shouts in Greek towards the village', moments later, '"[…]*Pezevenkler*!" He spits out the last word in Turkish'.[67] It is through a translingual investment in the shared culture of all Cypriots—in this case, a common swearword, *pimps*—that the partitions of nationalism—linguistic, domestic, as well as geopolitical—can be contested. For Ali, Cyprus has always been a site of 'bilingual' identities which cannot be martialled by a monocentric denial of cultural syncretism. In this explicitly-*transportal* story, a midwife from one ethnolinguistic background crosses a physical and symbolic limen to deliver a baby from an ethnolinguistically-Other mother, counter to the demands of the nationalist 'motherland'.

Papadakis similarly explores the linguistic heterogeneity of Cypriot vernaculars while learning Turkish and travelling across the historically-pluralist cities of Nicosia and Istanbul. Once home to varied ethnolinguistic communities who spoke Armenian, Arabic, Greek, and Turkish, both cities have become linguistically-homogenous following the emergence of nationalist movements from the early twentieth century onwards. As a countertraveller, Papadakis reveals how changes in his political and cultural identifications alter his understanding of the urban spaces around him. Notably, while the first chapter is titled 'Constantinople', when he describes revisiting the metropolis two years later, he does so in a chapter named 'Istanbul'. As he explains during his first stay, he begins 'feeling less that I was in Constantinople and more that I was in Istanbul'.[68] The imagined geography he experiences alters. Gradually, he revises his pre-existing history of the Mediterranean by destabilising the imagined

Byzantine and Hellenic fantasies he once projected onto Agia Sophia as a simulacrum of Greek nationalist identity. Travelling to the city and engaging with Turkish people allows him to re-write the discursive Constantinople of his Hellenocentric education.

Equally, in Cyprus, while crossing the capital's Buffer Zone from north to south, he reveals that 'I would never be able to go back to that place called Lefkosia. It could never be just Lefkosia again'.[69] The subsequent chapter is titled 'Lefkosha/Lefkosia'. Places are socially and psychologically constructed. As such, Papadakis enters a new psychic space, despite it being a physical return to the half he had previously been familiar with. He wrestles with the dictates of nationalism by rejecting the ethnocentrism which denies, in Ali's terms, the 'bilingual' identities of Cypriot places and peoples. By the final chapter, while walking across the border in 2003, he asserts that 'divided Nicosia became a mixed city once again… the others' language was heard everywhere'.[70] Like Ali's anthology, this is an integration of past, present, and future, where the idealism of what Cyprus can become alludes to its historic syncretism, aware, nonetheless, of the need for further progress rather than complacency. The self and 'other' binary safeguarded by formal partition begins to destabilise and the city has become audibly-heteroglossic for the first time since 1963. However, Papadakis emphasises, more than Ali, that this is a different space to the city/cities of the colonial era, of 1960, of 1974, and of the years preceding the border-opening.

There are echoes here of Montis' description of the newly-independent capital recalling 'its name' (as I detailed in the preceding chapter).[71] The triumphant opening of the Buffer Zone has an historical importance as great as decolonisation from the British Empire. Imperialism is mirrored with nationalist partition. Yet, as with the tainted promises of 1960, Papadakis tempers optimism with the practical needs to find methods to facilitate and increase trans-border dialogue. Interestingly, it is in this chapter that Papadakis exclusively refers to the capital as Nicosia. The English name offers a neutral idiom shared by all speakers as an intercommunal signifier, one that is more practical than the longer Lefkosia/Lefkoşa, but which also estranges Greek and Turkish from its identity.

The Transportal Language of the Buffer Zone

Both writers disavow the identities of locally-internalised nationalisms through a philological approach to worldliness which, according to Said's theory, 'opposes monocentrism, [or] ethnocentrism, which licenses a culture to cloak itself in the particular authority of certain values over others'.[72]

Ali, as editor and translator of the academic papers contained in *Turkish Cypriot Identity in Literature/Edebiyatta Kıbrıslı Türk Kimliği*, compiles a bilingual work in which the Anglophone versions of each essay are contained in the first half and the Turkish in the second. She directs her foreword to 'Cyprus…' or 'Kıbrıs…',[73] addressing the island and its inhabitants in more than one language. Similarly, and as to be discussed in more detailed, the poet Mehmet Yaşın publishes works in Turkish and English simultaneously. This form accommodates a broad readership beyond the confines of one linguistic community, allowing English speakers from both the south and the diaspora to consume literature or theory concerned with deconstructing social borders. It also provides for a larger, global audience, entering each corpus into the marketable categories of 'postcolonial' or 'world' literatures. Similarly, three of Nadjarian's narratives in *Ledra Street* were previously commended by the Commonwealth Short Story Competition.[74]

Throughout *Echoes from the Dead Zone*, intercommunal dialogue is a pertinent and recurring theme, illustrating the necessity for discourse to move across the Buffer Zone. While in Istanbul, Papadakis' discussions with his Turkish friends allow them all to question the educations they had received. He states in striking clauses that, 'We spoke for a long time. Something was wrong. Someone had been cheated'.[75] By learning Turkish and interacting with people othered by pro-Hellenic nationalist pedagogy, Papadakis is able to revise and repudiate the ideological barriers impeding peace in the Eastern Mediterranean. Equally, in the following subsection, Papadakis' friend, Erkin, informs him that the ring-wing in Turkey 'think that anyone who reads is a reactionary',[76] an assessment later compared with the censorship of left-wing intellectuals in Cyprus. Simple acts of speaking and reading are politically-potent tactics, threatening the nationalist establishments of Cyprus, Greece, and Turkey, and illustrating the need for publishing works which can be read beyond the local.

Accordingly, Papadakis goes on to metatextually discuss the important—yet problematic—role played by English as the medium of both his publication and intercommunal dialogue in Nicosia. For an island of refugees, the burden of language means that 'the exile was triple': firstly, there is no 'common medium of communication' between Greek- and Turkish-speakers; secondly, the vernaculars of Cyprus are marginalised in favour of the standardised 'mother-tongues' of Greece and Turkey; and, finally, Cypriots are compelled to speak the former colonial-tongue, English, to interact across the border and to appear 'western'.[77] English, therefore, occupies an ambivalent inbetweenness, like the Buffer Zone itself, which both facilitates cultural interchange while estranging oneself from one's first language(s). As Papadakis emphasises, however, one's 'native tongue' offers its own problems. As well as the issues already cited, both the standardised forms of Greek and Turkish maintain their respective 'official idiom' of discussing the conflict.[78] Most Greek-speakers commonly refer to the actions of Turkey in 1974 as an 'invasion' (as do most British officials), while most Turkish-speakers allude to it as an 'intervention' (as do some American officials).[79] English, therefore, despite its colonial legacies, seemingly offers a politically-neutral medium for necessary dialogue across a linguistically- *and* politically-divided island.

It is through this form that Ali, Papadakis, and their contemporaries chose to publish to ensure that their post-partition narratives are able to surmount the epistemic partition of standardised national languages. This transportal *self-translation* allows for a broad intercommunal reading experience to subversively destabilise the nationalist dichotomising of self and Other. As well as realising Hugo Meltzl's 'principle of polyglottism' by composing works for a polyglot audience,[80] this process exemplifies the relationship posited between translation and selfhood in Apter's *The Translation Zone* (2006). Her work—its title revealing interesting parallels with the politics of zonality also present in *Echoes from the Dead Zone* and *Forbidden Zones*—situates itself as a post-9/11 thesis which carves out territory in the liminal *zones* between monocentric cultural forms. According to Apter, '[t]ranslation is a significant medium of subject reformation and political change', allowing one to cultivate 'an idea that belongs to no one language or nation in particular' while 'rendering self-knowledge foreign to itself'.[81] It is precisely through this act of self-translation that Ali and Papadakis are able to perform acts of 'subject re-formation' across the Buffer Zone, eschewing nationalist identifications and, thus, anticipating 'political change' in relation to partition.

Notably, by using the non-nationalist Anglophone form, Papadakis routinely complicates Cypriots' nationalist perceptions of the purity of their languages by revealing their inherent intersectionality which, in turn, defamiliarises what Apter terms 'self-knowledge'. While in Istanbul, for instance, he learns that many idioms for cultural artefacts in Greek and Kypriaka, including words for food, music, and even religious practices, have Turkish or Arabic etymologies. For him, this is a means of 'self-revelation' whereby a new selfhood is constructed by de-exoticising Turkish while auto-exoticising Greek.[82] Exhuming the diachronic code-switching responsible for transporting loanwords between Mediterranean vernaculars, he finds that '[l]earning Turkish was an exploration deep into the subconscious of the Greek language' and which facilitates 'a welcome liberation to my mouth'.[83] His use of the term 'subconscious' illustrates Apter's theory that translation offers the ability to alter one's own cultural consciousness, freeing one from the coercive restrictions of nationalist dictates which attempt to purify languages and identities. The self of one nationalist discourse in Cyprus cannot exist without cultural remnants from, or associated with, the Other.

His commentary on the term *kalamarades*—'originally meaning scribblers' and used by Greek-speaking Cypriots to (sometimes pejoratively) denote people from Greece—reveals the ironic othering performed by Cypriots against discourses external to their own local context.[84] The *written* nature of Standard Modern Greek is rendered Other to the oral condition of Kypriaka. Greek-*speakers* in Cyprus view Greek-*writers* in Greece—those whose who codify the official, nationalist language—as Other. There is a cognitive dissonance between the local Kypriaka, with its dependence on the alterity of non-codified Turkish loanwords, and the external, seemingly-purified Greek standardised in Greece.

It is *within* the limens of self and Other that Cypriots understand their socio-linguistic subjecthood, an in-between that is both familiar and foreign to the standardised cultures of Greece and Turkey. In short, there are translingual words shared across Greece, Turkey, and both sides of the Cypriot Green Line. However, there also are words that Cypriots share only with either Greece or Turkey, rendering the standardised languages of the latter two partially foreign. It is only through English that Papadakis can elaborate on this linguistic intersectionality and which can reveal the doors, open or closed, between the various languages of the Eastern Mediterranean. By tracing what Lacan calls 'slippage' (or, '*glissement*') between linguistic forms,[85] Papadakis deconstructs the ostensible holisticism of each to decentre the metropoles associated with them. The medium of English, therefore, helps to foreignise the *metropolitan* discourses codified in either Athens or Ankara in order to destabilise the nationalist registers transported to *peripheral* Cyprus.

As Ali similarly states, she 'delight[s] in the play on words special to multilingual communities',[86] offering a poststructuralist wordplay that destabilises the formal conceits of official linguistic forms. As already observed, Ali's oeuvre regularly mixes English, Turkish and untransliterated Greek, blending the three into a uniquely Cypriot heteroglossia which, while understood by most Anglophone readers, has a specific intonation for those familiar with the Eastern Mediterranean. For both writers, *self*-translation is a necessary means of contesting nationalist segregation by creating a pan-Cypriot sprachbund—via a foreignised postcolonial English—that can be powerfully borne across borders. Doing so, they translate who the self and the Other are within a partitioned habitus.

Notably, both Ali and Papadakis repeat the term *mahallas/mahalle*, a shared Cypriot term for neighbourhood of Arabic etymology.[87] For the latter, the very word 'brought a certain sweetness to the mouth for many', contrary to the 'bitter' social antagonisms which are as unpleasant as eating 'a large mouthful of lemon'.[88] Alluding to Durrell once again, the binary of 'sweetness' and 'bitter' illustrates the satisfaction of cross-cultural imbrications in spite of the partitions inspired during the 1950s. Emblematised by a Cypriot word signifying the site of *homes*, polyglotism is used to construct a new cultural home for Cypriots which decolonises consciousness, not only from the discursive categories of British imperialism, but also from its equally-'bitter' ideological successor, nationalism. This is freedom from all epistemic violence against the tongue. Like common Cypro-Greco-Turkish culinary words, and following the connotations of taste, Ali and Papadakis create works to be *consumed* by all Anglophone Cypriots through textual exchanges which flow transculturally beyond the local by reconfiguring what 'the local' means in post-2003 Cyprus.

The Homes of the Buffer Zone

This concept of a new cultural home is contrary to the images of homelessness used to denote the subject position of refugees in contemporary

Cypriot writing. Literary spaces are figured as alternatives to the physical territory emptied of its exiled inhabitants and divided by sectarian politics. Indeed, the word 'home' appears on 57 pages across *Echoes from the Dead Zone*.

Continuing the references to Durrell, a subsection titled 'Home Sweet Home' details Papadakis' invitation to visit the home of a Turkish-speaking Cypriot refugee, Erkan, formerly inhabited by a Greek-speaking family before 1974. The section immediately follows the transcript of a nationalist postcard printed for Turkish soldiers visiting northern Cyprus, illustrating how 'home' is a construct imagined by discourses of political ownership. Erkan's home garden is vividly described, detailing 'shady lemon trees' and the leaves of an 'old olive tree… reflecting the sunrays in their silver underside'.[89] The echoes of *Bitter Lemons* and the mechanisation of nature into a metallic form represent the legacy of colonialist issues of land rights which resonate today. The motif of 'reflecting' sunlight symbolises how the solar imagery of the British Empire is reproduced in the 'postcolonial' and post-partition present and is filtered through the olive leaves metonymic of the flag of the Republic of Cyprus and the coats of arms of both south and north. The redistribution of Cypriot property after the 1960s and 1970s is a paradigm unique to this 'postcolonial' context in which land is interceded by competing political forces: those of British imperialism (the lingering solar rays between the bitter lemons), the concept of an independent Cypriot nation (the olive tree rooted to the land), and the nationalisms of Greece and Turkey (the textual postcard moving between Cyprus and one of its so-called motherlands). Crucially, the territorial colonisations of imperialism and nationalism are placed in parallel.

Here, the pastoral of Durrell's travelogue is devoid of all idealism as the home*land* is—like Ali's metaphor of pollution—scarred by politics. Erkan's home is subsequently described through the register of the unhomely, revealing how refugees are not only estranged from the place of their birth but also from the residences of their sanctioned rehousing. Papadakis asks, 'How does one enter and live in another's home? How long does it take to become your own?'.[90] For many rehoused refugees, they live as 'an invited guest' in another's legal property, motivating the narrator to question whether the 'reflections [of former occupants] fleetingly appear on the mirrors?'.[91] The recurring questions demonstrate the unresolved nature of the *status quo* in which issues of belonging remain unanswerable in an incomplete construction of both home and 'home-land'. This is supported by the doubleness of the mirror—the imagined ghostly apparitions which haunt one's domestic space—in opposition with the feigned homogeneity of the two national-ised parts of the island.

Another visited home in the north is shown to have salvaged all Orthodox icons, now accompanied on the walls by 'Arabic verses from the Koran'. The occupant corrects his grammar when speaking with Papadakis, explaining that the collection of icons 'used to belong… no, that *belongs*… to the owner'.[92] The shifts register the duality of the Cypriot home which not only moves between notions of pan-Cypriotism and imaginings of Greek and Turkish cultures, but between the two places a Cypriot refugee calls home on either side of the Buffer Zone. Home is inherently defamiliarised and, like the idea of a 'Cypriot nation' itself, is one with only partial commitment or sense of ownership. Imagining a photograph album left during the conflict of 1974, Papadakis describes various moments of a family's life before 'you turn a page – empty'.[93] Like the partition, an individual's existence is cut in two, creating a fragmented habitus, suspended and without completion. This metatextual motif of a book on (family) identity reveals the need for literature to offer a resolution to this inertia by creating a medium through which an alternative feeling of belonging can be cultivated.

Elsewhere, 'home' is represented as an estranged and politicised site of being. The 'Museum of Barbarism' in northern Nicosia, for instance, is described as appearing like 'an ordinary home, with a horrendous name'.[94] Papadakis also describes how, when he 'visited peoples' homes, I was struck by ammunition shells being used for decoration' alongside 'ashtray[s…] or plastic flowers'.[95] In both instances, war is internalised into quotidian, domestic spaces, as all areas of Cypriot life are corrupted by the traumas of conflict. The first 'home' becomes an explicit monument to warfare, while the latter demonstrates how symbols of death usurp those of life, like the dusty residue of an 'ashtray' or the lifeless 'plastic flowers' unable to propagate in the future. Home becomes a paradoxical inhibitor of life in a relatively-inert, post-traumatic society.

Similarly, in 'Forbidden Zone', Ali commences the narrative with an image, not of a home, but an abandoned hotel left languishing in decay since 1974. Unlike Baybars' and Montis' novels which begin with idealised images of their pre-1950s homes—and in opposition with colonialist travel writers' exoticist renderings of Levantine villas—Ali represents a generation of exiled Cypriot writers for whom the signifier 'home' has been emptied to the point of meaninglessness. She begins with disjointed images of violence: 'A cracked skull appeared beyond the hotel… Snuggled in the shape of a foetus. A larger head compared to the body… A large chunk missing. Jagged edged'.[96] Inverting the typical beginnings of the *bildungsroman*, birth is substituted by death with the perverse symbol of a foetal corpse representing an island prematurely destroyed in the early years of its independence. The ruptures in the human remains—the parts 'missing' and its disproportionate features—reflect the disjointed status of Cypriot society with its broken body politic and the '[j]aged edge[s]' of its partition.

The hotel is described as a 'square building twelve storeys high. Broad and full of bravado' with 'neat lined-up balconies as though at a military parade, reminders of the boom '70s package holidays'.[97] The male anthropomorphic idioms render the building a monolith of masculinist power, a projection of the phallic dominance over land desired by its architect. As a testament to the power struggles between male Cypriot politicians, the 'twelve storeys' correspond to the twelve years of intercommunal violence between 1963 and 1974, each layer now rendered defunct. Moreover, the hotel, explicitly built during 'the late 1960s early '70s',[98] is a metonym of conformity, modernisation, and Westernisation, revealing how nationalism constructs its identity as a capitalist imitation of preceding, colonially-imposed forms. Throughout the narrative the name of this liminal space is reiterated in Western European languages—'Forbidden Zone', 'Zone Interdite', and 'Verbotene Zone'—all discourses of partition written by, or from, the outside in three languages where 'Zone' is a common, totalising signifier of space, foreign to Greek and Turkish. The Cypriot *non-home* of the hotel represents how the island's domestic territory, throughout its history, has been estranged by the mediation of external forces—from colonialism and tourism, to nationalism and international diplomacy—which all share the same discursive methods of regulating this sought-after territory.

Imagining the tourists formerly occupying the hotel—'blonde' women observing 'the local tanned olive-skinned boys with erotic eyes'[99]—Ali visualises the subject position of neo/colonial travellers and the racialised and 'erotic[ised]' dynamics of First World travel, before reversing these conceits and revealing the sexual violence committed against Cypriot women in this post/colony. The 'package holidays' which have since resumed on both sides of the island, further defamiliarising Cyprus with new signs written in Northern European languages, are performed in wilful ignorance of the war enacted on its beaches decades earlier. This commentary on the unhomely world created by politics resonates with Huggan's theories of the 'postcolonial exotic' as well as Kincaid's diatribe against colonialism and tourism in *A Small Place*. The hotel mirrors Kincaid's satirical tour of Antigua and the 'monument[s] to rottenness' she details on the consumerist landscape, the 'style of building, ugly in any climate [but] especially ugly in a small, hot place'.[100] In Cyprus, the hotels trapped in the 'Forbidden Zones' of Nicosia and Famagusta are literally *rotting*, like the promise of the independent nation itself, with Ali detailing, with bodily imagery, '[t]he dark hollow body of the hotel [which] cannot prevent the echoes escaping from all its orifices'.[101] Embodied as a putrefying mass, it is nonetheless a source from which—using the same term as Papadakis—'echoes' are faintly discernible. These are *echoes* of truth-telling, personal testimony, anti-nationalism, and cultural heterogeneity which both Ali and Papadakis are attempting to salvage from the remains of destroyed buildings and lives, reconstructing an Anglophone corpus on modern Cyprus which writes-back against the expectations of neo/colonial travelogues and the divisive nationalisms exploiting a vulnerable society.

In this unhomely habitus, Ali isolates Varosha's 'modern houses' surrounded 'with trees transported from other parts of the Empire', including Australia, the Caribbean, Malaysia, and South Africa.[102] The Cypriot home and metonymic 'modern' nation are products of colonialism and, thus, of foreign influences imposed on the land and then naturalised. The semi-anachronistic allusion to 'other parts of the Empire', *after* 1960, is a marker of continuing neo-colonial remnants on the island's domestic policies. Similarly, the name of the hotel, Aspendia, the Greek name of an ancient city now in modern Turkey, reveals how quasi-domestic spaces on the island are arbitrary amalgams of external influences—the hotel's Western European architecture and its claimed Greco-Turkish identification—constructing spaces in which no Cypriot is fully at home. Indeed, the description of the garden correlates with the geopolitics of land detailed in Papadakis' text, and contrasts with the edenic space of Baybars' childhood home in *Plucked in a Far-Off Land*. Here, the 'postcolonial' garden is an unfamiliar space stripped of its pastoral, naive idealism.

In opposition with the innocence of youth imagined by Baybars, Ali portrays children as unconscious receptacles of ideology: the character Yorgos, for instance, watches his child and 'marvelled and worried at the capacity of the young to pick up so much which was not consciously taught them'.[103] In addition to the dangers of politicised pedagogy, this brutalised world is one without justice and which destroys intercommunal bonds. The lawyer Yorgos, before being murdered by Turkish-speaking soldiers, watches fires consume the 'doors of the District Court House', worrying about his 'fellow barrister', a Turkish-speaking friend, Mustafa.[104] The rule of law has been abandoned and the 'House' within which it was symbolically maintained, like all other homes, is demolished. With it, so are the relationships between Cypriot friends from different linguistic backgrounds: the 'House' in which Yorgos and Mustafa once worked is gone, as is their friendship. Conspicuously, both Baybars and Montis trained in law, a discipline they both abandoned as youths born in a colonised habitus, a discipline now abandoning all Cypriots in the 'postcolonial', nationalist alternative.

In the following subsection of the narrative, Yorgos is halted by a Turkish-speaking Cypriot soldier who communicates in Kypriaka. Nonetheless, all Yorgos 'could see was a rifle pointing at him', moments after having 'close[d] his eyes willing with all his powers that [Mustafa] be unharmed'.[105] The peaceful coexistence denoted by Yorgos' and Mustafa's companionship is *already* rendered a figment of the character's memory, existing only when he shuts his eyes. The island's *closed doors* are internalised to the barrier of the eyelids. Equally, Cypriot polyglotism dissolves as the universal signifier of war—a gun—usurps as the sole method of communication, over Cypriot vernaculars, in the exchange between soldier and civilian. It ultimately leads to the latter's death. This is the anti-home created by neo-colonial nationalist conflict to which Ali's writing reacts. Notably, her opening description of the 'skull… Snuggled in the shape of a foetus' is idiomatically echoed, later in the anthology, in her portrayal of her and Maro when the latter 'snuggles up' to read to Ali's short story with her.[106] Lacking a fixed Cypriot home, Ali imagines a newly-regenerated Cypriot society, following the opening the border, in which intercommunal bonds are revived through sharing discourse. When Ali closes her eyes embracing Maro, she re-opens them to a resumed friendship; a generation earlier, when Yorgos opens his eyes from memories of Mustafa, he sees the gun which portends his murder.

In *Echoes from the Dead Zone*, Papadakis elaborates on how, in the absence of a distinct territory to bear his allegiances, 'the Dead Zone became my real home', his 'own mother-fatherland'.[107] The place which facilitates and inspires his anti-partition research—including 'the voices I had carried over',[108] as a literal description of the act of translation—is the limen with which he identifies himself. Counter to the nationalisms of 'mother-fatherland[s]', he repudiates the concept of an unproblematic 'homeland' in favour of the limen as his 'real home'. Importantly, and like Ali, it is his unpacking of the Buffer Zone through counter-discursive writing that he challenges the geopolitics which compete to occupy Cypriot territory with ideology, soldiers, and partitions. For Ali and Papadakis, the Anglophone stories they compose and share is the only *home* to which they ascribe a feeling of belonging, a place where new identities are forged and an honest appraisal of history can be mounted. Re-writing the Buffer Zone is tantamount to deconstructing it.

Poems of Homelessness and the Unhomely

Prior to Papadakis' publication, there was a paucity of long prose works by Cypriots following the trauma of partition. The psychological and economic impact of war, as well as issues of censorship, rendered careers in the cultural representation of Cypriot politics, particularly from the Left, problematic. Nonetheless, many of the themes in the works of post-partition prose writers are anticipated in Mehmet Yaşın's influential poetry collection, *Don't Go Back to Kyrenia* (2001), an anthology of compositions from 1977 onwards. Rare for Cypriot publications, the text presents the original Turkish alongside English translations by Baybars on the opposing recto page.

Translation and self-translation are important to Mehmet's works. While primarily writing in Turkish, he occasionally integrates English and non-transliterated Greek words into his corpus. The poems he and Baybars chose for the new-millennium anthology were published as part of the Middlesex University Press World Literature Series, consciously entering the translingual texts into a planetary oeuvre. The title explicitly writes-back to Durrell's *Bitter Lemons* and the colonialist's translation of an Ottoman poem, 'Don't Go To Kyrenia'.[109] There is a fascinating intertextual movement between Ottoman Turkish, British English, Standard Modern Turkish, and the English of a British-Cypriot translator. In Mehmet's and Baybars' body of translation, intended by the former for an Eastern Mediterranean audience, the cooperative acts of composing and translating works about the island are reclaimed by dispossessed Cypriots who seek repatriation with their place of birth. The difference in titles, however, illustrates the problematic status of Cypriot refugees deprived of the basic human right to return—to go *Back*—to their homes. Mehmet's poetry describes the homelessness of refugees in implicit contrast with the holiday homes of exoticist travel writers. For an epigram, Mehmet quotes Durrell's Orientalist axiom that Cyprus 'was more Eastern than its landscape would suggest', inspiring the latter to 'c[o]me back always to the Kyrenia range',[110] a privilege now denied to thousands of contemporary Cypriots. Furthermore, as Kyrenia is in the predominately Turkish-speaking north, Mehmet uses this anti-colonial intertextuality to tacitly sympathise with Cypriots of other socio-linguistic backgrounds. While Mehmet, in 2001, cannot easily return to the southern Nicosia he knew as a child, it is his peers speaking Greek, Cypriot Arabic, and Armenian who cannot easily *go back to Kyrenia*. In addition to colonialism, therefore, Mehmet explores the related role performed by endo-colonial nationalisms on the freedom of movement, notably in opposition with his father, Özker Yaşın, whose own poetry routinely valorised Atatürk.

The motif of home commences in the collection's first poem, 'A Ghost'. It presents the speaker's inbetweenness, situated, like Papadakis' 'Dead Zone' and the figurative ghosts of Ali's hotel, between the states of living and death. He asserts that,

> Only as a ghost can I now return to my own home,
> emerging from blurred mirrors. I haven't much time.
> I throw the windows open [...]
> I shake the dust off the curtains,
> [...] bookshelves. I must also clean
> [...] the family pictures in frames.
> The avenging angels of this polyglot house, now silenced,
> Make every one who enters it, promise to write
> against wars, against everything jingoist, even tongues [...]
> ...[with] enchanted words [...]
> I'm a phantom...[111]

Speaking from a position of liminality, the figure of the 'ghost' or 'phantom' symbolises the Cypriot writer who moves between spaces and, like the supernatural beings, is uninhibited by physical structures. He overcomes the limitations of a war imposing its violence on the physical body, especially the 'tongue'. In this role, the 'ghost' has no reflection and the 'blurred mirrors' reveal a distorted and fragmented selfhood—both the adverse result of conflict dehumanising individuals, and a tactic of resistance that disavows a recognition of existing identity categories. Notably, this anti-subjecthood is accompanied by the necessity to challenge, or 'write/against', 'jingoist' discourses—colonial and nationalist—and their imposed homogenisation of 'tongues'. In his unpublished poem, 'The Boy of Tongues', it is his Greco-Turkish idiolect that overcomes this policing of linguistic identity, as is the process of translation across this anthology.

The 'home' is also a metaphor for the entire island, written from a position of dispossession in London: as a British-Cypriot 'ghost', Mehmet's works are present in the Cyprus of his past despite his physical absence from (at least half of) the island in the present. It is the urgent responsibility of Cypriot writers—they who 'haven't much time'—to restore the 'polyglot house' of history and to recount the cultural pluralism of the pre-1963 era through dialogue. To denounce sectarianism, the speaker recovers the 'book[s]', 'family pictures', and memories of quotidian life, as well as the experiences of partition's victims, 'now silenced'. As in Papadakis' depiction of the post-partition Cypriot home, it is the 'family pictures' of the *former* occupants of a house since reallocated to other refugees which should not be ignored. This act of forcing 'the windows open'—much like Ali's and Papadakis' complicity in breaking-down the walls of the Buffer Zone—symbolically deconstructs barriers through cross-cultural interaction and publication: powerful, 'enchanted words', themselves under threat from censorship or, worse, assassination. It is also an act of individual and social catharsis, a cleansing of trauma through a repudiation of markers of physical identity. According to the 'phantom' speaker, 'no one has even seen me', and hence he moves between internal/external, past/present, Turkish/Greek/English, free from the nationalist panoptic gaze.

A succeeding poem, 'Old Songs in Neapolis', is named after Mehmet's childhood home in Neapolis/Yenişehir (Greek and Turkish for *new city*), a 'mixed' suburb of Nicosia. In its first subsection, *Bitter Olive Tree*, the speaker, in parallel with Papadakis, laments how 'His silver leaves burn for me like incense,/dearest grandfather, Bitter Olive Tree'.[112] Following his dispossession, the olive tree represents the destruction of his ancestral roots. The olive 'leaves' which feature on the flag of the Republic of Cyprus, now used almost exclusively by Greek-speakers, reveal how this ruptured relationship with his home island was rendered 'bitter' by a colonialist martialling of land and discourse. As Mehmet is one of Cyprus' third generation of modern writers, it is Durrell who represents his literary 'grandfather'—before his Kemalist father—and whose textual 'leaves' the 'postcolonial' and post-nationalist poet must grapple with in his revisions of home. Moreover, by incorporating the Greek name for the suburb, the poem also pushes against the discursive expectations of Turkish nationalism by moving between taxonomic layers of old and *new*. It re-writes the diachronic ideological strata which claim land, from the *roots* of (British) imperialism to the sprouting of neo-colonial nationalism.

In 'The Swallow', the speaker recounts being troubled by 'dreams' which render him 'tongueless' and send him 'back to childhood,/the war hasn't broken out, my mothers are still living/and all the people I know haven't left the land'.[113] Awakening, he attempts to identify a 'turtledove' in the sky—the ironic symbol of peace used in the coats of arms for both the north and south—but cannot. His verse carries the acute awareness of an enduring loss, recollecting a home of the past before the 'war[s]' of intercommunal violence and the exile of those forced from 'the land'. It is a pre-1963 juncture in which he is a child victimised by the actions of an older generation, and where his multiple 'mothers'—those of the imagined 'motherlands'—are living peacefully. In this era, such identifications are pluralistic rather than homogeneous; the various socio-linguistic 'mothers' live harmoniously, and Mehmet's Kemalist father remains unmentioned.

Nonetheless, his poetry does not, like some 'postcolonial' literature, create idealised *dreams* of an edenic pre-colonial or pre-partition era. He chooses not to construct 'imaginary homelands' of the past. Instead, following Rushdie's theory, he demonstrates that while 'exiles or emigrants or expatriates, are haunted by some sense of loss, some urge to reclaim', one is not 'capable of reclaiming precisely the thing that was lost'.[114] As Hall similarly proposes, '[t]here can be no simple "return" or "recovery" of the ancestral past which is not re-experienced through the categories… the technologies and the identities of the present'.[115]

Indeed, far from idealism, the same poem describes 'our home in Lefka…/ [what? did I say *our h o m e* ?]/ Sometimes I find myself sobbing in my dreams'.[116] The 'dreams' are a source of anguish, envisioning a 'home' he no longer has. There can be no repatriation to the past and historiography must be critical in its appraisal of what has come before. Moreover, as his social anthropologist wife, Yael Navaro-Yaşın, discusses in the preface to her academic work, *The Make-Believe Space*, Lefka/Lefke was not his place of birth (Neapolis/Yenişehir) but the Turkish-speaking enclave to which his family was exiled between 1963 and 1974.[117] In the Cyprus of the years between independence and partition, *the very experience of home was already estranged*, having been dispossessed before moving abroad.[118]

In another subsection of 'Old Songs in Neapolis', *One Morning in Greece*, the speaker details how 'They wrote ΕΛΛΑΔΑ on our door while we slept... we now live like guests in our own house... our house is not ours'.[119] Set during a time of sleeping, anticipating his later nightmares, the speaker reports on when his home in Neapolis/Yenişehir was branded with the word 'ΕΛΛΑΔΑ', or Greece. As the recipient of an act of symbolic violence by Greek nationalist *discourse*, the speaker feels dispossessed to another country without having left his own property. Having rendered the first-person pronouns meaningless, the family's ownership rights and claims to ancestral land have been breached by a hegemonic assertion over territory by pro-*enosis* ideology. Like the dual 'guest'/owner paradigm expressed by Papadakis, home is defamiliarised and the colonialist *closed doors* depicted by Montis are now recalibrated as the demarcated spaces of post-independence enclaves.

These two poems manifest a subversive form of countertravel by representing the forced movements of refugees alongside the paradoxical non-travel of enclaved Cypriots imprisoned in the unhomely homes which have been symbolically dislocated by nationalism. Where local and foreign begin is dictated by hegemonic ideologies—as is the decision as to whom is identified as self or Other. For one, the village is in Cyprus; for another, it is in Greece. For one, the occupant is a neighbour; for another, he is a stranger. Counter to Durrell's autonomous movements, these are dead homes to which Mehmet cannot return and yet from whose haunting memories he cannot find freedom. The anthology is replete with images of the powerlessness and inertia refugees experience drifting in the tides of political upheaval over which they have had limited agency. Revisiting these homes through literature and translation, however, allows the poet to transport these spaces away from the sectarian hegemons which have previously vandalised the island with their discourses.

Manoeuvring between these ideological layers, the poem 'Aunt-ology' describes how the domestic space confines his teacher aunt's identity-identities. Baybars' title is an obvious play on the field of ontology which does not appear in the Turkish 'Teyzedil', or *auntie-tongue*, a play solely on mother-tongue instead. The first subsection is translated as '*Home-Life. Auntie-tongue*', elaborating on the imbrications between domestic and linguistic identifications. The hyphens also appear in the Turkish (*'Ev-Hayat Teyze-dil'*) but not in the title ('Teyzedil'), presenting identities as fragmented, disjointed, and inconsistent.

Accordingly, 'In the English era' Mehmet's aunt 'was Süreyya at home and Judith to all others,/Flax-haired Lâmia to her friends [...] And then, the Turks came./She was now Judith at home and Süreyya outside'.[120] The pressures of the public/private dichotomy martial an individual's subjecthood whereby the 'home' is the only space free from the demands of a publicly-appropriate identity but which then generates a sense of existential imprisonment. In this symbolic violence against the textuality of naming, Mehmet's aunt is forced to delimit her identity across three names, one of each language, Turkish, English, and Greek. During the colonial juncture, she is forced to assume an Anglocentric selfhood in her public career as a teacher, while her Turkish and Greek names remain in intimate yet sequestered spaces. The political shift denoted by the moment 'the Turks came' demonstrates how the cultural hegemony of British imperialism is usurped by Turkish nationalism (in this village). From this moment, she is compelled to use only her Turkish name among strangers, to reserve her English name for private, and to repudiate her Greek name completely. Lâmia is no longer mentioned in the poem, perhaps because her Greek-speaking 'friends' are isolated on the other side of the Buffer Zone. Any kind of jingoism, therefore, reduces agency and the ability to form linguistically- or culturally-plural identities.

The 'home' of this environment is never entirely free. Another poem is titled 'The Door' after the same structure Montis uses to mark political delineations. In it, behind such structures, 'Freedom is a prison of sorts...'.[121] Yael Navaro-Yaşın has investigated how the common expression used by some Turkish-speaking Cypriots to describe (pre-2003) northern Cyprus as 'an open-air prison' is complex and problematic.[122] Nonetheless, it illustrates how, in Cypriot vernaculars, one's 'homeland' often remains unhomely. For an internally-displaced person, there is a fine line between viewing the nation she/he is forced to move to as either 'home' or 'prison'. This includes Cypriots who view interventionist politics in 1974, either by Greece or Turkey, as attempted '[f]reedom'. Any perceived liberation offered by nationalism is capable of imprisoning individuals within narrow cultural confines—from the outside of one's house being forcibly marked 'ΕΛΛΑΔΑ', to one's public identity being forcibly homogenised by Turkish linguistic conventions.

Counter to these existential and linguistic standardisations, Mehmet's poetry expresses a heterogeneous, pan-Cypriot, and trans-border identity to resist division. In 'Flying Away to the Other Side', the imagery of birds is used, like that of ghosts, to imagine free movement across the Buffer Zone. The speaker defines himself as 'a poembird' representing 'my Generation'.[123] Metonymically, he switches regularly between the singular and plural first-person pronouns: 'Our birthplace is split in two and we/are caught on barbed wire – hybrids/Turk and Greek alike'.[124] Despite political attempts to segregate and imprison—to catch civilians like birds 'on the barbed wire' of the border—the speaker reclaims the colonialist term 'hybrid' to assert a dialectical culture which spans a shared, albeit partitioned, 'birthplace'.

He is subsequently asked,

> "Is it December is it July
> Choose your Side
> Are you Turkish or Greek
> [...]"
> I [...] asked a man
> – *Ποιός είμαι εγώ;*
> shell-shocked I questioned my place in the world
> – *Kimim ben?*
> [...]
> half of my heart opens in December, half in July
> Nothing is whole any more in my life[125]

In a society compelling him to take 'Side[s]', he rejects sectarianism by mourning the deaths and dispossessions of Cypriots in both *December* 1963 and *July* 1974. In raw numbers, the greater number effected by the former were Turkish-speakers, and the latter were Greek-speakers. As rendered in the English translation, when asked to commit to an existential category, he queries his subject position in this partitioned 'world' by asking *Who am I?* in both Turkish and Greek. The latter is also untranslated and untransliterated in the original. His is an identity of two interconnected 'half' pieces. The division of Cyprus does not inspire him to become an autonomous subject aligned with only one section of society, instead it divides his ontological being, his 'heart', and cultural allegiances into two.

This ambivalence towards using a literary language without affiliation to the nation with which it is typically associated is best articulated in

'Wartime'.[126] Like his aunt's home which insulates from social expectations, he reveals that 'I used to talk within myself so that no one could hear me'. For him, 'Turkish was dangerous', 'Greek was absolutely forbidden', while English was positioned 'in the middle,/a slender paper-knife for cutting schoolbooks' and for speaking 'with the Greeks'. Related to Baybars' own use of 'cutting' motifs to describe his relationship with English in *Plucked in a Far-Off Land*, the language is one of inbetweenness, privileged by Anglocentric curricula, yet also used for crucial intercommunal dialogue. In the middle of Greek and Turkish, it is a post/colonial language which both 'cut[s]' and unites a linguistically-plural island. The speaker uncertain which language to express his identity through—each tongue politicised for different reasons—chooses to produce a heteroglossia whereby 'in my poems, the three languages got into a wild tangle', a chaotic mixture defiant of linguistic purification and standardisation. *At home in none of the languages*, feeling dispossessed in a nationalist island, 'the life I lived wasn't foreign, but one of translation'. His identity mediates various, competing cultural strands, illustrating how identifications as a Cypriot are always associated with continual self-translation, anticipating the choice of post-partition prose writers to use English as a cross-cultural medium.

The speaker explains that 'my mother-tongue [is] one thing, my motherland another,/and I, again, altogether different…'. The emphasis on mothers relates to Mehmet's editorship of *Step-Mothertongue: From Nationalism to Multiculturalism* (2000), a trans-communal work which integrates theory, prose, and poetry, in English and translation, by writers from a range of socio-linguistic backgrounds. The overall aim of both 'Wartime' and *Step-Mothertongue* is to deconstruct the very notions of *motherland* and *mother-tongue* in order to uncouple language from national/ist affiliations and to diminish the promotion of the two nationalist ideologies as the prevailing existential modes. In doing so, he rejects these parental constraints and stresses, in another poem, that 'I was nobody's son'.[127]

Similarly, as alluded to earlier, 'Aunt-ology' is dedicated to the paternal aunt who raised Mehmet after his actual mother's death, the aunt who fluctuates between Turkish, Greek, and English names, and who is also depicted reading Arabic and writing Latin. Throughout, the speaker uses the term 'Auntie-tongue' to refer to this paradigm in which languages mix in the construction of the self, a poetic inheritance distinct from that of the symbolic Mother of the nation. Ultimately, he traces his

'Auntie-tongue' to the long-lost 'house with a garden at Neapolis', since destroyed by nationalist aggression, and to the late aunt he wishes to revive through verse: 'I carry [my family] in my heart/and so I carry a cemetery inside me, in my words/of love'.[128] He remembers a polyglot home of the past, to compare with the dispossession of the sectarian present, ultimately, to imagine a possible future where intercommunal dialogue resumes the construction of a Cypriot family home 'of love'—*within literature if not on the ground itself*. Laden with images of death, such an imagining is not an act of quixotism but a faint hope for a movement away from the ongoing political impasse. Poetry is characterised as a 'cemetery'; it is the place where his family now resides, rather than a living home. However, as he stresses in the opening poem, it is precisely as a *ghost* speaking from this war-ravaged subject position that he defies the chauvinist discourses rendering him—symbolically, if not actually—homeless: speaking of death to give voice to a new way of life.

These themes coalesce in 'Canticle for a Schoolteacher', in which the speaker observes the Buffer Zone. He describes how 'The City whose voice is split in two/exhausts its strength singing the same hymn./*hallelujah la ilahe ill'allah*/There's no longer a difference between life and death'. He concludes by asking, 'If I address my letters "To My Mother",/Where will they go?/If I write "Cyprus"... but where?'.[129] The wall parting Nicosia divides its speakers dualistically. As a consequence, the textual 'Cyprus' to which his identity and poetry belongs is riven, raising the problem of which 'Mother'-land he associates his language, literature, and selfhood with. As his poet sister, Neşe Yaşın, similarly asks in her often-quoted 'Which Half in Nicosia?' (1995): 'They say that a man must love one's country/My country/has been divided into two/Which of the two parts must I love?'.[130] The two choose to speak from the limens across 'the two parts' without literary or political allegiance to either of the national spaces existing north and south of the partition.

By referring to Nicosia as 'The City'—or, 'Şehir' in Turkish—Mehmet grounds himself to the Cypriot capital of his birth, without mention, across the collection, to the cultural centre of Istanbul, also known simply as The City—or, Polis in Greek. In a partitioned habitus, it is the *ghost* poet who assumes a dialectical position 'between life and death', and, in doing so, discerns the city's inherent syncretism. It is a syncretism understood by many to be dead or relegated to the past, but one that is exposed by the poet to be alive in the present. The alliterative and rhythmic parallels of the Judeo-Christian '*hallelujah*' and Islamic '*ill'allah*' showcase the intersectionality of the 'voice[s]' from south and north that echo one another. Like Mehmet's poetry, these translingual tongues overlap above and across the border, symbolising a shared Abrahamic and Middle Eastern heritage that transcends secularist nationalisms on the ground. Ghostly, intangible voices perform a social function opposite to that of physical walls, facilitating a fluid and intercommunal interaction within a realm above the corporeal: one that is sacred, lyrical, and free from imprisonment. His 'letters', therefore, cannot be addressed to one physical destination as they allude to, and are directed towards, an idea of a 'Cyprus', of a home, which does not (yet) exist on the politically-dissected land. This is a transportal mode which carries cultural forms across the ideological barriers imposed by hegemonic politics and publishing conventions. The motif of the hodja's prayer transcending physical parameters is one to be revisited in the succeeding chapter through Nadjarian's work.

Conclusions

From their very titles, the works of post-partition writers are deeply entrenched in the politics of the Buffer Zone. A comparison of Ali's *Forbidden Zones* and Papadakis' *Echoes from the Dead Zone*—one written by a Turkish-speaking Cypriot and the other, a Greek-speaking Cypriot—reveals inextricable parallels in the themes, linguistic forms, and generic fluidity of the two. Both prose works—one an academic travelogue, the other a series of stories based on global travel by an academic—reclaim these disciplines to speak for, and as, Cypriot refugees. Travel, as a model of narrativisation, is reviewed in terms of dispossession and exile, and both writers carve out a home within literature denied to many Cypriots exiled from their familial homes. As well as offering theoretical foundations which disavow the speaking of the Anglo-American academy over Cypriot individual experience, they repudiate the authorities of nationalist dominant discourses—both Greek and Turkish with equal vigour. The works—as well as Nadjarian's *Ledra Street*, and comparable to Mehmet Yaşın's translingual poetry collection translated by Baybars—use a heteroglossic Anglophone form. These self-translated narratives engage with the polyglotism of pre-partition Cyprus, allowing for a broad pan-Cypriot readership across nationalist-linguistic borders, and illustrate the heterogeneous sprachbund of the island. These transportal literatures embrace the cultural pluralism denied by the dualistic discourses of both Orientalising colonialism and homogenising nationalism, drawing on the historic imbrications of Greek, Turkish, English, and other Mediterranean *lingue franche* on the island.

Ali and Papadakis use these stylistic elements in their polemic reconstructions of Cypriot identifications by revising right-wing (Greek and Turkish) historiographies. The two writers advocate the importance of testimony in exposing war crimes against *both* Greek-speaking and Turkish-speaking Cypriots. The actual interviewees of Papadakis' travelogue are mirrored by the ostensibly-fictional interviewed ex-soldier in Ali's 'Forbidden Zone', as well as her intimate travels across the Green Line in 'Finding Maro' and 'The Midwife'. Ali and Papadakis similarly use the motif of travelling across the two halves of the city to illustrate how the Nicosia border can be physically surmounted and, with it, the symbolic demarcations of language and culture can be overcome. Their concerns with geopolitics is grounded with a consideration of land rights and the forced removal of Cypriots from their homes—in both 1963 and 1974—which has created a unhomely habitus desperately needing to be re-written.

Equally, this theme is at the centre of Mehmet's poetry, recounting his multiple dispossessions between villages and, ultimately, from the island. Like Papadakis' recurring image of the 'Dead Zone' or the rotting tourist hotel of Ali's 'Forbidden Zone', Mehmet imagines the figure of the 'ghost', an ethereal being emerging from a society of death but transcending the shackles of nationalism, hatred, and borders. As an ambulatory ghost poet, Mehmet's translated compositions pass through the Buffer Zone, even before the openings of 2003. His voice is a porous medium of transcultural exchange, like the symbolism of Nicosia's religious soundscape *echoing* across the capital, free from confinement. In some ways, it is a poetic revival of the bird-like outlaw, Hasanpouli.

For all three contemporary Cypriot writers, cultivating literary territory to challenge the Buffer Zone—the place where Papadakis finds his 'real home', metres away from the recreated, 'timeless' home of Ali's and Maro's childhood—is necessary in understanding what the concept of 'homeland' means, deconstructing the hegemonic colonialism and nationalisms used to build the ideology of partition within individual consciousness and on the streets. Notably, the writers, whether from an Armenian-, Greek-, or Turkish-speaking background, all share the same political vision for a reunified Cyprus, intertextually advocating the need for intercommunal peace through the physical and psychological dissolution of the Buffer Zone.

Notes

1. Aydın Mehmet Ali, 'Forbidden Zone', *Kunapipi*, 33 (2011), 188–201. Note that all further references to this narrative will be from its anthologised form in *Forbidden Zones* (2013).
2. Huggan, *The Postcolonial Exotic*, p. 177.
3. In an earlier version of this chapter, I suggested that Pyla/Pile was the last 'mixed' village in Cyprus. As Robert Young has kindly reminded me, the same terminology could be used to describe Rizokarpaso/Dipkarpaz. Near the northern-most tip of the island, it remains home to both Greek-speakers and Turkish-speakers.
4. Papadakis, p. 50.
5. Ali, *Forbidden*, p. 5.
6. Papadakis, p. xiii.
7. Papadakis, p. 2.
8. Papadakis, p. xiv.
9. Papadakis, pp. 171, 83.
10. Papadakis, p. 102.
11. Papadakis, p. xiii.
12. Peter Marcuse, 'The Layered City', in *The Urban Lifeworld*, ed. by Pete Madsen and Richard Plunz (London: Routledge, 2002), pp. 94–114.
13. Papadakis, p. 251.
14. Papadakis, p. 155.
15. Ali, *Forbidden*, p. 5.
16. Aydın Mehmet Ali, *Turkish Speaking Communities and Education: No Delight* (London: Fatal Publications, 2001), pp. 1–2.
17. Ibid., p. 2.
18. Aydın Mehmet Ali, 'Foreword' and 'Opening Remarks from the Chair', in *Turkish Cypriot Identity in Literature/Edebiyatta Kıbrıslı Türk Kimliği*, ed. by Ali (London: Fatal Publications, 1990), pp. 7–10, 127–128 (pp. 8–9). All further references to this text will be cited as Ali, *Identity*.
19. Papadakis, p. 170.
20. Ali, *Identity*, p. 8.
21. Ali, *Forbidden*, p. 25.
22. Ali, *Forbidden*, pp. 24–25.
23. Papadakis, p. 174.
24. Papadakis, p. 172.

25. Ali, *Forbidden*, pp. 24–25.
26. Ali, *Forbidden*, p. 5.
27. Papadakis, p. 175.
28. Papadakis, p. 67.
29. Tom Nairn, *The Break-Up of Britain: Crisis and Neo-Nationalism* (Altona, VIC: Common Ground, 2003), p. 347.
30. Papadakis, p. 39.
31. Papadakis, p. 14.
32. Papadakis, p. 39.
33. Papadakis, p. 31.
34. Papadakis, p. 176.
35. Ali, *Forbidden*, p. 191.
36. Ali, *Forbidden*, p. 191.
37. Ali, *Forbidden*, p. 192.
38. Ali, *Forbidden*, p. 193.
39. Ali, *Identity*, p. 7. It is worth noting the parallel image in Papadakis' *Echoes*… which describes his newly-awakened impression of northern Nicosia during the moment after '[r]ain washed away the city dust, and the sun was shining brightly above Lefkosha [… and] in Lefkosia as well, only a few hundred metres away' (p. 87).
40. Ali, *Forbidden*, p. 12.
41. Ali, *Forbidden*, p. 27.
42. Ali, *Forbidden*, p. 10.
43. Ali, *Identity*, p. 7.
44. Papadakis, p. 177.
45. Ali, *Identity*, p. 7.
46. Papadakis, p. 169.
47. Ali, *Identity*, p. 7.
48. Papadakis, p. 2.
49. Papadakis, p. 2.
50. Nora Nadjarian, *Ledra Street* (Nicosia: Armida, 2006), p. 41.
51. Bhabha, *The Location of Culture*, p. 92.
52. Papadakis, pp. 40, 25, 28.
53. Papadakis, pp. xiv, 13, 43.
54. Ali, *Forbidden*, p. 228.
55. Ali, *Forbidden*, p. 189.
56. Ali, *Forbidden*, pp. 25, 219, 223.
57. Paul Gilroy, *Against Race: Imagining Political Culture Beyond the Color Line* (Cambridge, MA: Belknap Press, 2000), p. 8.
58. Ali, *Forbidden*, p. 207.
59. Ali, *Forbidden*, p. 208.
60. Ali, *Forbidden*, p. 206.
61. Ali, *Forbidden*, pp. 202, 209.

62. Ali, *Forbidden*, p. 222.
63. Ali, *Forbidden*, pp. 224–225.
64. Ali, *Forbidden*, pp. 214–215.
65. Ali, *Forbidden*, p. 215.
66. Ali, *Forbidden*, pp. 218–219.
67. Ali, *Forbidden*, p. 219.
68. Papadakis, p. 19.
69. Papadakis, p. 135.
70. Papadakis, p. 243.
71. Montis, *Closed*, p. 115.
72. Edward W. Said, *The World, the Text, and the Critic* (Cambridge, MA: Harvard University Press, 1983), p. 53.
73. Ali, *Identity*, pp. 7, 127.
74. Nadjarian, *Ledra*, p. 1.
75. Papadakis, p. 15.
76. Papadakis, p. 15.
77. Papadakis, p. 173.
78. Papadakis, p. 173.
79. Central Intelligence Agency, *The CIA World Factbook 2017* (New York: Skyhorse, 2016), p. 226. It describes how a 'Greek-government sponsored attempt to overthrow the elected president of Cyprus was met by military intervention from Turkey' in 1974.
80. Hugo Meltzl, 'Present Tasks of Comparative Literature', in *Comparative Literature: The Early Years*, ed. and trans. by Hans-Joachim Schulz and Phillip H. Rhein (Chapel Hill: University of North Carolina Press, 1973), pp. 53–62 (p. 58).
81. Emily Apter, *The Translation Zone: A New Comparative Literature* (Princeton, NJ: Princeton University Press, 2006), p. 6.
82. Papadakis, p. 13.
83. Papadakis, pp. 12–13.
84. Papadakis, p. 5.
85. Jacques Lacan, *Ecrits: The First Complete Edition in English*, trans. and ed. by Bruce Fink (New York: W. W. Norton, 2006), p. 817.
86. Ali, *Forbidden*, p. 222.
87. Ali, *Forbidden*, p. 188; Papadakis, pp. 54–56.
88. Papadakis, p. 56.
89. Papadakis, p. 98.
90. Papadakis, p. 99.
91. Papadakis, pp. 99–100.
92. Papadakis, p. 100.
93. Papadakis, p. 99.
94. Papadakis, p. 83.
95. Papadakis, p. 96.

96. Ali, *Forbidden*, p. 9.
97. Ali, *Forbidden*, p. 9.
98. Ali, *Forbidden*, p. 9.
99. Ali, *Forbidden*, pp. 9–10.
100. Kincaid, *A Small Place*, pp. 69, 62.
101. Ali, *Forbidden*, p. 11.
102. Ali, *Forbidden*, p. 20.
103. Ali, *Forbidden*, p. 16.
104. Ali, *Forbidden*, p. 19.
105. Ali, *Forbidden*, pp. 19–20.
106. Ali, *Forbidden*, pp. 9, 209.
107. Papadakis, pp. 138, 181.
108. Papadakis, p. 142.
109. Durrell, p. 16.
110. Mehmet, *Kyrenia*, p. 1.
111. Mehmet, *Kyrenia*, p. 3.
112. Mehmet, *Kyrenia*, p. 7.
113. Mehmet, *Kyrenia*, p. 5.
114. Rushdie, *Imaginary Homelands*, p. 10.
115. Stuart Hall, 'New Ethnicities', in *Stuart Hall: Critical Dialogues in Cultural Studies*, ed. by David Morley and Kuan-Hsing Chen (London and New York: Routledge, 1996), pp. 441–451 (p. 449).
116. Mehmet, *Kyrenia*, p. 5.
117. Yael Navaro-Yashin [*sic*], *The Make-Believe Space: Affective Geography in a Postwar Polity* (Durham and London: Duke University Press, 2012), p. x.
118. Navaro-Yashin, p. 221.
119. Mehmet, *Kyrenia*, p. 11.
120. Mehmet, *Kyrenia*, p. 67.
121. Mehmet, *Kyrenia*, p. 93.
122. Navaro-Yashin, p. 71.
123. Mehmet, *Kyrenia*, p. 19.
124. Mehmet, *Kyrenia*, p. 17.
125. Mehmet, *Kyrenia*, p. 17.
126. Mehmet, *Kyrenia*, p. 25.
127. Mehmet, *Kyrenia*, p. 47.
128. Mehmet, *Kyrenia*, pp. 66–67.
129. Mehmet, *Kyrenia*, pp. 54–65.
130. Neşe Yaşın, 'Which Half of Nicosia?', quoted in Anna M. Agathangelou and L. H. M. Ling, *Transforming World Politics: From Empire to Multiple Worlds* (London and New York: Routledge, 2009), p. 119.

CHAPTER 5

Re-gendering Borders: Partitions in Contemporary Cypriot Women's Writing

There is an intricate relationship between the partition of Cyprus and the borders of gender. The project to re-write the political division of the island stands alongside recognition of the gendered parameters of both imperialism and nationalism, and the need to integrate these concerns into resistance writing. As has been demonstrated throughout this book, particularly in the second chapter, the discursive representation of politics and conflict cannot be individuated from questions of gender and sexuality. As McClintock summarises, 'women and men do not live postcoloniality in the same way, nor do they share the same singular post-colonial condition'.[1] When complicating definitions of postcolonialism, it is vital to do so while considering its relationship with gendered power and disparity.

This is a reality from which the Cypriot context is not exempt. The persistent masculinist imagery of warfare on the island, which presents men as agents in the nationalist construction of the land, often relegates women to the margins of the experience of conflict. While men are framed in iconographic monuments as noble soldiers or politicians, women are either absent from such motifs or imagined as elderly widows and, thus, passive victims far from the front lines. The Liberty Monument in southern Nicosia, for instance, presents a bronze scene of male soldiers, priests, and prisoners of war, alongside only two women: a hunched, elderly woman aided by a young man and the Classical female abstraction of Liberty herself. This is corroborated by the androcentric nature of most

D. Nunziata, *Colonial and Postcolonial Cyprus*,
https://doi.org/10.1007/978-3-030-58236-4_5

Cypriot writing until the twenty-first century, in which the established oeuvres of Montis' generation included few women writers. Instead, images of womanhood constructed by men—the ubiquitous icon of one's respective '*mother*land', presented in terms of purity or virginity—exist in lieu of the actual voices of individual Cypriot women. Nationalist men occasionally speak of the victimisation of women in 1974 but without risking the perceived societal or familial shame of women vocalising their own persecution.[2]

Consequently, among the images of valiant Cypriot men, and of black-veiled older widows, what of the younger women in 1974 and their lives since? If war is understood through a gendered lens, then so too is the experience of it. Emblematic of the fact that postcoloniality is lived differently according to gender is the reality that, between 1963 and 1974, Cypriot women became targets of sexual violence. It was of such severity that the government of the Republic of Cyprus legalised abortion in 1974, as a consequence.[3] This was an ethically-complex decision which bypassed the island's religious conservatism, not as a peacetime recognition of women's rights over their bodies, but as a desperate response to an indiscriminately violent war and the fear of the 'miscegenated' products of rape in a racialised society shaped by gendered notions of 'honour' and 'shame'. These women are rarely discussed in the male-dominated landscape of nationalist historiography. They are either erased from communal memory or sporadically instrumentalised in graphic polemics by men seeking to prove the barbarism of the Other. Women do not freely express their own suffering; it is a suffering appropriated by men to create dualistic narratives of the ethnolinguistic self through binaries of active men and passive women, and moral self and perverse Other.

As Papadakis observes, 'History was always a history of war; of men; self-centred'; routinely '[t]he nation was shown as strong, united, equal, single-purposed and male'.[4] In other words, the historiography surrounding nation-writing employs misogynistic discourse to marginalise sections of society considered too weak to represent the ideal of the powerful, monocentric homeland. Difference, not only from the ethnic Other, *but also the sexual or gendered Other*, is erased as a threat to the demands of homogeneity. One cannot understand the writing of partition without an awareness of its gendered constitution and how gender disparity pervades all areas of Cypriot life. Traditionally, in both the north and south, free time is occupied by men in the communal coffee shop while women are confined to the home. In a space of multiple perceived cultural differences, the coffee-shop *status quo* of gender is an important, yet unfortunate, symbol of the actual homogeneity of pan-Cypriot everyday life. Equally, poetry recitals and duals in all Cypriot vernaculars are traditionally performed by men only, excluding women from these ostensibly pre-colonial modes of cultural expression. In both cases, culture is partitioned across the portals of public and private.

It is necessary, therefore, to evaluate the generic and linguistic form Cypriot women writers appropriate to challenge these gendered borders. This chapter will again focus on travel writing and the motif of the home to understand how the personal testimony of women is used to challenge the orthodoxies of masculinist literatures, primarily considering two texts by Nadjarian and Neşe Yaşın.

Rewriting History from the Periphery

As has already been demonstrated, the oeuvre of their contemporary, Ali, is consciously invested in 'giving voices to the silenced. She who feels it knows it', identifying her writings as part of an emphatic 'HERSTORY'.[5] *His*tory, a pun only possible in English, is essentially an androcentric discipline. Signalling how the dominant discourses involved in martialling historiography exclude the experiences of women, Ali revises these epistemic silences through counter-histories which are anti-colonial, anti-nationalist, *and* feminist. These themes are integral to the short stories 'Finding Maro' and 'The Midwife' in *Forbidden Zones* which deprovincialise homosocial dialogue between Turkish-speaking and Greek-speaking women: Ali and Maro, and Ali and Γιανούλλα/Yianoulla, respectively. Reclaimed from the margins, women from north and south are re-positioned at the centre of narratives of Cypriot history as agents of peaceful collaboration across the Buffer Zone. Counter to the 'self-centred' images of war that Papadakis describes,[6] Ali is invested in a re-positioning of centre and periphery, not only in relation to colonialist and nationalist dichotomies, but to the parallel opposition of gender. In antithesis to masculinist nationalisms, this challenge to partition is doubly impactful in its simultaneous rejection of ethnolinguistic segregation and gender disparity.

The marked increase in publication by Cypriot women after 2003 reveals how the border opening not only inspired a rise in demand for Cypriot voices but facilitated the publication of women. It allowed for gender division to be questioned, and it introduced potential literary media that enabled Cypriot women to be widely read. In other words, there is a relationship between deconstructing the division of Cypriot languages in 2003 and contesting the marginalisation of women from mainstream cultural production. Following the opening of the Buffer Zone, and its implications for linguistic, literary, and cultural movement, publishers not only sought women writers but aimed to revive forgotten works for dissemination across the re-opened island and the global marketplace. Ali's *Forbidden Zones* (2013), Nadjarian's *Ledra Street* (2006), and the English translation of Neşe Yaşın's *Rose Falling Into Night* (2017) are all heteroglossic *anthologies* created for Anglophone audiences.

While the three employ different forms (Ali's and Nadjarian's short stories in contrast with Neşe's poetry), they can all be read as subversive examples of travel writing. Challenging this genre as a colonialist, androcentric discipline—much like historiography as a whole—their *herstories* provide personal testimonies of the self beyond rigid literary standards. Here is the complex layeredness of their discursive resistance: Cypriot writers must destabilise (at least) three distinct languages in their standard use. English, Greek, and Turkish are all metropolitan discourses of power which, historically, have erased the experience of women in their corresponding literary outputs.

This is where the politics of power intersects with those of language and gender. VassosArgyrou has summarised the view, not necessarily his own, that '[b]y embracing a *hegemonic* identity, [Cypriot women] may be able to achieve legitimation *as a woman*. At the same time, however, inadvertently but inevitably, she reproduces the conditions of being dominated *as a Cypriot* [...] actively participating in one's own domination'.[7] While partly attuned to the issues surrounding the claimed dichotomy of local anticolonialism versus 'Western' or global feminism, this is nonetheless a reductive assessment for multiple reasons. Not least, it presupposes a gender-neutral figure of 'a Cypriot' which experiences postcoloniality in a uniform manner—to paraphrase McClintock. It, therefore, fails to expound how British colonialism dominated Cypriot women *as Cypriots and as women* simultaneously and fails to consider the imperialism of standard Greek and Turkish cultural dissemination. Cypriot women writing in nationalist languages would also be 'participating in one's own domination' by a foreign hegemon. These Greek and Turkish hegemons are equally patriarchal and do not allow one 'to achieve legitimation as a' *Cypriot* of any gender. None of the conventional languages of literary production—standardised English, Greek, or Turkish—allow for power as a Cypriot, or a woman, or both. It is a fallacy of nationalist rhetoric that the dominant discourses of Greece and Turkey are significantly less imperialist than the English similarly standardised, and introduced from, abroad. Where does local and foreign begin and end, and where are women offered a literary space to discuss their multiple colonisations freely?

It is useful here to invoke Rushdie's advice that, 'if you want to give voice to the voiceless, you've got to find a language... Use the wrong language, and you're dumb and blind'.[8] His expression closely echoes Ali's aforementioned mantra of 'giving voices to the silenced'.[9] The established question of what discourse can be used to recover power for the most oppressed strata of a society is understood by these two Anglophone prose writers in terms of linguistic efficacy. It is interesting to note that, following the paucity of works by Cypriot women writers published before 2003, after the border-opening the efflux was largely in English. Alongside Ali and Nadjarian, as well as Neşe's translated anthology, others chose the same language: Andriana Ierodiaconou's *Margarita's Husband* (2007) and *The Women's Coffee Shop* (2012); Christy Lefteri's *A Watermelon, A Fish, and A Bible* (2011); and Eve Makis' oeuvre largely set in London, beginning with *Eat, Drink and Be Married* (2004). All are composed in English and most with titles alluding to the gastronomical: a global English used, nonetheless, to convey the local, private, and domestic. It is in this linguistic medium that *coffee-shop* gender roles can be represented and questioned most powerfully, outside the pressures of andro-nationalist publishing industries. Writing in national/ist languages does not allow for freedom from their patriarchal assumptions, from their ethnolinguistic sectarianism, or from the limits it would place on the size and demographics of the readership.

I, therefore, seek to analyse Cypriot women's writing through a slight amendment to Spivak's theory on subalternity. Although she considers the notion of 'translation as reading',[10] it is important to enquire after the role of *translation as writing*. For Spivak, the act of withholding is one of empowerment for the subaltern. Instead, she implores readers, critics, and theorists to 'learn her mother-tongue'.[11] What happens, however, when the subaltern has no so-called mother-tongue? What if the official languages of the postcolonial nation are not the same as non-codified vernaculars? For Cypriot women writers, there is no viable alternative to the plural dominant *discourses* which each perform a different and specialised kind of epistemic violence. There is no uncomplicated pre-colonial, postcolonial, antinational, *and* pan-Cypriot language. For Cypriots who do not necessarily see standardised Greek or Turkish as their 'mother-tongue', they consciously chose to disavow the island's official languages in order to repudiate their attendant political problems. In its place, there is, I would argue, 'gendered agency' within *acts of translation and self-translation*, appropriating dominant discourses to deconstruct authorised ideologies from within.[12] Publishing in English is chosen over silence—the silence of the pre-2003 period. All major, institutional languages spoken in Cyprus have been introduced by patriarchal colonisations throughout its history.

While I wholeheartedly agree with Spivak's insistence on learning other languages—Cypriot schools should introduce Turkish language classes in the south and vice versa—as this is not yet the case, Cypriot women writers composing in the international auxiliary language prevent their works from *falling silent for potential (women) readers living on the other side of the Buffer Zone*. Here, 'translation as reading', is then an act of resistance to nationalist partition by allowing for trans-cultural contact and the moving of voices beyond the silencing border. More needs to be done translating works across English, Greek, and Turkish, but failing that, English is the already-translated medium that anticipates the largest possible audience. Having works translated can often be a luxury for writers from small countries who struggle to be published in one language to begin with. As Ketu Katrak emphasises, 'given our neocolonial legacies, it is only after third world writers have been published in metropolitan areas that they are recognized in their home territories'.[13] The context's complex political past means that subaltern Cypriots are not only silenced by gendered (neo-)colonialisms—which appear in at least three guises—but are silenced from each other because of the violence of physical and cultural sectarianism. This chapter, subsequently, will examine Nadjarian's and Neşe's works by considering their metatextual representations of language in relation to the intersecting ventures of probing the partitions of nation and gender.

First, however, it is important to note both similarities and differences in the way they structure this. As identified previously, Nadjarian's text is an anthology of short stories composed in English. Several were previously published independently and were recognised by various awarding bodies, notably the Commonwealth Short Story Competition for 'Ledra Street' (2001), 'Spoon Sweet' (2002), and 'No-Man's-Land' (2005), all to be discussed presently. Having also been acknowledged by institutions across Western Europe, including the *The Guardian* in 2004, Nadjarian's publishing history demonstrates the global reach of her audience.[14] Utilising English as a cross-cultural and Commonwealth language allows her stories to be read across national borders, not only in Cyprus, but the entire decolonising world. English becomes the language of anti-nationalism through a conscious act of divorcing the work from either the Hellenosphere or Turkosphere. The Anglophone form enters the writing into an intercontinental body of 'world literatures' rather than simply the 'Greek world' or 'Turkish world' of literary production.

Neşe's *Rose Falling Into Night*, on the other hand, while also an anthology, is of English translations of poems originally composed in Standard Modern Turkish. Neşe, born to the poetry-producing, Turkish-speaking Yaşın family, spearheaded the pan-Cypriot, left-wing 'Rejection Front', using her cultural products to resist the nationalist *status quo*. After 1974, in part due to restrictions on her literary freedom in the north, she migrated to the south, a relatively unprecedented phenomenon. In the south, where she eventually began teaching at the University of Cyprus, she composed the Turkish-language poetry collections from which this Anglophone anthology derives its material: *Doors* (1992), *The Moon is Made of Love* (2000), *Chambers of Memory* (2005), and *Chilling Birds* (2016). Translation is a key aspect of trans-border interchange, realised by Neşe's Anglophone performances of her works outside northern Cyprus, her translated life as a migrant of the north living in the Greek-speaking south, and her frequently-translated poetic oeuvre. It is through practices of translation that her poem 'Which Half of Nicosia?' (1995) has been regularly reproduced in parallel English, Greek, and Turkish stanzas as the motto of the anti-nationalist Left. Similarly, the collection, *Rose Falling into Night*, is a collaborative venture with illustrator Hara Savvidou whose post-modern representations of natural imagery cover the work and bookmark its subsections. In addition, Ali translates many of the included poems. The final product is a multimedia artefact by Cypriot women, two Turkish-speaking and one Greek-speaking, who intersect the borders of genre to construct a cohesive cultural product of borderlessness. The placement of Neşe's biography on the inside front-cover, and of Savvidou's on the inside back-cover, mirror the two and represent their dual authorship. Images which need no translation suitably accompany this work of textual translation. Indeed, most of the images resemble aerial views of barren trees and, consequently, offer a literal *distanced reading* of the conflict on the ground. Likewise, the English translation offers a *distanced reading* of Neşe's experiences of the conflict for a widened readership. Neşe's work is a transportal poetry of anti-partition translationality radically counter to the parochial expectations of the national/ist poem.

Despite formal differences, there are important stylistic and thematic parallels between Nadjarian's and Neşe's post-2003 anthologies, including their semantic questionings of linguistic restrictions which intersect with their related critiques of both the political border and gender inequality. The two works are examples of travel writing which draw heavily on their individual experiences of trans-border movement, alongside representations of fathers and male lovers as symbols of patriarchal dominance. The potential freedom of movement is placed in contrast with the restrictions enforced by androcentric institutions. For both writers, as well as Ali, their embrace of the fragmented form of short texts amalgamated into a single body reveals—in accordance with the theories of feminist, postcolonial travel writing—how the genre of the holistic novel elected by many postcolonial male authors has failed Cypriot women.

Similarly, Nadjarian's work puts pressure on generic conventions to the point where it can be read as prose poetry. Her use of metaphor, anaphora, repetition, and other poetic figures of speech provides her prose with a distinctive rhythm. Notably, her repetitions recur across the short stories causing them to appear less as discrete narratives but rather vignettes within a continuous series with a shared setting (quotidian Cyprus) and common characters: the speaker, her parents, and her past lovers. This has two effects. First, it illustrates the discursive limits of the domestic and the familiar, revealing, with claustrophobia, the roles in which Cypriot women are trapped and the spaces in which they are confined. Homes, words, gender performativity are all marked by internal borders analogous to the external buffer zone. Second, it reveals the importance of the anthology in collecting texts *which can only be read in unison* as the constituent parts of a new work—or, hypertext—which draws disparate threads of experience into one heterogeneous whole. Neşe's collection similarly selects and arranges works to illustrate persistent themes across her career. Like the claustrophobic familial homes of *Ledra Street*, Neşe repeats several idioms throughout: 'doors', 'love', 'silence', 'birds', 'loneliness'. These themes form a trajectory tacitly linking all the poems to create—almost as a metaphor for the island's future—a united narrative giving new life to old works through acts of suturing and translation. It is oneness from disparate discursive elements.

For instance, 'Doors', the second of the collection and one of the earliest compositions (from the book of the same name published in 1992), is joined, for the first time, with 'Variations on a Theme of Doors', near the end of the anthology and originally published in 2016. They mirror each other like Neşe's and Savvidou's biographies, two artists brought together for a common socio-political goal.

Both Nadjarian and Neşe, therefore, can be understood as using poetic devices to construct generically-subversive counter-travelogues which elaborate on the intersecting politics of nationalism and gender. While the significant difference between the two should not be underestimated—poetic *prose* against free *verse*—it is necessary to consider how each is related to the individual author's chosen language of composition. Nadjarian's prose is already Anglophone, allowing for a pan-Cypriot and global *readership*. Neşe's verse, on the other hand, may originally have been written in Turkish, but her delivery of works translated by others illustrates how she self-translates her voice during performances for pan-Cypriot and global *audiences*. Poetry intended for recitation is translated ahead of performance, whereas prose is self-translated ahead of publication. Both authors seek to have their works transcend the limits of the local, electing specific forms, languages, and dissemination methods to ensure this. Preserving Neşe's diverse works into a single book, the Anglophone *Rose Falling Into Night* is a celebration of this process: breaking-up and reforming Neşe's oeuvre for *readers* on both sides of the border.

Re-claiming Gendered Spaces

Unlike many male contemporaries, Nadjarian's and Neşe's concerns with the spatial politics of borders specifically relate to the literary and gendered spaces occupied—and unoccupied—by women. These themes are apparent in the former's 2003 English poem, 'Don't Forget'.[15] The title explicitly evokes the polemic calls for Cypriots from multiple ethnolinguistic communities to always remember the island's violent history: in Greek, *ΔενΞεχνώ*, *DhenKsehno*, *I Don't Forget*; in Turkish, *Unutmayacağiz*, *We will not forget*. Ironically, it is an expression shared by almost all Cypriots, but divided by language and nationalist politics of selective recollection. What a Greek nationalist remembers and forgets is often the polar opposite of a Turkish nationalist, and vice versa. A Greek nationalist may choose to forget attacks on Turkish-speaking Cypriots in 1963 and 1964, and yet this will form the mainstay of Cypriot history that is part of the *unutmayacağiz* of the north. Here, the Anglophone form crucially brings the parallel expressions together allowing Nadjarian to critique the inherent forgetfulness of nationalist historiographies caused by a *lack of dialogue* between Cypriots of different linguistic backgrounds. The 'neutral' English allows Cypriot readers to recognise their shared subject position as victims of the same conflict, a position nonetheless divided into opposing worldviews by nationalisms. Through the estrangement of translation—by uttering a vital phrase of nationalist historiography in a non-nationalist language—the poem facilitates a radical defamiliarisation of the discourses of historical and cultural identity.

In addition, the title draws on the experiences of women forgotten by official histories of war, from monuments to nationalist poetry. Instead, the text describes how the Greek-speaking woman speaker crosses the border opened in the year of its composition, meeting the Turkish-speaking woman who now resides in the home the former was made refugee from in 1974. It is a quintessential experience lived by many Cypriots since the border opening. The poem's exilic movements across the Buffer Zone afford the speaker a literal and figurative *translation* of her selfhood, re-remembering and reviewing the limits of extant historicist writing, and using *trans-lingual dialogue between women* to rewrite andro-nationalist assumptions. As such, the binaries of both gender and the border are contested together. Anderson, similarly discussing the 'characteristic amnesias' of nationalisms, details their resulting 'narratives [...] set in homogenous, empty time'.[16] For Nadjarian, the 'empty time' which has existed almost literally between 1974 and 2003, sits alongside the *empty space* of the other side, unseen for decades yet falsely remembered by narratives of non-forgetting. The poem, like Neşe's oeuvre, seeks to inhabit this 'empty time' and space and, doing so, destabilise the 'homogenous' nationalist narratives claiming them. Further to Anderson's gender-neutral thesis, the two explicitly interrogate the empty spaces devoid of women—spaces both physical and cultural—doubly effaced by the selectively-amnesiac discourses of nationalism.

> At the poem's opening, the speaker details how:
> The past came to visit again last night,
> wrapped her arms around my neck
> and whispered: It's me. Don't forget.
> I knocked at a door which a woman opened.
> She said in Turkish: [...]
> *Hoşgeldiniz.Hoşgeldiniz.*

> She handed an album of photos to me,
> [...] this house,
> pre-1974. The blue album. My living room.
> [...]
> I thanked her in Greek. *Efcharisto poli.*

Represented here is the translingual interchange between two women who use English as the medium through which to share Turkish and Greek words—'*Hoşgeldiniz*', or welcome; '*Efcharisto poli*', or many thanks—and to exchange the photo album. The photo album is not a textual body, instead it is a book of visual media which conglomerates debris-like vestiges of individual experience beyond the realm of the discursive. A testament to phenomenology, like Ali's aforementioned insistence of feeling over knowledge, it is an anthology not unlike *Ledra Street* or *Rose Falling Into Night*. Specifically, it is a memorial to a lost space of the 'pre-1974' era, now radically altered and uninhabitable. Like the colour 'blue' and its political connotations, the speaker recognises that the *empty space* of the 'blue'-and-red past cannot be revived, but the two instead re-remember and recreate the domestic space of the present. In this post-1974, post-2003 home, beyond the formation of the pure nationalist 'blue' or red oeuvres of the past, revived dialogue allows new cultural works to be formed. The Cypriot 'living room', the domain of women, *unlike the coffee-shop*, is re-formed through transportal acts of countertravel. Indeed, it is now a *living* space, counter to the epistemic and discursive void which existed before, separating southern and northern Cypriots through sealed 'door[s]' of silence.

The imagery of an unhomely home throughout—including the subsequent questioning, 'One of us was guest, the other hostess – but which?'—resonates with the motifs of returning refugees depicted by Ali, Papadakis, and Mehmet Yaşın. However, like Ali in particular, Nadjarian's poem sees peaceful interaction across partition, its closed 'door', through dialogue between Greek-speaking and Turkish-speaking women who do not suppress their linguistic difference but who also appropriate English to facilitate their discourse. As with 'Finding Maro' and 'The Midwife', Nadjarian contests the epistemic marginalisation of women by framing the domestic as the site of successful anti-partition movement, in tacit contrast with the failed dialogue of male politicians in lofty, unseen spheres. Indeed, in the *Ledra Street* story, 'The Cyprus Problem', male politicians are lampooned for their tautological rhetoric which leads to no syntactic conclusion or political solution: 'Let's just cut the crap because what we are basically saying is that we are talking crap because there is no solution to the Cyprus problem. Because there is no solution to the Cyprus problem. Because [etc.…]'.[17] The poem, instead, emphasises the importance of the characters' gender as 'two sisters who were mothers, wives, daughters', whose shared testimonies afford a unique worldview counter to stubborn ethnocentric men. What they have in common is more important than the nationalisms that attempt to divide them. Even the abstract of time is feminised, 'wrapp[ing] her arms around' them, signalling the importance of excavating the *herstory* of women, relegated within official discourse. The idiom of intimacy closely echoes Ali's narratives; like Ali and Maro, Nadjarian's speaker and her Turkish-speaking counterpart 'leant like two friends over a secret', bonding over their related experiences as Cypriot women which they share, almost esoterically, in a habitus of male-generated borders.

Between them, speaking different languages while comparing their lives on the same island, they create '[a] tiny space the size of a pinhead', a common 'space' outside the demarcations of territory and of literary space defined by men. It is negligible, even invisible, in size, but is one which belongs to them solely. Correlating with McClintock's insistence that men and women live postcoloniality differently, Nadjarian defies the *empty spaces* of gendered nationalism and forges a 'space […] between each word' for women's trans-border, trans-lingual, and transportal voices. This is especially notable given women's historically-limited property rights and the denial of maternal refugee status in the south. Following the *closed doors* of colonialism and nationalism alike, it is pertinent that, here, the woman speaker 'knocked at a door which a[nother] woman opened' as the very first stage in a process which transformed 'patterns of the future on the walls' of the domestic, the literary, and the socio-political. Like Bakhtin's theories of heteroglossia, the polyphonic dialogue between linguistically-different women illustrates how 'each character's speech possesses its own belief system, since each is the speech of another in another's language'.[18] Through English, Nadjarian recognises different 'belief system[s]', without effacing cultural difference, integrating 'a second language',[19] the voice of the Other, into a single body of text in which both Greek and Turkish are equally-foreign but equally-represented. It is through the *buffer* of 'another's language', English, that the Cypriot heteroglossia can be most easily expressed, allowing 'the speech of [the O]ther' to be recognised and included as vital in the peace process.

This construction of a women's literary space marks a resistance to the structural barriers of gender depicted across Neşe's oeuvre, as well as *Ledra Street*. In the eponymous short story of the latter, the narrator describes her movements in the southern Nicosia of the present, remembering the day, decades earlier and before 1974, when a local coffee-shop owner, Andreas, was killed in a car accident, detailing her and her parents' responses. As the first story in the collection, it importantly introduces the recurring concern with the divided city as well as the theme of complex parental relationships further explored in 'No-Man's-Land' and 'Spoon Sweet'. Early in the text, space is presented as a gendered construct, not least due to the account of the coffee-shop from which 'the men gathered round' to observe the aftermath of the accident.[20] Conspicuously, the narrator is the only female character present in this scene which opens the Cypriot setting according to a public/private dichotomy of gender: the coffee-shop paradigm.

In Nadjarian's story, the father is shown 'with a pic-measure in his hand [...] as if to measure the life and death left in the body'.[21] Analogising the trauma of that day with the events of July 1974, she asserts that these were the moments her 'memory was divided into important and less important things'.[22] In this episode, it is 'men'—the patriarchal figure of the father as well as the uncharacterised male politicians marking out their imagined 'fatherlands'—who 'measure' and 'divide' space, history, and memory according to their values of 'importan[ce]'. These values are subsequently adopted and internalised by women. In contrast, however, it is the female narrator who uses the first-person: 'I read panic again in my father's eyes'.[23] By employing the active/passive binary of writing and reading, it juxtaposes 'men' who 'measure' cartographically and empirically with women as passive recipients of the former's discursive observations.

Notably, the narrator's 'read[ing]' is not of a text, but a re-'read[ing]' of the male body. Men's bodies become scrutinised through a reclaimed first-person narration, reviewing the male-dominated landscape of pre-1974 Cyprus through a subversive counter-gaze. If her 'memory was divided' for her in the 1970s, in the present, she re-defines what is important according to her own *subjective* values. The opening paragraph repeats this idiom, re-centring a woman's quotidian life as one of 'the less important things' nonetheless at the commencement and core of this depiction of Cyprus.[24] This story, named 'Ledra Street', is not concerned with transcendental politics of the border opening—the most iconic 2003 crossing was here—but with the experiences of a young woman in relation to a single death now completely overshadowed and forgotten by the catastrophes of war. In a prolepsis to the twenty-first century, the narrator marks her own measurements of the partitioned city, counting the distance from the extant coffee-shop to the border as 'fifty-two steps to freedom, fifty-two steps to captivity'.[25] Transcending the authorised quotas of sanctioned methods—a woman's body's own 'steps' instead of feet and inches—the measurement once again re-centres the seemingly-'less important things' of individual experience. The coffee-shop of her *personal history*, and not the monumentalist history of a partitioned city in the much-mythologised Eastern Mediterranean, becomes the chosen gauge with which to conceptualise political terrain. Moreover, it explicitly complicates official nationalist quantifications by manifesting the aporia surrounding which side of the border is truly the 'freedom' or 'captivity' each ideology claims it to be. Set on the island's limen, the narrative puts pressure on the stability of the dualisms of male/female, objective/subjective, past/present, south/north, Greek/Turkish, as arbitrary categories—like her father's measurements—gradually losing their (cultural) value. It provides a sense of catachresis which, alongside the estrangement of the English form, renders nationalist signifiers foreign.

When the narrator states that 'I can only imagine the other side',[26] she expresses an explicit acknowledgement of the limitations of one's subject position. The dipolar 'side[s]' of nationalist alterity—like gender—are Anderson-esque 'imagine[d]' spaces rendered objective entities by patriarchal authorities. Indeed, the subsequent images she conjures of the north are explicitly, and satirisingly, exoticist, and Orientalist: 'My father's [pre-1974] shop hidden in a souk. Labyrinths of spices, hands dripping gold, a tree of idleness, Bellapaix, la belle paix'.[27] These are overt intertextual allusions to Durrell's *Bitter Lemons* and its exoticising accounts of the tree of idleness in Bellapaix, now north of the buffer zone. Nadjarian engages with the project of writing-back to the imperialist *forefather* and his urtext, and well as the neo-colonial and neo-Orientalist nationalisms which have usurped his discourse when describing 'the other side'. Nadjarian's narrators contend, not simply with a 'double colonialism', but the triple layers of imperialist, nationalist, and anti-feminist ideologies which intersect to limit Cypriot women's self-representation. Here, the narrator can only 'imagine the other side' through access to, and repetitions of, the passively received discourses of politically-biased men:

her Cypriot father or the imperial forefather in this patrilineal literary genealogy. In other words, she depends on the latter's depictions of a Kyrenia to which she cannot freely *go back* (to paraphrase both Durrell and Mehmet Yaşın).

Reflecting on her past, the narrator laments, 'I would like to say this to the sky [...] like the hodja [...] But somehow it doesn't seem important any more. It sounds silly, even'.[28] In an example of the poeticism of Nadjarian's prose, the repetition of the concept of importance emphasises the ostensible triviality and ineffability of the narrator's experiences. Stressed by the hypothetical modal, 'I would like', women in a religiously-conservative, patriarchal society cannot (easily) find a voice within the island's power structures. Unlike the male hodja with whom she associates herself, her words cannot resonate across the partitioned landscape. As was discussed in the preceding chapter, the Islamic call to prayer is used by Cypriot post-partition writers as a symbol of discourse that can overcome the border and be heard on both sides of Nicosia. Here, however, it is presented as a uniquely-male voice, revealing how Cypriot women's words, deemed '[un]important' or 'silly', are afforded neither respect nor the power to cross the divide. *The subaltern cannot speak.* Who is able to *transport* words depends on their gender.

Crucially, to return to my theory of the translator-as-writer, modifying Spivak's terms, it is through a rejection of 'native' Cypriot languages, by inhabiting English, that Nadjarian can, not only be read, but read across the Buffer Zone. It is a transcendental linguistic form which enters her narrations into 'the sky' of a global marketplace, above the constraints of gender on the ground. By comparison, in fact, the Turkish-speaking hodja would have sounded the call to prayer in Arabic, assuming linguistic power *through translation into a transcontinental lingua franca*. The religious conventions of Koranic Arabic would, nonetheless, exclude its efficacy for the secular, non-Muslim author. English is almost paralleled with the religious tongue as performing an ecstatic function, raising the individual from the limits of the corporeal—the marked, gendered body. However, unlike religious Arabic—or the epic pathos of Greek and Turkish nationalist rhetoric—English also accommodates bathetic representations of the quotidian. Through it, she freely expresses the 'silly' aspects of her identity otherwise effaced in a heavily-regulated society dictated by the expectations of nation, religion, and the shame/honour codes of gender. In stories like 'No-Man's-Land' and 'Coffee Cup', for instance, she describes taboo coital and post-coital scenes, sometimes with men of different ethnicities. Such scenes, especially from a woman's perspective, might well be censored by many (Greek-, Turkish-, and Arabic-language) publishers across the Eastern Mediterranean.

Similarly, the rest of 'Ledra Street' details the unequal relationships between the narrator's father and mother—as well as the late Andreas and a prostitute, Maria—in terms of literary, social, and economic disparity. The narrator begins by describing her parents' reaction to the accident through repetitions of idioms used earlier, including the active/passive binary of textual consumption:

> It was in the paper the next day. My father [drank…] coffee from the little cup, and read – possibly to himself, possibly to my mother: "Andreas Demetriou, 41, killed […]" My mother said: "And his wife? And his children? Don't they ever write about those that are left behind?"
>
> I am now the one left behind. Behind a wall, behind a checkpoint […] Counting the steps to the other side. Wondering where unimportance ends and importance begins.[29]

Reading and writing are represented as male homosocial practices whereby sanctioned discourse—including sanctioned newspapers composed in the standardised national language—is produced and consumed by men. The association with drinking 'coffee', an echo of the coffee-shop paradigm, is a tacit reminder of the gendering of cultural consumption on the island. The mother, whose literacy is never established, is merely a passive listener of information shared—wittingly or otherwise—by her husband. She is an eavesdropper to the voice of a disinterested husband within a relationship devoid of dialogue. Yet, the narrator gives voice to the mother character who denounces the silencing of women's lives through an expression with a triple meaning: the specific women 'left behind' in the newspaper *miseen abyme*; all the women 'left behind' from the coffee-shop sphere within which the newspaper report is set; and the women 'left behind' in conflict and masculinist narratives of such conflict. Subsequently, the narrator pronounces that 'I am *now* the one left behind' (*emphasis mine*)—the common fate of Cypriot women which she has inherited.

In resistance, the narrator concludes by excavating the *herstorical* past of her mother and the woman Andreas left behind, Maria, by reading between the aphasias of the dominant discourse. She also achieves this throughout by dissolving the traditional unities of (empty) time and space when leaping between decades and through the disjointed tangles of repetition. In doing so, she complicates the conventions of English prose in the construction of a text which challenges both the island's gendered networks of production and the uniform stability of the venerated 'emblem of the English book'.[30] When describing her mother, the narrator draws on the former's wedding album—like the photo album of 'Don't Forget'—imagining the moment through the lens of the bride: 'I will not mention the groom, only the bride'.[31] In this reverse-marginalisation, she excludes the experiences of Cypriot men in favour of reclaiming matrilineal ancestry. As in 'Don't Forget', it is a *non-textual book* which acts as the object of cultural dissemination between women, not the textual products of patriarchal politicians and journalists. The photo album is in opposition to the father's newspaper. It is also worth noting that when introducing the album's constituent images, her sardonic parenthesis on English collective nouns—'an admiration of bridesmaids (a flock of birds, a pride of lions, an admiration of bridesmaids)'—queries the conceits of a gendered language, foreignising obscure English conventions.[32]

Overall, the narrator searches for fragments of women's lives beyond, and within, the limits of the discursive. To little avail, the figure of the mother-bride on her wedding day is represented as a silent 'sylph' surrounded by the 'noise of happiness'.[33] As a 'sylph', she has an air of unreality; an imagined construct in a 'nois[y]' semiotic system of gender within which she is the voiceless, fantastical conception of others. This noise includes the religious sounds on Victoria Street: 'Church bells rang [...] the hodja sang in the minaret [...] And suddenly overnight everyone hated each other. [...] Anyone can see [in the photograph] that the [couple] are strangers, it is an arranged marriage, that love is absent from the photo, that my mother's frozen smile is really a sigh in disguise'.[34]

Although this commences as a symbol of peaceful pre-1963 Cyprus—Christian and Muslim coexistence on the colonially-named street, well before Cypriots 'hated each other'—it shatters the quixotic idea of the pre-partition island as an idyll. It is, instead, a religiously-conservative society in which the discourse of empowered men drowns out the voice of women to that of a barely-perceptible 'sigh'. The sound of the hodja, as demonstrated earlier, still exists, as does the narrator's feeling of being 'left behind' like her mother. It is a society where women, without agency, are coerced into forced and 'arranged marriage[s]'; the static mother-wife role within the nationalist 'mother-fatherland'. It is also a colonial space designed by British imperialist men, valorising their empress while codifying conquered territory with women's names. The 'postcolonial' narrator tacitly warns that women's rights should not be 'frozen' like that of the *empty space and time* of the border; attitudes to gender should progress and contemporary readers of historical documents, like photographs, should not aspire to the restrictive socio-religious traditions of the pre-partition era. Like the postcolonial invention of the purely 'pre-colonial', mythologising the past may appear as a benign tactic of anti-partition historiography, but is in fact one which is insensitive to the limitations of the period it describes.

For Nadjarian, post-partition movements must look to the future, including progressive attitudes towards gender and sexuality, however problematically 'Western' in origin, rather than revert backwards. The wedding may have happened before Cypriots politically 'hated each other', but it was also when some women 'hated' their arranged marriages. Nadjarian uses this English—an English of Victoria Street, one into which Greek and Turkish, or Orthodox and Muslim, vestiges diffuse—to appropriate its present-day feminist-postcolonial tools and interrogate the 'unimportant' stories of women. Crucially, these stories risk being forgotten by right-wing, misogynistic nationalists *and* left-wing idealists alike. Nadjarian begins with the simple 'sigh' of the subaltern woman to begin to tell this story. Notably, however, in the position of *translator*-as-writer, she does not speak on behalf of the—or, her—mother, but discerns a narrative from her own interpretation of historical remains. Recognising that this interpretation is itself a translation, she does not speak-over the mother, but elaborates on her own understanding of the genealogy of which she is a product and the society within which she 'now' is threatened with being 'left behind'. Instead, reversing the subject-object ordering, Nadjarian actively *leaves* behind this gendered world through the self-estranging process of writing in English. Elsewhere in the collection, stories express vehement disconnect with the expectations of contemporary arranged marriages, especially in 'Spoon Sweet'. The narrator, observing, through repetition, how the 'frozen' city still maintains the sounds of hodjas and church bells, as well as the threat of arranged *lives* for women, seeks to defrost this stagnation by moving away from the andro-nationalist discourses which preserve it.

Subsequent to the mother's story, the narrator exposes the hidden lives of prostitutes searching for 'custom' on Regina Street, perhaps ironically named after a queen.[35] Central is Maria who is shown to have formed a romantic relationship with the late Andreas. In the coffee shop, Maria's contact details, including her name, 'were hidden, in fact, under a framed picture' of Sophia Loren looking 'like an amazon'.[36] Within this metaphor, 'the woman's name'—'[t]he small word' she had etched on the façade of this homosocial space—is obscured by an icon of womanhood positioned by the male owner.[37] In Cyprus, these defining images fall into the binary of mother and lover: the narrator's mother and a prostitute. The photograph of Loren sits in parallel with the earlier photograph of the mother; the 'frozen' Cypriot role of wife-mother in ostensible competition with Loren, the 'Western', sexualised embodiment of femininity. However, the narrative destabilises these oppositions. Loren's posture, as a *translation* of a Classical Greek 'amazon', is neither entirely foreign nor local. Equally, Maria's identity, a sex-worker named after the virgin mother Mary, is controversially liminal, accounting for Andreas' panic to keep her 'hidden'. Loren, as 'an actress',[38] symbolises the performativity of gender and ethnicity which Cypriot women are forced to mediate—especially as the central/southern Italian star internalised by 1950s Anglo-Saxon Hollywood represents this struggle between the Mediterranean local and Anglophone global. Yet, it is Andreas—whose name means *man* in Greek—who 'straightened the picture frame'.[39] It is Cypriot men who, *not only control local nationalist discourse*, but who martial Anglo-American, global imports of womanhood. Cypriot women are expected to stay 'frozen' in order to honour antiquarian traditions, while their male counterparts are able to engage with, and exploit, modern cultural trends.

Before his death, Andreas speculated whether the narrator will 'grow up to be as pretty as her', Loren.[40] The objectified narrator is compelled to balance local and foreign expectations of femininity which, like Maria, obscure her own discursive identity—within an increasingly-postcolonial society which is, nonetheless, wary of feminism as 'Western' neo-colonialism. Like the internationally-disseminated image of Loren—and, even, Victoria—this is a global framing of womanhood which Nadjarian seeks to discuss through a global language. She pushes aside the national icons of 'frozen' women's roles to expose 'hidden' realities in a medium to be read more widely than that of the narrow readership embodied by the father consuming his coffee and national/ist newspaper. In the narrative's allegorical economy of gender, Andreas (*man*) is owner of his business producing local goods, while Maria (southern Cyprus' most common female name) is economically-dependent on men—even if through subversive means. His death signals the end of this dependence, but it also introduces a looming uncertainty and 'silence' in Maria's life,[41] resulting in the story's uncomfortable anti-climax. His death does not portend liberty for Maria but unstable economic isolation without any promise of change. Between the 'frozen' mother, the daughter who inherits the fear of being 'left behind', and the 'silence' of Maria's 'hidden' and economically-insecure existence, the women of this story are trapped within the borders of gender which, like the Buffer Zone, are lingering, circular, and repetitious remains which need to be re-read and rewritten. Maria, searching for the deceased Andreas, does not know he is dead, *possibly because she cannot read the newspaper*.[42] Instead, 'she looked to see him, but the place was shut, the door bolted, a silence hanging like the black night'.[43] The *closed doors* of colonialism and nationalism here meet those of gender which Nadjarian wishes to force open through transportal Anglophone works that can express that which cannot be said—which remains silent, 'hidden'—in nationalist discourse.

These themes resonate throughout the collection which uses parallelism to connect the individual narratives into a larger, singular nexus of experience. The constant recurrence of the same motifs of family life mimetically represents the claustrophobic imprisonment of women trapped by domestic constraints. In one of the subsections of 'Ten Little Tales of Love and Hate', for instance, the family's disintegration is represented by '[a] broken vase. A broken marriage'.[44] In this scene, the father is once again depicted 'watching the news on television', a modernised alternative to the newspaper, while, in an echo of the aforementioned photo albums, the narrator desperately attempts to repair the metonymic vase, 'like a photograph pieced together after it had been ripped'. The mother, meanwhile, is figured having written her exasperation in a diary only her daughter reads. The words of the subaltern woman remain unexpressed before her husband and are only covertly unveiled by the daughter who translates—and, therefore, releases—their content away from the restraints of the domestic and the hidden. The narrator stresses that with the vase, like the analogised photograph, 'the glued bits showed, always'. Restoration leads to a new object, not a return to the original. Comparable are both the *Ledra Street* anthology and 'Ten Little Tales…', within which their constituent stories are contained. Translation-as-writing allows for the creation of a new cultural body which is divorced from its original source material. This montage of fragmented texts brings each narrative together, allowing them to receive new meaning from their proximity. Yet, this fragmentising, like the repaired vase, reveals the breaks between them. It disrupts rhythm and continuity. Self-translation, likewise, allows one to break-up and reorder the materials of one's experiences, constantly reminded of the 'broken' nature of the society it describes. Through a metaphorical break from Cypriot national languages, the 'broken' state of its gender conventions—like the 'broken' map of the island—can be viewed from a distance, allowing one to interrogate those breaks, rather than permit them to remain concealed in private. As Michelle Kelly observes of J.M. Coetzee's use of a related motif, the 'private diary will not be subject to official censorship'.[45] The personal diary for a solitary reader is metatextually juxtaposed with the publically-released anthology and the international readership afforded by its Anglophone form. This enables a re-reading of discourse from an alternate subject position, like the photo album in 'Don't Forget' given new life through the transaction between linguistically-different women, and like the photographs of the mother and Sophia Loren re-viewed in 'Ledra Street'.

Through her own album of stories, Nadjarian radically reviews gender on the island through access to moments of quotidian life reassembled distantly by self-translation. *This is not simply the distant reading of Moretti, but an act of distanced writing*. From the outside position of English, the author-translator re-reads, and then exposes, the secret lives of women marginalised locally. The fragmented nature of these lives—caused in part by a fragmented island—can only be observed from a distance, like a glued photograph. From this distance, these pieces can be showcased and evaluated through a discourse uncoloured by the pressures of local, nationalist textualities—textualities composed and consumed by fathers, not mothers. This *distanced* writing exposes the borders within the Cypriot home often ignored by local political discourse only concerned with the outside border of the Buffer Zone. This is not to say that the local does not offer a cultural space for Cypriot women but rather that how the local is understood must be redefined, deconstructing the binary of local and global in order to revaluate the limits of domestic gender roles. Through distance, the categories of domestic, local, global, worldly, national, transnational, and foreign are contested by women readers and writers.

The *Closed Doors* of Gender

Further to these concerns with the domestic borders of Cypriot life, Nadjarian's 'Spoon Sweet' returns to the dynamic between mother and (narrating) daughter to articulate the latter's resistance to the former's calls for an arranged marriage. This story elaborates on a world where the mother's 'exasperated, high-pitched word[s], always repeated twice, would travel from one kitchen cupboard to the other'.[46] This is a symbolic representation of women's discourse trapped within the confines of the domestic—particularly the kitchen space—denied, not only the 'travel' of free movement across the border, but also complete freedom within the spaces they do occupy. Beyond the topos of the refugee's unhomely home in Papadakis' and Mahmet Yaşın's works, the home of Cypriot women (refugees or not) are presented by Nadjarian as inherently limiting. These constraints then reduce the freedom of 'word[s]', with their 'repeated' nature once again representing the claustrophobia of discursive gender roles. For the narrator, arranged marriages are analogised with 'a solemn, white-faced, taffeta-feathered dove' locked 'in a cage'.[47] Similarly, in 'Curtains', she describes the archetypal Cypriot bride as 'a trapped bird', wearing white on her wedding day, 'frozen in that smile, like a bird's eyes'.[48] As well as echoing motifs from 'Ledra Street', demonstrating a fear of inheriting her mother's 'frozen' fate, the imagery illustrates the incarceration associated with extant marriage conventions. In particular, the white 'dove', the ironic emblem of both government administrations of north and south, expresses how the violence of the island is not limited to a genderless discussion of geopolitics but also manifests itself in overlooked areas of quotidian life. Women have been especially failed by the unrealised promise of the dove of peaceful independence. While the island is not yet fully decolonised, neither are the lives of its women.

'Spoon Sweet' complicates this *status quo* by characterising the mother's adopted misogyny as a result of internalising discursive hegemony. While pressuring her own daughter into an arranged marriage, 'her voice was anything but sweet'.[49] The narrator-daughter goes on to say, 'I couldn't possibly live in bitterness. There was too much of that already on the island'.[50] These intertextual allusions to Durrell demonstrate how patriarchal discourse—colonial as well as nationalist; *Bitter Lemons* as well as the Cypriot newspaper—are not only pervasive and restrictive but (unconsciously) absorbed by the women it seeks to disempower. The mother, a product of the island's social conditioning, is now an agent of the arranged marriage which once *froze* her own freedom. Her ***unsweet*** voice is a translation of the ***bitter*** words of masculinist political domination, reformed and repeated within the confines of the 'kitchen'-'cage'. She is an embodiment of Ngũgĩ's theory that, if a hegemonic ideology can 'control the self-perception of those who are being controlled, they will never in fact need police'.[51] For the narrator, with all the political 'bitterness' in Cyprus, contesting this area of oppression is her aim. Yet, she does not reject the possibilities of translation. Counter to 'bitterness', she imagines love marriage as a spoon sweet, '*Glykotoukoutaliou*'.[52] She marvels at how, during their manufacturing, fruit 'preserved their essence, while becoming something else!'.[53] Alongside Greek descriptions of desserts—including the un-glossed, un-italicised 'almond daktyla', or fingers—she and her forbidden lover play with the linguistic structures of English's sweet idioms: 'The words "honey" and "moon" had never held so much meaning for me as they did in that moment [...] married like bride and groom [in...] Kostas' mouth. A moon of honey, yes, I liked that. A honey-filled moon, yes.'.[54]

All these offer important metaphors of translation. Like the preservation of spoon sweets, translation into English allows one to utilise local materials, maintaining their 'essence', while transforming them into a new, more palatable entity. Synthesis and translation, like the puns on honeymoon, allow new significations to emerge, the denotations of which are subversive, idiosyncratic, and liberating. English is not reduced to the 'bitter' connotations of its (increasingly-antiquated) colonial discourse. Here, instead, a 'postcolonial' woman writer is able to transmute its cultural values, reforming the language and its semiotic system from within. In addition, it is through this process of transmutation that English offers an alternative to the mother's auto-oppressive 'voice' in a national language. Regardless of the culpability of British imperial discourse, nationalist languages have themselves become 'bitter'. Comparable are colonially-inherited laws and customs limiting women's rights which have since been rewritten in standardised Greek and Turkish as languages *preserving* hegemonic inequality. No written language is immune from this constant reinterpretation of oppressive discourse—but through an active wresting, polyphonising, and foreignising of dominant discourses, new alternatives can be produced which put pressure on the originals' authority. A ***distanced*** writing, in translation, searches for new tools to usurp the patriarchy of the local, itself a nationalist translation of colonial violence. The result is the 'married' integration of local and foreign. It is free from the social expectations of either and is as private as the narrator's romance outside the gaze of dominant power structures.

These themes closely echo those of Neşe's *Rose Falling Into Night*. The selection of poems in the collection is able to showcase the intersections between their individual concerns and motifs. Notably, the arrangement of the first two poems, 'Unsent Letters' and 'Doors', both originally published in 1992 and translated by Ali, illustrates how the broad political imagery of the former is subsequently understood in more nuanced, gendered terms by the latter. In addition, the anthology brings together 'Doors' with the much later, 'Variations on a Theme of Doors', originally published in *Chilling Birds* (2016), demonstrating their intertextual links as diachronic treatments of the same subject. In short, 'Unsent Letters' uses the imagery of love to lament the tragic division of the border, while the speaker and translator of 'Doors' explicitly repeats many of its idioms to show how the condition of partition is understood and experienced specifically by women. 'Variations…' then consciously re-engages with these earlier works to demonstrate, with resignation, the unresolved nature of these existing divisions after 2003.

As the metatextual titles suggest, Neşe's works repeatedly employ the topos of doors. They exhibit how the *closed doors* of British colonialism and of nationalism manifest themselves in the island-wide division of gender. As such, her poetry writes-back, not simply to the conceits of colonialism, but to the patriarchal suppositions of male Cypriot writers. In particular, she re-writes the androcentricity of Montis' *Closed Doors*, stressing the culpability of masculinist nationalism in erecting contemporary social barriers—a culpability equal to, if not greater than, the colonialism Montis interrogates.

Like Nadjarian, Neşe also makes sporadic allusions to Durrell, alongside references to Classical Greek works and *The Arabian Nights*. This intertextual range reveals the importance of translation to her oeuvre. It is one of the methods of crossing doors and, to evoke the title of 'Unsent Letters', it allows one's discourse to be disseminated and received. Although composing in standardised Turkish, she emphasises the limits of claimed nationalist purity. In addition, she shows how hegemonic ideologies are translations of one another—gendered borders are translations of national borders, themselves translations of colonial divide-and-rule. Comparatively, her transportal poems are Turkish *translations*—not only of Greek myths or Arabic fairy-tales—but of a Greek-speaking, androcentric writer (Montis) who metaphorically *translated* the Anglophone travel writing of a British imperialist (Durrell). In addition, much like Nadjarian, Neşe's discussion of her estranged relationship with her father—the poet, Özker—*translates* his nationalism from the other side of the border, following her exilic 'migration'. Like Papadakis, physically travelling across the Buffer Zones allows her to reconsider the limits of her cultural identity. Consequently, living on 'the other side' is itself a life of translation—like her writing—and she encourages her allusions to Durrell, Montis, and Özker to be transported by translation, partly by reading Anglophone versions in London and Nicosia.

Notably, the collection allows for her multiple allusions to doors to come into focus. For instance, in 'Seven Little Puppies' (originally composed in 2001) and 'Ode to Love' (2016), the discourse of love poetry is used to express the separation of Cypriots on either side of the Buffer Zone. While Nadjarian uses translation and word-play to illustrate how pluralistic Cypriot culture can be 'married like bride and groom' in a single annunciation,[55] albeit rarely, Neşe shows how linguistically-dissimilar Cypriots are divided by sectarianised cultures. In the former poem, the speaker describes how her loved-one is wrest 'from the door of my joy', with the two now existing 'on either side of a closed door'.[56] Equally, in the latter, she draws on the 'shuttered doors' of society which love is willing—but often unable—to cross.[57]

In 'Unsent Letters', as well as allusions to divided love, metatextual references to Neşe's career as a translated poet illustrate problems in, and solutions to, overcoming partition. The poem details how the allegorical figure of the Cypriot on the other side, 'Took your voice and left', causing the speaker to watch 'the empty space' of the Buffer Zone.[58] Accordingly, '[t]here is no access [...] without orders from the Commander',[59] a metaphor of both the physical impediments to free movement before 2003 and the symbolic martialling of culture by nationalist authorities. The figure of the male nationalist demarcates the free cultural expression of Cypriots' 'voice[s]'. For Neşe's speaker, this is resisted through acts of love within, and across, 'the empty space'. Politicising love—in all its forms of compassion, sympathy, and empathy—she states that 'Love has been detained in no-man's land' primarily because 'love is a national traitor' and is the 'non-recognition of borders'.[60] (Note here the intertextual echo in Nadjarian's short story title.) Challenging nationalism is the primary condition of a love that seeks to repudiate sectarian divisions and reunite displaced Cypriots. The world she conjures without this love—the

Cyprus in which she is an alien living in the south—is one of acute 'loneliness' and 'longings'; she repeats the phrase 'I am alone' three times.[61] In addition, it is a habitus with 'a bitter taste, confusion'.[62] Alluding to Durrell, she reveals the cultural layers involved in the creation of a chaotic political landscape over which she has limited agency. As a result of this segregation, Greek-speaking and Turkish-speaking Cypriots—analogised as forbidden lovers—are forced '[t]o live in separate cells/to love in silence'.[63] Cyprus is not only a prison-like space, 'empty' of hope, but one where the so-called love of anti-nationalists is effaced by epistemic 'silence'.

Subsequently, the motif of doors obviously permeates 'Doors', the eponymous poem giving the 1992 collections its name. It is used to signify the multifaceted ways in which women are segregated from positions of power, agency, and freedom in modern Cyprus through feminist writings-back to Montis. Through discursive echoes of the preceding 'Unsent Letters', 'Doors' reveals that, unlike the 'love' needed for reconciliation, there is false love within arranged marriages which, like Nadjarian's representations of her mother, coerces women into limited gender roles martialled by the *closed doors* of domesticity. In addition to the political borders of national spaces are the gendered borders of the home.

The opening lines state that 'Once there were knocks on doors/and women used to open them/life used to pass by/dusted and polished each day/[...] long[ing] for a great love /[...] to be frozen like a painting was their desire'.[64] Drawing on women's dependence on male suitors, it reveals how women are trapped by rigid roles related to the spaces they are forced to occupy. It draws on women's lack of social mobility and the domestic gender roles—those of cleaning, 'dust[ing] and polish[ing]'—which keep the 'doors' of freedom firmly shut. The first two lines, in the original Turkish, read as: 'Kapılarçalınırdı/vekadınlaraçarladıkapıları'[65] (literally: *The doors were knocked on/and women opened the doors*, my translation). Rhyme and alliteration are used to align women ('kadınlar') and doors ('Kapılar')—emphasising the limens through which society prevents them from passing—as well as the acts of knocking ('çalınırdı') and opening ('açarladı'). Women are associated with static objects while men are implicitly linked to the verbs through which motion and change are facilitated. In this binary of active and passive, women's agency is nullified in a world where men control the portals of movement, power, and subjectivity. The alliteration adds audible claustrophobia while the repetition of the poem's first stanza as the last is metonymic of the 'doors' remaining closed throughout the poem's duration. In addition, the verb 'çalınırdı', which can also convey stealing or playing (an instrument), tacitly gestures to how these symbolic 'doors' are stolen from women within a habitus where men have creative dominance over music and other art forms. Similarly, the concept of the Cypriot woman becoming 'frozen like a painting' emphasises this inertia with women presented as objects of a medium created and observed by the male gaze. Echoing the photograph of Nadjarian's 'frozen' mother in 'Ledra Street',[66] it demonstrates the continuities of how Cypriot women of various ethnolinguistic backgrounds are contained in a society where they are routinely excluded from the subjecthood of cultural production. Like Nadjarian's mother, marriage is a source of social confinement. Trapped in vacuums of cultural and socio-economic inertia, these women have their lives suspended, waiting on men who act as the authors of nation-building and architects of their daughters' and wives' existences.

Elsewhere in 'Doors', the speaker stresses that there was 'never a knock on the door' for the multiple kinds of women affected by gender inequality: the brides made victim by 'dowries'; the women of war left isolated in 'cold widow rooms'; and, again like Nadjarian, the prostitutes who 'took to the streets' in desperation.[67] Evoking the women failed by the island's conflict, it shows how, in their reliance on men, they wait for arrivals that may never happen. While married women are trapped within the home, expectant of their husband's return, prostitutes are on the other side of the 'doors', forever excluded from mainstream society. Metonymically, widows are locked in a war narrative which sees them passively confined to lonely domestic spaces, removed from political, social, and economic agency, in a nationalist conflict defined by the actions of men. Indeed, the idiom of 'loneliness' used in 'Unsent Letters' is repeated here,[68] demonstrating how the experience of women is a specific manifestation of the island's isolating divisions. It is a ubiquitous 'loneliness' that, for the speaker, cannot be removed from dialogue on partition. Throughout the poem, the borders of the political are rewritten as gendered to illustrate the layered impact on women often elided in sanctioned, nationalist accounts of modern Cypriot history.

The 'days spent in *longing*', due to the lack of 'permission to cross' the Green Line, in 'Unsent Letters', is reiterated in 'Doors' as the image of women who, in their patriarchal dependence on men, '*longed* for a great love' to become their custodians (*both emphases mine*).[69] Across 'Doors', women are shown to be controlled by men throughout their lives. 'From little girls', daughters are shaped into 'docile saplings' who, through the public performance of the wedding ceremony, 'entered prisons/like white doves'.[70] In addition to the internment camps and enclaves of the 1950s onwards—the 'cells' of partition detailed in 'Unsent Letters'[71]—are the 'prisons' of unequal marriages. Notably, like Nadjarian, the comparison with the 'white doves' of Cypriot political emblems (and even with the 'saplings' of olives used on the two sides' coat of arms and the flag of the Republic of Cyprus) illustrates how the marginalisation of women is a specific manifestation of physical and symbolic violence in post-independence Cyprus. In the preceding poem, the motif of the 'bird' was used to figure the overcoming of borders, much like in Mehmet Yaşın's poetry.[72] Here, the parallelism demonstrates how, in this political landscape, women are reduced to motionless, caged birds denied the right to sing for themselves, not unlike the title of Maya Angelou's famous autobiography.[73] In this transmedial, intertextual nexus, Neşe draws on the political insignias of the island, on the narratives of male Cypriots, and on the anti-colonial writings of other non-Western-European women to carve out her own experiences of confinement and censorship as a 'postcolonial' woman erased from the androcentric archives of history. Expressing her own identity hitherto locked behind the *doors* created by both her father and his nationalist writings, she reveals how the national symbols of the island do not represent her, or other Cypriot women, who have little voice in the production of political, historiographical, or cultural works. The Cypriot home, a place described with exoticism by imperialist writers and with political idealism by nationalists, is here rendered a defamiliarised place for women. Their claims to land are doubly effaced by the numerous colonising agents who have come before. In turn, their claims to the languages of the *home*-land are forever displaced as the discursive forms which define geography always exclude the experiences of women. The domestic home, the political home, and the home-tongue of a nationalist ideology are all unhomely for the women marginalised by their gendered limitations.

In 'Variation on a Theme of Doors', these motifs all repeat, drawing on Neşe's specific relationship with the border as an émigré to the post-2003 south. Its short, broken stanzas, most only two lines and almost all using the word 'door', offer a fragmented and tautologous image of suffocating imprisonment. Her speaker asks, for instance, 'Why is every door/related to closing?',[74] recognising the continuance of this phenomenon even after the *opening* of the seven crossings. Echoing Montis, the *closed doors* are always gendered and linguistic. Describing one such door, the speaker declares that '[t]here was a woman behind the door' being trapped by a man sealing her into this position, having 'took the slam of the door with him'.[75] In addition to confinement, women are left in symbolic silence as men control the only possible sounds associated with the border. For the speaker, this silent isolation means that, 'The door's memory/is of leaving'.[76] The 'doors' are the limits placed on Neşe as a left-wing, woman writer in the north, now restrained in the Greek-speaking south by the Green Line.

As a consequence, she states: 'My sentences cut in two/are behind the doors now' and that 'Doors talk always/in time's alphabet'.[77] The island is a textual body carved into segments, much like the fragmented stanzas, dictated by the politicised semiotic systems containing history, and subsequently containing women *within* that history. As a trans-border, translated poet, Neşe's words are always 'cut in two' or more pieces, never finding a cultural home in any one place. Language is a source of division, complicit in its writing of gender, which illustrates the need for translation, travel, and dialogue across the 'doors' that detain cultural identity. The poem is mostly a nihilistic engagement with this process; translation is one of *cutting*, like the cutting of English in Baybars' *bildungsroman*. It is both necessary and limiting. However, she actively deconstructs the purist, complete 'sentences' and 'alphabet[s]' of nationalist discourse. In one stanza, she promises that '[t]he archives [...] of the women behind doors/are flowing towards the city'.[78] This is *Şehir*in Turkish, or, *The City*, Nicosia.[79] The border capital, increasingly re-multilingualised by intercommunal dialogue, usurps London as a place of exchange *because* of a polemic assault by the Left, exposing lost 'archives' of experience denied by the homogenous linguistic spaces of pre-2003 (southern) Lefkosia and (northern) Lefkoşa. It is women now writing-back to the dichotomies of gender and language. Indeed, one stanza details 'a sad door/appearing suddenly/İn front of us'.[80] The translator's decision to include the Turkish dotted *İ* to spell an English word offers a brief example of how the divided 'alphabet[s]' of the island can 'cut' and splice into each other, removing their former segregation. It is only a small gesture, and one that does not include the more distinct Greek alphabet, but it nonetheless engages with Neşe's life of translation constantly reading English versions of her compositions with a Turkish nuance in linguistically-neutral spaces.

Rejecting the 'Provincial' Through Translation as Resistance

Countering both the *closed doors* of nationalism and gender, Neşe's poetry frames itself—transportal literature—as the means through which ideological 'cells' and 'prisons' can be destabilised. Returning to 'Unsent Letters', the speaker summarises that, 'if love exists, it can only be as poetry [...] overflowing uncontrollably'.[81] The tactic of resistance is the composition of poetry which is represented as the material form of this compassionate 'love'. Its words, free from all constraints, aim to 'overflow' barriers, breaking the limits of the dam-like border as well as those of linguistic form. This is a problematic task. 'To touch you/first I need paper and pen', she states: writing is the method through which Cypriots can reach out to one another. Yet, two lines later, she laments, 'How can I touch you?' as a weightless one-line stanza.[82] Playing with literal and figurative meanings of 'touch', it is clear that the physical demarcation is, in the 1990s, insurmountable. Dejected, she offers lines of this paradoxical separation in such as small island: 'If only the address of the two of us was the same', she considers, before asking, 'Can you not even fly me a message?'.[83] Alongside the physical division is a textual one. The discursive 'address' of the *nation* is what is dissimilar for Cypriots, not the actual land. Equally, the 'message', tacitly drawing on the imagery of a paper plane, is embargoed at the border and cannot glide over. This is one of several rhetorical questions throughout, mimetically demonstrating the lack of dialogue between the sides.

The speaker, in conversation with herself, also asks, 'where shall I go?/Who shall understand my language?/the love of a provincial girl'.[84] Here, she introduces the important nexus of place, language, and gender. Not knowing where to stake her claims of identification—drawing explicitly on Neşe's decision to 'migrate'—the speaker expresses her doubts over the effectiveness of her chosen literary 'language' and over the impact of her gender on her reception. She wonders, practically, how she will be 'underst[ood]' as a Turkish-speaker in the south; how her left-wing worldview will be 'underst[ood]' by a largely-nationalist audience; and how Turkish-language poetry will be 'underst[ood]' when establishing intercommunal dialogue. Regarding the last, each national language of Cyprus is itself 'provincial' and fails to offer an effective trans-border medium. Such cultural provinciality—which she redresses by immersing herself in life on 'the other side'—leads to further 'silence'. In addition, concerned with being denigrated and infantilised as a 'girl', she expresses the significance of her gendered identity on her subject position as poet but also how it leads to yet further silencing by andro-nationalist audiences. The 'silence[s]' caused by nationalism, linguistic difference, and anti-feminism coalesce in her doubt that her left-wing 'message' will ever be heard.

As partitioned Cyprus is an *empty space*, as Cypriots do not share a single physical or discursive 'address', and as each national language is 'provincial', Neşe offers only one viable alternative: translation abroad. In the latter half of the poem, the speaker describes a literary breakthrough. In a society martialled by the capitalised 'Army', she tells the reader, 'Your message for a meeting has reached me/in a different country/at a different time'.[85] In a representation of her readings in Britain, 'message[s]' between divided Cypriots can be articulated, shared, and published 'in a different country', away from the cultural regulations of domestic militaries and local censorship. In an estranged 'time' and space, ironically, Cypriots born on either sides of a thin buffer zone are able to communicate for the first time. In the vacuum of 1990s Cyprus, Britain offers a neutral surrogate space where dialogue can be fostered and produced. The *Rose Falling into Night* anthology, drawing on this heritage, uses English translation in the creation of a pan-Cypriot literary project which, in the post-2003 island, can finally exist locally. Almost prophetically, Neşe's words have now 'reached' its audience, '*at a different time*' (*emphasis mine*) in Cypriot history, with her translated 'message' successfully delivered to southern Nicosia—not via British seminars, events, or publishers. In the poem, she subsequently pleads, 'Wait for me/take me in your arms/I will say "miow" to you in Turkish'.[86] It is a promise of translingual exchange, speaking Turkish to those from non-Turkish-speaking communities. The emphasis on the animal noise draws on seemingly universal, onomatopoeic, and untranslatable expressions unrestrained by codification. Somewhat realising this promise, her public readings embrace her translated works to speak the ineffable to linguistically-diverse audiences across the planet. That quasi-universal 'miow' (or, *niaou* in Greek and *miyav* in Turkish) sounds almost the same when the poem is performed solely in Turkish or in English.

Throughout the poem, the speaker tacitly alludes to her gender in relation to this counter-discursivity. Her imaginings of a post-partition future are marked, for instance, as 'my dreams[,] those of an adolescent girl'.[87] Three short stanzas later, she asks 'how a man [can] love/overcoming all obligations'.[88] As 'love' is frequently analogised with poetry throughout, she goes on to gender her writing by concluding that 'to love like a woman is the implication' in her desire for 'peace/between woman and man'.[89] These sporadic allusions to men and women frames the political *status quo*, and the literary tactics used to counteract it, in gendered terms. She argues that Cypriot men struggle to transcend the limits of their nationalist social conditioning because of the 'obligations' they are forced to assume as active agents of andro-nationalist institutions. She indicates the difficulty of observing the problems of a system one is enmeshed in, consciously or otherwise. As such, she suggests that men ought to sympathise with the social position of women in order to correct this myopia and that a literary movement which places the voices of women at its centre can provide this. The 'love' she encourages within her writing seeks to move away from masculinist cultural ideals. For Neşe, women and girls offer the antidote to male-authorised discourses of division, including the ideological conflict 'between woman and man' in parallel with the lack of 'peace' between north and south.

She closes the poem by elaborating on the writing of '[m]y homeland'—an echo of her famous 'Which Half of Nicosia?', explicitly ambiguous as to where, or what, her 'homeland' is. Doing so, she argues that 'my heart is the most genuine document' while, by contrast, 'History did not love those who loved'.[90] Like her translator, Ali, phenomenology is juxtaposed with the dominant discourse of official 'History', comparable to the sanctioned media internalised domestically in Nadjarian's narratives. Her poetry, described as 'genuine', is framed as an authentic product of individual experience and sympathy for the Other. On the other hand, dominant historiographies are neither accurate depictions of the organic lives they claim to represent, nor products which encourage 'love' towards those marked by categories of otherness. They are uncompassionate and ethnocentric. If translated works can be understood through processes of *distanced reading*, then history books are here marked as poor translations of the real, problematically at a *distance* from both the pathos of individual suffering and the lives of those outside the confines of the idealised nation. In opposition, Neşe focuses on the intimate psyche of the conflicted individual who struggles with the ethnolinguistic and gendered identities she is compelled to embody. The resulting 'document' can then be borne across borders without being confined, like nationalist histories, by the demarcations of their own imagined nation.

In parallel, Apter suggests that, '[c]ast as an act of *love*, and as an act of disruption, translation becomes a means of repositioning the subject in the world and in *history*' (*emphases mine*).[91] For both, who employ a similar idiomatic register, there is an important relationship between 'love', trans-border dialogue, and counter-history which affords literature an inherent readiness to be translated. Similarly, for Spivak, '[t]ranslation is the most intimate act of reading'.[92] Neşe both celebrates this intimacy with the subject of her verse and facilitates it by personally transporting her writing across borders. In this regard, she is comparably a self-translator in her physical act of bearing her own works across linguistic and national lines. Her poem, alluding to unrealised 'dreams' of a peaceful resolution challenging official 'History', echoes Bhabha's analysis that, '[t]he racism of colonial empires is [...] part of an archaic acting out, a dream-text of a form of historical retroversion', resistant to concepts of 'hybridity'.[93] Neşe's work is a counter-discursive 'dream-text' which imagines its positioning both locally and globally, through dialogue and cultural exchange across multiple linguistic and geographic frontiers, offering a vision of the present and future which defies the racialised sectarianism of colonialist and nationalist textualities. Building on Bhabha, this reductive *performance*, or 'acting out', is vehemently not restricted to British imperialism but is embodied by nationalist and anti-feminist discourses which imbricate in their expunging of heterogeneity and difference. In her 'act of love', she radically translates this existing historiographic material into a revised form of transportal travel writing, imagining a 'dream-text' of attempted dialogue. Not only is she what Spivak describes as an 'intimate reader',[94] but an intimate writer. She does not simply 'surrender to the text', but surrender's to the text's inevitable afterlife across socio-linguistic frontiers.

In 'The Seven Gates of Poetry' (2016), Neşe's speaker positions herself on the limens of the Buffer Zone and promises that 'the poem is not afraid'; instead, the '[t]he uprising begins/with the lips'.[95] In a poem drawing on the imagery of Janus, as well as the seven border crossings erected in the years prior to composition, Neşe expresses the voice of inbetweenness. Like the Roman god, she articulates a double annunciation which looks to both sides of the partition, to both past and present, and to the multifaceted cultural identifications of Cyprus as a once-Roman province whose citadel walls were Venetian constructs. She translates this heritage in the present, exploring vestiges of history beyond trite repetitions of Greek/Byzantine, Turkish/Ottoman, and British remains. Space and literature are elided and the poem is consciously aligned with a spatial politics of pluralism, not singular purity. It is through *words* that resistance is mounted—specifically words that can overcome borders and, like Janus, look to both sides of a boundary simultaneously. If 'Janus is the God of Poetry', and if he is associated with the seven crossings of the island,[96] then the text infers that Cypriot literature must always be positioned liminally, willing to express itself with two separate but intersecting voices, showcasing the power and importance of (self-)translation. Neşe, the poet often reading her words in translation, is Janus: one individual speaking two voices at once. In turn, the poet and Janus are metonyms for what the island should be according to the former's worldview, a pluralist space with linguistic crossings allowing each tongue equal prominence.

The poem 'Ode To Love' shares the same symbolism of seven, referring to the speaker's 'seventh night of love'.[97] Translated by Ali, it also repeats the imagery of exile and cultural segregation from 'Unsent Letters', echoing motifs of love, silence, and writing. Its speaker, for instance, describes how one 'would wake up to the verses of/your distant land' while passing through 'shuttered doors' which only elevate the paradox of being 'strangers while close/and close while strangers'.[98] Its compactness emphasises the unhomeliness of the sevenfold border and the inevitable uncanniness between Cypriots, 'close' yet 'distant', simultaneously. Its tacit preoccupation with the translatedness—or, crossings—of culture reveals how all Cypriot cultural exchanges involve forms of 'distant' reading which mediate the dual closeness and differences of Cypriot lives. All inhabitants of the island are physically proximal and share a common history, but linguistic (and political) disparities impose 'doors' between their dialogue and 'verses'. Whether these 'doors' are truly opened or whether they remain *closed*, despite the fanfare of 2003, is one of the main preoccupations of Neşe's work and one which fuels her desire to dismantle their presence altogether.

In an explicit echo of 'Unsent Letters', 'Ode to Love' articulates a poetic call to arms to challenge problems in cultural dissemination and reception: 'If ever this poem comes flying to you/Cling onto its wings/Don't let this bittersweet memory of the heart/be orphaned'.[99] These, the lines of the final stanza, use the image of the Cypriot dove to imagine an emblem of peaceful literary production which can surpass the limits of the terrestrial and to which all Cypriots are implored to embrace. Notable, in particular, are the motifs of 'bittersweet' and a child being orphaned. The former, like the use of the adjective 'bitter' in 'Unsent Letters', invariably echoes Durrell, while the latter draws on Neşe's complex relationship with her nationalist father who lived on the other side of the border. Within this idiom, Cypriot history, communal 'memory', and literary heritage are all the *offspring* of colonial and national patriarchs. Like Nadjarian, Neşe seeks to wrest Cyprus from their hands, creating a shared cultural product which will disavow the bitterness of neo-colonialism while also avoiding the rejection—being 'orphaned'—which befalls most left-wing material by the nationalist-aligned majority. It is anti-colonial and anti-nationalist simultaneously, alluding, in the same sentence, to the pain of contemporary Cypriots' relationships with generations of androcentric political ideologies. Neşe's 'poem[s]', which *fly* across borders aided by translation and intercommunal dialogue, are manifested as the *offspring* of a woman writer contesting the conceits of hegemonic father-figures by cherishing, rather than repudiating, egalitarian literary exchange.

In addition to the father, in 'The Light Rising Inside Me' (2005), the speaker laments how her 'history teacher/read out lies at the gates of Heaven'.[100] Once again, sanctioned discourse is dismissed as a false corruption of memory. Pedagogy, particularly the official teaching of 'history', is shown to be the product of an older generation complicit the construction of borders. As a being between these boundaries, the poet illustrates how the 'gates' which divide are relative in their signification; the 'Heaven' of one is the prison of another, just as the concepts of afterlife in Christianity and Islam are not necessarily compatible. Deconstructing the claimed objective truths of one cultural body, she signals that the proud, edenic nation of one right-wing policy is a false-paradise sustained by propaganda—for both the right on the other side *and* the left on both sides. This is the same discipline of regulatory 'history' described in 'Unsent Letters'; the same controlled by men at the highest echelons of Cypriot governance; and the same associated with Durrell, the colonial 'history teacher'. Equally, this specific 'history teacher', never explicitly described in a school setting, may simply be Neşe's father and his indoctrinating depiction of contemporary political events. This 'history' is always separate and diametrically-opposed on either side of the Buffer Zone's 'gates', and 'the book of fate' delimiting cultural expression is an essentialised product of an ethno-racial destiny from which the offspring of the nation struggles to escape.

Choosing a transportal move to the other side of the 'gates', Neşe's subject position is comparable to that of Nadjarian in 'Ledra Street'. As the latter states, 'I am now the one left behind. Behind a wall, behind a checkpoint [...] Wondering where unimportance ends and importance begins'.[101] Neşe, instead, not only recalibrates that which is important, but denounces nationalist values as 'lies' to be disavowed alongside the *closed* 'gates' they have constructed.

Translating Across Mother-Tongues and Father-Tongues

Neşe's most recent poems, from 2016's *Chilling Birds*, bring the themes of 'native language' and (un)translatability to the fore. In doing so, she addresses the gendered and ethnolinguistic divisions which persist into the twenty-first century. It is *within* standard modern Turkish that she unpacks the limitations of the form and illustrates its ineffability for left-wing women writers.

In two of the poems, the speaker characterises this through references to the suffering of women in Classical literature. In 'Ode to Love', she alludes to Daphne, the nymph metamorphosed into a laurel after being pursued by Apollo, to describe contemporary Cypriot women: 'We were like the broken branches during the last looting'.[102] This intertextuality draws on both the Greek narrative and Neşe's own recurring use of nature—'saplings' and 'branches'—to imagine the destruction of female selfhood by men who 'loot' both women and land. In 'Penelope', the abandonment of widows and other women from the 1960s onwards is placed in parallel with the title character's wait for Odysseus. The poems, therefore, offer three important functions. Firstly, they demonstrate the timelessness, even universality, of the oppression of women which can be liberally transported between the cultures of different times, places, and languages. Secondly, this cultural mixing allows for modern, Turkish-language interpretations of Greek myth, deconstructing the holistic bounds of either tradition by 'enter[ing] your kingdom/Through shuttered doors', as she states in the former.[103] These are, once again, the *closed doors*, of neo-colonialisms being shattered by linguistic transportation. It is through the liminal 'shutter[s]' that her *intimate* readings and writings of Eastern Mediterranean texts slip osmotically. Thirdly, they are feminist writings-back, or translations, of androcentric literary traditions offering the perspective of oppressed women. The dehumanised 'branches' of ancient myth write-back. History, or *herstory*, is being rewritten through a process of translation blurring linguistic boundaries in order to undermine centuries-old notions of gender dimorphism. Notably, the original myths all depict women being passively *transported* from one form to another by omnipotent, male deities. Neşe, on the other hand, is an active agent in processes of cultural production and literary exchange.

Summarising all this, the speaker of 'Penelope' asserts:

> The footprints of the visible/are traced in the gaze of others/from the gates of grief […] don't come back/The woman in waiting/vanished… /in the silence of other women[104]

The poem demonstrates how the marks of men on much-contested land—their very 'footprints'—are being reviewed and repaved by the subversive 'gaze of others', if not, indeed, the Other. This 'gaze' rereads established literature and the divisions—or, 'gates', like those of the History teacher—it erects between Greek-speakers and Turkish-speakers, and men and women. Unlike Homer's Penelope, Neşe's figure renounces her fidelity to a man. It is by embracing 'silence', in Spivakian terms, that she aligns herself with 'other women' of different ethnolinguistic traditions, the Turkish-speaking poetic speaker and Greek-speaking Penelope. Doing so, she rejects any allegiance to the male protagonist of androcentric tales of travel and conquest, including the *Odyssey* as the Classical travelogue *par excellence*.

Notably, the opening lines directly contrast with the opening stanza of 'Unsent Letters' where the patient speaker, encumbered by nationalist segregation, observes how 'your footprints did not disappear', in relation to those lost by war and partition.[105] Instead, the speaker of 'Penelope' disavows the expected role of Cypriot women waiting for husbands (or, more loosely, fathers, military commanders, politicians) to approve of their speech and movements. Amidst its resigned tone is the emphatic 'don't come back'—a woman utilising the phrase often repeated as *don't go back to Kyrenia*. Indeed, having crossed to the other side, and 'vanished' from the men who impeded her freedom in youth, Neşe's words are now often censored into 'silence' in the Turkish-speaking north and only given life through translation by 'other women', including Ali. This translation of Greek into Turkish awaiting further translation, positions itself firmly *on* 'the gates', aware that any manifestation of the work is affected by the paradox of translation overcoming, yet also creating, different forms of 'silence' simultaneously. Her works are silent in the north, but given a new voice in the south and the Anglosphere. Yet, as translation results in the loss of some original meaning, these versions contain within them a different kind of epistemic 'silence'. This is a problem acutely felt by 'women' writers for whom entering into *any* language involves a translation of selfhood into an androcentric mode.

Indeed, throughout her later poetry, allusions are made to recognising and advocating the ineffability of all literary expression. As such, she undermines the perceived stability of any singular linguistic system and thus demonstrates how translation between languages is no less effective in conveying meaning than attempting to carry meaning between two individuals within the same language. In the appropriately named 'Broken Words Symphony', the speaker addresses the weight of established literary modes: 'As your gaze saddens mine/I go to the lake of gazelles/trailing after broken words'.[106] Elsewhere, it is a dominant discourse personified with a 'virgin blood stain on your forehead'.[107] Here, dominant discourse is embodied as a gendered semiotic system complicit in violence against women through its male 'gaze'. The reference to 'gazelles', a common dehumanising trope of Persian and Ottoman *ghazal* poetry, directs the focus here, not to Classical literature, but to early modern precursors to contemporary Turkish literature and its objectification of women. For the speaker, the language which is expected to be her own is, in fact, rendered distant due to its antiquarian and exclusionary depiction of women. As a consequence, for women writers, this literary legacy is a 'broken' system which cannot fully express the experiences of contemporary life and which women must continue to deconstruct. It is by breaking-down the language that a new voice can be formed from the reconfigured remains. In short, the language intended to be one's 'native language' is unhomely and unsuitable for women interpolated into that national cultural sphere. It is, rather, a *father*-tongue which excludes women's subjectivity and promotes their social marginalisation.[108] Once again, it is the language of the father and the history teacher, not the words of the 'adolescent girl' described in 'Unsent Letters'.[109] Counter to Spivak's calls for the subaltern to be read and heard in her 'mother-tongue',[110] Neşe illustrates that no such system exists. All discourses are dominant due to their historical standardisation by men. Hence, translation from Turkish (or, Greek) into

English is a movement from one problematic language to another—and not a relinquishing of a subaltern mode to a dominant alternative.

It is *within* Standard Modern Turkish that Neşe deconstructs the authority of this one system. Metatexually positioning herself alongside the Lacanian 'slippages' of the form, she showcases the ineffability of any single linguistic body. Like her Classical allusions, she ruptures the cohesiveness of one cultural tradition by putting pressure on its internal limitations. In 'Broken Words Symphony', she describes her discourse as 'flitting meanings of wordlessness', as 'disjointed meanings' and 'whispers', and as 'a dead language' once having belonged to a man.[111] Elsewhere, 'Poison Apple' outlines 'my voiceless voice' as a poet attempting to carry 'every heartbroken woman's voice'.[112] Like Nadjarian, Neşe employs a combination of what can and cannot be said. Rejecting the idiomatic 'language' system of a patriarchal and ethnocentric discourse, she chooses to create—or, at least, gesture towards—a new lexicon and a new space in which to create it. Unlike the poetry of her brother, Mehmet, Neşe achieves this, not by coining new portmanteau terms, but through the equally-powerful act of withholding. Through 'wordlessness' and a 'voiceless voice' she, almost directly echoing Spivak, deconstructs the authority of standardised Turkish through what she does not say, showcasing the lacunae and elisions inherent in the cultural habitus. Like her Penelope, she abandons the domination of men and their discourse by actively choosing to be *absent* while writing.

This, therefore, illustrates parallels with, and differences from, Nadjarian's own linguistic form. The latter rejects the dominance of Standard Modern Greek by self-translating her subject position into English—a process which also creates a 'voiceless voice', one that cannot be heard in either of the nationalist languages of the island and one which has its local nuances altered by its conversion to an Anglophone form. On the other hand, Neşe *demonstrates* the 'voiceless voice' of a left-wing Cypriot women writing in Standard Modern Turkish by using said language to showcase its ineffability for writers who challenge the nationalist, patriarchal nature of its extant use. Not least, this is the case when her words are censored in northern Cyprus. Given its rare circulation in the north, her metatextual allusions to the limits of all semiotic systems open her poetry up to transport and translation and allow her to create spaces of dissemination where her 'voiceless[ness]' is countered through the process of what Boehmer calls 'cross-border transaction'.[113] It is by embracing the paradox of translation and creating a 'voiceless voice'—aware that the same problems occur when a woman writer translates herself into the patriarchal father-tongue of her birth—that she allows for traces of her subjecthood—even if mere 'whispers'—to emerge unrestrained. She undermines the limits of one of Cyprus' nationalist languages from within, and by rendering it 'dead', she allows for future translation to perform the act of reincarnation. Both Neşe and Nadjarian metaphorically kill their respective standardised *father-tongues*—the Turkish of Ankara and the Greek of Athens—by living literary lives of translation. While the latter does so from the moment of composition, the former does so during: using Turkish to reduce it into 'a dead language' from which her 'voice' is revived through published translation by peers, locally or abroad. She revives her selfhood through the sutures of 'broken words' reformed, of 'wordlessness' given meaning through substitution, and performances of poetry in southern Cyprus and London where her 'voiceless voice' is given a new voice to inhabit and survive.

This ultimately showcases Walter Benjamin's theory that 'translation issues from the original – not so much from its life as from its afterlife'.[114] In 'Broken Words Symphony', this is literally figured in the image of 'a dead language' allowing for a resurrected cultural *afterlife* to emerge. It is a motif related to the *ghosts* of Mehmet's poetry and illustrates the need to deconstruct existing social assumptions in the redevelopment of the island's post-partition identity. It is an identity which consciously overcomes partition through the willed death of the structures of a dominant discourse. Neşe's play on the stability of the great national language echoes Butler's assessment that '[c]cultural translation is also a process of yielding our most fundamental categories, that is, seeing how and why they break up and, require resignification when they encounter the limits of an available episteme'.[115] To return to McClintock's emphasis on post-coloniality being lived differently by women, Butler's *Undoing Gender* (2004) illustrates the importance of a translational perspective for post-colonial women writers wishing to 'break'—an idiom shared by Butler and Neşe—the ideological confines of nationalist patriarchy. For Cypriots, in particular, however, translation is necessary for revising both the dimorphism of male/female and Greek/Turkish which consolidate each other in the formation of epistemic borders. Symbolically killing the stability of standardised Turkish and Greek allow Neşe and Nadjarian, in different but related ways, to put pressure on these neo-colonial binaries.

These themes coalesce in 'AlashyaThe Little Match Girl'. The poem imagines the union of the speaker and her male lover resulting in a metaphorical 'daughter', named Alashya after one of the earliest designations for Cyprus in the Bronze Age. Eliding the production of poetry and of children, this fantastical Alashya, an allegory of the island and its cultural output in the twenty-first century, is the consequence of an increasingly mixed and linguistically-diverse present which looks back on Cypriot history critically. The very name itself rejects the nationalist historiographies which circumscribe memory to that of one cultural tradition and begin Cypriot history with either the Mycenaean or Ottoman eras. This product of the post-partition age is a necessary outcome of the present but also one which re-remembers the island's pre-Ottoman, pre-Greek identity. It is the same name that Papadakis alludes to when discussing the theory that the Asian continent gained its name from its westernmost island.[116] As such, Alashya—or, Alashiya, Alasia—represents one of the few vestiges of a truly pre-colonial identity which draws on a period before all European occupations and settlements. Its etymological connection with mainland Asia stresses its use as an anti-Eurocentric moniker. Powerfully revising the past illustrates what Cypriots can create in the present in this *consciously* paradoxical double-image of ancient history and new birth. The speaker excavates a past which unravels and disempowers the conceits of Greek and Turkish nationalist histories, of their discursive labels for the island, and of Eurocentric distortions of geography. The name, of uncertain etymology, offers an alternative to Greek and Turkish which dismantles their authority in claiming and organising the territory. Like McClintock's analysis of men imposing their patronymic names onto their offspring, Neşe's symbolic daughter is given a name predating the father-tongues of both Greek and Turkish.[117] It is simultaneously pre-nationalist and post-nationalist, with the two temporalities consolidating each other.

Crucially, this process is performed by the speaker as a mother-poet, not by a male writer imagining the fatherland. It is a dissident vision of Cyprus-as-daughter and of the literary agent as mother. Counter to the exclusion of women from the historical record, it is a (figurative) mother who assumes the first-person and who revises the androcentric historiographies which have excluded both her experiences as a woman and the pre-colonial junctures deemed problematic by nationalists. This is a gesture to the possibility of a *mother*-tongue which incorporates, while subverting, dominant discourses. Equally, the use of the second-person across the poem stresses that this 'daughter' is a product of speaker and listener, signifying how a new Cyprus can be born through the dialogism of sharing culture. The listener includes the translator and those consuming the work in translation, showcasing how these inevitable processes of her trans-border poetry is integral in the re/construction of an alternative Cyprus which recovers historical junctures repudiated by nationalist writers. Parallel to the motif of an *afterlife*, Neşe's work imagines the creation of *new life*. It is the product of various vestiges of Cyprus' cultural past being revived and reincorporated by a mother, counter to the distilling of this past into segregated layers by patriarchal nationalisms. In addition, the very paradox of a fledgling Cyprus as the reincarnation of its most ancient identity parodies the inherent contradiction of nation-building using this doubleness to the advantage of the political left and by destabilising local pedagogy which fails to teach the earliest, pre-Greco-Turkish centuries of the island's history.

Echoing the notion of 'a dead language', 'Alashya…' details how the parents of this new Cyprus 'didn't speak to each other/had forgotten every language/in our stammering passion'.[118] A reunited Cyprus can only emerge when intercommunal expression evades the strictures of 'every' national 'language' and finds dialogue through nonhegemonic, nonmetropolitan forms. It is a salvaging of the love supressed in the first poem of the collection, 'Unsent Letters', finding freedom by escaping the limits of ethnolinguistic segregation, both physical and symbolic. As such, it creates a Cyprus which aspires towards an identity independent from 'every' foreign hegemony for the first time since it was called Alashya—centuries before its colonisations by Mycenaeans, Ottomans, Western European powers, and now the nationalisms of Athens and Ankara. Indeed, translation is itself an act of 'forg[etting] language' as a work finds new life in another.

Throughout the poem, the couple are figured attempting to converse outside standardised forms; the mother tries desperately to 'decode your secret alphabet',[119] notably in an island home to more than one. The resulting daughter is said to have 'spoke bird language'.[120] The image, which draws on the dove of political emblems and the imprisoned birds detailed across Neşe's (and Nadjarian's) oeuvre, illustrates the formation of a Cypriot cultural expression outside authorised forms, through a pidgin mode. The actual realisation of the peace symbol can only be achieved by rejecting the dominant linguistic conventions which impede intercommunal dialogue. The 'bird language' represents, like translation, words that are in constant motion and can fly across the borders demarcating the Cypriot cultural and political habitus. This 'bird language', therefore, implicitly draws on translations—of *bearing across*—in the construction of a literary discourse which is precisely non-dominant because of its view to transcend the parochial and 'forg[et]' all national affiliations in its fluid movement between voices. The mother-speaker, in her subversive mother-tongue, creates this new Cyprus by speaking an idiolect which, while drawing on extant conventions, leaves their semiotic and political constraints 'dead' in pursuit of creating a free, mobile, diglossic alternative within the post-partition present. Nationalism is killed in favour of the long-erased Alashya, the unrealised dove, the unused act of translation, and the unspoken mother. They are all revived in order to correct the epistemic silences which have dogged the historiography, peace, dialogue, and women's rights of a politicised Cyprus and its selective memories.

Confronting Father-Tongues in the *No-Man's-Land* of Translation

The themes of mother- and father-tongues introduced by Neşe reappear in Nadjarian's metatextual commentary on translation in 'No-Man's-Land' and its depiction of the bordered nature of Cypriot society. The short story, like others in the collection, draws on the style of prose poetry with its use of symbolism, quasi-real dreamscapes, and idiomatic repetition. It is roughly divided into three temporal segments. In the present, the narrator watches her childhood home in the Green Line being demolished. This results in two analeptic scenes: recalling the death of her Cypriot father in a local hospital alongside her mother, step-mother, and half-brother; and remembering her English lover, John, whom she met while studying at a British university. These vignettes are, nonetheless, linked by their tacit relationship with language and its gendering on the island.

In this merging of various memories—combining past and present, reality and fiction—the narrator portrays herself as a trans-historical countertraveller revisiting an intimate Nicosia soon to be consigned to history. Doing so, it forces her to 'look with my eyes half-shut, at a world half in focus', gazing at where the house's 'half-walls had [once] stood still'.[121] She reiterates the motifs of *half*-ness employed in both colonialists' ambivalence towards in-between cultures and nationalists' fears of ethnic impurity. Their connotations are as fleeting as the physical structures demolished by conflict. Across the text, the narrator embraces an inevitable subject position of half-ness. Her dual perspective from the 'eyes' of Anglophone and Cypriot worldviews draws on her doubleness as a British-educated Cypriot and as a woman. The discourse of preceding male writers is ultimately re-written to express the double identity of a diasporic woman recounting, not epics of monumentalist *His*tory, but the intricacies of her personal *herstory*. It is the unassuming—*unimportant*—places of her life which are transformed into monuments warranting an excavation of the past. Crucially, it is as a woman writer-narrator that she deconstructs and reconstructs the Cypriot home once controlled, legally and discursively, by the colonial administration or the nationalist father. These memories of half-ness also stress the inherent fictiveness of all discourse—'half' real and 'half' imagined—putting pressure on the reliability of all received historiography.

The pun of the title draws on the narrator's attempts to carve out textual territory outside the rule of men. This work with *no man* as its author, is only achieved, within the narrative, following the death of her father and end of her relationship with John. Comparable to Neşe, Cypriot and British men are decentred from the historiography of partition. Throughout the text, the idioms of 'loneliness' and 'lonely' are used to describe both the Green Line and the narrator's migration to England.[122] Unlike Neşe, however, this 'loneliness' is not only symptomatic of the island's sectarianism, but also affords the opportunity for the narrator's budding independence. In a work of *half* affiliations—positioned between Cyprus and England, Greek and English—every word has double connotations of loss and possibility. The same is true for the limits and prospects afforded by translation. It is her identity between colonial periphery and centre and situated on the Ledra Street border, that allows her to explore her relationship with language. Translation, for all its problems, enables her to play with, and manifest, an identity as an anti-partition woman writer in ways sanctioned nationalist discourse would not allow. Translation attempts to overcome the borders of national spaces *and* puts pressure on the divisions of gender dimorphism. In short, linguistic translation and gender subversion consolidate one another across Nadjarian's oeuvre. Showing interesting parallels with Matthew Reynolds' theory of translation, the title exposes the 'no-man's land that readers of one language can enter to make sense of writing in another'.[123] Here, it is the translator-as-writer who performs this *reading* and allows the signifiers of two cultural spheres to interact, mix, and learn from each other. The tools of a 'Western' feminist criticism meet the individual experiences of an anti-colonial, anti-nationalist writer trapped in a neo-colonial conflict outside the 'West'. In this 'no man's land between languages',[124] Nadjarian wrestles with a 'postcolonial', gendered identity that can never be fully expressed by one linguistic form, especially as almost all language is institutionally codified and standardised by 'man'.

Instead, she deconstructs the authority of written discourse, playing with the fictiveness of historiography and, in particular, how men are written about. Reversing the male gaze, her translation inverts gender conventions and places men under the scrutiny of her narration. Beginning the analeptic description of her youth and her relationship with her father prior to his death, she states that 'my childhood… is always autumn'.[125] It is another symbol of liminality, here at the heart of the story-telling process. She goes on to clarify, however, that '[t]here is no autumn on Mediterranean islands […] There is no autumn, so I make it up, from what I have read in books, seen in films'.[126] She does so because she wishes her 'father has died in an English autumn' rather than the tortuous heat 'of a Cypriot summer'.[127] From this, she confesses that she doctors this quasi-real *bildungsroman*, '[i]n the same way I make up the stories my father never told me, about life, and love'.[128]

In short, her personal histories are fictions mediated by other genres, 'books' and 'films', imported from the 'West'. Illustrating how nationalist histories of the father(land) are fictions based on a 'Western' model, it reveals the unreliability of authors describing the past in order to demonstrate how *all writing is an act of translation*. In particular, 'postcolonial' authors must always mediate between 'Western' form—the 'books' depicting 'an English autumn'—and local materials—the topographies of the post-Ottoman, post-British house crumbling next to a 'stoic palm tree' in 'a Cypriot summer'.[129] The two extremes re-write one another until a third possibility emerges between 'then' and 'now', 'autumn' and 'summer', English and Cypriot, one which cannot be read without counter-reference to the other. The city becomes a hypertext and the author-narrator uses an Anglophone form to represent its intertextual translingualism. She alludes to traces of Persian, Venetian, and English,[130] all former languages of administration and Mediterranean *lingue franche*. With the notable absence of Greek and Turkish, and the obvious irregularity of 'Cypriot' as a geopolitical adjective with no definite language attached, she enters the most recent international auxiliary language to reconstruct the city, its houses, and its fictions anew. The transportal medium associated with Hollywood 'films' is used for her filmic depiction of Cyprus on the cusp of the global and the local. If all writing is translational, then writing in any one linguistic form involves a partial translation of the self: a process from which the standard forms of Greek and Turkish in 'books' and 'film' are not exempt. All writing is imitational, intertextual, and heteroglossic, merging the real with the imagined in their attempts to *translate* experience into narrative. Metonymic of the necessity of English, however, is the narrator's account of walking along the Green Line as a child with her father. The latter would implore, 'Listen to the story on the other side'.[131] Like the subject of Neşe's poetry, the two attempt to communicate across the partition but in ways which, within the narrative, amount to little more than a symbolic gesture. (Outside it, however, the Anglophone mode allows for publication and dissemination across 'side[s]'.) This statement is followed by the confession that representations of her father were falsified as well as the discovery of her father's extramarital affair and remarriage. Dissolving the truthfulness of stories told of, and by, her father, it reveals the internal borders between truth and fiction impacting all discourse and which require movements *between* voices, perspectives, and temporalities to arrive at the most comprehensive summary of events. The genre of Nadjarian's texts, situated within the *no-man's-land* between fiction and travel writing—thematically and linguistically between Cyprus and the Anglosphere—textualises the partitions of the island and its diametrically-opposed histor*ies* as overlapping sites of transportal crossing.

In a short story beginning with an idealised childhood with the father, the midpoint, around his death, introduces the voice of the mother to re-write the narrator's naïve patriarchal myths. The narrative surrounding the great father figure—in parallel with Venizelos and Atatürk—is being revised. She achieves this through one of the non-*father-tongues* of the Republic, English, using the form both to question Cypriot nationalist-patriarchal conventions and to undermine the fantasies of the 'West' acculturated from 'books' and 'films'. It showcases the problems of translating experience into a discourse with inherent cultural biases, either towards the Cypriot father or an idyllic England, which produce tinted images of the past and one's identity. It is a critique of Cypriot cultural consumption, alluded to through the motifs of how 'time engulfed' the house's markers of trans-historicity and 'ate them'.[132] In this metatextual narrative, Cypriots 'engulf' either Western imports (the 'English autumn' of false memories and the house's 'colonial etchings') or nationalist historiography (the hagiographic image of the father). Instead, and like in Neşe's poetry, the mother's 'words', and her voice of painful 'truth', are rarely heard. In Nadjarian's narrative, it is only recognised after the father's death and after the relationship with John in England has ceased. Interestingly, the mother's voice cannot be expressed freely in its *mother-tongue*, that of a Cypriot vernacular (like Kypriaka). Consequently, the narrator chooses not to present it, or her own voice, through one of the *father-tongues* of standardised national languages (Greek, Turkish, and possibly Armenian).

For Nadjarian, Cypriot women's writing cannot successfully challenge patriarchal nationalism through a father-tongue. Yet, the use of English must also destabilise its links to English topologies: 'English autumn' giving way to the Cypriot palm tree. This is a Cypriot English, or a globalised English, not an English of the British metropole. She metatextually translates the history of writing history by re-building the archetypical Cypriot house. Simultaneously excavating its chronological layers, as well as her relationship with men, she constructs a counter-discursive present from the ruins of the past, utilising the remains of a decolonised English to make sense of the newly-fragmented border. Never pure, this self-reflexive, nonlinear, and repetitious perspective, consciousness of its inherent 'half[ness]', forges a female voice in 'No-Man's-Land' which rejects male-centred histories of false absolutes and blind idealism. Aware of her own unreliability, she repeatedly relishes in having 'ma[d]e it up'; travel writing, the *bildungsroman*, and historiography are all fictionalised in her deconstruction of these genres from within. Countering the destruction of land, buildings and lives committed by men—be it the house's demolition or the lies told by her father—the speaker ultimately creates the textual house of Nadjarian's poem, 'Don't Forget'.

The narrator, therefore, constructs a home in the lacunae of an extant—but abandoned—form. The house becomes a metonym of a self-translated and transportal English. Her fragmented memory, like discursive 'dry leaves [and] messages on yellow paper', are 'messages I cannot catch or read [as] they fly away'; they are juxtaposed with the image of 'sparrows building nests in the gaps' of the derelict building.[133] The landscape is analogised with writing, evoking a historical linguistic form within which the speaker has little agency. The 'yellow paper', denoting an aged semiotic system, represents a tradition over which she has limited control. In this epigraphical scene, she is excluded from dominant discourses which, through parallelism with memory, are shown to corrupt the ways history is remembered through text. For the self-translated Nadjarian, whose internal monologue and memories are not in English, the language of these memories fails her when attempting to engage in the literary tasks of 'read[ing]' and writing. In short, Standard Modern Greek fails as a possible linguistic form within which she can freely represent herself. However, like Neşe, motifs of birds and flying are used to re-imagine subjecthood. Counter to the nationalist discourses—Greek and Turkish—which impede self-expression and cause individual autonomy to 'fly away', Nadjarian's speaker creates a transient 'nest' within the ostracon-like debris of the fallen house. Unlike the Cypriot emblems of doves, the image of 'sparrows' rejects the symbolism of purity in favour of everyday birds. Quotidian experience trumps a reliance on monumentalist national symbols. Even the 'yellow paper' illustrates how the once-pure eventually succumbs to the corruption of time.

Unable to associate herself with ostensibly-*pure* national languages, the speaker creates an allegiance with the house: a heterogeneous, heteroglossic, and trans-historical site on the limens of time as well as nations. The house becomes a *transnation*. Despite being destroyed by others—indicated by the subject of the story's opening line, '*they* pulled down the house' (*emphasis mine*)—she actively 'resurrect[s]' the building by suturing its disparate parts back together.[134] She creates a linguistic form, her idiomatic English, which crosses temporalities and spaces, and darts between realism and dreamscapes, to make a claim to land which disavows purist nationalist allegiances.

The house itself, with its 'colonial etchings', remnant 'costumes', and echoes of 'polite conversations', an adjective regularly associated with British high society, recalls the homes of British travel writers, including Durrell and Scott-Stevenson.[135] It is not unlike latter's, in which '[t]he floor was covered with cool Turkish matting, while a few pieces of English furniture gave quite a comfortable appearance', alongside 'divans' and 'verses from the Koran' which are 'translated to' her.[136] Specifically, however, it echoes Durrell's representation of his village abode 'in the purest peasant tradition – domed Turkish privies [...] bearing the faint traces of a Venetian influence' alongside 'old-fashioned mouldings' from where he can discern the distant music of mandolins.[137] Nadjarian's narrator revisits the Cypriot homes of pre-1960 Anglophone prose and, consequently, re-inhabits the English form which now exists as 'half' of what it was, foreignised and rearranged. The building and the language may not be structures she owns completely, but she maintains an unbreakable bond with both. The house allows her to recapture a diverse history within which she is now an agent, reconstructing uncomfortable memories of the 'colonial' past without rejecting all of what Britain introduced to the Cypriot sprachbund. It is a rewriting of Durrell, of the English language, and of the androcentric, 'colonial' textualities—imperialist and nationalist—which have built the island as it currently exists. The childhood home of the Cypriot woman writer, displacing the dramatic unities of time and space upon which objective historiography is founded, usurps the long tradition of Cypriot topologies being contained by androcentric dogmatism. Notably, she describes the bordered capital without explicit reference to any of the political bodies, movements, or leaders culpable in the walls' erection or the ethnolinguistic communities on either side.

Indeed, when she describes how she 'stood some distance away from the rubble and dust',[138] she illustrates her *distanced* reading and writing from the remains of a crumbling form—the translator-as-writer appropriating a language, English, increasingly losing its colonial power. As for the textualised remnants of the house, she claims 'time engulfed them, sucked them in, ate them'.[139] Comparatively, she consumes Anglophone literary practices—vampirically and cannibalistically—before regurgitating them to produce a new, foreignised form. 'Then' and 'now' coalesce as the history of English literature confronts the postcolonial present. What remains with any sense of permanence is the 'tall palm tree in No-Man's-Land' and 'its fringe of leaves swaying above my head in the slight breeze'.[140] It is a symbol of the local being read in English, from 'some distance'. She goes on to detail how the palm is 'pulled and pushed by an invisible wind, now from the south, now from the north'.[141] All this is in contrast with the metaphorical wind which blew her memories and words—like 'dry leaves' and 'yellow paper'—from her. The 'leaves', in its double-meaning as pages, represent the narrativising of the island. She has no control over the winds of nationalism which dispel her attempts to speak freely. Nonetheless, by self-translating, Nadjarian appropriates English in order to create new 'leaves' representing Cyprus, 'leaves' which Mediterraneanise the language itself by synthesising local topographic materials with external textual structures. On the limens of the border, and of a global yet localised English, she cultivates a literary mode which frees her from restrictive political allegiances of the nation, of the 'north' and 'south' vying for control of the land. She can only achieve this by reinventing English from within to deconstruct the symbolic borders of inside and outside which define both homes and nations.

Distanced Readings of Gender

The idiom of *distanced reading* recurs subsequently in the depiction of the narrator's mother and the gendered implications of reading and writing the Cypriot political context. In the hospital scene, the mother—the dying father's ex-wife—is presented as distracted, as if 'she was watching activities taking place in another world, activities invisible to the rest of us', creating 'a strange distance between us'.[142] Multiple terms are repeated from earlier in the story—'distance', the motif of worldliness, and the invisibility associated with the political winds—reframed with specificity and immediacy to explore the psyche of the post-1974 Cypriot woman. The mother becomes the *distant reader*, observing a 'world' unreadable and unread by others. The self/Other binary of pronouns, her and 'us', transforms the existential divisions commonly associated with the Cyprus dispute into the lived division of Cypriot mother-wife and the rest of the society. This 'distance' in individual experience creates different 'world'-views; she is confined in a gender-demarcated 'world' which is not synonymous with the global and which is routinely excluded from established literary representations. What she sees is unreadable because it is so often ignored—like historical accounts of women's experiences of the Cyprus conflict. Once again, the *mother-tongue*, and perspective of the mother, while alluded to, cannot find articulation in writing. To continue the filmic register, it exists off-screen. Yet, as the narrative progresses, not only is the daughter's viewpoint explored, but it slowly integrates the mother into the Anglophone prose.

This is achieved by further displacing the role of the patriarch. In the same paragraph, the father's death creates 'a total blank we now had to face'.[143] As with earlier metatextual images of writing, the 'blank' page opened up by the death of the father—counter to the aged 'yellow paper'—presents the need to write and create anew. In a scene replete with comparable motifs, including the deathbed's 'folding sheets', the focus shifts to 'the sound of [the] mother's words [which] emerged from her mouth'.[144] It is only as the father departs from the narrative that the mother's voice begins to be discerned, filling the void and usurping the presence of her former-husband. It is a subversive counter-reading and -writing which gestures to a 'world' which had existed but the narrator and her external readers had been ignorant of. For a moment, the mother's voice appears to be 'solely addressing the nurse'.[145] Given the gendered stereotypes associated with the profession, this scene suggests a performed homosocial—and, even, esoteric—dialogue between two women. One is the unnamed mother and wife of previously-introduced protagonists; the other is an unnamed, unvoiced nurse on an island with gendered disparity within its medical professions. The two are trapped in their respective gendered roles. Nonetheless, their dialogue, to which the daughter-narrator is privy, allows for discursive exchange between women outside the authority of the late husband and the absent doctor—like the two women in Nadjarian's 'Don't Forget', and the pairs of women across Ali's short stories. It overrides the male gaze of the husband and the medical gaze of the doctor and manoeuvres the narrative's perspective between the experiences of women observing, discussing, and appraising men.

Indeed, while her father lies in the hospital bed, the narrator describes herself with 'tissues in hand', which she discards into a 'small bin full of cotton wool and elastoplast, injections which may have held traces of my father's body hair, his skin, his blood. We were the four people who witnessed my father's death'.[146] A person's life is framed, almost nihilistically, as a fleeting collection of fragmented textualities created by both the individual and others, occasionally read and interpreted by selected 'witness[es]', and then cast-off. As a metatextual symbol of writing, it illustrates the discursivity of ontology. Each character is a simulacrum formed from heteroglossic perspectives which consume elements of the real—the biological, corporeal, medical—in the creation of a textual construct. This is a deconstructed reading and writing of the father, demonstrating the constructivist nature of said process, counter to nationalist essentialism. It is also one where three readers, those who 'witnessed', with its judicial connotations, are women: the narrator, her mother, and her step-mother. Not only does this put pressure on sanctioned masculinist discourse, but it also acts as a symbol of Cypriot linguistic heterogeneity. The translator-as-reader and -as-writer producing this Anglophone account assumes only one of four distinct, yet *related*, perspectives. The mother, step-mother, and half-brother—in their echoes of phrases like mother-tongue—emblematise the various vernaculars Cypriots inherit, share, and exchange. In Nadjarian's actual family, they include Greek, Kypriaka, Armenian, and English. These tongues consequently allow the habitation of different worldviews, each informed by other sociological factors, including gender. As with allusions to halfness throughout, the narrator is conscious that her own worldview is always only 'half', or part, of a greater whole. She attempts to redress and complicate her biases by integrating others' perspectives, showing how the self imagines the Other through the former's peculiar cultural lens, and vice versa.

Living a life between languages, the narrator details her 'double vision' while grieving.[147] Comparable to the aforementioned account of occupying 'a world half in focus',[148] she reads her immediate society through two simultaneous and overlapping perspectives. She follows the description of her tears by stating that her step-mother looked 'ugly' while weeping, despite 'how gentle her eyes' were, before imagining how her own crying must render her 'ugly' in the eyes of her half-brother.[149] In this paragraph replete in images of eyes, the narrator shifts between multiple viewpoints in their shared, but independent, visions of the dying father-husband. Much like Agnes Smith's shifts between the worldviews of 'Western' and 'native' in *Eastern Pilgrims*, Nadjarian's narrator imagines the perspective of the Other—here, however, that of a man of the same nationality. Similar to the sibling-like connection between Standard Modern Greek and Kypriaka—and the coexistence of all vernaculars on the island—the narrator symbolically code-switches, embodying different linguistic systems in order to consider a single subject which affects all Cypriots, regardless of their familial ethnolinguistic background. Smith's translations between English, Greek, and Arabic was used to highlight differences between inside and outside, or colonised and coloniser. For Nadjarian, however, exploring linguistic families, alongside her own genealogy, is a tool for understanding the polyphonic heterogeneity *within* Cyprus. Her family, while composed of many branches, have an inherent unity, even if it is marred by distrust and division. The half-siblings may represent the difference between standard and vernacular linguistic forms; the historic synchronicity of Greek and Turkish in the Eastern Mediterranean sprachbund; or even how Indo-European languages, such as Armenian, English, and Greek, are related despite their lack of mutual intelligibility. However, these Cypriot siblings see the world, and in whatever language they communicate, they still occupy and observe the same island. They also confront the same problems—those of cultural identity in relation to mythic fathers—and they cry the same 'ugly' tears over the cycles of violence which define Cypriot modern history. It is through English, nonetheless, that Nadjarian allows these parallels and slippages to become apparent, using a language that no Cypriot claims as the dominant father-tongue.

The *closed doors* which splinter postcolonial Cypriot ontology—especially for women—are exemplified by the British university space: 'in

England I was desperately lonely [in…] a small room overlooking the quadrangle'.[150] Sharing the dormitory with a 'young Asian man', she found herself '[t]oo homesick to notice anything around me, too self-conscious of my accent to talk to anyone'.[151] In this diasporic space, the sense of exilic estrangement not only prevents dialogue with her neighbours—a condition of modernity *par excellence*—but also limits her visual abilities. Repeating the emphasis of 'eyes' from the preceding hospital scene, she is given a position of panoptic power 'overlooking' her surroundings, yet she fails 'to notice' them. She lacks, therefore, the capacity to be *an active reader or writer*, despite the panopticism afforded by an Anglophone setting or form. It is discursive power from which she feels excluded. Her aporia prevents her from reading the space-as-text, or to freely speak or compose in an 'accent'-inflected English.

Instead, she telephones her mother, complaining of her disappointment towards Britain, ushered 'in whispered tones, though I was not speaking in English'.[152] The weight of her English institutional surroundings puts pressure on her ability to loudly and robustly speak non-English. This is a potent symbol of Cyprus itself and the hegemony of English—and other, foreign dominant discourses—over local academic, political, and cultural spheres. Notably, here and elsewhere in the collection, Nadjarian chooses not to identify the language her narrator uses with her mother. What is the *mother-tongue*: Kypriaka, Standard Modern Greek, Armenian, or an uncodified pidgin of the three (with or without additional English loanwords)? On the one hand, it illustrates, like Baybars, how English *cuts* into one's mother-tongue and erases its identity. On the other, it demonstrates how Cypriots have no single linguistic alternative to English and, given the diglossia or triglossia of individuals, Cypriots perhaps do not have a single mother-tongue. Equally, if it does exist (as a pidgin or creole), there is no single name to describe it. As such, the narrator and her mother speak an imprecise 'not[-]English', while the former speaks English at university (and with her lover). This is, in opposition to Derrida, the *multilingualism of the Other*. The false binaries of global and local, standard and dialect, or metropole and periphery, all rely on the arbitrary division of linguistic systems into dyads. In reality, various linguistic forms leach into each other in daily use. English as an international auxiliary language cannot exist without its relationship to the not-Englishes feeding it loanwords and sustaining its socio-academic dominance through contrast.

Adding to this confusion, the narrator expresses how her expectations of England have shifted. Not unlike George Lamming's accounts of colonial migrant disappointment towards a formerly-idealised England, she states that 'I hate[d...] my first autumn... the English autumn'.[153] In contrast with her earlier desperation to experience this month, the reality does not fulfil her quixotic expectations inspired by literary and filmic depictions of the country. The narrator uses English to re-write the androcentric archive of representations of the country which have been disseminated globally. As a 'postcolonial' woman, a figure associated with the outside, she enters the country and language to deconstruct its conventions from within. Nonetheless, English is also the language of her dialogue with her British lover, John. It becomes the symbolic product of exchange across cultural and colonialist frontiers, reimagining the 'irrational love of England' described by Durrell as an egalitarian relationship detailed with *realism* by a woman agent examining the lives of the men around her.[154]

The narrator's account of her affair with John, a poet, plays with this literary and linguistic history by directly comparing their romantic bed with her father's 'lifeless... hospital bed'.[155] Here, the ending of *Othello* is rewritten with a Cypriot (Eastern Mediterranean) woman describing her relationship with an English (Western European) man. It is *he* who is the object of *her* scrutinising, academic gaze—she states that 'I studied his eyelids' while closed—and who is presented as voiceless—'his lips exhausted from my kisses'.[156] She is the subject of the prose, a sexual agent, and the arbiter of what is seen and spoken. She goes on to fetishise his haunting 'pale blue eyes',[157] which both reverses the exoticist discourse used to represent ethnic otherness in Orientalist writing, and evokes the Levantine blue beads which ward off the evil eye, symbolising, in this Anglophone work, an act of corporeal commodification according to a local, Mediterranean frame of reference. As the beads have an ambivalent meaning, she uses both their folkloric association with the evil eye and their desacralised (and touristic) reduction to the level of the aesthetic to simultaneously denigrate and idolise a British man. Her intended meaning, transecting local and global readings of blue eyes, remains obscure. The beads exist as a signifier often switching between the discourses of tradition and modernity, from important cultural artefact to an oft-reproduced trifle of tourist shops. In 'No-Man's-Land', they evade translation as a mode of expression which transcends the (Anglophone, androcentric) written form, used by a woman writer to denote her own ambivalence towards a foreign(ised) man. This is the touristic gaze in reverse.

Within this creation of a semiotic idiolect *within* English, the narrator rewrites Shakespeare's seminal play. She, unlike Desdemona, does not die at the story's conclusion. Instead, the two beds are used to symbolise the termination of her relationships with men. In addition to the death of her father, she represents the end of her complicated affair with John through motifs of silence. She details, for instance, how John 'keeps [his] words inside, the words that are on the tip of his tongue are left unsaid. They must be the most terrible words I have heard, the loudest silence'.[158] It is an ambivalent passage. On the one hand, it shrouds the British poet in 'silence', removing his vocal agency by presenting his English words as untranslatable within the narrative of her travels, despite its Anglophone form. It symbolises how, despite writing in an English mode, it is not the same as his, complicating the notion that writing in translation necessarily means entering the cultural system of the Other, at the expense of abandoning all of the self's social identity. Nadjarian creates an English distinct from that of the pre-1960 British writings of the island, reversing the binary of speech and 'silence' which juxtaposed coloniser and 'native'.

On the other hand, the palpability of his 'silence' illustrates the insidious power of English discursive dominance, not from speaking, but withholding. Although Spivak advocates silence as a tactic of the subaltern, this representation of John shows that those with systemic power over speech acts can also affect power through their own staged withholdings. His 'silence', paradoxically, becomes tangible 'words I have heard'. Moreover, parallelism is used to contrast them with her mother's earlier speech exposing her father's affairs, then 'the most painful words I had ever heard'.[159] The two hyperbolic phrases diametrically oppose the former lover's unspoken English with the mother's unidentified mother-tongue. The former is associated with terror; the latter with pain. It emblematises the colonialist violence of English—or, any dominant discourse—against the language of the 'native'. It is also a gendered act of linguistic disparity. This double reading, in which the narrator conquers her poet-boyfriend's speech and is yet 'terri[fied]' by its lingering possibility to return, demonstrates her dual relationship with English. It is a source of both power and powerlessness, allowing her (limited) literary agency while also casting a shadow which estranges her, painfully, from her native-tongue(s).

The paragraph is concluded by a repetition of her father's aforementioned advice when standing at the border: 'Shhh! Listen to the story on the other side'.[160] It demonstrates the violence of dialogue always split according to sectarian 'side[s]', comparing the divisions in an ethnolinguistically-diverse Cyprus with the impenetrability of understanding between a romantic couple from different ethnicities and genders. Meaning, even when expressed through a single language, is always divided existentially between self and Other, creating an untranslatable *buffer zone* which can be listened to but never fully crossed. In the narrative, language consistently creates borders which are contested by the narrator but are seldom dissolved entirely. The repeated 'Shhh!', for instance, marks the control patriarchal men hold over women's discursive agency, in parallel with how ethnolinguistic borders control the movement of transcultural expression. These epistemic silences follow the narrator from the Nicosia Buffer Zone to her university lodgings in Britain as sites of simultaneous connection and estrangement. Cultures meet at these points but do not fully interact or exist equally.

Ultimately, the two beds analogise the father and John, symbolising the base inevitability of death and sexual reproduction in a hetero-patriarchal cycle within which women are trapped. The borders outside are reproduced internally through domestic borders demarcating the individual. Comparatively, in the hospital, the narrator's step-mother is marked 'opposite me, on the other side of the bed'.[161] Women are divided across a male-generated buffer zone, unable to communicate beyond the divisions of a society which reduces women to the roles of wives, mothers, and daughters. This lack of communication also reveals how the narrator, forced to interact with dominant father-tongues, cannot freely engage with the island's diverse vernaculars. In other words, she speaks Standard Greek and English but not Turkish; she writes in English but not Kypriaka.

Nonetheless, she wrests from her father's 'Shhh!', and her British poet-lover's control over 'words' spoken or withheld, through the active role of writing in English. Notably, in the succeeding paragraph, she describes her dreams. Entering into a transcendental realm of being, she arrives at an imagined 'library' of the mind where she escapes the physical bounds of borders, hospitals, and beds. She states that, on the evening of her father's death, she dreamt of her university years, envisioning 'a corner of the library, hunched over titles, reading and not reading, distracted by the sweet smell of the English summer', being 'lured by the freedom of daydreaming and covering the margin of my notepad with snippets of poems' as they manifested themselves, like a 'breeze'.[162] In this other-worldly place, she breaks from the realism of the narrative, mixing actual experience with fantasy, blurring her lives in Cyprus and England, cross-remembering the last day of her late father and her last months with her former-boyfriend. Emblematic of this is the idiom 'English summer', a portmanteau-like amalgam of the oft-repeated 'English autumn' and 'Cypriot summer' from earlier in the text. In this dream state, these two topologies and their associated cultural influences finally merge with fluency; it is a symbol of realising an English self-translation of her Cypriot background.

This place of 'reading' and writing, books and 'poems', offers a 'freedom' for literary voices to exist beyond the division of languages and nations. Selectively 'reading and not', she moves on to *writing as an intertext of cultural, poetic ostraca*, decentring the authority of monophonic, realist prose forms. Most importantly, the image of marginalia, like annotations, offers a symbol of translation itself: that which reinterprets the original, post-margin text. Here, her metatextual and post-modern self-translation reinterprets the genres and languages she engages with, subsequently defamiliarising and foreignising both. Pushing back on the silencing and silence of the Cypriot father-tongue, and of androcentric English, she creates a unique voice independent from their respective cultural conventions. It is reducible to neither binary of 'Cypriot summer' or 'English autumn'. As a whole, *Ledra Street* offers a fragmented series of stream-of-consciousness vignettes, not unlike a developed oeuvre of marginalia, rejecting the elevated form of the holistic novel in its existential and philological excavation of the literary, ethnolinguistic, and gendered self. The marginal and marginalised are re-centred and the voice of the Cypriot woman, while irrevocably cut-off from her mother-tongue in this juncture of twenty-first-century publishing, resists the aphasias inflicted by male-dominated cultural practices. Parallel with the home of 'Don't Forget', the narrator of 'No-Man's-Land' constructs a new 'library', or archive, satiating the lacunae of experience hitherto excluding the lives of women between, and against, ontological borders. Filling these gaps, her words are compared with a 'breeze', a new force implicitly counter to the winds of dominant discourse which had overwhelmed her earlier in the story. Past the *closed doors* of colonialism and nationalism, moving through the 'gates' routinely described by Neşe, Nadjarian creates a new site of belonging as both a Cypriot and a woman representing herself in the post-partition present.

Conclusions

As the works of Ali, Nadjarian, and Neşe Yaşın have shown, contemporary Cypriot women writers contend with the intersectional colonisations of British imperialism, Greek and Turkish nationalisms, and patriarchal ideologies which, themselves, may be imperialist, nationalist, or religious in origin. In particular, they demonstrate the inherent masculinist bias of historiography, including the writing of the (postcolonial) nation, which marginalises the experiences of Cypriot women in both war and peacetime. Complicating these paradigms, they discern the internal borders of gender disparity which exist alongside the partition of the Green Line. The binary of male and female is placed in sharp relief alongside that of south and north, and Greek and Turkish. Doing so, they confound the very juxtaposition of inside and outside, both illustrating *internal* barriers within the ostensibly-homogenous nation, and putting pressure on the fallacy that nationalist hegemonies are not neo-colonial products from the outside.

Re-writing two key themes of modern Cypriot literature—historiography and the home—they demonstrate the unreliability of nationalist selective elisions of women's oppression and they reimagine Cypriot homes away from the binaries of domestic and public. Challenging the coffee-shop *status quo*, women are shown either reoccupying public spaces—Nadjarian's coffee house in 'Ledra Street' and her role as a countertraveller in 'No-Man's Land'—or redefining the home as the space where intercommunal dialogue is revived, counter to the failed talks of male politicians. Ali's home where she, a Turkish-speaker, revives dialogue with Greek-speaking peers, Maro and Yianoulla, is comparable to the home in Nadjarian's poem 'Don't Forget', its title playing on the parallel Greco-Turkish slogans of nationalist historiography, and to the Cypriot intertextual home of Neşe where allusions to Abrahamic, Classical, and Ottoman poetic traditions coalesce in the birthplace of paradoxically new-yet-ancient Alashya. The home is a partitioned, prison-like structure in Nadjarian's and Neşe's works, representing a social confinement exclusively for women but analogous to the partition of the island.

They vehemently demonstrate that the layeredness of their social and literary identities is more complex than gender-neutral theories of the colonial/native dichotomy. Ali, Nadjarian, and Neşe must contend with the strata of imperialism, multiple nationalisms, and patriarchy, filling the lacunae created by each while attempting to merge, not the traditions of oppressor and oppressed, but the experiences of Cypriot women from either side of the Buffer Zone. Beyond notions of 'double colonisation', these writers challenge the masculinist biases across layers of Cypriot, Greek, Turkish, and British literatures.

The three works also repudiate the linguistic conventions of nationalist dominant discourses, albeit in different ways. For Ali and Nadjarian, Anglophone self-translation allows them to escape the discursive limits of the andro-nationalism heavily bound to the Turkish and Greek standardised by men. While they recognise the issues of using an Anglophone form, they see all dominant tongues as equally patriarchal and foreign in their codification by men and their relative inability to *translate* the movements of women to the page. The languages of Atatürk and Venizelos are not languages of gendered or postcolonial liberation, even if English is similarly tied to its own andro-imperialist past. Neşe, on the other hand, composes in standardised Turkish, using the form employed by her nationalist father poet to re-write the genre from within, and to deconstruct the gendered semiotic limits of Turkish through translations of ancient Greek myth. Nevertheless, Neşe's life of travel and translation—an exile in southern Cyprus frequently reading her own poems in English at symposiums—is the inspiration for *Rose Falling Into Night*. A collaborative work with Cypriot translators and artists from both sides of the partition, including Ali, its publication is a product, not only of the border-opening, but of Neşe's conscious commitment to cultural exchange between ethnolinguistic communities. Ali's and Nadjarian's works equally have the ability to circulate globally, relinquishing identification with the ideas of 'Turkey' or 'Greece'.

Slightly counter to Spivak's concept of 'translation as reading' and the need for withholding, Ali, Nadjarian, and Neşe illustrate the importance of *translation as writing* as a tactic of literary resistance against subalternity. The latter two, by modifying the inside and outside binary, reveal that Cypriot women have no (literary) mother-tongue. While Spivak implores the reader to learn the subaltern's 'mother-tongue', Nadjarian and Neşe show that Cypriots only have *father-tongues* at their dispersal: the language of the father reading the sanctioned newspaper; the form of the nationalist father-poet. They investigate the language of the mother—the voice of truth on the father's deathbed; the hypothetical voice of Alashya's mother—but it is always transient, marginalised, and overpowered by the literary father-tongue of nationalist discourse. If the local does not afford a cultural habitus for Cypriot women—such as the public performances of orature which have typically excluded them—then they must break-down the juxtapositions between local, worldly, and global. They draw on global mediums to illustrate the shared lives of Cypriot women which exceeds the bounds of one demarcated ethno-linguistic community. They speak of, and to, women, not only silenced by nationalist discourses, but *silenced from one another* by partition.

Writing-back to both traditions symbolised by Durrell and Montis, they expose the *closed doors* extant in contemporary Cyprus. Beyond simply the doors of colonialism are those of nationalism and patriarchy: the doors that conceal women within the domestic space and in arranged marriages; the doors that prevent women from being widely published prior to 2003; and the doors dividing Cypriot women living on either side of the partition. Ali, Nadjarian, and Neşe seek to break these doors while simultaneously deconstructing the limits of genre and disavowing linguistic convention. Doing so, Cypriot women are able to share an intersectional cultural habitus where all are welcome, symbolised by the house in Nadjarian's 'Don't Forget' where the words *efcharisto poli* and *hoşgeldiniz* exist equally within the buffer of English. Without a so-called mother-tongue, and rejecting the authority of father-tongues, they form a subversive literary domain which is fragmented, heteroglossic, and free from the masculinist drive to conquer land and languages.

Notes

1. McClintock, p. 14.
2. The concepts of 'honour' and 'shame' have been treated extensively in relation to the Mediterranean, beginning with the influential work of Cypriot sociologist, Peristiany. See, J.G. Peristiany, 'Honour and Shame in a Cypriot Highland Village', in *Honour and Shame: The Values of Mediterranean Society*, ed. by Peristiany (Chicago: University of Chicago Press, 1966), pp. 171–190.
3. Maria Hadjipavlou, *Women and Change in Cyprus: Feminisms and Gender in Conflict* (London and New York: I.B. Tauris, 2010), p. 65.
4. Papadakis, pp. 178, 155.
5. Ali, *Turkish Speaking*, p. 2.
6. Papadakis, p. 178.
7. VassosArgyrou, *Tradition and Modernity in the Mediterranean: The Wedding as Symbolic Struggle* (Cambridge: Cambridge University Press, 1996), p. 174.
8. Rushdie, *Imaginary Homelands*, p. 115.
9. Ali, *Turkish Speaking*, p. 2.

10. GayatriChakravortySpivak, *Outside in the Teaching Machine* (Oxford and New York: Routledge, 2009), p. 201.
11. Spivak, *Outside*, p. 215.
12. Spivak, *Outside*, p. 201.
13. Ketu H. Katrak, *The Politics of the Female Body: Postcolonial Women Writers* (London and New Brunswick, NJ: Rutgers University Press, 2006) p. xxv.
14. Julian Evans, 'Continental Shelf', *The Guardian*, 30 April 2004. https://www.theguardian.com/books/2004/may/01/featuresreviews.guardianreview34 [accessed 21 April 2017].
15. Nora Nadjarian, 'Don't Forget', in *Creativity in Exile*, ed. by Michael Hanne (Amsterdam and New York: Rodopi, 2004), pp. 121–122.
16. Anderson, p. 208.
17. Nadjarian, *Ledra*, p. 23.
18. Bakhtin, p. 315.
19. Ibid.
20. Nadjarian, *Ledra*, p. 9.
21. Nadjarian, *Ledra*, p. 9.
22. Nadjarian, *Ledra*, p. 9.
23. Nadjarian, *Ledra*, p. 9.
24. Nadjarian, *Ledra*, p. 9.
25. Nadjarian, *Ledra*, p. 10.
26. Nadjarian, *Ledra*, p. 10.
27. Nadjarian, *Ledra*, p. 10.
28. Nadjarian, *Ledra*, p. 10.
29. Nadjarian, *Ledra*, p. 11.
30. Bhabha, *The Location of Culture*, p. 102.
31. Nadjarian, *Ledra*, p. 11.
32. Nadjarian, *Ledra*, p. 11.
33. Nadjarian, *Ledra*, p. 11.
34. Nadjarian, *Ledra*, p. 12.
35. Nadjarian, *Ledra*, p. 13.
36. Nadjarian, *Ledra*, p. 12.
37. Nadjarian, *Ledra*, pp. 12–13.
38. Nadjarian, *Ledra*, p. 13.
39. Nadjarian, *Ledra*, p. 13.
40. Nadjarian, *Ledra*, p. 13.
41. Nadjarian, *Ledra*, p. 13.
42. The subsequent and final paragraph is simply a repetition of Andreas' one-line obituary, italicised to emphasise Maria's obliviousness to its existence.
43. Nadjarian, *Ledra*, pp. 13–14.

44. Nadjarian, *Ledra*, p. 61. All subsequent references to this story are from this page.
45. Michelle Kelly, '*The Master of Petersburg* (1994)', in *A Companion to the Works of J.M. Coetzee*, ed. by Tim Mehigan (New York: Camden House, 2011), pp. 132–147 (p. 134).
46. Nadjarian, *Ledra*, p. 48.
47. Nadjarian, *Ledra*, p. 49.
48. Nadjarian, *Ledra*, pp. 72, 74.
49. Nadjarian, *Ledra*, p. 48.
50. Nadjarian, *Ledra*, p. 49.
51. Ngũgĩ, 'Borders and Bridges', p. 122.
52. Nadjarian, *Ledra*, p. 48.
53. Nadjarian, *Ledra*, p. 49.
54. Nadjarian, *Ledra*, p. 50. Note that, in Greek, honeymoon is *minas toumelitos* (month of honey) and, in Turkish, it is *balayı*, derived from *bal* (honey) and *ay* (moon). I am here reminded of Spivak's observation on 'the irreducible hybridity of all languages' (*Death of a Discipline*, p. 9).
55. Nadjarian, *Ledra*, p. 50.
56. Neşe, *Rose Falling Into Night* (Nicosia: Heterotopia Publications, 2017), pp. 47–48.
57. Neşe, *Rose*, p. 65.
58. Neşe, *Rose*, p. 8.
59. Neşe, *Rose*, p. 9.
60. Neşe, *Rose*, pp. 9–11.
61. Neşe, *Rose*, pp. 8, 16, 19.
62. Neşe, *Rose*, p. 11.
63. Neşe, *Rose*, p. 9.
64. Neşe, *Rose*, p. 24.
65. Neşe Yaşın, *Kapılar: Şiirler* (Istanbul: Cem Publications, 1992), p. 19.
66. Nadjarian, *Ledra*, p. 11.
67. Neşe, *Rose*, pp. 25–26.
68. Neşe, *Rose*, pp. 8, 26.
69. Neşe, *Rose*, pp. 18, 24.
70. Neşe, *Rose*, p. 24.
71. Neşe, *Rose*, p. 9.
72. Neşe, *Rose*, pp. 8, 15.
73. Maya Angelou, *I Know Why The Caged Bird Sings* (New York: Random House, 1969).
74. Neşe, *Rose*, p. 89.
75. Neşe, *Rose*, p. 90.
76. Neşe, *Rose*, p. 87.
77. Neşe, *Rose*, pp. 87, 90.

78. Neşe, *Rose*, p. 87.
79. Interestingly, it is not Istanbul, the metropolis typically referred to as *Şehir* in Standard Modern Turkish.
80. Neşe, *Rose*, p. 88.
81. Neşe, *Rose*, p. 13.
82. Neşe, *Rose*, p. 20.
83. Neşe, *Rose*, pp. 14–15.
84. Neşe, *Rose*, p. 12.
85. Neşe, *Rose*, p. 18.
86. Neşe, *Rose*, p. 19.
87. Neşe, *Rose*, p. 8.
88. Neşe, *Rose*, p. 8.
89. Neşe, *Rose*, p. 15.
90. Neşe, *Rose*, p. 22.
91. Apter, p. 6.
92. Spivak, *Outside*, p. 205.
93. Bhabha, *The Location of Culture*, p. 356.
94. Spivak, *Outside*, p. 205.
95. Neşe, *Rose*, p. 80.
96. Neşe, *Rose*, p. 80.
97. Neşe, *Rose*, p. 67.
98. Neşe, *Rose*, pp. 65, 69.
99. Neşe, *Rose*, p. 69.
100. Neşe, *Rose*, p. 62.
101. Nadjarian, *Ledra*, p. 11.
102. Neşe, *Rose*, pp. 65–66.
103. Neşe, *Rose*, p. 65.
104. Neşe, *Rose*, p. 71.
105. Neşe, *Rose*, p. 8.
106. Neşe, *Rose*, p. 72.
107. Neşe, *Rose*, p. 72.
108. Aamer Hussein, 'Mother Tongue, Father Tongue', *Journal of Postcolonial Writing*, 47 (2011), 199–204.
109. Neşe, *Rose*, p. 8.
110. Spivak, *Outside*, p. 215.
111. Neşe, *Rose*, pp. 72–73.
112. Neşe, *Rose*, p. 93.
113. Boehmer, *Empire, the National, and the Postcolonial*, p. 51.
114. Walter Benjamin, 'The Task of the Translator', trans. by Harry Zorn, in *Illuminations*, ed. by Hannah Arendt (London: Pimlico, 1999), pp. 70–82 (p. 72).
115. Judith Butler, *Undoing Gender* (New York and Oxford: Routledge, 2004), p. 38.

116. Papadakis, p. 67.
117. McClintock, p. 29.
118. Neşe, *Rose*, p. 82.
119. Neşe, *Rose*, p. 83.
120. Neşe, *Rose*, p. 83.
121. Nadjarian, *Ledra*, pp. 25–26.
122. Nadjarian, *Ledra*, pp. 27, 29.
123. Matthew Reynolds, *Translation: A Very Short Introduction* (Oxford: Oxford University Press, 2016), p. 4.
124. Reynolds, *Translation*, p. 3.
125. Nadjarian, *Ledra*, p. 26.
126. Nadjarian, *Ledra*, p. 27.
127. Nadjarian, *Ledra*, p. 27.
128. Nadjarian, *Ledra*, p. 34.
129. Nadjarian, *Ledra*, p. 26.
130. Nadjarian, *Ledra*, pp. 25–27.
131. Nadjarian, *Ledra*, p. 26.
132. Nadjarian, *Ledra*, p. 26.
133. Nadjarian, *Ledra*, pp. 25, 27.
134. Nadjarian, *Ledra*, p. 25.
135. Nadjarian, *Ledra*, pp. 25–26.
136. Scott-Stevenson, pp. 96–97.
137. Durrell, pp. 47–48.
138. Nadjarian, *Ledra*, p. 25.
139. Nadjarian, *Ledra*, p. 26.
140. Nadjarian, *Ledra*, p. 26.
141. Nadjarian, *Ledra*, p. 32.
142. Nadjarian, *Ledra*, p. 28.
143. Nadjarian, *Ledra*, p. 28.
144. Nadjarian, *Ledra*, p. 28.
145. Nadjarian, *Ledra*, p. 28.
146. Nadjarian, *Ledra*, pp. 28–29.
147. Nadjarian, *Ledra*, p. 28.
148. Nadjarian, *Ledra*, p. 26.
149. Nadjarian, *Ledra*, p. 28.
150. Nadjarian, *Ledra*, p. 29.
151. Nadjarian, *Ledra*, p. 29.
152. Nadjarian, *Ledra*, p. 30.
153. Nadjarian, *Ledra*, p. 30. This corresponds with Lamming's '*idea* of England', part of 'a seed of [a psychological] colonisation which has been subtly and richly infused with myth'. George Lamming, *The Pleasures of Exile* (Ann Arbor, MI: University of Michigan Press, 1991), p. 26.

154. Durrell, p. 130.
155. Nadjarian, *Ledra*, p. 30.
156. Nadjarian, *Ledra*, p. 30.
157. Nadjarian, *Ledra*, p. 31.
158. Nadjarian, *Ledra*, p. 31.
159. Nadjarian, *Ledra*, p. 28.
160. Nadjarian, *Ledra*, pp. 26, 31.
161. Nadjarian, *Ledra*, p. 28.
162. Nadjarian, *Ledra*, p. 31.

CHAPTER 6

Conclusions

Travel writing on Cyprus, from the late nineteenth century to present, is redolent with images of doors, windows, and the boundaries of the home. In short, these portals and limens are metonymic of the island's cultural, geographic, and political liminality which writers examine in the creation of what I have dubbed *transportal literatures*. These acts of literary transportation are able to reveal Cyprus' layered colonialisms as a space not yet fully decolonised but one for which the field of postcolonialism is crucial in understanding the identities (or, identifications) of its inhabitants over the very long twentieth century. The layers of British imperialism (past and present), Greek and Turkish nationalisms, and of competing patriarchal discourses all compel writers of Cyprus to use literary forms which place movement, modification, and interchange at the heart of projects which resist what Said describes as 'the binary oppositions dear to the nationalist and imperialist enterprise'.[1] This involves transporting literary representations of the island through various linguistic forms, from the writing of the Victorian polyglot Agnes Smith to the self-translations of Cypriot authors since 1960. These works attempt to unshackle the island from hegemonic discourses which erect sectarian dyads—between coloniser and colonised, men and women, Greeks and Turks, and various standardised languages—in order to, from the 'emergency' onwards, challenge the partition made physical by the walls of 1974.

Counter to these physical, symbolic, and linguistic walls are the gateways of literature through which multicommunal, heteroglossic, and

D. Nunziata, *Colonial and Postcolonial Cyprus*,
https://doi.org/10.1007/978-3-030-58236-4_6

cross-cultural dialogue can exist. Using Anglophone works, the form of the vast majority of texts considered in this book, Greek-speakers can purchase and understand the sentiments of Turkish-speakers ostensibly-stranded in a figurative elsewhere by partition, and vice versa. Equally, the words of British and Cypriot women are given literary voice in a sea of androcentric political jargon. The (neo-)colonialist dichotomy of self and Other—or, coloniser and Orientalised 'native', later internalised as that between 'Greeks and Turks' or 'Turks and Greeks'—is revised, complicated, and sometimes rescinded. Moreover, as this inheritance of colonialist discourses illustrates, the travel writing of Cyprus exists in a large, diachronic hypertext, and it is necessary to unpack the inter-textual portals between these voices: British women writers challenging the limitations of British male contemporaries; Cypriot anti-colonialists writing-back to British imperialism as a whole; Cypriot post-partition writers analysing and contesting British imperialism *as well as* Greek and Turkish nationalisms *and* the gendered implications of all these male-dominated geopolitical paradigms. These are acts of literary trans-portation across times, in addition to the physical space of the Buffer Zone. Anglophone works allow these textual exchanges to be apparent, from echoes of *Othello* across nineteenth-century travelogues to allusions to Durrell repeating in the narratives of writers as diverse as Montis and Nadjarian. Anglophone writing is also chosen, especially after the actual portal openings of 2003, as a counter-discourse to the standard-ised languages of Greece and Turkey which exist in an ambivalent midway between local and foreign. It is this dichotomy—elsewhere calibrated as local and global, internal and external, home and homeless—which the doors of transportal literatures open and expose. It is from the portal or the *parergon* that countertravel can start to take place, allowing authors to forge nonmetropolitan counter-travelogues which reveal paranational alternatives to various, competing metropoles.

As noted in the first and second chapters, since Cyprus was acquired by the British Empire in 1878, it has been considered the *key* through which imperial power might cross the gateway between continents, or between the Orient and Occident and Christian and Muslim 'worlds'. It is evident here how metaphors are carriers of meaning with Cyprus being *freighted*, a code for transportation, with this sense of inbetweenness. Cyprus is a metaphorical limen through which power is manoeuvred but it is also, according to European colonisers, a dangerous site carrying disease and facilitating unspeakable interracial relations and hermaphroditism.

The image of the 'door' repeats in the works of Dixon and Mallock to figure their desired segregation from Orientalised Cypriots[2]; yet, for the latter in particular, it also suggests a conscious movement away from the heteronormative regulations of the British metropole in their expression of homoerotic motifs deemed natural in the effeminised Orient. Playing with this intermediation between metropolitan and nonmetropolitan, contemporaneous British women writers—notably Brassey, Scott-Stevenson, and Smith—seek to complicate the patriarchal discourses of imperialism. Brassey, for instance, assesses 'the spaces between' herself, soldiers, and Cypriots,[3] while Scott-Stevenson's attention to the *Home* of her work's time explores the limits of internal and external. The doors of the courthouse, for her, mark the constrictions of her power in relation to her husband, yet the echo of the same motifs to describe the Muslim girl 'Mariehou' at her private door illustrates how power and imperialism are layered given the author's control over a primitivised Cypriot woman. Sympathy with the 'native' as a figure comparably on the fringes of British imperial domination is rarely, if ever, made. Comparable is the door between Dixon and his eroticised servant Hassan, or the window between Angela Carter and the Levantine girl she encounters in the 1970s. If women writers—and men writers seeking to escape heteronormative conventions—use the Cypriot setting to *transport* their identities and glean modes of authority denied inside Britain, then it is performed at the expense of silenced, subaltern Cypriots. Scott-Stevenson is excluded by her husband, Captain Andrew, from politics, but she consequently reimagines herself as Queen Victoria to the Cypriot women she denigrates as racially inferior. Likewise, for Smith, the Cypriot woman is always the Other and she is useful primarily as a literary commodity to exchange for publication.

These problematic representations of Cyprus resulted in intertextual acts of writing-back by authors of the 'Cypriot Renaissance', including Baybars and Montis. As the third chapter demonstrates, the two respond directly to the discourse of Durrell and his predecessors by focusing on the homes of Cypriots affected by poverty and colonially-induced conflict. While both use different linguistic forms, their related genres, themes, and motifs—from the figure of the father reading the newspaper (later repeated by Nadjarian) to nationalist parades (later discussed by Papadakis)—reveal the transportal nature of these works which realise the onset of a hitherto-undiscovered pan-Cypriot literary movement. Both *Plucked in a Far-Off Land* and *Closed Doors* consider the epistemic violence of language, imperialism, and nationalism and how the three 'cut' Cypriots apart. Explicitly this is achieved through the 'closed doors' of British internment camps; tacitly, it is also performed inside the buildings promoting sectarianism, from nationalist schools to American-centric cinemas. It is inside the homes of Cypriots where politics is manoeuvred on a daily level, from the reception of British, Greek, or Turkish news to the domestic inclusion of, and subsequent disillusionment towards, Venizelos and Atatürk. It is these homes, and the authors' movements to Britain and Ireland, which offer counter-images to Durrell's holiday rentals and which begin a continuity of literatures by Cypriots considering the figure of the homeless refugee.

The final two chapters have demonstrated how, after the opening of seven portals though the Buffer Zone in 2003, post-partition writers began publishing works which wrote-back to the hegemons of British imperialism and Greek and Turkish nationalisms with equal force. Ali, Papadakis, Nadjarian, and the two Yaşın siblings have constructed modes of countertravel which challenge the assumptions of British colonial discourse, often through intertextual allusions to Durrell, while also framing Greek and Turkish cultural hegemonies as modes of (neo-)colonialism partially culpable in the segregation of Cypriots along ethnolinguistic lines. To this end, the Anglophone counter-travelogues of the three prose writers considered in these chapters use the language to complicate the internal biases of Standard Modern Greek and Standard Modern Turkish from a distance. Unable to write and/or publish in the island's pre-twentieth-century vernaculars (Kypriaka and Kıbrıslıca), English is a quasi-neutral *buffer* which enables cross-cultural readerships without the authors being forced to make nationalist literary affiliations. These works, as a whole, challenge partition through transportal perspectives. Ali, a refugee, as well as Nadjarian and Papadakis, detail their travels across southern and northern Nicosia, as well as Istanbul and Britain, through literary forms which destabilise the expectations of preceding discursive representations of the Cypriot capital or the Eastern Mediterranean (and 'Middle East') more broadly. They re-examine all areas of Cypriot textualities, including the recurring image of the photograph album in Nadjarian's, Papadakis', and Mehmet Yaşın's works. Ali, Mehmet, and Neşe also allude to birds as emblems of a perspective which passes-through, or above, the strictures of the ground, drawing on the anti-colonial history of the bird-like outlaw, Hasanpouli, and the failed dove symbolism used by both the Republic of Cyprus and the 'TRNC'.[4]

Mehmet's goal is to 'throw the windows open' of 'my own home', his 'polyglot house', a motif echoed later in his poem, 'The Door'.[5] The refugee home is an unavoidable image in all twenty-first-century literatures from Cyprus. Comparably, two of Neşe Yaşın's major poems are 'Doors' and 'Variations of a Theme of Doors'. Indeed, her anthology, created for the most recent generation of post-2003 pan-Cypriot readers, repeatedly draws on portals to express her polemic resistance to sectarianism. In addition, through echoes of Montis' *Closed Doors*, she seeks to give needed representation to the perspectives of Cypriot women often elided by patriarchal discourses—and imperialist British women's writing—over the past century. Like Ali and Nadjarian, both of whom detail post-partition homes where Greek- and Turkish-speaking women meet and talk, interchange between Cypriot women is pertinent. Even *Rose Falling Into Night* symbolises this co-operation through translations by the Turkish-speaking Ali and transmedial illustrations by the Greek-speaking Hara Savvidou. The portals between politics, gender, ethnicity, language, form, medium, and cultural identities are all opened wide.

Notes

1. Said, *Culture and Imperialism*, p. xxviii.
2. Dixon, p. 91; Mallock, p. 85.
3. Brassey, p. 271.
4. Ali, *Forbidden*, p. 27.
5. Mehmet, *Kyrenia*, pp. 3, 93.

Bibliography

Print sources

Achebe, Chinua, *Hopes and Impediments: Selected Essays* (New York: Doubleday, 1990).

———, *Things Fall Apart* (London: Heinemann, 1958).

Agathangelou, Anna M., and L.H.M. Ling, *Transforming World Politics: From Empire to Multiple Worlds* (London and New York: Routledge, 2009).

Ahmed, Sara, *Strange Encounters: Embodied Others in Post-Coloniality* (Oxford and New York: Routledge, 2000).

Ali, Aydın Mehmet, 'Forbidden Zone', *Kunapipi*, 33 (2011), 188–201.

———, *Forbidden Zones: Short Stories & Others* (London: Fatal Publications, 2013).

———, 'Foreword' and 'Opening Remarks from the Chair', in *Turkish Cypriot Identity in Literature / EdebiyattaKıbrıslıTürkKimliği*, ed. by Aydın Mehmet Ali (London: Fatal Publications, 1990), pp. 7–10; 127–128.

———, *Turkish Speaking Communities and Education: No Delight* (London: Fatal Publications, 2001).

An, Ahmet, 'The Cypriot Armenian Minority and Their Cultural Relationship with the Turkish Cypriots', in *The Minorities of Cyprus: Development Patterns and the Identity of the Internal-Exclusion*, ed. by Andrekos Varnaca, Nicholas Coureas, and Marina Elia (Newcastle upon Tyne: Cambridge Scholars, 2009), pp. 282–298.

Anderson, Benedict, *Imagined Communities: Reflections on the Origin and Spread of Nationalism* (London and New York: Verso, 2006).

D. Nunziata, *Colonial and Postcolonial Cyprus*,
https://doi.org/10.1007/978-3-030-58236-4

Angelou, Maya, *I Know Why The Caged Bird Sings* (New York: Random House, 1969).

Appadurai, Arjun, *Modernity at Large: Cultural Dimensions of Globalization* (Minneapolis: University of Minnesota Press, 1996).

Apter, Emily, *The Translation Zone: A New Comparative Literature* (Princeton, NJ: Princeton University Press, 2006).

Argyrou, Vassos, *Tradition and Modernity in the Mediterranean: The Wedding as Symbolic Struggle* (Cambridge: Cambridge University Press, 1996).

Arondekar, Anjali, *For the Record: On Sexuality and the Colonial Archive in India* (Durham, NC: Duke University Press, 2009).

Arvaniti, Amalia, 'Linguistic Practices in Cyprus and the Emergence of Cypriot Greek', *San Diego Linguistic Papers*, 2 (2006), 1–24.

Ashcroft, Bill, 'Transnation', in *Re-Routing the Postcolonial: New Dimensions for the New Millennium*, ed. by Janet Wilson, Cristina Sandru, and Sarah Lawson Welsh (Oxford and New York: Routledge, 2010), pp. 72–85.

Ashcroft, Bill, Gareth Griffiths, and Helen Tiffin, eds., *The Empire Writes Back: Theory and Practice in Post-Colonial Literatures* (London and New York: Routledge, 1989).

Baker, Samuel W., *Cyprus, As I Saw It in 1879* (London: Echo Library, 2007).

Bakhtin, Mikhail, *The Dialogic Imagination*, ed. by Michael Holquist, trans. by Caryl Emerson and Michael Holquist (Austin: University of Texas Press, 1981).

Baybars, Taner, *Narcissus in a Dry Pool* (London: Sidgwick & Jackson Limited, 1978).

———, *Plucked in a Far-Off Land: Images of Self-Biography* (London: Victor Gollancz Ltd., 1970).

———, *Plucked in a Far-Off Land: Images of Self-Biography* (Nicosia: Moufflon Publications, 2005).

———, *To Catch a Falling Man* (London: Scorpion Press, 1963).

Beauvoir, Simone de, *The Second Sex*, trans. and ed. by H.M. Parshley (London: Vintage, 1997).

Behn, Aphra, *Oroonoko: Or, The Royal Slave* (London: William Canning, 1688).

Benjamin, Walter, 'The Task of the Translator', trans. by Harry Zorn, in *Illuminations*, ed. by Hannah Arendt (London: Pimlico, 1999), pp. 70–82.

Bhabha, Homi K., 'Introduction: Narrating the Nation', in *Nation and Narration*, ed. by Homi K. Bhabha (London and New York: Routledge, 1990), pp. 1–7.

———, *The Location of Culture* (London and New York: Routledge, 1994).

Boehmer, Elleke, 'A Postcolonial Aesthetic: Repeating Upon the Present', in *Re-Routing the Postcolonial: New Dimensions for the New Millennium*, ed. by Janet Wilson, Cristina Sandru, and Sarah Lawson Welsh (Oxford and New York: Routledge, 2010), pp. 170–181.

———, *Colonial and Postcolonial Literature: Migrant Metaphors*, 2nd edn (Oxford: Oxford University Press, 2005).

———, *Empire, the National, and the Postcolonial, 1890–1920: Resistance in Interaction* (Oxford: Oxford University Press, 2002).

———, *Empire Writing: An Anthology of Colonial Literature, 1870–1918* (Oxford: Oxford University Press, 2009).

Bohls, Elizabeth A., 'Introduction', in *Travel Writing 1700–1830: An Anthology*, ed. by Elizabeth A. Bohls and Ian Ducan (Oxford: Oxford University Press, 2005), pp. xiii–xxvii.

Bond, Lucy, and Jessica Rapson, 'Introduction', in *The Transcultural Turn: Interrogating Memory Between and Beyond Borders*, ed. by Lucy Bond and Jessica Rapson (Berlin: De Gruyter, 2014), pp. 1–26.

Bourdieu, Pierre, *Masculine Domination*, trans. by Richard Nice (Stanford: Stanford University Press, 2001).

———, 'The Field of Cultural Production, or: The Economic World Reversed', trans. by Richard Nice, in *The Field of Cultural Production: Essays on Art and Literature*, ed. by Randal Johnson (Cambridge: Polity Press, 1993), pp. 29–73.

———, 'The Forms of Capital', trans. by Richard Nice, in *Handbook of Theory and Research*, ed. by John G. Richardson (New York: Greenwood Press, 1986), pp. 241–258.

Brah, Avtar, *Cartographies of Diaspora: Contesting Identities* (London and New York: Routledge, 1996).

Brassey, Mrs [Annie], *Sunshine and Storm in the East: Or, Cruises to Cyprus and Constantinople* (London: Longmans, Green, and Co., 1880).

Brown, Laura, *Ends of Empire: Women and Ideology in Early Eighteenth-Century English Literature* (New York: Cornell University Press, 1993).

Bunbury, E.H., 'Cyprus', *The Academy*, 6 December 1879, pp. 402–403.

Burton, Richard F., ed., *A Plain and Literal Translation of the Arabian Nights' Entertainments, Now Entitled The Book of The Thousand Nights and a Night*, 10 vols (London: Kama Shastra Society, 1885).

Butler, Judith, *Bodies That Matter: On The Discursive Limits of "Sex"* (Oxford and New York: Routledge, 1993).

———, *Undoing Gender* (New York and Oxford: Routledge, 2004).

Buzard, James, 'Postcolonial Valediction: Durrell's *Bitter Lemons of Cyprus* and the Legacies of the Grand Tour', in *The Legacy of the Grand Tour: New Essays on Travel, Literature, and Culture*, ed. by Lisa Colletta (Lanham, Maryland: Fairleigh Dickinson University Press), pp. 115–131.

Calotychos, Vangelis, '"Lawrence Durrell, the Bitterest Lemon?": Cyprus and Brits Loving Each Other to Death in Cyprus, 1953–57', in *Lawrence Durrell and the Greek World*, ed. by Anna Lillios (Selinsgrove: Susquehanna University Press, 2004), pp. 169–187.

Canetti, Elias, *Crowds and Power*, trans. by Carol Stewart (London: Phoenix Press, 1962).

Carlson, Marvin, *Performance: A Critical Introduction*, 2nd edn (London and New York: Routledge, 1996).

Carter, Angela, 'Triple Flavour', *New Society*, 25 (1973), 268–269.

Casanova, Pascale, *The World Republic of Letters*, trans. by M.B. DeBevoise (Cambridge, MA: Harvard University Press, 2004).

Central Intelligence Agency, *The CIA World Factbook 2017* (New York: Skyhorse, 2016).

de Certeau, Michel, *The Practice of Everyday Life*, trans. by Steven Rendall (Berkeley, CA: University of California Press, 1984).

Chakrabarty, Dipesh, *Provincializing Europe: Postcolonial Thought and Historical Difference* (Princeton, NJ: Princeton University Press, 2007).

Chanda, Nayan, *Bound Together* (New Haven and London: Yale University Press, 2007).

Chevalier, Tracy, ed., *Contemporary Poets* (Chicago and London: St James Press, 1991).

Churchill, Winston, *The War Speeches of the Rt. Hon. Winston S. Churchill: From June 25, 1941 to September 6, 1943* (Cambridge: The Riverside Press, 1953).

Clarke, Robert, 'Toward a Genealogy of Postcolonial Travel Writing: An Introduction', in *The Cambridge Companion to Postcolonial Life Writing*, ed. by Robert Clarke (Cambridge: Cambridge University Press, 2018), pp. 1–17.

Clifford, James, *Routes: Travel and Translation in the Late Twentieth Century* (Cambridge, MA: Harvard University Press, 1997).

Colenso, Frances Ellen, *History of the Zulu War and Its Origins* (London: Chapman & Hall, 1880).

Colley, Linda, *Britons: Forging the Nation, 1707–1837* (New Haven: Yale University Press, 1992).

Colton, Walter, *Ship or Shore; or, Leaves from the Journal of a Cruise to the Levant* (New York: Leavitt, Lord & Co., 1835).

Conrad, Joseph, *Heart of Darkness* (London: Penguin, 1994).

Constantinou, Costas M., 'Cyprus, Violent Cartography and the Distribution of Ethnic Identity', in *The New Violent Cartography: Geo-Analysis After the Aesthetic Turn*, ed. by Samson Opondo and Michael J. Shapiro (Oxford: Routledge, 2012), pp. 195–213.

Cunningham, H., 'Leisure and Culture', in *The Cambridge Social History of Britain, 1750–1950, Volume 2: People and Their Environment*, ed. by F.M.L. Thompson (Cambridge: Cambridge University Press, 1990), pp. 279–340.

Damrosch, David, *How to Read World Literature* (Oxford: Wiley-Blackwell, 2017).

Defoe, Daniel, *A Journal of the Plague Year* (New York: Dover, 2001).

———, *The Life and Strange Surprizing Adventures of Robinson Crusoe* (London: William Taylor, 1719).

Demetriou, Nicoletta, and Jim Samson, eds, *Music in Cyprus* (Surrey: Ashgate, 2015).

Derrida, Jacques, *Adieu to Emmanuel Levinas*, trans. by Pascale-Anne Brault and Michael Naas (Stanford: Stanford University Press, 1999).

———, *Archive Fever: A Freudian Impression*, trans. by Eric Prenowitz (Chicago and London: University of Chicago Press, 1996).

———, *Monolingualism of the Other; or, The Prosthesis of Origins*, trans. by Patrick Mensah (Stanford: Stanford University Press, 1998).

———, *Of Grammatology*, ed. by Judith Butler, trans. by GayatriChakravortySpivak (Baltimore: John Hopkins University Press, 2016).

———, *The Truth in Painting*, trans. by Geoffrey Bennington (Chicago: University of Chicago Press, 1987).

Diez, Thomas, 'Introduction: Cyprus and the European Union as a Political and Theoretical Problem', in *The European Union and Cyprus: Modern Conflict, Postmodern Union*, ed. by Thomas Diez (Manchester: Manchester University Press, 2002), pp. 1–13.

Dixon, William Hepworth, *British Cyprus* (London: Chapman & Hall, 1879).

Du Bois, W.E.B., *A W.E.B. Du Bois Reader*, ed. by Andrew G. Paschal (New York: Collier Books, 1971).

Durrell, Lawrence, *Bitter Lemons of Cyprus* (London: Faber and Faber, 2000).

Equiano, Olaudah, *The Interesting Narrative of the Life of Olaudah Equiano* (London: n.p., 1789).

European Commission, 'Europeans and their Languages: Report', European Commission, Special Eurobarometer 386 (Brussels: The Gallup Organisation, 2012).

———, 'Europeans and their Languages: Summary', European Commission, Special Eurobarometer 243 (Brussels: The Gallup Organisation, 2006).

———, 'User Language Preferences Online: Analytical Report', European Commission, Special Eurobarometer 313 (Brussels: The Gallup Organisation, 2011).

———, 'Youth on the Move: Analytical Report', Special Eurobarometer 319b (Brussels: The Gallup Organisation, 2011).

Fanon, Frantz, *A Dying Colonialism*, trans. by Haakon Chevalier (New York: Grove Press, 1967).

———, *Black Skin/White Masks*, trans. by Charles Lam Markmann (London: Pluto Press, 1986).

———, *The Wretched of the Earth*, trans. by Constance Farrington (New York: Grove Press, 1968).

Fusaro, Maria, Colin Heywood, and Mohamed-Salah Omri, eds, *Trade and Cultural Exchange in the Early Modern Mediterranean: Braudel's Maritime Legacy* (London and New York: I.B. Tauris, 2010).

Galloway, J.H., *The Sugar Cane Industry: An Historical Geography from Its Origins to 1914* (Cambridge: Cambridge University Press, 1989).

Gibran, Kahlil, *The Prophet* (Hertfordshire: Wordsworth Editions Limited, 1996).

Gilroy, Paul, *Against Race: Imagining Political Culture Beyond the Color Line* (Cambridge, MA: Belknap Press, 2000).

———, *Darker Than Blue: On the Moral Economies of Black Atlantic Culture* (Cambridge, MA: Harvard University Press, 2010).

———, *Postcolonial Melancholia* (New York: Columbia University Press, 2005).

———, *The Black Atlantic: Modernity and Double Consciousness* (Cambridge, MA: Harvard University Press, 1993).

Given, Michael, '"Father of his Landscape": Lawrence Durrell's Creation of Landscape and Character in Cyprus', *Deus Loci: The Lawrence Durrell Journal*, 5 (1997), 55–65.

Graham, James, *Land and Nationalism in Fictions from Southern Africa* (Oxford and New York: Routledge, 2009).

Greenslade, William, *Degeneration, Culture, and the Novel, 1880–1940* (Cambridge: Cambridge University Press, 1994).

Gulle, V. Ozan, 'Structural Borrowings in Cypriot Turkish from Cypriot Greek', *Mediterranean Language Review*, 18 (2011), 91–113.

Gutzmer, Alexander, *Brand-Driven City Building and the Virtualizing of Space* (Oxford and New York: Routledge, 2014).

Hadjioannou, Xenia, StravoulaTsiplakou, and Matthias Kappler, 'Language Policy and Language Planning in Cyprus', *Current Issues in Language Planning*, 12 (2011), 503–569.

Hadjipavlou, Maria, *Women and Change in Cyprus: Feminisms and Gender in Conflict* (London and New York: I.B. Tauris, 2010).

Hall, Stuart, 'New Ethnicities', in *Stuart Hall: Critical Dialogues in Cultural Studies*, ed. by David Morley and Kuan-Hsing Chen (London and New York: Routledge, 1996), pp. 441–451.

Hasikou, Anastasia, 'The Emergence of European Music', in *Music in Cyprus*, ed. by Nicoletta Demetriou and Jim Samson (Surrey: Ashgate, 2015), pp. 103–127.

Haubrich, William S., *Medical Meanings: A Glossary of Word Origins* (Philadelphia, PA: American College of Physicians, 2003).

Hegel, Georg Wilhelm Friedrich, *The Philosophy of History*, trans. by J. Sibree (Mineola, New York: Dover Publications, 2004).

Herodotus, *The History*, trans. by David Grene (Chicago: University of Chicago Press, 1987).

Holland, Patrick, and Graham Huggan, *Tourists with Typewriters: Critical Reflections on Contemporary Travel Writing* (Ann Arbor: The University of Michigan Press, 1998).
Huggan, Graham, *Extreme Pursuits: Travel/Writing in an Age of Globalization* (Ann Arbor: University of Michigan Press, 2009).
———, *The Postcolonial Exotic: Marketing the Margins* (London and New York: Routledge, 2001).
Hussein, Aamer, 'Mother Tongue, Father Tongue', *Journal of Postcolonial Writing*, 47 (2011), 199–204.
Ierodiaconou, Andriana, *Margarita's Husband: A Fable of the Levant* (Nicosia: Armida, 2007).
———, *The Women's Coffee Shop* (Marston Gate: Amazon, 2012).
Ioannides, Panos, 'Cinyras', trans. by David Bailey, in *Gregory and Other Stories* (Nicosia: Armida, 2009), pp. 82–133.
JanMohamed, Abdul, 'The Economy of the Manichean Allegory: The Function of Racial Difference in Colonialist Literature', *Critical Inquiry*, 12 (1985), 59–87.
Jones, Sadie, *Small Wars* (London: Chatto & Windus, 2009).
Kant, Immanuel, *Theoretical Philosophy After 1781*, ed. by Henry Allison and Peter Heath, trans. by Gary Hatfield, Michael Friedman, Henry Allison, and Peter Heath (Cambridge: Cambridge University Press, 2004).
Kappler, Matthias, 'Remembering a Childhood in Cyprus: Taner Baybars' "Smellscape" and Multiculturalism in His Autobiography, *Plucked in a Far-Off Land*', in *Turkish Literature and Cultural Memory: "Multiculturalism" as a Literary Theme After 1980*, ed. by Catharina Dufft (Wiesbaden: Harrassowitz Verlag, 2009), pp. 207–224.
Karayanni, Stavros Stavrou, 'Gender and Transformative Possibilities in Cypriot Narratives of Displacement', in *On the Move: The Journey of Refugees in New Literatures in English*, ed. by Geetha Ganapathy-Doré and Helga Ramsey-Kurz (Newcastle upon Tyne: Cambridge Scholars Publishing, 2012), pp. 57–75.
Katrak, Ketu H., *The Politics of the Female Body: Postcolonial Women Writers* (London and New Brunswick, NJ: Rutgers University Press, 2006).
Kazantzakis, Helen, *Nikos Kazantzakis: A Biography Based on His Letters*, trans. by Amy Mims (New York: Simon & Schuster, 1968).
Kazantzakis, Nikos, *Journeying: Travels in Italy, Egypt, Sinai, Jerusalem and Cyprus*, trans. by ThemiVasils and Theodora Vasils (Boston: Little, Brown and Company, 1975).
Kelly, Michelle, '*The Master of Petersburg* (1994)', in *A Companion to the Works of J.M. Coetzee*, ed. by Tim Mehigan (New York: Camden House, 2011), pp. 132–147.
Kincaid, Jamaica, *A Small Place* (New York: Farrar, Straus and Giroux, 1988).

Kipling, Rudyard, *Kim* (London: Macmillan and Co., 1901).

Klein, Herbert S., *The Atlantic Slave Trade* (Cambridge: Cambridge University Press, 2010).

Lacan, Jacques, *Ecrits: The First Complete Edition in English*, trans. and ed. by Bruce Fink (New York: W. W. Norton, 2006).

Lange, Matthew, *Educations in Ethnic Violence: Identity, Educational Bubbles, and Resource Mobilization* (Cambridge: Cambridge University Press, 2012).

Larson, Jennifer, 'Greece', in *The Cambridge Companion to Ancient Mediterranean Religions*, ed. by Barbette S. Spaeth (Cambridge: Cambridge University Press, 2013), pp. 136–156.

Lawrence, T.E., *Seven Pillars of Wisdom: A Triumph* (New York: Anchor Books, 1991).

Lee, Dennis, *Body Music* (Toronto: Anansi, 1998).

Lefebvre, Henri, *Critique of Everyday Life Volume II: Foundations for a Sociology of the Everyday*, trans. by John Moore (London: Verso, 2002).

Lefteri, Christy, *A Watermelon, a Fish and a Bible* (London: Quercus, 2010).

Lewis, Reina, *Gendering Orientalism: Race, Femininity and Representation* (London and New York: Routledge, 1996).

Lisle, Debbie, *The Global Politics of Contemporary Travel Writing* (Cambridge: Cambridge University Press, 2006).

Lobby for Cyprus, 'A Call to End Impunity and Reject Segregation', *Lobby for Cyprus News*, 27 (2014), 2.

———, 'Ankara Calls the Shots in Occupied Cyprus' and 'The True Face of Bizonalism', *Lobby For Cyprus News*, 28 (2015), 1–3.

———, 'The 10th Anniversary of the Annan Plan Referendum', *Lobby For Cyprus News*, 27 (2014), 2.

Low, Gail Ching-Liang, *White Skin/Black Masks: Representation and Colonialism* (London: Routledge, 1996).

Lowe, Lisa, *Critical Terrains: French and British Orientalisms* (New York: Cornell University Press, 1994).

Lukács, Georg, *The Theory of the Novel: A Historico-Philosophical Essay on the Forms of Great Epic Literature*, trans. by Anna Bostock (Cambridge, MA: MIT Press, 1971).

MacNiven, Ian S., and Carol Peirce, 'From the Editors', *Deus Loci: The Lawrence Durrell Journal*, 4 (1996), vi–vii.

Makdisi, Saree, 'Postcolonial Literature in a Neocolonial World: Modern Arabic Culture and the End of Modernity', in *The Pre-Occupation of Postcolonial Studies*, ed. by Fawzia Afkal-Khan and Kalpana Seshadri-Crooks (Durham, NC: Duke University Press, 2000), pp. 266–291.

Makis, Eve, *Eat, Drink and Be Married* (London: Black Swan, 2004).

———, *Land of the Golden Apple* (London: Black Swan, 2008).

———, *The Mother-in-Law* (London: Black Swan, 2006).

Mallock, William Hurrell, *In an Enchanted Isle, Or, A Winter's Retreat in Cyprus* (London: Richard Bentley & Son, 1892).

Marcuse, Peter, 'The Layered City', in *The Urban Lifeworld*, ed. by Pete Madsen and Richard Plunz (London: Routledge, 2002), pp. 94–114.

McClintock, Anne, *Imperial Leather* (London and New York: Routledge, 1995).

Meltzl, Hugo, 'Present Tasks of Comparative Literature', in *Comparative Literature: The Early Years*, ed. and trans. by Hans-Joachim Schulz and Phillip H. Rhein (Chapel Hill: University of North Carolina Press, 1973), pp. 53–62.

Mohanty, Sachidananda, 'Introduction: Beyond the Imperial Eye', in *Travel Writing and the Empire*, ed. by Sachidananda Mohanty (New Delhi: Katha, 2003), pp. ix–xxi.

Montis, Costas, *Closed Doors: An Answer to* Bitter Lemons *by Lawrence Durrell*, trans. by David Roessel and Soterios G. Stavrou (Minneapolis, MN: Nostos, 2004).

Montis, Costas, and Andreas Christofides, 'Introductory Remarks', in *Anthology of Cypriot Poetry (From Ancient Times Until Today)*, ed. by Costas Montis and Andreas Christofides (Nicosia: Cultural Service of the Ministry of Education, 1974), pp. i–v.

'More About Cyprus', *The Saturday Review*, 6 December 1879, pp. 701–702.

Moretti, Franco, 'Conjectures on World Literature', *New Left Review*, 1 (2000), 54–68.

———, *Distant Reading* (London and New York: Verso, 2013).

Morgan, Tabitha, *Sweet and Bitter Island: A History of the British in Cyprus* (London and New York: I.B. Tauris).

Moroz, Grzegorz, and Jolanta Sztachelska, 'Preface', in *Metamorphoses of Travel Writing: Across Themes, Genres, Countries and Literary Traditions*, ed. by Grzegorz Moroz and JolantaSztachelska (Newcastle upon Tyne: Cambridge Scholars Publishing, 2010), pp. ix–x.

Morton, Stephen, *States of Emergency: Colonialism, Literature and Law* (Liverpool: Liverpool University Press, 2013).

Murphy, Rosalie, ed., *Contemporary Poets of the English Language* (Chicago and London: St James Press, 1974).

Nadjarian, Nora, 'Don't Forget', in *Creativity in Exile*, ed. by Michael Hanne (Amsterdam and New York: Rodopi, 2004), pp. 121–122.

———, *Ledra Street* (Nicosia: Armida, 2006).

Naipaul, V.S., *Miguel Street* (London: André Deutsch, 1959).

Nairn, Tom, *The Break-Up of Britain: Crisis and Neo-Nationalism* (Altona, VIC: Common Ground, 2003).

Navaro-Yashin [*sic*], Yael, *The Make-Believe Space: Affective Geography in a Postwar Polity* (Durham and London: Duke University Press, 2012).

Ngũgĩ wa Thiong'o, 'Borders and Bridges: Seeking Connections Between Things', in *The Pre-Occupation of Postcolonial Studies*, ed. by Fawzia Afzal-Khan and Kalpana Seshadri-Crooks (Durham: Duke University Press, 2000), pp. 119–125.

Nkrumah, Kwame, *Neo-Colonialism: The Last Stage of Imperialism* (New York: International Publishers, 1965).

Oyěwùmí, Oyèrónkẹ́, *The Invention of Women: Making an African Sense of Western Gender Discourses* (Minneapolis: Minnesota University Press, 1997).

Papadakis, Yiannis, *Echoes from the Dead Zone: Across the Cyprus Divide* (London and New York: I.B. Tauris, 2005).

Pattie, Susan, 'Imagining Homelands: Poetics and Performance Among Cypriot Armenians', in *Cyprus and the Politics of Memory: History, Community and Conflict*, ed. by Rebecca Bryant and Yiannis Papadakis (London and New York: I.B. Tauris, 2012), pp. 140–167.

Peristiany, J.G., 'Honour and Shame in a Cypriot Highland Village', in *Honour and Shame: The Values of Mediterranean Society*, ed. by J.G. Peristiany (Chicago: University of Chicago Press, 1966), pp. 171–190.

Petersen, Kirsten Holst, 'First Things First: Problems of a Feminist Approach to African Literature', *Kunapipi*, 6 (1984), 35–47.

Pollis, Adamantia, 'Intergroup Conflict and British Colonial Policy: The Case of Cyprus', *Comparative Politics*, 5 (1973), 575–599.

Pratt, Mary Louise, *Imperial Eyes: Travel Writing and Transculturation* (Oxford and New York: Routledge, 1992).

Reynolds, Matthew, *Translation: A Very Short Introduction* (Oxford: Oxford University Press, 2016).

Roufos, Rodis, *The Age of Bronze* (London: Heinemann, 1960).

Rushdie, Salman, *Imaginary Homelands: Essays and Criticism, 1981–1991* (London: Granta Books, 1992).

———, *The Satanic Verses* (London: Vintage Books, 1988).

Said, Edward W., *Culture and Imperialism* (London: Vintage Books, 1994).

———, 'On The University', in *Edward Said and Critical Decolonization*, ed. by Ferial J. Ghazoul (Cairo and New York: The American University in Cairo Press, 2007), pp. 26–36.

———, *Orientalism* (London: Penguin, 1995).

———, *Reflections on Exile and Other Essays* (Cambridge, MA: Harvard University Press, 2001).

———, *The World, the Text, and the Critic* (Cambridge, MA: Harvard University Press, 1983).

Salih, Tayeb, *Season of Migration to the North*, trans. by Denys Johnson-Davies (Oxford: Heinemann, 1991).

———, 'The Cypriot Man', in *Arabic Short Stories*, trans. by Denys Johnson-Davies, ed. by Roger Allen (Berkeley: University of California Press, 1994).

Schneider, Edgar W., *Postcolonial Englishes: Varieties Across the World* (Cambridge: Cambridge University Press, 2007).

Scott-Stevenson, Mrs [Esmé], *Our Home in Cyprus* (London: Chapman & Hall, 1880).

Seal, Graham, *Outlaw Heroes in Myth and History* (London: Anthem Press, 2011).

Seferis, George, *A Levant Journal*, ed. and trans. by Roderick Beaton (Jerusalem: Ibis, 2007).

Shakespeare, William, *The Oxford Shakespeare: Othello*, ed. by Michael Neil (Oxford: Oxford University Press, 2006).

———, 'Venus and Adonis', in *The Oxford Shakespeare: The Complete Sonnets and Poems*, ed. by Colin Burrow (Oxford: Oxford University Press, 2002), pp. 175–236.

Shemak, April, 'Refugee and Asylum Seeker Narratives as Postcolonial Travel Writing', in *The Cambridge Companion to Postcolonial Life Writing*, ed. by Robert Clarke (Cambridge: Cambridge University Press, 2018), pp. 188–201.

Simmel, Georg, 'Bridge and Door', *Theory, Culture & Society*, 7 (1994), 5–10.

Smith, Agnes, *Eastern Pilgrims: The Travels of Three Ladies* (London: Hurst and Blackett, 1870).

———, *Through Cyprus* (London: Hurst and Blackett, 1887).

Soule, Richard, *A Dictionary of English Synonyms* (Boston: Little, Brown, and Company, 1871).

Spivak, Gayatri Chakravorty, *Death of a Discipline* (New York: Columbia University Press, 2003).

———, *Outside in the Teaching Machine* (Oxford and New York: Routledge, 2009).

———, *Toward a History of the Vanishing Present* (Cambridge, MA: Harvard University Press, 1999).

Stepan, Nancy Leys, *The Hour of Eugenics: Race, Gender, and Nation in Latin America* (New York: Cornell University Press, 1991).

Stevens, Peter A.J., *Ethnicity and Racism in Cyprus: National Pride and Prejudice?* (London: Palgrave Macmillan, 2016).

Thubron, Colin, *Journey into Cyprus* (London: Vintage, 2012).

Tiffin, Helen, 'Post-Colonial Literatures and Counter-Discourse', *Kunapipi*, 9 (1987), 17–34.

Tofallis, Kypros, *The History of Cyprus: From the Ancient Times to the Present* (London: The Greek Institute, 2002).

Tsiplakou, Stavroula, 'Code-Switching and Code-Mixing Between Related Varieties: Establishing the Blueprint', *International Journal of Humanities*, 6 (2006), 46–66.

Wächter, Bernd, 'Recent Trends in Student Mobility in Europe', in *Internationalisation of Higher Education and Global Mobility*, ed. by Bernhard Streitwieser (Oxford: Symposium Books, 2014), pp. 87–97.

Whitlock, Gillian, 'Outlaws of the Text: Women's Bodies and the Organisation of Gender in Imperial Space', in *The Post-Colonial Studies Reader*, ed. by Bill Ashcroft, Gareth Griffiths, and Helen Tiffin (London and New York: Routledge, 1995), pp. 306–308.

Wilde, Oscar, *The Picture of Dorian Gray* (London: HarperCollins, 2010).

Williams, Raymond, *Marxism and Literature* (Oxford and New York: Oxford University Press, 1977).

———, *The Country and the City* (Oxford and New York: Oxford University Press, 1973).

Wolseley, Sir Garnet, *Cyprus 1878: The Journal of Sir Garnet Wolseley*, ed. by Anne Cavendish (Nicosia: Cyprus Popular Bank Cultural Centre, 1991).

Woolf, Virginia, *A Room of One's Own* (Toronto: Broadway Press, 2001).

Yashin [*sic*], Mehmet, *Don't Go Back ToKyrenia*, trans. by Taner Baybars (London: Middlesex University Press, 2001).

———, ed., *Step-Mothertongue: From Nationalism to Multiculturalism: Literatures of Cyprus* (London: Middlesex University Press, 2000).

Yaşın, Neşe, *Ay AşktanYapılmıştır* [*The Moon Is Made of Love*] (Istanbul: Gendaş, 2000).

———, *BellekOdaları* [*Chambers of Memory*] (Istanbul: Dünya, 2005).

———, *Kapılar: Şiirler* [*Doors: Poems*] (Istanbul: Cem, 1992).

———, *Rose Falling Into Night* (Nicosia: Heterotopia Publications, 2017).

———, *ÜşümüşKuşlar* [*Chilling Birds*] (Istanbul: Ayrıntı, 2016).

Yeğenoğlu, Meyda, *Colonial Fantasises: Towards a Feminist Reading of Orientalism* (Cambridge: Cambridge University Press, 1998).

Yiangou, Anastasia, *Cyprus in World War II: Politics and Conflict in the Eastern Mediterranean* (London: I.B. Tauris, 2010).

Young, Robert J.C., *Colonial Desire: Hybridity in Theory, Culture and Race* (London and New York: Routledge, 1995).

———, 'Postcolonial Remains', *New Literary History*, 43 (2012), 19–42.

———, *Postcolonialism: A Very Short Introduction* (Oxford: Oxford University Press, 2003).

Zeiger, Dinah, 'That (Afghan) Girl! Ideology Unveiled in *National Geographic*', in *The Veil: Women Writers on its History, Lore, and Politics*, ed. by Jennifer Heath (Berkeley and Los Angeles: University of California Press, 2008), pp. 266–280.

Zonana, Joyce, 'The Sultan and the Slave: Feminist Orientalism and the Structures of *Jane Eyre*', *Signs*, 18 (1993), 592–617.

Online sources

'Arts in Cyprus', www.kypros.org/CyprusPanel/cyprus/arts.html [accessed 13 October, 2016].

Campbell, John C., 'The Mediterranean Crisis', *Foreign Affairs* (1 July 1975). https://www.foreignaffairs.com/articles/cyprus/1975-07-01/mediterranean-crisis [accessed 14 June 2018].

'Cyprus Convention', in Wikisource. http://en.wikisource.org/wiki/Cyprus_covention [accessed 11 August 2018].

Davidson, Roderic H., 'Where Is The Middle East?', *Foreign Affairs* (1 July 1960). https://www.foreignaffairs.com/articles/middle-east/1960-07-01/where-middle-east [accessed 14 June 2018].

Evans, Julian, 'Continental Shelf', *The Guardian* (30 April 2004) https://www.theguardian.com/books/2004/may/01/featuresreviews.guardianreview34 [accessed 21 April 2017].

Gorvett, Jonathan, 'Cyprus in the Middle: Nicosia Holds the Keys to Syria, the Migrant Crisis, and Gas in the Eastern Mediterranean', *Foreign Affairs* (12 January 2016). https://www.foreignaffairs.com/articles/cyprus/2016-01-12/cyprus-middle [accessed 14 June 2018].

Statement of U.S. Policy Toward Cyprus', National Security Council 6003, Department of State (9 February 1960). https://history.state.gov/historicaldocuments/frus1958-60v10p1/d347 [accessed 21 April 2020].

'The Sykes-Picot Agreement', in Wikisource. http://en.wikisource.org/wiki/The_Sykes-Picot_Agreement [accessed 11 August 2018].

'Treaty of Guarantee', in Wikisource. http://en.wikisource.org/wiki/Treaty_of_Guarantee [accessed 11 August 2018].

United Nations Development Programme, 'Gender Inequality Index' (2006). hdr.undp.org/en/composite/GII [accessed 11 February 2018].

Wiseman, Eva, 'Small Wars by Sadie Jones', *The Guardian* (22 August 2009). www.theguardian.com/books/2009/aug/23/jones-soldier-small-wars [accessed 14 December 2014].

Author Index

D. Nunziata, *Colonial and Postcolonial Cyprus*,
https://doi.org/10.1007/978-3-030-58236-4

Subject Index

D. Nunziata, *Colonial and Postcolonial Cyprus*,
https://doi.org/10.1007/978-3-030-58236-4

Printed by Printforce, United Kingdom